TEACHING IMPROVEMENT PRACTICES

CENTER FOR TEACHING EFFECTIVENESS
111 Pearson Hall
University of Delaware
Newark, DE 19716-1106

TEACHING IMPROVEMENT PRACTICES

Successful Strategies for Higher Education

W. Alan Wright

Dalhousie University

and Associates

Foreword by
Wilbert J. McKeachie and Barbara K. Hofer

ANKER PUBLISHING COMPANY, INC.
BOLTON, MA

TEACHING IMPROVEMENT PRACTICES
Successful Strategies for Higher Education

ISBN 1-882982-06-1

Composition by Alta Zena Graphics.
Cover design by Deerfoot Studios.

Anker Publishing Company, Inc.
176 Ballville Road
P.O. Box 249
Bolton, MA 01740-0249

À
Marie-Jeanne,
Marianne,
William,
et
Adam

Contents

Foreword

Faculty development is flourishing. In Chapter 15 of this volume, George Gordon and Patricia Partington tell us that every university in the United Kingdom now has a director of faculty development. Growth has also been dramatic in the United States. In the past, many administrators, department heads, and faculty members knew and cared little about what went on under the rubric of "faculty development." Now, however, faculty development is increasingly seen as vital to universities facing the problems of growing enrollments, inadequate budgets, and pressures from governments, funding agencies, and the public. Thus, this book provides a valuable resource for faculty developers, for deans and department heads who have responsibilities for the quality of teaching and research, and for faculty members who may not be aware of opportunities for continued growth. Individuals seeking a model of how these groups might work together to further teaching improvement would do well to read the chapter by Mary Deane Sorcinelli and Norman D. Aitken; they draw on their collaboration at the University of Massachusetts to describe partnerships between academic leaders and faculty developers.

The unique contribution of this book comes not so much from its outstanding group of chapter authors as from the foundation laid by Alan Wright and Carol O'Neil's survey of faculty developers in Australasia, Canada, the United Kingdom, and the United States. The survey results broaden our understanding of perceptions of current practices, point the way toward needed research, and substantiate the need to work on multiple fronts to improve teaching. Although many faculty developers may have previously concentrated their efforts on direct service to individual faculty members, the current view of the practitioners surveyed seems to be that the most important means of improving teaching is to affect institutional climate through greater recognition of teaching.

When we think of an institutional climate that facilitates fine teaching, we usually think first of whether institutional personnel policies reward teaching. But this is simplistic. In fact, a heavy emphasis on evaluation of teaching for personnel decisions may well be counterproductive. What counts in an institutional climate supportive of teaching is a set of norms that encourage conversations about teaching among faculty members, conversations that include students and administrators as well, conversations that are enriched by faculty understanding of teaching and learning (as described in several chapters of this volume), and conversations stimulated by a faculty development program dealing with the issues in each of the chapters that follow. Yes, we need to be sure that good teachers do not feel they are exploited by institutional personnel policies; we need to be sure that faculty members feel that good teaching is recognized and appreciated by peers, administrators, and students. Appreciation is important, but it needs to be supported by opportunities for continual growth in skill, understanding, and enjoyment.

As Wright and O'Neil and other authors suggest, an effective faculty development program typically uses a variety of approaches, just as effective teachers vary their strategies depending upon their goals, students, content, the stage of the course, and the demands of the immediate situation. Faculty developers seeking ideas for improving their own practices will find clear conceptions of programs and approaches by experts in the field. For example, Milton Cox describes 15 years of experience with a multi-faceted program for new faculty at Miami University in Ohio, a program that was recognized nationally in the US with the 1994 Hesburgh Award. Similarly, James Eison and Ellen Stevens draw on extensive successful experiences with faculty workshops and a summer institute for faculty to offer useful guidelines and strategies for others.

Several themes emerge across a number of chapters. One of these is the importance of deep processing both in student and faculty learning. The deep versus surface approach to learning derived from Craik and Lockhart's levels of processing theory of cognition and applied to university learning by Ference Marton and his associates is essentially picked up under the rubric of "elaboration" or the catch-all term "active learning." The theoretical underpinnings are derived from the elaboration theories of Craik and Watson and Anderson and Reder. Essentially, the point is that we need to get students and teachers to *think* about their learning. Learning is more likely to be remembered and used if it is meaningful. Meaningful theory is an aid to application appropriate to a given situation, as opposed to mindless use of particular methods or techniques that may have great virtue in many (but not all) situations. Probably the most important thing we have learned from research on university teaching and learning is that nothing works all the time, in every situation.

A second theme is that of the importance of methods of assessing learning in influencing for good or ill the kind and amount of learning that occurs. In the earlier chapters, we are reminded that students do not use deep processing when examinations require only memorization of facts; in the chapters dealing directly with faculty development, we find a similar concern about the influence of methods of evaluation on teacher motivation. The threat of evaluation can generate crippling anxiety both for students and faculty members. We note that classroom peer observation, as well as end-of-term student feedback for summative purposes, were among the items rated, in the survey of faculty developers as least likely to be helpful. Organizational assessment can have similarly negative effects. Yet we are told that an accounting firm recommended to the Committee of Vice-Chancellors and Principals in the United Kingdom that they develop a system of sanctions to use in conjunction with their Academic Audit.

Readers will note that several chapters deal with items that did not receive high ratings in the international survey, or that were not surveyed directly. This did not seem to us to be a fault, and the logic becomes apparent in the reading. Faculty workshops, for example, did receive high ratings across the institutions surveyed, and the editors have wisely included chapters on topics of current interest to those planning such workshops. A particularly timely contribution is that of Nancy Van Note Chism and Anne S. Pruitt on "Promoting Inclusiveness in College Teaching," which examines both curricular issues and teaching methods and provides suggestions for implementing faculty development programs that address student diversity. Laurie Richlin reminds us that faculty preparation begins in graduate school and offers models for TA training and development.

Items which received low ratings may have received attention for other reasons. For example, survey results indicated fairly low confidence in the use of the teaching portfolio *as a teaching improvement practice*, but as the editor notes, use of the portfolio approach is booming. Faculty developers who may have viewed the teaching portfolio as a useful device for personnel decisions, but who have been less likely to acknowledge its role in teaching improvement, may find the chapter by Seldin, Annis, and Zubizarreta enlightening. This chapter makes a particularly valuable contribution to the field and is one we are eager to circulate among our own staff. The authors highlight the benefits of the preparation process, emphasizing the value of deliberate reflection upon teaching that this necessitates and the potential for consultation between the instructor and a mentor during the preparation. Other chapters give excellent suggestions about how such things as peer observation, books and newsletters, seminars on student learning, and videotaping can be effective components of a faculty development program.

The book offers a wealth of good ideas in its descriptions of exemplary programs and practices and enables faculty developers to learn from one another across cultures. Graham Gibbs, for example, offers an unusually rich level of expertise in responding to issues of teaching large classes that should benefit others. His description of organizing a nation-wide project that led to the training of 8,500 faculty is useful for those addressing similar concerns; he also offers insight into recent changes in higher education in the UK and his perceptions of comparative responses in the US.

While these chapters deal specifically with faculty development in primarily English-speaking countries, we believe that they will be valuable to faculty developers and university administrators all over the world. The need is great; the book is timely; the content is thoughtful and helpful.

Wilbert J. McKeachie
Barbara K. Hofer
Center for Research on
    Learning and Teaching
University of Michigan
September, 1994

REFERENCES

Anderson, J.R., & Reder, L. (1979). An elaborative processing explanation of processing. In L.S. Cermak & F.I.M. Craik (Eds.), *Levels of processing in human memory*. Hillsdale, NJ: Lawrence Erlbaum Associates

Cermak, L.S., & Craik, F.I.M. (Eds.). (1979). *Levels of processing in human memory*. Hillsdale, NJ: Lawrence Erlbaum Associates.

Craik, F.I.M., & Lockhart, R.S. (1972). Levels of processing: A framework for memory research. *Journal of Verbal Learning and Verbal Behavior, 11*, 671-684.

Craik, F.I.M., & Watkins, M.J. (1973). The role of rehearsal in short-term memory. *Journal of Verbal Learning and Verbal Behavior, 12*, 599-607.

Marton, F., & Säljo, R. (1976). On qualitative differences in learning: I. Outcome and process. *British Journal of Educational Psychology, 46*, 4-11.

Preface

BACKGROUND AND RATIONALE

This book examines the most successful recent initiatives to enhance the quality of higher education through systematic efforts to improve teaching. Drawing on the research and practical experiences of leading American, Canadian, British, and Australian scholars, this collection of essays identifies the issues, reviews the literature in the field, describes successful implementation strategies, and outlines prospects for the future.

The contributed chapters are supported by the findings of recent surveys of teaching improvement specialists in the United States, Canada, the United Kingdom, and Australasia. All respondents to the international surveys have responsibilities at the institutional level for what is typically called *faculty development* or *instructional development* in North America and *staff, academic,* or *educational development* in Australasia and the UK.[1] The survey data, which emanate from over 330 post-secondary institutions, demonstrate the relative levels of confidence of leading members of the academic community in a wide variety of policies and practices designed to improve teaching. A questionnaire was distributed exclusively to degree-granting colleges, universities, and polytechnics; however, the essential findings and their practical implications outlined in Chapter 1, and the suggestions offered in the 14 contributed chapters in this volume, apply to teaching improvement efforts in any tertiary-level institution. The terms *college* and *university* tend to be used interchangeably in this volume. The same holds true for the terms referring to academic teaching staff in these institutions: *instructor, professor,* and *faculty member* are also used interchangeably and are not, generally, meant to specify rank and seniority.

The data generated by the surveys, undertaken with Carol O'Neil, afforded the researchers a unique vantage point from which to write the introductory chapter and to lend perspective to the contributed chapters. What is the promise, for example, of academic staff development workshops? Do faculty developers believe that peer consultation has significant potential to improve instruction? What is the impact of mentoring on the pedagogical development of junior faculty? What is the role of academic administrators in improving college teaching? The survey results and analysis undertaken in Chapter 1 begin to situate these questions; the chapters which follow capitalize on the contributers' understanding of the issues surrounding individual practices and on their extensive practical experiences in the field to provide the academic readership with the best information and advice available. The contributors to this book have demonstrated their ability to bridge the gap between theory and practice; this uncommon attribute is reflected in every chapter. This book offers the reader credible paths of activity and direction to implement successfully the instructional development practices under consideration.

The volume appears during a period when the vast majority of institutions are forced to cope with increasing public expectations and decreasing public financing. Major change, re-organization, and amalgamation have been undertaken in higher education in Australia and the UK in recent years, and few North American colleges and universities have escaped the ordeal of increased scrutiny, accountability to external bodies, and the exigencies of bureaucratic rationalization processes. Yet many observers feel that colleges and universities face even more difficult times ahead, that they may be obliged to make sweeping changes in a crisis situation. This scenario is likened, rather ominously, by Jon Wergin of the American Association for Higher Education, to a great, rolling snowball on the mountainside, gaining both volume and momentum as it bears down on the sleepy village of academe in the valley below. In the face of the impending avalanche, a quick "taking of stock" leads us to conclude that our principal resource for survival is the scholarly and pedagogical talents of the professoriate. Plans for expansion could be put on hold as we look to members of the faculty for ingenuity to avert disaster and for dedication to dig us out. Faculty and educational developers, members of instructional development teams, representatives on teaching and learning committees, and academic administrators would be called upon to provide leadership in the efforts to re-establish the academic community.

This metaphor illustrates the belief that, in a time of financial restraint and crisis of public confidence, in a time of renewal, those responsible for the quality of teaching and learning should take a leadership role. The teaching improvement practices advocated in this book are well-founded, research-based, field-tested avenues to improving both faculty morale and teaching quality, as well as learner motivation and performance.

Major studies published over the last several years have heavily criticized academic programs in higher education and advanced proposals to enhance both the quality and the status of university teaching. Boyer (1990)[2] called for a second look at the issue of "what it means to be a scholar," suggesting that it was essential to re-vamp the faculty reward system to recognize the scholarship of teaching on an equal footing with discovery research and thus serve students better, unlock faculty creativity, and pursue appropriate institutional goals (p. 2). Smith (1991), in a study commissioned by the Association of Universities and Colleges of Canada, found that teaching was seriously undervalued in universities and recommended steps to improve the status of teaching in higher education. Australia's Higher Education Council (1990) issued recommendations designed to ensure the quality of teaching and to enhance the status of teaching in that country's transformed national system. How have institutions responded to the challenge of reform? Observers in the UK claim that academic staff development is "still at a primitive and uneven state of advancement" and that one must look carefully at development programs to ensure that institutional responses to "government pressures… to demonstrate commitment" are not simply "pious statements" and "empty rhetoric" rather than useful programs (Smith & Smith, 1993, p. 5).

In the wake of the many critical reports on higher education we must not overlook the promising work of instructional developers and their faculty associates in scores of institutions. This book turns to the inventory of successful faculty development strategies in order to demonstrate that, inspired by the accomplishments described by our contributors, significant improvements in the quality of teaching can, in fact, be realized in the academy. The book seeks to raise the credibility and broaden the circle of influence of faculty developers, who are too often content to exchange success stories among themselves without presenting a convincing case to the academic community at large. Every chapter brings scholarly reflection, professional insight, and organizational knowledge to a topic of unquestionable relevance and potential to improve university teaching and learning.

OVERVIEW OF THE CHAPTERS

Chapter 1, by Alan Wright and Carol O'Neil, reviews the results of an international survey of faculty developers and others responsible for teaching improvement programs in colleges and universities. The chapter looks at the teaching improvement practices rated by survey respondents and discusses the potential of each practice in the context of a comprehensive instructional development program. Many of the practices are taken up in greater detail in subsequent chapters. Although there are no clearly delineated sections to this book, the chapters have been grouped by themes.

Chapters 2 and 3 focus on teaching and learning in higher education. Canada's Christopher Knapper provides a significant starting point for the remaining chapters by underlining the importance of increasing professors' understanding of student learning. Keith Trigwell of Australia complements Knapper's chapter by describing how faculty development programs can incorporate research findings on how university teachers conceptualize and approach teaching.

The next three chapters describe specific approaches to teaching and learning and how they can be presented to faculty in the context of an instructional development strategy.

Canadian David Kaufman discusses the considerable potential of problem-based learning and makes practical recommendations for the preparation of faculty tutors. Barbara Millis provides insights into the workings of cooperative learning, which is becoming increasingly popular in university classrooms in the United States and elsewhere, and makes suggestions for introducing this approach to academic staff. Elizabeth Hazel, a second Australian contributor, offers many sound, research-based recommendations for improving laboratory teaching and for working with faculty colleagues to introduce change in the laboratory teaching and learning setting.

The three chapters which follow deal with well-known and effective strategies often employed by faculty development specialists as they work with academics to improve college and university teaching. Canadian Richard Tiberius contributes a fascinating account of the changing practices employed by faculty developers and consultants to help teachers fulfill their roles in higher education. James Eison and Ellen Stevens of the United States take up the subject of organizing faculty workshops for maximum benefit. The teaching portfolio is used more and more frequently as a tool to record the professor's teaching accomplishments and to improve teaching in higher education. Peter Seldin, Linda Annis, and John Zubizarreta delve into the nature and the benefits of the portfolio concept as it attracts phenomenal interest in the United States and beyond.

Under the theme of the professionalization of teaching in higher education, Laurie Richlin addresses the question of the preparation of college and university teachers, and Milton Cox focuses on the development of new and junior faculty as teachers. The authors draw on a vast experience in higher education in the United States to present these issues.

The next two chapters emphasize the establishment of partnerships to implement change in the institutional setting. Mary Deane Sorcinelli and Norman Aitken illustrate that much can be accomplished when faculty development specialists work with academic administrators to launch and support teaching effectiveness programs. Nancy Van Note Chism and Anne Pruitt offer advice on implementing programs on teaching for diversity. All four authors are from the United States.

The final chapters in the book study the impact of national programs, policies, and developments on teaching, learning, and faculty improvement in the institutional setting. Graham Gibbs reports on a national-scale faculty development effort on the theme of teaching large classes in the United Kingdom. George Gordon and Patricia Partington describe and assess national developments in the UK designed to improve the quality of instruction in higher education.

The many contributors from several different countries bring a variety of perspectives, as well as a wealth of experience in higher education, to the chapters described above. I hope the reader will find each chapter both intellectually stimulating and immediately useful for reflecting on ideas and designing projects to improve the quality of teaching and learning in higher education.

ACKNOWLEDGEMENTS

This publication required the collaboration of a large number of people. First and foremost, I would like to thank my chief associate in this undertaking, Carol O'Neil.

Carol has worked in partnership with me from the beginning of the project. I have relied on her to coordinate the survey and to compile the results, to interpret the results with me and to join me in writing Chapter 1, to critique contributed chapters and to participate at every phase of the enormous task of editing this volume. Carol's thoughtful comments on the manuscript, based on her excellent insights into teaching and learning in higher education, have been extremely valuable to me at every stage of this process.

Janice MacInnis has also played a critical role in bringing this project from proposal to finished publication. Janice was responsible for the word processing and formatting of all texts, tracking version upon version of the various chapters as we worked with some 20 contributors to add, delete, cut, paste, modify, and massage the material until all parties were satisfied that it represented their best work. Janice not only did an excellent job of error detection and discovering incomplete references, but also offered many suggestions for improving the manuscripts. She won the appreciation of the contributors for her energy, her commitment to the project, and her good-natured attention to their needs.

I would like to thank Eileen Herteis for the many hours she volunteered to review manuscripts and for the many improvements which resulted from her efforts. Eileen's knowledge of the English language and of faculty development were great assets to the publication.

The contributors did an excellent job of writing and revising their manuscripts. I am most grateful that these talented individuals agreed to submit chapters to this book despite hectic schedules and many other commitments. I would also like to thank those contributors who offered suggestions to improve other chapters, as well as Neil Fleming, Andy Farquharson, Dale Roy, and Geraldine Thomas for their comments, Jenny Winterfield, Leo Bartlett, and Bruce Zimmer for supplying source documents used in the book, and Barbara Hofer for all her help via electronic mail.

James D. Anker, President of Anker Publishing Company, was generous with friendly advice, encouragement, and assistance through all stages of this project. My thanks to Jim for his valuable guidance and support.

The Professional and Organizational Development Network (US), the Standing Committee on Educational Development (UK), and the Higher Education Research and Development Society of Australasia are to be thanked for their assistance with the international survey of instructional developers.

I wish to express my gratitude to my gracious hosts at Macalester College, St. Paul, where I spent several enjoyable months preparing this book and collaborating with faculty on a teaching improvement project.

Finally, I wish to thank Dalhousie University and President Howard Clark for facilitating the publication of this book.

W. Alan Wright
Halifax, Nova Scotia
July, 1994

NOTES

[1] These terms are discussed further in Chapter 1 under "Structure and Organization."

[2] See the references at end of Chapter 1 for the publications mentioned in the Preface.

1.

Teaching Improvement Practices: International Perspectives

W. Alan Wright
M. Carol O'Neil

Individuals with formal responsibility for the improvement of teaching in higher education provide important insights on the potential impact of a variety of activities, programs, and policies designed to improve the quality of instruction. International perspectives on strategies to enhance teaching can inform program design and help establish priorities at the institutional level. The essential leadership role of deans and heads, the benefits of recognizing teaching in personnel decisions, and the importance of building a comprehensive instructional development program are stressed.

INTRODUCTION

This chapter describes the results of an inquiry into the perceived impact of teaching improvement practices in higher education institutions in the United States, Canada, the United Kingdom, and Australasia. Utilizing survey research, the study recorded the perceptions of key campus participants active in the area of instructional and faculty development regarding the teaching improvement potential of a variety of institutional policies and programs.

The compiled data yields a broad international portrait of which kinds of teaching improvement initiatives professionals in the field consider most promising and which are considered of secondary importance. A close analysis reveals information about patterns of agreement and disagreement, first and foremost from one national group to the next, but also according to the size and type of the institution, as well as the specific role and function of the respondents within their colleges and universities. While the potential of some teaching improvement practices appears to be a function of prevailing local conditions, the relative place of many others in the hierarchy of faculty development values transcends international borders and institutional type.

Several implications arise from our findings and subsequent analysis. First of all, the reader is given a clear picture of "what works" in the opinion of faculty development specialists. The faculty development community's perceptions of the value of each of the elements could help the decision-maker to lay out the options for an action plan for an instructional development program. The survey results might also prompt academics committed to improving post-secondary education to explore the teaching improvement practices likely to have an impact on their campuses when used *in combination*. A judicious blend of teaching improvement strategies might well add up to much more than the sum of its parts.

We hope that this chapter will prompt readers to introduce evaluation schemes into instructional development programs currently underway or to incorporate such schemes when devising teaching improvement programs and introducing policy. Faculty developers' perceptions of the relative value of policies and practices could provide the starting point for measures of effectiveness; there is a great need to demonstrate the impact of faculty development activities in terms of demonstrable change in teaching and student learning. Our hope, then, is that the international survey and our analysis of the results presented here will stimulate individuals and campus groups to probe further into the realm of university pedagogy and changing professional practice in the institutional setting, for it is ongoing, informed dialogue about teaching and learning which lies at the heart of the process of change.

METHOD

The purpose of the study is to examine how key instructional development people at universities and colleges in several countries perceive the potential impact of various teaching improvement practices. Information was gathered and analyzed to permit insights into the perspectives of the faculty development community in higher education within a given country and to allow comparisons on an international scale.

The data for this study were collected through surveys administered during 1992 and 1993. The survey respondents included people responsible for teaching improvement activities on campus: instructional development professionals, members of faculty, and administrators. In all but a few cases, a questionnaire was addressed directly to appropriate respondents whose names were identified through directories of teaching improvement personnel and lists of members of representatives to organizations concerned with teaching in higher education. The sample included only one individual for each institution or semi-autonomous campus.

The survey included two parts. The first section of the questionnaire asked for background information on the specific role of the respondent in teaching improvement activities, the structures designed to enhance teaching (offices, committees, etc.) and the size of the student population (full-time equivalent enrollment). In the second section of the survey instrument respondents were asked to rate each of 36 items (activities, policies, and practices) "to indicate the confidence you have in its potential to improve the quality of teaching in your university." Ratings for each item were based on a numeric scale of 1 ("least confident") to 10 ("most confident"). The responses were compiled and each item was ranked according to its mean.

The items were then grouped into nine previously defined categories of practices, with four related items in each category[1]. This classification scheme provides a framework for analysis by grouping related policies and practices. The categories themselves were then ranked according to the mean of the four-item aggregate rating. Multivariate tests of significance showed significant means differences within the nine categories at the $\alpha 0.05$ level for each of the four countries. While differences in category means between countries were also found, it is necessary to take into account the varying "cultures of measurement" at play. Specifically, respondents from the United Kingdom (UK) were less likely to give ratings at the highest levels (for example, the highest category mean for the UK group was 26.78 compared to 28.39 for Canada, 28.73 for Australasia, and 30.85 for the United States). For this reason, we chose to compare the results on the basis of a high to low mean ranking for each of the countries.

The surveys sent were identical, except that minor changes were made to reflect local terminology and that some additional information was collected for some countries. We describe the approach to conducting the research on a country-by-country basis below.

Canada

One questionnaire was sent to each of the 58 degree-granting institutions in Canada. A French-language version of the instrument was ad-

dressed to the 12 universities in which French is the language of instruction. Fifty-one completed questionnaires (41 English, 10 French) were received, an overall response rate of 87.75%, which closely reflects the
proportions of English and French universities in Canada.[2] For each college or university, the respondent was a person responsible for teaching
improvement activities on campus and was identified through the process
described above. In many instances, the respondents were active members
of Canada's Society for Teaching and Learning in Higher Education, but
membership in the Society was not a requirement. In each case, the appropriate institutional respondent was defined as "a director of a faculty development centre, a head of a committee on teaching and learning, or an
academic whose specific responsibility is faculty development." A question on the survey asking the respondents to indicate the nature of their
involvement in teaching improvement activities provided a means of ensuring that the individuals were indeed members of the target group.

United States

The US sample was drawn from the membership of the Professional
and Organizational Development Network in Higher Education (POD),
an organization devoted to improving teaching and learning in post-secondary education whose members have a high degree of involvement in
the enhancement of teaching and learning in higher education. The US
portion of this study was undertaken with the support of the 1993-94 POD
Grant Program. Questionnaires were sent to 290 individual POD members
who work in colleges and universities. Only one questionnaire was sent to
each university, college, or semi-autonomous campus, and an attempt was
made to identify the most appropriate respondent in institutions with
multiple members in POD. The survey instrument itself was similar to the
Canadian version, except that the Carnegie Classification (The Carnegie
Foundation for the Advancement of Teaching, 1987) was used to identify
the nature of the institution in the United States. The initial mailing and
follow-up process yielded 165 completed questionnaires, a response rate
of 57%. A database was then developed, applying the same model as described for the Canadian sample.[3]

United Kingdom

In the case of the UK, we obtained the support of the Standing Conference on Educational Development and the Society for Research into Higher
Education's Staff Development Group[4] (Small Grants Scheme for Research
and Development in Staff and Educational Development) to carry out the
survey. Minor modifications of terms, titles, and spellings were made to
the survey instrument before sending it to 151 members of the two organi-

zations in the United Kingdom. Information on the type of institution was also requested. Eighty-two completed questionnaires were received, a return rate of 53.6%. Data were then compiled as above.

Australasia

The Higher Education Research and Development Society of Australasia (HERDSA) was instrumental in forwarding the appropriate list of faculty developers for the conduct of our survey in the region in which the Society is active. Fifty-one surveys were sent to the 38 individuals on this list, as well as to 13 additional Australian universities.[5] We received 33 responses: 27 from Australia, 5 from New Zealand, and 1 from Fiji, for a response rate of 64.7%. We refer, throughout the rest of this chapter, to the "four country and regional surveys" because this survey extended beyond Australia. The Australasian data were treated in the usual manner and the results of the four surveys were then compiled to create the database including all respondents.

RESULTS

The compiled data from the international survey of teaching improvement practices were drawn from 331 responses. Several tables serve to illustrate the results and to provide a reference when reading our analysis, interpretation, and discussion of the results.

Table 1, "Respondents' Profile," displays information concerning the respondents' involvement in teaching development activity. The largest group consisted of full-time directors of instructional development offices or teaching centers. Respondents were also part-time directors, professors who chair institutional committees on teaching and learning, and academics whose duties include teaching enhancement on campus. A discussion of the relationship between the role of the respondent and the results of the questionnaire is undertaken below (see "Other Observations").

Table 2, "Size of Institution," categorizes the institutions involved in the study by student enrollment. Totals are provided for the entire sample, and a breakdown by country or region adds detail and facilitates comparisons of institutional size. About one-half of the colleges and universities surveyed enroll between 5,000 and 20,000 students. The role the "size of institution" plays in the rating of individual teaching improvement practices is examined below in the section "Other Observations."

Table 3, "Type of Institution," provides additional information on respondents' institutions in the US and UK, the two countries where such classifications are in widespread use.

Information regarding the existence of "Institutional Structures Devoted to Teaching Improvement" in the colleges and universities involved in our survey appears in Table 4. Note that over 60% of the institutions have centers or offices devoted primarily to the improvement of teaching, while the majority also have faculty committees on teaching.

A rank-ordering by mean of the combined ratings of all respondents of the 36 items on the questionnaire is found in Table 5, "Teaching Improvement Practices: Items by Rank." The table also provides standard deviations for each item internationally, as well as the corresponding results by country and region. This important table clearly displays the potential of the individual teaching improvement practice as seen by faculty developers in several different countries. It allows the reader to compare, at a glance, the rankings of a particular item as evaluated by respondents from one survey to the other.

Table 6, "Teaching Improvement Practices: Categories by Rank," introduces the nine categories, consisting of four questions each, which are used to organize the analysis of the results of the questionnaire. "Categories by Rank" includes aggregate means and standard deviations for the overall sample as well as for the four national and regional surveys. Table 5 and Table 6 constitute key references for the analysis and discussion of findings which follow.

ANALYSIS OF RESPONSES BY CATEGORY

This section provides an analysis of the responses to the four questions in each of the nine categories. The categories are considered by descending order of international rank, from "Leadership: Deans and Heads" through "Summative Evaluation of Instruction." The relevant parts of Tables 5 and 6 appear under each of the nine sub-titles.

Leadership: Deans & Heads

All Respondents		United States		Canada		United Kingdom		Australasia	
Rank	*Mean*	*Rank*	*Mean*	*Rank*	*Mean*	*Rank*	*Mean*	*Rank*	*Mean*
1	29.25	1	30.85	2	28.39	1	26.78	1	28.73

Items: Deans/heads foster importance of teaching responsibilities (2)
       Deans/heads promote climate of trust for classroom observation (4)
       Deans/heads praise and reward good teaching (8)
       Deans/heads give funds/opportunity for classroom research (14)

TABLE 1
Respondents' Profile

Respondent's Involvement in Teaching Improvement Activities	All Respondents N	%	United States n	%	Canada n	%	United Kingdom n	%	Australasia n	%
Full-time director of instructional development office	110	33.6	42	25.5	8	15.7	36	43.9	24	72.7
Part-time director of instructional development office	53	16.2	30	18.2	13	25.5	7	8.5	3	9.1
Full-time faculty member & Chair of teaching committee	44	13.5	28	17.0	9	17.6	7	8.5	Ø	Ø
Person responsible for (among other things) faculty dev.	53	16.2	34	20.6	5	9.8	9	11.0	5	15.2
Other*	67	20.5	29	17.6	15	29.4	22	26.8	1	3.0
Missing	4	1.2	2	1.2	1	2.0	1	1.2	Ø	Ø
Total	331	100%**	165	100%	51	100%	82	100%	33	100%

* Other includes: Non-teaching staff professional (n=7)
Dean (n=6)
Vice-President, Associate Vice-President, vice-recteur (n=4)
Directeur de l'Enseignement & de la Recherche ou d'Affaires (n=2)
Tutor/Lecturer in Education or Teaching (n=2)
Provost (n=1)
Chair of Faculty (n=1)

Senate President (n=1)
Research Fellow (n=1)
Head of Research Unit (n=1)
Chair of Planning Committee for Teaching Center (n=1)
Director, Educational Media (n=1)
Academic Support Services for Students (n=1)
Director, State-wide Program (n=1)
Did not specify (n=33)

** Because of rounding, figures do not always total 100%

TABLE 2
Size of Institution

Student Enrollment*	All Respondents		United States		Canada		United Kingdom		Australasia	
	N	%	n	%	n	%	n	%	n	%
<1,000	22	6.9	14	8.5	4	7.6	4	4.9	Ø	Ø
1,001 to 2,500	41	12.4	30	18.2	7	13.7	4	4.9	Ø	Ø
2,501 to 5,000	45	13.6	26	15.8	8	15.7	7	8.5	4	12.1
5,001 to 10,000	81	24.5	31	18.8	9	17.6	30	36.6	11	33.3
10,001 to 20,000	79	23.9	27	16.4	10	19.6	30	36.6	12	36.4
>20,000	50	15.1	32	19.4	12	23.5	Ø	Ø	6	18.2
Missing	13	3.9	5	3.0	1	2.0	7	8.5	Ø	Ø
Total	331	100%	165	100%	51	100%	82	100%	33	100%

* Full-time equivalent

TABLE 3

Type of Institution: US and UK

Carnegie Classification of Institution (US)	N	%
Research University I	33	20.0
Research University II	12	7.3
Doctorate-Granting University I	11	6.7
Doctorate-Granting University II	4	2.4
Comprehensive University or College I	36	21.8
Comprehensive University or College II	16	9.7
Liberal Arts College I	11	6.7
Liberal Arts College II	8	4.8
Two-Year Community, Junior, or Technical College	14	8.5
Professional School or Other Specialized Institution	15	9.0
Missing	5	3.0
Total	165	100.0
Type of Institution (UK)	N	%
University	69	84.1
College of Higher Education	9	11.0
College of Further Education	1	1.2
Mixed Further/Higher Education	2	2.4
Other	1	1.2
Total	82	100.0

TABLE 4

Institutional Structures Devoted to Teaching Improvement

Structure	All Respondents (331)		United States (165)		Canada (51)		United Kingdom (82)		Australasia (33)	
	N	%	n	%	n	%	n	%	n	%
A center or office devoted primarily to the improvement of teaching	205	61.9	98	60	22	43	56	69.1	29	93.5
A standing faculty committee on teaching	140	42.3	66	40	22	43	40	49.4	12	38.7
An *ad hoc* faculty committee on teaching	59	17.8	24	15	17	33	16	19.8	2	6.5
Other**	56	16.9	28	17	9	18	18	22.2	1	3.2

* Some institutions have more than one of these structures.

** Includes planning bodies for a teaching center or standing committee, pedagogical resource centers, advisory panels, teaching awards and grants committees, and structures related to curriculum development and student needs. In the UK, this includes development units and committees for all staff, Enterprise in Higher Education units, academic standards committees, and various other committees.

TABLE 6

Teaching Improvement Practices Categories by Rank

Category Name	All Respondents			United States			Canada			United Kingdom			Australasia		
	Rank	Mean	S.D.	Rank	Mean	S.D.	Rank	Mean	S.D.	Rank	Mean	S.D.	Rank	Mean	S.D.
"Leadership: Deans & Heads"	1	29.25	6.41	1	30.85	5.95	2	28.39	6.45	1	26.78	6.94	1	28.73	4.95
"Employment Policies & Practices"	2	28.26	6.13	2	29.43	6.18	1	29.73	5.68	3	25.45	5.43	2	27.21	5.87
"Development Opportunities & Grants"	3	27.15	5.75	3	28.18	5.91	6	26.53	5.86	2	26.12	5.21	5	25.48	5.25
"Formative Evaluation of Instruction"	4	26.05	5.49	4	26.81	5.63	7	26.49	5.56	4	25.13	5.29	7	23.88	4.43
"Structure & Organization"	5	25.65	5.46	7	25.57	5.50	5	26.61	5.52	5	25.04	4.85	3	26.06	4.27
"Leadership: Senior Administration"	6	25.55	7.28	6	25.85	7.32	3	27.06	7.36	6	23.87	7.42	4	25.94	6.08
"Educational Events"	7	25.46	5.59	5	26.12	5.92	4	26.73	5.71	7	23.76	5.13	6	24.39	6.04
"Developmental Resources"	8	24.42	4.92	8	24.78	4.95	8	25.75	5.04	8	23.16	4.61	8	23.70	4.81
"Summative Evaluation of Instruction"	9	22.25	6.17	9	22.78	6.46	9	22.47	6.53	9	21.18	5.70	9	21.91	4.98

TABLE 5

Teaching Improvement Practices
Items by Rank

"Rate each item to indicate the confidence you have in its potential to improve the quality of teaching in your university." (Scale: 1 = least confident 10 = most confident)

Teaching Improvement Practice	All Respondents N=331		
	Rank	Mean	S.D.
Recognition of teaching in tenure and promotion decisions	1.	8.24	1.60
Deans/Heads foster importance of teaching responsibilities	2.	7.94	1.70
Center to promote effective instruction	3	7.50	1.89
Deans/Heads promote climate of trust for classroom observation	4.	7.47	2.12
Mentoring programs and support for new professors	5.	7.38	1.60
Grants to faculty to devise new approaches to teaching	6.	7.31	1.86
Workshops on teaching methods for targeted groups	7.	7.30	1.72
Deans/Heads praise and reward good teaching	8.	7.29	1.90
Hiring practices require demonstration of teaching ability	9.	7.21	2.07
Consultation on course materials with faculty peers (formative)	10.	7.20	1.60
Senior admin. give visibility to teaching improvement activities	11.	7.17	1.89
Temporary workload reduction for course improvement/revision	12.	7.13	1.83
Availability of expert teaching consultant	13.	7.04	1.91
Deans/Heads give funds/opportunity for classroom research	14.	7.03	2.08
Regular (non-t&p) review of faculty teaching effectiveness	15.	6.86	2.04
Videotaping classroom teaching for analysis & improvement	16.	6.81	1.94
Faculty review of academic program to improve instruction	17.	6.75	1.82
Seminars on understanding student learning	18.	6.72	1.72
Funds for faculty to attend conference/course on teaching	19.	6.69	1.76
Classroom observation by peers for improvement purposes	20.	6.63	1.85
Mid-term student feedback to instructor (formative)	21.	6.59	1.96
Conference on teaching and learning held on campus	22.	6.56	1.89
Teaching dossier recognized record of teaching accomplishments	23.	6.48	2.08
Sabbatical leaves for improving teaching	24.	6.43	2,17
Senior admin. foster instit. pride to stimulate effective instruction	25.*	6.31	2.20
Course materials reviewed in univ. review process (summative)	25.*	6.31	2.01
Importance of teaching made public by senior administrators	27.	6.28	2.41
Senior admin. emphasizes how research supports teaching	28.	6.16	2.25
Faculty committee with mandate for improving instruction	29.	5.92	2.02
Teaching recognition programs (e.g., awards)	30.	5.88	2.02
Annual report on teaching accomplishments (summative)	31.	5.73	2.15
Circulation of articles and newsletters on teaching	32.	5.59	1.80
Classroom observation by peers/heads for summative purposes	33.	5.31	2.11
End-of-term student feedback for summative purposes	34.	5.22	2.34
Speakers on issues in higher education	35.	5.02	1.93
Readily accessible professional library	36.	4.55	2.09

* denotes tie

United States n=165			Canada n=51			United Kingdom n=82			Australasia n=33		
Rank	Mean	S.D.	Rank	Mean	S.D.	Rank	Mean	S.D.	Rank	Mean	S.D.
1.	8.30	1.65	1.	8.68	1.64	1.	7.83	1.53	1.	8.27	1.16
2.	8.13	1.66	4.	7.60	1.94	2.	7.63	1.74	2.	8.24	1.23
4.	7.72	1.93	3.	7.70	1.52	9.	6.79	1.99	3.	7.82	1.61
3.	8.00	1.87	26.	6.43	2.35	5.	7.24	2.15	7.*	6.94	2.12
6.	7.63	1.60	7.	7.39	1.46	7.	7.04	1.48	6.	6.97	1.93
7.	7.63	1.82	22.	6.67	1.85	4.	7.26	1.92	10*	6.88	1.60
13.	7.31	1.80	5.	7.55	1.64	3.	7.35	1.42	14.	6.73	2.08
5.	7.65	1.77	8.*	7.31	2.03	11.*	6.73	2.08	10.*	6.88	1.54
9.	7.48	2.10	2.	7.98	1.64	16.	6.30	1.98	12.	6.85	1.94
10.	7.43	1.58	8.*	7.31	1.63	8.	6.85	1.59	13.	6.79	1.54
11.	7.34	1.86	10.	7.30	1.84	10.	6.78	2.06	5.	7.12	1.60
15.	7.20	1.84	17.	6.77	1.95	6.	7.22	1.84	4.	7.15	1.60
14.	7.29	1.92	11.	7.12	1.85	14.	6.51	1.90	7.*	6.94	1.84
8.	7.55	1.90	6.	7.45	1.79	23.	5.86	2.15	15.	6.67	2.06
16.	7.09	2.11	23.	6.66	2.02	13.	6.63	1.91	18.	6.57	2.00
12.	7.33	1.81	12.	6.90	2.04	22.	6.04	1.91	26.	6.03	1.65
24.	6.70	1.93	14.*	6.82	1.89	11.*	6.73	1.60	9.	6.91	1.72
21.	6.96	1.69	16.	6.78	1.65	18.	6.26	1.78	17.	6.58	1.62
17.	7.08	1.76	18.	6.76	1.88	17.	6.27	1.50	30.	5.63	1.56
22.	6.94	1.78	27.	6.41	1.99	15.	6.40	1.79	28.	5.97	2.06
19.	7.04	1.96	20.	6.73	2.01	26.*	5.67	1.76	20.	6.46	1.64
20.	7.01	1.73	14.*	6.82	1.73	29.	5.62	1.90	22.	6.30	2.08
18.	7.07	1.88	21.	6.71	2.10	31.	5.29	2.08	23.	6.12	1.71
23.	6.84	2.00	24.	6.60	2.17	26.*	5.67	2.48	27.	6.00	1.64
25.	6.52	2.23	25.	6.45	2.13	24.	5.79	2.20	21.	6.31	2.01
26.	6.34	2.16	29.	6.20	1.97	20.	6.22	1.88	19.	6.55	1.56
28.	6.11	2.43	13.	6.84	2.58	21.	6.15	2.44	16.	6.61	1.82
27.	6.32	2.17	19.	6.74	2.14	28.	5.51	2.44	24.	6.09	2.04
30.	5.85	2.12	28.	6.36	1.77	25.	5.73	1.94	25.	6.06	2.00
31.	5.79	2.04	31.	6.00	2.18	19.	6.23	1.91	32.	5.27	1.86
29.	5.91	2.23	33.*	5.71	2.23	30.	5.41	2.04	29.	5.64	1.85
32.	5.74	1.87	30.	6.10	1.65	32.	5.03	1.75	31.	5.39	1.46
33.	5.74	2.04	36.	4.96	2.18	33.	4.93	1.99	35.	4.76	2.33
34.	5.25	2.35	32.	5.73	2.52	34.	4.89	2.18	33.	5.13	2.27
35.	5.07	1.92	33.*	5.71	1.83	36.	4.58	1.99	34.	4.79	1.76
36.	4.34	2.12	35.	5.14	1.99	35.	4.65	2.12	36.	4.39	1.92

The category "Leadership of Deans and Department Heads" was ranked highest by All Respondents with a category mean of 29.25. Respondents in each of the US, UK, and Australasian portions of the survey accorded this category top ranking, while the Canadian respondents ranked the category second. Individual items ranked between second and 14th in the All Respondents listing.

The item "Teaching is fostered as an important aspect of academic responsibility by Deans and Department Heads" ranked second in the All Respondents listing of 36 items. Each of the national and regional surveys ranked the item second overall, except for the Canadian survey, which ranked it in fourth position.

According to the authors of one major study on the dynamics of the academic department, the head "may well represent the single most important factor in determining whether or not a department actively supports teaching." Faculty in 20 colleges and universities interviewed about their working environments "cited the crucial role the chair plays in creating an environment conducive to effective teaching" (Massey, Wilger, & Colbeck, 1994, p. 17).

Some researchers have found that departments and department heads could, in fact, be doing more to foster teaching as an important academic activity.[6] According to an Australian study (Moses, 1988), faculty "felt that teaching was not encouraged enough" by their departments. In cases where teaching *was* considered, it was seldom with a view to improving quality: "the department's preoccupation is with getting the teaching done, not with doing it well" (p. 88). Faculty also perceived their departments "as being largely indifferent to organized professional development," the majority seeing their academic units as having "no policy, no opinion, providing no encouragement for staff to avail themselves of existing professional development opportunities" (p. 88). Faculty call for frequent departmental discussions of teaching and course content as well as encouragement to attend teaching development courses in order to improve the status of teaching in their departments. Even "informal acceptance and approval of teaching" is seen as "positive" (p. 91).

The promotion of excellence in teaching should be constantly on the departmental agenda (Moses & Roe, 1989). Department heads can enhance the quality of teaching in their departments by ensuring that course syllabi circulate throughout the department, by starting a department library on teaching, by establishing a committee on teaching, by capitalizing on formal and informal discussions of teaching, and by making "teaching effectiveness a high priority goal in the department" (Lucas, 1990, p. 392).

The item, "Climate of trust created by Deans and Department Heads which supports classroom observation," ranked fourth in the All Respondents listing. It ranked third among US respondents, fifth among UK respondents, and seventh among Australasian respondents. Canadian respondents, curiously enough, ranked this item only 26th. Ambiguity in the wording of this item (the lack of a clearly defined purpose for the "classroom observation") makes us reluctant to draw conclusions from these results. However, there is a pattern of response from the Canadian group who tend to have lower levels of confidence in a number of survey items dealing with the review or evaluation of teaching by someone other than the teacher being assessed.

Classroom observation, in its various forms, is thought by professors in higher education, as well as by faculty developers, to have considerable potential. Faculty complain that teaching is "not monitored," that they receive "no feedback" regarding their work in the classroom. They recommend peer observations of teaching and regular evaluation of teaching with follow-up discussions (Moses, 1988). The department head can help create the "climate of trust" to which we alluded in the survey item in order to make visiting colleagues' classrooms a supportive activity which is both "acceptable and non-threatening." Classroom observation can be either informal or conducted in the context of a mentoring system in which faculty work in pairs as teacher and observer over a period of a semester (Lucas, 1990, pp. 392, 394).

Perhaps the reason faculty developers have confidence that classroom observation can improve teaching is that this approach has the potential to foster a refreshing openness about teaching, to break down the barriers among teaching colleagues, and to stimulate productive discussions about teaching. While many of our respondents are themselves perceived as the campus "experts" on teaching in higher education–the ones to turn to for the correct "answer" to problems of post-secondary pedagogy–they nonetheless express a belief in the capacity of faculty members to provide one another with meaningful feedback and advice on teaching with minimal guidance from central agencies in the institution. The departmental setting has enormous potential for significant teaching improvement, if only its members would emphasize the pooling of their own pedagogical experience and collective wisdom. Instructional developers seeking to improve teaching on a collective, rather than an individual, basis would be well advised to assist departments in realizing this potential.

One department head advocates going "beyond self-interest" and moving towards "dependence on each other," all the while lamenting the tendency to leave a great potential untapped: "In our department, we are likely already to possess what we need to know about good teaching–what it is, and how to do it–but that knowledge is now fragmented and locked in the isolated experience of individual faculty members, unshared among colleagues who separately go about their common business" (Trask, 1989, p. 101). Where effective teaching is not formally encouraged and where there are no demands for accountability, teaching may be "swept under the carpet," and faculty are left to "operate in isolation... in a vacuum" (Moses, 1988, p. 90).

The item "Good teaching is praised and rewarded by Deans and Department Heads" ranked eighth in the All Respondents listing. The item ranked fifth in the US sample, eighth in the Canadian, 10th in the Australasian, and 11th in the UK. Our findings are consistent with an earlier teaching improvement practices survey in which Canadian faculty developers ranked the item "Department head praises/rewards good teachers" in a tie for third (out of 15 items) with "Department Head says teaching is important" (Schulz, 1988). Praise and reward for teaching accomplishment are key factors in motivating faculty to invest in the improvement of their teaching. Many faculty feel that teaching is "certainly not rewarded" at the departmental level, and one of their recommendations, not surprisingly, is that teaching be recognized in a more tangible fashion in tenure and promotion decisions (Moses, 1988, p. 90). Short of the ultimate "acknowledgement" (Moses & Roe, 1989, p. 19) of an individual's important contribution to the departmental teaching effort through the granting of tenure or promotion, faculty developers insist that praise, internal acknowledgement, nomination for a teaching award, recognition in the academic community, and positive reinforcement can go a long way to promoting teaching improvement among faculty members (Lucas, 1990; Moses & Roe, 1989).

The fourth item in this category measured the potential of deans and heads providing "opportunities and funding for professors to engage in classroom research for the purpose of improving instruction." The overall rank for this item was 14th. The item fared particularly well in North America, where Canadian respondents ranked it sixth and US respondents ranked it eighth. In Australasia, it ranked 15th, while in the UK, it ranked only 23rd.

Perhaps the higher ratings of this item by faculty developers in North America compared to the moderate confidence professed by their counterparts in Australasia and the UK can be attributed in part to the remarkable work of Americans Patricia Cross and Thomas Angelo, whose books, articles, and workshops on the subject have been very well received in Canada and the US. Classroom research, and its informal version called *classroom assessment techniques*, aim to provide faculty and students with information and insights to improve teaching effectiveness and the quality of learning. Classroom research views teaching as a dynamic activity in which professors monitor learning, collect feedback from students, and adjust pedagogical practices to better meet the goals of the course (See Angelo, 1991; Angelo & Cross, 1993; Cross & Angelo, 1988).

Faculty expect their departments to demonstrate commitment to teaching enhancement through the allocation of resources; the establishment of a fund to support classroom research would constitute a tangible and workable example of such a resource allocation. A plan to support classroom research would motivate faculty for whom "excellence in teaching is seen... as a scholarly activity for which they strive" (Moses, 1988, p. 93).

Institutional support for research on teaching appears low when compared with the considerable potential it has in the minds of faculty developers. In one study, chief academic officers at colleges and universities in the United States ranked research on teaching the lowest of 25 measures of institutional commitment to teaching and learning (Cochran, 1989). The Commission of Inquiry on Canadian University Education (Smith, 1991) found that research on university teaching was underdeveloped and "not highly regarded in most... universities" and recommended national initiatives to redress the situation by fostering "growth and maturation in the field of educational research" (p. 89).

The notion that deans and heads have an essential role to play in improving the quality of teaching in their colleges and departments has wide support. Chairs are in "a singular position" to make departments "places where people can share a sense of excitement" and where professors can make strong commitments to exchanging successful teaching strategies and identifying means of overcoming difficulties associated with teaching a specific discipline. Teaching improvement must begin in the department because "faculty's primary allegiance in a college or university is to the department" (Lucas, 1990, p. 395). The role of the department head is critical to the pursuit of teaching (and research) excellence because the department is an "organizational structure... which ideally unites a community of scholars with interest in a discipline in a situation where inspiration and intellectual challenge may be experienced" (Moses, 1985, p. 337).

Deans and chairs are seen to have considerable influence in colleges and universities due to their intellectual authority and their actions as important agents of socialization into the academic profession and as transmitters of academic culture (Neumann, 1992). The authors of a report on the evaluation of the Lilly Teaching Fellows Program in the United States concluded that "many incentives to encourage good teaching may be fruitless" without the active support of department heads (Rice & Austin, 1990, p. 39).

Faculty developers have a great deal of confidence in the potential of various actions of deans and department heads to improve teaching in colleges and universities. If department heads and chairs are increasingly rec-

ognized as "key agents for maintaining and enhancing the quality of undergraduate education" and, further, if the contention "that those chairpersons with the best knowledge and resources related to college teaching
and learning will be the most effective agents" is valid, what are faculty
developers doing to work with heads and other academic administrators
to promote teaching effectiveness on campus (Lucas, 1989a, p. 1)? A number of contributors to this book (Cox, Kaufman, and Sorcinelli and Aitken)
emphasize the importance of working closely with academic administrators at all levels to promote faculty development programs and to introduce change.

Employment Policies and Practices

All Respondents		United States		Canada		United Kingdom		Australasia	
Rank	*Mean*	*Rank*	*Mean*	*Rank*	*Mean*	*Rank*	*Mean*	*Rank*	*Mean*
2	28.26	2	29.43	1	29.73	3	25.45	2	27.21

Items: Recognition of teaching in tenure and promotion decisions (1)
     Hiring practices require demonstration of teaching ability (9)
     Regular (non-tenure and promotion) review of faculty teaching
     effectiveness (15)
     Teaching dossier recognized record of teaching accomplishments (23)

Respondents had high confidence in the potential of employment policies and practices to improve teaching on their campuses. This category
ranked second overall with a four-item aggregate mean of 28.26 and a first
to third ranking in the four countries and regions. With one exception, there
was a fair degree of inter-country variation, however, among the individual
items in this category.

Of all the survey items, respondents expressed the highest level of confidence in the recognition of teaching in tenure and promotion decisions;
this item achieved a first-place ranking in each of the country and region
sub-groups. The respondents clearly see a direct relationship between the
quality of teaching and the reward system; linking faculty career advancement to teaching performance is perceived as an important avenue to improving teaching.

There were interesting differences among the national groups' levels of
confidence in the remaining items in this category. The Canadian group
differed from the other groups in its strong support for the practice of requiring a demonstration of teaching ability during hiring procedures, which
ranked second for this group. Other national groups were less confident

that this practice would improve teaching in their institutions, with the UK group expressing the least support with a rank of 16.

Respondents had only moderate confidence in the teaching improvement potential of the practice of requiring a regular review of faculty teaching effectiveness, which ranked 15th overall. The Canadians' comparatively low level of support for this practice (ranking it 23rd) is part of a pattern of low confidence expressed by this group in a variety of evaluation of teaching activities described in this and other categories. There would appear to be more resistance among the Canadians to the idea of administrative control.

There were wide-ranging degrees of confidence in the use of the teaching portfolio (or *dossier*, as it is called in Canada) as the recognized record of teaching accomplishments, indicating a substantial lack of agreement among respondent groups about the teaching improvement potential of this practice. The teaching portfolio is defined by the Canadian Association of University Teachers as "a summary of a professor's major teaching accomplishments and strengths," a document to parallel "lists of publications, grants, and academic honors" in the field of research (Shore et al., 1986, p. 1). The portfolio is being used both for purposes of improvement and in the context of gathering and presenting files for tenure and promotion. One university president describes the benefits of a teaching portfolio guide as "help[ing] us not only to document teaching accomplishment more effectively, but also to encourage improvements in our teaching performance, and make it possible to recognize and reward those who display particular excellence in their teaching activities" (Clark, 1993, p. vii).

The overall ranking for this item was 23rd. Moderate confidence was expressed by the US, Canadian, and Australasian groups at 18th, 21st, and 23rd. The UK respondents had little confidence in this practice, ranking it a low 31st. Because of the teaching portfolio's development and longer history of use in North America, the lack of strong support from US and Canadian respondents is one which we did not anticipate.

A chapter in this volume (Seldin, Annis, & Zubizarreta) documents the tremendous upsurge of interest in the teaching portfolio on campuses in the United States and Canada. And faculty developers have been at the forefront of a movement to harness the potential of the teaching portfolio strategy to further their collective agenda of improving the status of teaching in their institutions. The enthusiasm of the faculty development community in North America for the portfolio approach (if the proliferation of conferences, articles, papers, and books on the subject is an indication) is not reflected in the results of this survey. The reasons for the somewhat lackluster confidence in this process of documentation and performance review are not clear; whether it is due to inexperience with, or even negative experience with, the teaching portfolio approach, or to some other cause, those interested in furthering the use of the portfolio would do well to investigate.

Correspondents prominent in the UK faculty development community, though they themselves support the portfolio concept, are not surprised that the item fared poorly in the UK. They observe that the concept is not widely known in the UK and that higher education is slow to adopt new procedures such as those associated with the portfolio approach. They went on to point out, however, that the time is ripe to explore the concept further on a national and international scale (G. Gibbs, personal communication, May 9, 1994; G. Gordon, personal communication, May 10, 1994). In Australia, the portfolio approach has not been implemented, but it may help answer some problems in documenting teaching at a time that coincides with moves toward greater accountability in universities (N. Fleming, personal communication, July 27, 1994). Perhaps the true potential of the portfolio concept remains a relatively unknown commodity despite the flurry of activity relating to the portfolio in many higher education settings in recent years.

A great deal of attention has been focused on the question of whether extrinsic rewards for faculty and changes in personnel decision-making practices to recognize effective teaching have a positive impact on the quality of teaching. It is clear that many authorities believe that they do.

The high level of confidence of the survey respondents in the overall potential impact of employment policies and practices on teaching quality is evident throughout the higher education community. Cochran (1989), in his study of over 1,300 chief academic officers at universities and colleges in the United States, recorded a high level of institutional commitment to the use of "employment policies and practices to support instructional effectiveness" (p. 70). A recent survey of over 20,000 administrators, deans, and department heads in the United States found that a majority would support "an effort to modify the [reward] system to recognize and reward teaching" (Diamond, 1993-94, p. 1). Other studies confirm that research accomplishment remains the primary determinant of career and salary advancement for university and college faculty (The Carnegie Foundation for the Advancement of Teaching, 1991; Fairweather, 1993; Moses, 1987; Smith, 1991). These authors and others (Eble, 1990; Konrad, 1983; Shore, 1974) contend that personnel decisions which recognize and reward effective instruction will lead to improved teaching performance.

However, some writers such as Ramsden (1992) disagree, arguing that emphasis on increasing extrinsic rewards as a means of improving teaching ignores the dynamics of teaching improvement or research into the impact of extrinsic rewards (See also Centra, 1993; Miller, 1988). Centra and Ramsden suggest that an accent on extrinsic rewards may have a significant *negative* impact by reducing the motivation that comes from intrinsic rewards. Simply put, faculty members frequently cite the enjoyment of teaching as a primary reason for being in the profession; focusing on tangible rewards to encourage improved teaching overlooks this fundamental motivation. A teaching improvement program which places undue attention on eventual rewards such as promotion, tenure, and merit pay may create an environment which actually undermines efforts to improve teaching and learning.

Ramsden makes a stong case for a teaching improvement strategy which is broader in scope than that represented by improved employment policies and practices which focus on individual teachers. The high level of confidence the survey respondents expressed in the teaching improvement potential of the reward system is, no doubt, an indication that institutions are failing to demonstrate that teaching is valued. While the importance of an improved reward system should not be overlooked, we should also keep in mind the warnings of Ramsden, Centra, and others, that the recognition and reward of effective teaching performance is not enough to ensure the creation of institutional structures and culture dedicated to educational excellence.

Development Opportunities and Grants

All Respondents		United States		Canada		United Kingdom		Australasia	
Rank	*Mean*	*Rank*	*Mean*	*Rank*	*Mean*	*Rank*	*Mean*	*Rank*	*Mean*
3	27.15	3	28.18	6	26.53	2	26.12	5	25.48

Items: Grants to faculty to devise new approaches to teaching (6)
Temporary workload reduction for course improvement or revision (12)
Funds for faculty to attend conference/course on teaching (19)
Sabbatical leaves for improving teaching (24)

The category "Development Opportunities and Grants" ranked third in the All Respondents listing, with an aggregate mean of 27.15. The relative category rankings for the national and regional groups, however, ranged from second and third in the UK and the US to fifth and sixth in Australasia and Canada. The individual items ranked from sixth to 24th in the All Respondents listing, as faculty grants scored highest, followed by workload reductions, funded course and conference attendance, and sabbaticals for teaching improvement.

Faculty developers in the UK, the US, and Australasia ranked the item "Grants for faculty members to develop new or different approaches to courses or teaching" fourth, seventh, and tenth, respectively. The Canadian group, exceptionally, ranked this item only 22nd. Surveys have established that the practice of institutional funding systems for classroom teaching innovation is widespread in colleges and universities in Canada and in the United States (Erickson, 1986; Wright, 1993). Teaching development funds are administered by teaching improvement centers, faculty committees, senate committees on instructional development, or the office of a senior academic officer such as a vice-president or provost. Individual grants range from $250 (US) to $5000 (US) (Weimer & Lenze, 1991; Wright, 1993). Various institutional documents describing the grants state that they are designed to test teaching strategies, to stimulate the development of improved course materials, and to facilitate student learning. Examples of funded projects include the production of a guide for teaching assistants, the organization of a conference on language teaching, and the study of independent learning methods in a given discipline (Wright, 1993). Note that some universities also offer large grants (up to $40,000 US) to departments and multi-departmental coalitions to promote major curriculum revision and pedagogical change (Wright, 1993), but this practice was not evaluated by means of our international questionnaire.

Grants for instructional improvement projects have been a part of the faculty development repertoire of strategies since the 1960s; their use is widespread, and they are well received by faculty. Yet there has been remarkably little study of the outcomes of these awards in terms of pedagogical effectiveness or student learning (Weimer & Lenze, 1991). Our faculty development respondents expressed strong confidence in the potential of the grants, but higher education institutions appear, in general, to have been remiss in not measuring the impact of this approach on improving instruction.

Another strategy to facilitate new course development and course revision is to grant temporary workload reductions, usually in the form of a "course release," to individual professors. Internationally, our respondents ranked the potential of this practice 12th overall, though a close look at the rankings in individual countries and regions shows that faculty developers in the UK and Australasia have very high confidence in the practice, while faculty developers in North America express less confidence. Although granting a temporary workload reduction is usually the prerogative of departments and faculties, teaching development committees in some institutions exercise this responsibility. At York University (Canada), the Senate Committee on Teaching and Learning administers Release-Time Fellowships to provide professors with "the opportunity to develop innovative teaching and learning projects or to enhance their own skills (as opposed to disciplinary competence), when such development or enhancement could not take place in the context of a full teaching load" (Wright, 1993).[7] We have little hard evidence of the overall impact of course-release plans, though personal experience leads us to conclude that such a system does, indeed, have considerable potential to improve instruction.

A third item in this category concerned the potential of "Funds for faculty members to attend conferences or take courses related to their improvement as teachers," and ranked 19th overall. Three of the national surveys yielded rankings of 17th and 18th for this item, while the Australasians ranked the item only 30th. Some institutions provide travel fees and expenses for courses and conferences through their teaching development committees described above, while others, such as Wilfrid Laurier University (Canada), have dedicated structures to facilitate this activity (The Instructional Development Travel Grant Program) (Wright, 1993). Most colleges and universities encourage the active participation of academic staff in courses and conferences by means of funding mechanisms of one sort or another, but, when separate funds for the two types of activity do not exist, events which accent the teaching of one's discipline take a back seat to the traditional discipline-based research meetings. Many academics who have opted to attend the annual conferences sponsored by their national organizations for the promotion of teaching have found them to be very stimulating: the meetings tend to provide a refreshing change of atmosphere and format, involving participants in an ongoing dialogue regarding pedagogical issues and avenues of response.[8]

The use of sabbatical leaves for the purpose of developing one's teaching does not appear to be a common practice internationally among postsecondary academic staff, nor did the approach garner very high scores among the faculty developers we asked to rate its potential. Some of our respondents may have been altogether unfamiliar with the concept. It ranked 24th in the All Respondents listing with little variation among the country and regional groups. National surveys on sabbatical leave policies have tended to concentrate on gathering data on *prevalence* and *percent of salary* earned during the period of the leave (Erickson, 1986, p. 189). A study of universities in Atlantic Canada, however, pinpoints several instances in which institutional policy statements and union contracts allude to teaching improvement as an intended *outcome* of a sabbatical leave; one document explicitly refers to supporting sabbatical projects "directed primarily toward enhancement of teaching" (Brooks, 1993, p. 1).

There is a fair amount of support, then, in the faculty development community internationally for structures, programs, and policies which provide development opportunities and grants to faculty in order to foster teaching improvement. But, generally speaking, the confidence level regarding individual grants and workload reductions is somewhat higher than for conference/course participation and sabbaticals dedicated to improving teaching.

Formative Evaluation of Instruction

All Respondents		United States		Canada		United Kingdom		Australasia	
Rank	*Mean*	*Rank*	*Mean*	*Rank*	*Mean*	*Rank*	*Mean*	*Rank*	*Mean*
4	26.05	4	26.81	7	26.49	4	25.13	7	23.88

Items: Consultation on course materials with faculty peers (formative) (10)
Videotaping classroom teaching for analysis and improvement (16)
Classroom observation by peers for improvement purposes (20)
Mid-term student feedback to instructor (formative) (21)

Formative evaluation refers to diagnostic assessment aimed at talent development (not to be confused with performance assessment for administrative and personnel decision-making, or summative evaluation). Teachers may use a variety of formative evaluation techniques to aid in independent self-assessment of teaching performance, or they may choose to engage the assistance of a trained observer (usually a teaching specialist or knowledgeable colleague) to provide additional feedback and advice. Ideally, formative evaluation is a continuous process of information gathering, interpretation, planning, and action, followed by another cycle which assesses the impact of changes.

Because formative evaluation is undertaken with the single goal of enhancing performance, we expected the survey respondents would express fairly high levels of confidence in the teaching improvement potential of the items in this category, which ranked fourth overall and for the UK and US respondent groups. The Canadian rank was seventh, but the difference among the means of the fourth- to seventh-ranked categories, while statistically significant, was small and, in this case, the rankings may exaggerate actual results. However, the seventh-place ranking from the Australasians reflects a greater variation in means, clearly differentiating the confidence level of this group from the others (see Table 6).

Consultation on course materials (e.g., outlines, readings, and evaluation procedures) with faculty peers ranked tenth overall and each respondent group gave this item the highest ranking in the category. This is a common activity (Erickson, 1986) which is very much in keeping with traditional academic interaction: discussion of the literature, exchange of information and opinion about important research in the field, and the orderly transmission of a particular body of knowledge. Consultation on course materials focuses not only on course content and organization, but on such specifics as the construction of examinations and assignments and their impact on students (Do tests and assignments encourage "deep" or "surface" approaches to learning? Do they measure desired learning objectives? Are student workloads reasonable?).

As faculty developers, survey respondents know that this activity is a good way to encourage a collegial approach to teaching improvement. This approach is also less intimidating to faculty than are other practices in this category which focus on an individual's classroom performance. Weimer (1990) recommends that those promoting course materials consultation ensure that the specific activities and their benefits are fully explained to prospective faculty participants.

Videotaping classroom teaching for analysis and improvement (often including consultation with a teaching expert) is frequently cited in the faculty development literature as a useful formative evaluation technique (Weimer, 1990; Weimer and Lenze, 1991). This item received an aggregate ranking of 16, indicating moderately high levels of confidence. But the national and regional group responses differed notably. Both North American groups expressed a fairly high degree of confidence in this item, each giving it a rank of 12. Less supportive of the teaching improvement potential of videotaping were respondents from the UK (rank 22) and Australasia (rank 26).

In comparison with their ranking of video observation, respondents overall had less confidence in classroom observation by faculty peers for formative purposes (rank 20). The UK group was much more supportive of peer observation than were any of the other groups (rank 15, compared to the US at 22 and Canada at 27). The Australasians were particularly consistent in their lack of confidence in classroom observation techniques of either kind. They ranked peer observation at a low 28.

On the whole, these results are somewhat surprising, since peer consultation programs have gained increasing popularity over recent years. The relatively low confidence of respondents in this activity may be a reflection of the deeply ingrained view that teaching is essentially a private activity, or at least a recognition that faculty themselves hold this view and may thus be resistant to opening their classrooms to others. That the UK group expressed moderately high confidence in peer observation may be a reflection of a more collegial academic culture.

Overall in this category, the use of mid-term student ratings of instruction for purposes of improvement registered the least support, with an aggregate ranking of 21st, ranging from 19th to 26th in the national and regional surveys. This widespread practice has been the subject of considerable research which provides evidence that, when properly designed, administered, and interpreted, mid-term student ratings of instruction can provide the basis for enhanced teaching performance. This is the case particularly when such evaluations form part of a broader diagnostic and consultation process (Aleamoni, 1978; Areola & Aleamoni, 1990; Cohen, 1980, 1990; Franklin & Theall, 1990; Gil, 1987; McKeachie, 1987; Stevens, 1987; Weimer, 1990). Centra (1993) argues that student ratings for improvement purposes are most effective when instructors learn something new about their teaching, when they value the information, when they know or are advised about how to improve, and when they are motivated to change.

Participants did not express a high degree of confidence in the formative evaluation techniques contained in the survey. In spite of this, if we are inclined to follow the lead articulated in the work of faculty developers like Centra (1993), Ramsden (1992), Weimer (1990) and others, it is clear that formative evaluation should play a part in a comprehensive teaching improvement strategy:

> *Our aim should be the development of a self-critical, reflective academic community which constantly seeks internal and external comment on the quality of its teaching, and has the knowledge base and the sense of inner security to act wisely and temperately in the light of the judgements it makes of itself. (Ramsden, 1992, p. 247)*

Structure and Organization

All Respondents		United States		Canada		United Kingdom		Australasia	
Rank	*Mean*	*Rank*	*Mean*	*Rank*	*Mean*	*Rank*	*Mean*	*Rank*	*Mean*
5	25.65	7	25.57	5	26.61	5	25.04	3	26.06

Items: Center to promote effective instruction (3)
        Faculty review of academic program to improve instruction (17)
        Faculty committee with mandate for improving instruction (29)
        Teaching recognition programs (e.g., awards) (30)

The establishment of ongoing, supportive institutional structures helps to ensure a measure of permanence for teaching improvement efforts and signals the level of institutional commitment to educational quality. The All Respondents ranking of the category "Structure and Organization" was 5th of the nine categories, ranging from a high of 3rd for the Australasians to a low of 7th for the US group.

Survey results highlight the importance of establishing an institutional unit to promote effective instruction and to enhance the development of faculty in their roles as teachers: the item dealing with the potential of a center to improve teaching ranked third overall, third in both Canada and Australasia, fourth in the US, and ninth in the UK.

It would appear that, in the eyes of many of our respondents, the work of an instructional or faculty development center is fundamental to the enterprise of successful teaching improvement in the institutional setting. The units charged with the task of improving the quality of teaching and learning are variously called the office of instructional development, the center for university teaching and learning, the center for the support of teaching, the center for teaching enhancement, the teaching excellence center, the learning development office, the center for academic practice, and the educational development service, as well as the academic staff development office (UK), the "service de l'aide à l'enseignement" and "les services pédagogiques" (Canada), and, simply, the education centre (New Zealand) or the center for teaching (US). Differences in the resources, policies, and programs of the units appear to bear no relationship to their names as listed above. As the field of improving teaching in higher education developed, observers distinguished between the work of developing "the skills and knowledge of the teaching staff" (faculty development)[9] and efforts to improve "other parts of the educational process... such as the quality of instructional materials... or the relative value placed on teaching by the institution" (instructional development) (Shore, 1974, p. 45). While these distinctions are still useful in describing the foci of specific programs and activities, few professionals in the field would admit to directing a center which attempted *either* to have some impact on the abilities and performance of teaching staff *or* to influence educational offerings and the status of teaching in the institution: most are active on *both* fronts.

A teaching development center with a permanent academic and support staff and a clear mandate and reporting structure can make a significant impact on the quality of teaching in a college or university through a sustained, multi-faceted program of activities and policy development. The successful work of a center can be appraised in many ways: through the educational events it sponsors and organizes, through the publications it produces, through the influence it has in involving supportive academic administrators in its programs, and through its impact on institutional policies with respect to teaching. The center can, ideally, play a leading role in the implementation of many of the teaching improvement practices which were the subject of the international survey discussed here.

The respondents had a wide range of opinions on the potential of faculty involvement in "periodic, comprehensive reviews of academic programs for the purpose of improving instruction." The All Respondents ranking for this item was 17th, but the individual country and regional surveys produced rankings from 9th in Australasia to 11th in the UK, 14th in Canada, and 24th in the US. Perhaps this is an example of a survey question which was influenced both heavily and legitimately by a wide variety of local conditions and practices with respect to the history of faculty involvement in academic program review. Do American faculty developers feel that professors have had a fair amount of experience with program review in a country which tends to renew curriculum relatively easily because of dynamic contemporary pressures? Do they conclude that this is not, then, a relatively fruitful orientation in terms of teaching improvement results? And what to make of our Australasian respondents' relative confidence in the potential of this practice? Australian universities have experienced major amalgamation and reform: how does the recent past influence the attitudes of faculty developers towards program review at this point in time? Further investigation is necessary to understand these marked differences.

We think that faculty involvement in periodic program review has great potential to improve instruction. Faculty developers should seize every opportunity to work with department heads and review committees to ensure that program reviews go beyond questions on sequencing of courses and units and examinations of various traditional ways of "covering the content"; the reviews could be an excellent means of stimulating faculty discussion on alternative teaching methods and the need to develop new pedagogical strategies to deliver the components of the curriculum.

Survey respondents expressed a clear preference for the establishment of a faculty development center (rank 3) as opposed to a "broadly based faculty committee with a mandate for improving the quality of instruction" (rank 29 overall, ranging from 25th in Australasia and the UK to 30th in the US). Though centers flourish partly because of "passionate directors and dedicated change agents," faculty development programs run by committee *can* have a positive impact when organizers "have both the responsibility and the authority to carry out the work" (Lunde & Healy, 1991, p. 15). In some instances, to be sure, centers and committees co-exist in colleges and universities, and directors work with committee members to further a common teaching improvement goal. But relying solely on a committee to advance the instructional development project at an institution has its risks: such a system is highly dependent, over time, on the generosity, availability, and vision of many dedicated faculty working in a voluntary capacity.

According to our survey, teaching recognition programs, or "teaching awards," were not considered to have great potential to improve teaching. The item placed 30th of 36 items in the All Respondents listing, with rankings of 31st in the US and in Canada, and 32nd in Australasia. The item fared somewhat better in the UK, which listed the item in 19th place.

Though teaching awards are a common means of recognizing teaching accomplishment (Erickson, 1986), faculty developers view their impact as limited (Schulz, 1988). However, many faculty developers support the process of selecting award-winning teachers in their institution and, in fact, are often called upon to organize the process. Faculty development centers and committees are frequently charged with the preparation of the dossiers of candidates nominated by the institution or chief academic officer for awards at the regional, national, and international levels. Why, then, do our respondents express relatively little faith in the potential of the awards to improve instruction yet remain active supporters of teaching awards in their institutions? The answer to this question has, in our view, several dimensions. The first element relates to the nature of the awards themselves: they tend to be made in *recognition* of excellence in teaching rather than as an *incentive* to great teaching. Though many recipients state that they are grateful for the honor brought by their awards, the emphasis tends to be on acknowledgement of past service rather than to spur teachers on to "greater heights." In this sense, they are somewhat like a letter of thanks for a job well done: one would not undertake the task in order to receive such a letter, though one certainly appreciates the recognition and thanks when it arrives. Teaching awards are the decent thing to do.

The second element involves the aspect of public recognition and celebration of teaching excellence, which has some significance in an institutional setting where there is a premium on honors bestowed. The awards are often presented at public gatherings, at convocations, at formal dinners. The events frequently offer award-winning professors their first opportunity to articulate their philosophies of teaching in public. This brings us to the third element: teaching awards are about honors and recognition, but they fall short of rewards for teaching. As we have seen in the discussion of Employment Policies and Practices, faculty developers want to go beyond introducing peripheral improvements to the place of teaching in higher education. In order to effect major change, teaching awards may play a part in an overall strategy, but our respondents see a more significant impact at the level of changing the whole reward structure in colleges and universities.

Teaching awards may have a limited impact in and of themselves, but teaching centers can use the awards to further their aims of raising the profile of teaching on campus and proliferating knowledge of effective teaching. Award-winners are often interviewed by the campus newspaper, and some are also asked to write on their teaching philosophy or to offer teaching tips in a pedagogical guide or newsletter on teaching. For example, York University's (Canada) *Core* newsletter and Dalhousie University's *Focus on University Teaching and Learning* bulletin have featured such contributions. Some award-winning teachers are required to make a presentation on teaching excellence to their colleagues, and most of them welcome the opportunity. Winners of the annual Association of Atlantic Universities (AAU) Distinguished Teacher and Instructional Leadership Awards are granted financial support for a speaking or workshop tour of universities in the Atlantic Provinces. At Dalhousie University, the President's Graduate Teaching Assistant Award was established at the initiative of the Office of Instructional Development and Technolgy (OIDT). The Award has drawn attention to the important pedagogical role of the teaching assistant, provided faculty with the opportunity to formally nominate their teaching assistants for an honor, served as an incentive to graduate students to compile excellent teaching portfolios, and identified outstanding young teachers to whom the OIDT could turn for leadership in designing professional improvement programs for teaching assistants. The impact of awards, considered in isolation, would seem small, but when one includes the possible "spin-off" effects, the positive outcomes appear to be more significant.

Leadership: Senior Administration

All Respondents		United States		Canada		United Kingdom		Australasia	
Rank	*Mean*	*Rank*	*Mean*	*Rank*	*Mean*	*Rank*	*Mean*	*Rank*	*Mean*
6	25.55	6	25.85	3	27.06	6	23.87	4	25.94

Items: Senior administration gives visibility to teaching improvement activities (11)

Senior administration fosters institutional pride to stimulate effective instruction (25*)

Importance of teaching made public by senior administrators (27)

Senior administration emphasizes how research supports teaching (28)

Four of the 36 items on the international survey related to the potential of senior academic leaders to bring about improvement of teaching in higher education. In the discussion of responses in this category, we include presidents, academic and research vice-presidents, and their associates, as well as such officers as provosts and deputy provosts, in the discussion of responses in this category.

The most highly ranked item by All Respondents dealt with teaching improvement activities being given "high visibility by senior administration in order to illustrate their importance." The Australasian group ranked this item 5th, while the remaining countries had somewhat less confidence (10th to 11th rank). Senior administrators can go beyond lip-service in support of teaching by actively promoting instructional development programs, thus sending a clear message to the academic community that the institution is committed to teaching enhancement and to initiatives designed to further this commitment. Presidents can send personalized letters to newly hired faculty underlining the importance of orientation to teaching sessions and urging newcomers to participate fully in instructional development activities. Academic vice-presidents can put teaching improvement on the agenda of meetings of deans and department heads, collaborating with faculty development personnel to generate a program and specific items for consideration. Provosts and their associates can go beyond the perfunctory "guest appearance" at teaching improvement events by becoming involved in their promotion and joining in as interested participants. Giving high visibility to teaching improvement means placing instructional development efforts near the top of the priority list and, as far as possible, becoming actively involved in strategies designed to link the quality of teaching to the heart of the institutional mission.

Respondents, internationally, ranked the potential of senior administrators fostering "a feeling of institutional pride that stimulates effective classroom instruction" 25th. Once again, the rankings of responses by country were very consistent, with the US and Canada ranking the item 25th, the UK 24th, and Australasia 21st. As stated above, academics tend to owe loyalties to their disciplines and departments more than to their institutions; is it rather old-fashioned or impractical to think that senior administrators could significantly influence the quality of teaching by instilling a sense of "institutional pride" in the teaching staff? Perhaps.

What is the potential of statements emphasizing "the importance of teaching by senior university administrators in speeches and public presentations" in terms of their impact on teaching improvement? The All Respondents ranking for this item is only 27th, though faculty developers outside of the US express a somewhat higher level of confidence in the power of public pronouncement by senior administrators. It is interesting to note that this precise item ranked at the top, in terms of "perceived commitment" on the part of chief academic officers, of a list of five "strategic administrative actions in support of instructional effectiveness" in a nation-wide survey, conducted in the United States (Cochran, 1989, p. 100).

According to the survey respondents, emphasizing "the ways in which research and scholarly activity can be used to reinforce or support effective teaching" has even less potential to improve teaching than the other items in this category. It ranked 28th in the All Respondents listing, though it ranked slightly higher in the Canadian and Australasian surveys. The "teaching-research nexus" (Higher Education Council, 1990) has, in recent years, received a considerable amount of attention in the literature on higher education as well as in governmental reports (See, for example, Neill, 1989; Smith, 1991; Weaver, 1989). The debate tends to revolve almost solely around the question of whether an individual's on-going involvement in discovery research leading to publication constitutes a prerequisite to achieving teaching excellence. Some writers wisely "leav[e] aside" the unproductive consideration of "anecdotes about the capacity of the best researchers as teachers," suggesting that while research is an essential element in "an institution's profile of activities," there are "many ways to be a good academic" (Higher Education Council, 1990, p. 37). But much work has to be done concerning the conditions under which research can and does, in fact, support effective teaching. There is a need for more dialogue and new insights into how research activity can–for specific courses and specific disciplines–enhance teaching and learning in the laboratory and in the classroom. Academic administrators, faculty development specialists, and outstanding researchers and teachers should lead the way.

Despite the fact that faculty developers responding to our survey consider the potential of specific items relating to the actions and behaviors of senior administrators significantly weaker than that of items relating to the comportment of deans and heads, we contend that senior administrators can play an essential role in the success of campus teaching improvement initiatives. Senior administrators can influence the distribution of resources and exercise "their persuasive powers to create new priorities and mobilize faculty energies behind them" (Bok, 1986, p. 183). Further, the creation of a campus climate "that supports and rewards effective teaching and accord[s] such teaching a status equal to that of scholarly research and publication" has been called a "turnabout" that "can take place only at the initiative and with the guidance of the institution's administrative leaders" (Seldin & Associates, 1990, p. xviii). The four items on our international survey refer to ways in which senior administrators can exercise their "symbolic leadership" to "influence the organizational culture," thereby enhancing the prominence of both teaching and faculty development policies and programs on campus (Green, 1990, p. 46, 48-51). Finally, we would warn faculty developers prone to ignore or minimize the role of the senior academic administration that they do so at their peril. Although the *positive* impact of the senior administrator's attempts to bolster teaching in the institutional setting may be a matter of debate, the *negative* impact of the senior administrator's attitudes, words, and actions is clear: many programs and policies, as well as centers themselves, have failed miserably when a key senior administrator is not convinced that they are a priority.

Educational Events

All Respondents		United States		Canada		United Kingdom		Australasia	
Rank	*Mean*	*Rank*	*Mean*	*Rank*	*Mean*	*Rank*	*Mean*	*Rank*	*Mean*
7	25.46	5	26.12	4	26.73	7	23.76	6	24.39

Items: Workshops on teaching methods for targeted groups (7)
        Seminars on understanding student learning (18)
        Conference on teaching and learning held on campus (22)
        Speakers on issues in higher education (35)

The category "Educational Events" ranked 7th in the All Respondents listing. Rankings by country varied: 4th in Canada, 5th in the US, 6th in Australasia, and 7th in the UK. Workshops on teaching methods for targeted groups such as new faculty and teaching assistants ranked seventh among All Respondents. UK respondents had the most confidence in workshops, as the item placed third in their overall ranking. In Canada, the item fared almost as well, ranking fifth, but workshops placed only 13th and 14th in the US and in Australasia. Other surveys show workshops on teaching strategies and techniques to be both very prevalent in higher education (Erickson, 1986; Schulz, 1988) and very highly rated by faculty developers (Kapp, 1994). For many faculty development committees and centers, the faculty development workshop is their "bread and butter" activity, the most visible of services for professors on campus. Are faculty development workshops effective? The answer is complex, but researchers report that participants often consider the events "useful, relevant, and informative," particularly the longer programs requiring greater commitment and involvement (Weimer & Lenze, 1991, p. 304). As it is hard to imagine *any* active instructional or faculty development program without faculty workshops, perhaps the best we can do is to offer some suggestions to optimize impact, based on experience and observation. Individual workshops should be planned thoroughly and publicized widely; they should address the pedagogical problems and concerns of a wide range of faculty; they should be led by facilitators with a vast knowledge of the subject *and* proven expertise in workshop methodology; they should engage the participants in active learning; and they should be evaluated by means of a brief participant questionnaire on site.

Many faculty development centers find the "isolated," short workshop of limited value and prefer to organize series, often linking the events to an overall program theme or broader faculty development initiative. At Dalhousie University, we have adopted several strategies of this kind to ensure the success of our workshops. For example, workshops on the teaching dossier or portfolio were linked to policy development on the subject by the Senate Committee on Instructional Development and the publication of a guide to the creation of the teaching portfolio (O'Neil & Wright, 1993). In the case of the issue of how to help students to improve their writing, the teaching center organized an initial major workshop with a well-known speaker, mounted several more modest workshops in which professors explored techniques they had tried in their courses, and followed with the publication of a collection of assignments for students and teaching techniques (Herteis & Wright, 1993). All of the activities were organized in cooperation with the members of the university's Writing Across the Curriculum Committee. For a detailed discussion of workshops and their longer counterparts, sometimes called faculty development institutes, see the chapter by Eison and Stevens in this volume.

Seminars on understanding student learning, which deal with issues of modes of inquiry, learning styles, and developmental patterns, ranked 18th in the All Respondents listing of teaching improvement practices. The item ranked from 16th (Canada) to 21st (US) in the regional and national surveys. Critics of traditional approaches to university and college teaching claim that lecturers pay little attention to the learning process *per se*, that they lack knowledge of the learning process and ignore research in the field, and that they make few efforts to monitor closely the effectiveness of their teaching in terms of student learning.

There is a growing interest in the faculty development community in addressing questions related to student learning and the outcomes of teaching. The chapter by Knapper in this book treats the subject of student learning directly, while several other contributors take into account questions of student learning in their recommendations for faculty development programs.

Conferences on teaching and learning conducted on campus and open to faculty from all disciplines were the subject of a third item in the category Educational Events. It ranked 22nd in the All Respondents listing, but there was wide variation among the responses of the regional and country groups: from a high rank of 14 for Canada to a low of 29 for the UK. Well-organized teaching and learning conferences held on campus have several potential advantages over educational events staged in distant places, in that the host teaching center can involve many professors in the program design, as presenters and as participants. Local conferences often provide unique opportunities, at low cost, for faculty to speak about their own pedagogical breakthroughs and to attend stimulating sessions by academics from other disciplines. Ideally, first-time teaching and learning conference attendees become interested to the point of pursuing pedagogical ideas and events in the months and years to follow.

The fourth item in this category, speakers on issues or trends in higher education, ranked only 35th in the All Respondents listing, and the four regional and country rankings ranged from 33rd to 36th. It is clear that our respondents do not consider this kind of "event" specific enough to be of great use in improving instruction.

Faculty developers favor workshops, a term with connotations of involvement and active learning. They prefer organizing events for "targeted groups," faculty with specific needs. They express moderate confidence in the "seminar" format, particularly as applied to its potential to address questions of student learning. Interdisciplinary conferences on teaching and learning are thought to have less impact; faculty developers no doubt see these events as requiring less commitment on the part of participants and offering few direct solutions to discipline-based classroom concerns. In organizing "educational events," faculty developers should maximize impact on the academic community by keeping in mind the following keys to effectiveness: specificity, practicality, involvement, relevance, and assessment. Further, they should attempt to integrate the activities into a broad campus strategy to enhance teaching.

Developmental Resources

All Respondents		United States		Canada		United Kingdom		Australasia	
Rank	*Mean*	*Rank*	*Mean*	*Rank*	*Mean*	*Rank*	*Mean*	*Rank*	*Mean*
8	24.42	8	24.78	8	25.75	8	23.16	8	23.70

Items: Mentoring programs and support for new professors (5)
      Availability of expert teaching consultant (13)
      Circulation of articles and newsletters on teaching (32)
      Readily accessible professional library (36)

The category "Developmental Resources" ranked eighth out of nine categories in the All Respondents listing. Results were consistent, as the four regional and national surveys also ranked the category in eighth place. It is important to emphasize, however, that respondents generally rated the potential of the practices dealing with *human* resources quite favorably, while they rated the items involving *print* resources very unfavorably. Earlier Canadian studies published similar findings (Konrad, 1983; Schulz, 1988).

Respondents gave high marks to the item designed to measure the potential of "mentoring programs which include such activities as peer consultation and faculty support systems for new professors." The item ranked fifth in the All Respondents listing, and sixth or seventh in the regional and national surveys. Mentoring programs ranked first of six practices designed to improve instruction in another international survey involving faculty developers in 110 colleges and universities (Shackelford, Seldin, & Annis, 1993).

Mentoring programs, particularly those designed to lend a helping hand to new faculty, enjoy widespread interest and popularity. Plans which pair beginning professors with senior colleagues (not necessarily from the same departments) facilitate discussion of concerns related to course planning, teaching techniques, grading, student ratings, grant programs, and institutional tenure and promotion policies. New faculty report many benefits: advice which helps them avoid costly or embarrassing mistakes, ideas and resources to address classroom problems as they arise, and a sense of having an important place in the department and the institution (Wilfrid Laurier University, 1993a, 1993b). Mentoring appeals to the ideals of faculty developers, as well as to the sense of community of senior and junior faculty. For teaching centers, the concept of a mentoring program epitomizes the collegiality and openness in teaching in higher education which they are determined to promote. Although centers often take the initiative to establish mentoring programs, to organize pairs, and to assess results, it is the faculty members themselves who provide the essential expertise in this developmental program. Senior faculty can derive great satisfaction from participation in the program, drawing on a wealth of experience to support new colleagues and revitalizing their own approaches to teaching in the process. New and junior faculty feel less isolated as they turn to established members of the academic community for counsel and encouragement.

Unfortunately, efforts to measure the impact of mentoring programs in terms of improved teaching practices and enhanced learning outcomes have been minimal (Weimer & Lenze, 1991). See, however, a description of one successful program in the chapter by Cox in this volume.

The availability of expert consultation services regarding such areas as course planning, test construction, and teaching skills ranked 13th in the All Respondents listing. Australasian respondents ranked this item seventh, Canadian respondents ranked it 11th, US and UK, 14th. The results of our survey indicate that expert services are important to improved teaching, but that even the experts themselves (our respondents) see more potential in a judicious exploitation of the collective wisdom of experienced faculty through the kinds of peer and mentorship programs described above.

Expert consultation on matters of pedagogy became widely available in many colleges and universities in the 1980s (Erickson, 1986), and services of this type continue to grow. Kapp (1994) reported that more than 90% of the faculty development units he polled in his international survey provide consultation services. For an account of the evolution of consultation services in higher education, see the chapter by Tiberius in this book. Researchers caution that the high regard for expert consultation in some academic circles is largely founded on measures of client and consultant satisfaction rather than observable change in teaching behaviors and learning outcomes (Weimer & Lenze, 1991).

The two items dealing with the potential of print resources to improve teaching ranked near the bottom of the All Respondents listing: the circulation to faculty of newsletters and articles pertinent to teaching improvement ranked 32nd, while a readily accessible professional library concerned with such subjects as instructional methodology and teaching skills ranked last among the 36 items. The perspectives of our respondents did not vary significantly by country, as each of the national and regional surveys ranked the newsletter and article item between 30 and 32, and the professional library item either 35th or 36th. The two practices, according to at least one previous survey, are fairly common in higher education (Erickson, 1986).

Why do faculty developers, many of whom edit the campus newsletters and mount the professional libraries, have little regard for the impact of print resources of this kind? We can only speculate that our respondents see the value of print resources when used in concert with other faculty development strategies: a book may be of interest after a consultation regarding small group discussion, an article becomes relevant once a mentor suggests exploring learning styles, a guide is useful when the department chair recommends developing a teaching portfolio. Academics read widely in their disciplines as a matter of pride and professional interest. The same cannot be said of their reading on college and university pedagogy; faculty need a *reason* to read about teaching. One of the functions of the teaching center is to provide good reasons to read about effective teaching and learning, and to integrate the strategy of combining print resources with other elements of a comprehensive instructional development program (Weimer, 1988).

Summative Evaluation of Instruction

All Respondents		United States		Canada		United Kingdom		Australasia	
Rank	*Mean*	*Rank*	*Mean*	*Rank*	*Mean*	*Rank*	*Mean*	*Rank*	*Mean*
9	22.25	9	22.78	9	22.47	9	21.18	9	21.91

Items: Course materials reviewed in university review process (summative) (25)
   Annual report on teaching accomplishments (summative) (31)
   Classroom observation by peers/heads for summative purposes (33)
   End-of-term student feedback for summative purposes (34)

Summative evaluation of instruction, or performance assessment for personnel and other administrative decision-making purposes, is perhaps one of the most contentious issues in higher education today. The question of whether the quality of teaching performance can be enhanced through requiring faculty to demonstrate their pedagogical effectiveness arises in part from influences outside the university and in part from within. Shrinking budgets, public cries for greater accountability, criticisms about the direction and quality of higher education, and concerns about encroachments on academic freedom all contribute to make discussion about the evaluation of teaching performance both more sensitive and more agonizing than it was in a time of structural stability and financial security. Against this backdrop, the survey respondents' generalized lack of confidence in the improvement potential of performance assessment policies and practices came as no surprise.

The category "Summative Evaluation of Instruction" ranked last overall and for each of the four national and regional groups. This result may be explained by the fact that the items in this category are concerned only with assessing the quality of teaching, not with improving it. However, in view of the strong support of respondents for employment policies and practices which reward effective teaching, summative evaluation of instruction can hardly be ignored in a comprehensive teaching improvement strategy. If the potential positive impact of a reward system which values teaching is to be realized, methods of assessing teaching must have the support of faculty, administrators, and students. Appropriate mechanisms for assessing teaching performance build confidence that effective teaching is recognized and that the extrinsic rewards (and sanctions) for teaching performance are distributed equitably. While it may be difficult to demonstrate that fair, appropriate methods of summative evaluation have a direct, positive impact on the quality of teaching, their absence can certainly have a direct, negative impact.

Respondents had the most confidence in those summative evaluation practices over which faculty have the most control. The review of course materials, such as outlines, readings, and evaluation methods, as part of university review procedures, ranked 25th overall, with the greatest support from the Australasian and UK groups (rank 19 and 20, respectively) and the least from the Canadian group (rank 29). Preparing an annual report of one's teaching accomplishments ranked 31st (a range of 29 to 33 internationally). The teaching improvement potential of these practices may lie primarily in their symbolic value. An institution sends a clear message about the importance of educational practices by ensuring that they are scrutinized as a part of regular review procedures. Such review will also help to engender the type of ongoing discussion about educational objectives, methods, and outcomes which is central to a comprehensive teaching enhancement program.

The remaining items involve assessment practices over which the instructor has little control and which can be more stressful. Classroom observation by peers and department heads and end-of-term student ratings of instruction, both for summative purposes, ranked 33rd and 34th, respectively. The impact of such practices is probably indirect. If employment policies and practices have the potential to improve teaching, then methods of determining teaching quality for performance evaluation purposes must also have an impact by building (or undermining) confidence in the reward system and the tangible incentives it offers.

Exploring the role of faculty developers in the area of summative evaluation raises some important questions. Although it is not always easy to do so, most faculty developers avoid involvement in the summative evaluation process because it undermines faculty confidence in their ability to act independently and in a purely supportive role. As Moses (1987) points out in her review of faculty development in the US, Britain, Australia, Germany, and Sweden, there are often different (and competing) expectations of developers' roles from the perspectives of administrators and of faculty. In her discussion of the Australian context, she notes the particular problems which can arise:

> *There is possible tension between wanting to work for and with staff and also having to work for and on behalf of the institution. This tension is most noticeable in the area of personnel reviews. If a staff member is being evaluated on his/her own initiative by [faculty development] unit staff, who owns the data? Can the administration ask a center to conduct an evaluation of one of the staff members, of one of the courses?... Evaluation is seen by unit staff primarily as [a] developmental tool, by administrators primarily*

as evidence for decisions. Units have to respond creatively to the
challenge of reconciling different expectations. (Moses, 1987,
p.457)

It seems that faculty developers who are directly involved in the summative evaluation of performances do their cause of improving teaching no good. Indeed, "Who but a fool would share his or her problems in teaching with colleagues who are involved in gathering information to make judgments about one's professional ability, in matters as important as tenure?" (Ramsden, 1992, p. 261). However, faculty developers have an important role to play as advocates of appropriate assessment mechanisms. Using their expertise to determine what constitutes effective instruction and to gather and interpret reliable, valid data on teaching performance, faculty developers can influence the design and implementation of appropriate evaluation policies and practices.

Two examples of interventions by teaching centers illustrate various aspects of this complex question. One is drawn from our experience at Dalhousie University in the area of student ratings of instruction for summative purposes. The Senate Committee on Instructional Development and the Office of Instructional Development collaborated to undertake an institutional survey of departmental practices, an inventory of student rating instruments, and the compilation of faculty views and attitudes towards student ratings of teaching. While academic units were eager to receive advice on student ratings, they rejected the concept of a common rating form and procedures for all departments. Consequently, the Senate Committee and the Office developed and approved a set of *guidelines* for the design of student rating instruments and the adoption of sound practices.[10] In this instance, the instructional development center played a leadership role in a practice related closely to the evaluation of instruction without becoming involved in the evaluation process *per se*.

The second example is drawn from the experience of Concordia University (Canada) where the teaching center processes all of the student rating of instruction forms. According to a consultant from the center, the fact that the unit keeps these records of teaching performance (which are also filed with departments and can be used for purposes of summative evaluation) does not "keep teachers away" and does help the center to "better serve" faculty seeking advice to improve their teaching (M. MacKinnon, personal communication, July 15, 1994). Two elements of the "confidential service" are of interest in the context of this discussion. After classroom observations and other aspects of the consultation have been completed at Concordia, the professor receives a written report from the consultant. The report then becomes the "property" of the professor and can be submitted with tenure and promotion files. In at least one controversial tenure case, the consultant's report tipped the balance in favor of the candidate.

The second element involves what might be termed "inappropriate referrals." On occasion, a department head referring a teacher to the center does not act "in good faith" and lays out very unrealistic expectations for the process of pedagogical consultation. A center must be alert and prepared to deal with such rare incidents to avoid undermining the reputation of its services among members of the faculty who are making legitimate attempts to improve their teaching performance.

There is yet another area which poses both problems and opportunities for faculty developers. The increasing popularity of "performance-based funding formulas," wherein institutional funding allocations are linked to a variety of performance measures, also has implications for those involved in teaching improvement efforts (See Astin, 1993 for a discussion of the problems associated with performance-based funding). The summative evaluation practices included in this survey focused on the assessment of individuals. Performance-based funding usually focuses on the departmental, program, or institutional level. An unexpected benefit of this process could be that the emphasis of teaching evaluation is shifted away from the individual instructor to the collective performance of a particular unit, potentially resulting in the kind of teaching improvement programs recommended by Ramsden (1992) which focus "more on good teaching than on good teachers" (p. 254). Teaching centers and academic units, working together, could have a broad impact on the quality of teaching by concentrating on systemic improvement rather than individual development.

OTHER OBSERVATIONS

Our discussion so far has concentrated on international aggregate results and national/regional comparisons. Further analysis focuses on a comparison of the responses of respondents with different types of roles or from different sized institutions. The responses were grouped by degree of confidence in each activity's potential to improve instruction: "low" (1 to 3 on the scale), "moderately low" (4 to 5), "moderately high" (6 to 7), and "high" (8 to 10). Cross-tabulated results for each of two variables–the respondent's role in teaching improvement activities and the size of the respondent's institution–were examined for variations among the views of respondents. We found no major or consistent differences in the patterns of response for either the groups based on role or those based on size.

Respondents shared similar views about the relative teaching improvement potential of the highest- and lowest-ranked items. For each of the 8 highest-ranked items, at least half of all respondents accorded a "high con-

TABLE 7

"Recognition of Teaching in Tenure and Promotion Decisions"
Distribution of Responses by Role of Respondent

	Low 1-2-3	Moderately Low 4-5	Moderately High 6-7	High 8-9-10	Row Total
Full-time director n=110		4.5 (1.6)	21.8 (7.5)	73.6 (25.2)	100% (34.2%)
Part-time director n=51		2.0 (.3)	23.5 (3.7)	74.5 (11.8)	100% (15.8%)
Full-time faculty / Chair of teaching committee n=44	2.3 (.3)	4.5 (.6)	25.0 (3.4)	68.2 (9.3)	100% (13.7%)
Non-faculty n=52	1.9 (.3)	5.8 (.9)	21.2 (3.4)	71.2 (11.5)	100% (16.1%)
Other n=65	3.1 (.6)	6.2 (1.2)	27.7 (5.6)	63.1 (12.7)	100% (20.2%)
Column Total N=322	(1.2)	(4.7)	(23.6)	(70.5)	(100%)

Figures in brackets = percentage of N
Number of missing observations: 9

TABLE 8

"Deans and Heads Foster Importance of Teaching Responsibilities"
Distribution of Responses by Role of Respondent

| | | Confidence Level | | | |
	Low 1-2-3	Moderately Low 4-5	Moderately High 6-7	High 8-9-10	Row Total
Full-time director n=108	.9 (.3)	7.4 (2.5)	23.1 (7.8)	68.5 (23.0)	100% (33.5%)
Part-time director n=53		5.7 (.9)	32.1 (5.3)	62.3 (10.2)	100% (16.5%)
Full-time faculty / Chair of teaching committee n=44	6.8 (.9)	2.3 (.3)	25.0 (3.4)	65.9 (9.0)	100% (13.7%)
Non-faculty n=53	1.9 (.3)	11.3 (1.9)	13.2 (2.2)	73.6 (12.1)	100% (16.5%)
Other n=64	1.6 (.3)	4.7 (.9)	35.9 (7.1)	57.8 (11.5)	100% (19.9%)
Column Total N=322	(1.9)	(6.5)	(25.8)	(65.8)	(100%)

Figures in brackets = percentage of N
Number of missing observations: 9

fidence" (8 to 10) rating. For each of the 8 lowest-ranked items, less than 25% of respondents gave "high confidence" ratings. The following examples are illustrative of the distribution of responses.

The practice which ranked first overall (recognition of teaching in tenure and promotion decisions) was rated in the "high" confidence range by 70.5% of respondents and in the "moderately high" range by a further 23.6%. This pattern is largely consistent for the various types of respondents (See Table 7). Different types of respondents express similar agreement about the potential of the second-highest item (deans and heads fostering the importance of teaching responsibilities) with the exception that *Non-faculty* rate this item slightly higher and *Others* rate it slightly lower than the remaining groups (See Table 8). However, this pattern is not observed for the other items pertaining to the role of deans and heads, nor does it appear throughout the rest of the survey. We conclude that the precise role of the respondent in teaching improvement activities does not appear to significantly influence responses in this survey. This finding is not unexpected, since the respondents were all involved in teaching enhancement efforts and had similar roles and responsibilities. Further research which compares the views of instructional development practitioners, faculty members, students, and administrators would provide useful information about the perspectives of disparate groups.

We also examined correlation between size of institution and the responses for each of the items. About one-half of the institutions represented enroll from 5,000 to 20,000 students, while about one-third have smaller student bodies, and the remainder have higher student populations (see Table 3). Student enrollment profiles are similar in Canada and the United States, with relatively few institutions in the smallest category and a fairly even distribution over the remaining categories. Patterns of institutional size in the United Kingdom and Australasia were also similar to one another; for both groups, about 70% of institutions fell in the range of 5,000 to 20,000 students, with few institutions in the very small and very large categories.

Analysis of the correlation between the respondents' ratings of teaching improvement practices and the size of the institution provided interesting results. The most frequent inter-group variation occurred between the largest and the smallest institutions, although the small sample size in the case of institutions under 1,000 students (21, of which 14 are located in the US) makes us reluctant to draw conclusions from this observation.

The other pattern of response is more intriguing and occurs between the two largest institution groups. These groups show varying degrees of confidence in a number of important items, including the consideration of teaching performance in tenure and promotion decisions and the practice

TABLE 9

"Recognition of Teaching in Tenure and Promotion Decisions" Distribution of Responses by Size of Respondent Institution

Size		Confidence Level				
		Low 1-2-3	Moderately Low 4-5	Moderately High 6-7	High 8-9-10	Row Total
<1000	n=22	4.5 (.3)	9.1 (.6)	13.6 (1.0)	72.7 (5.1)	100% (7.0%)
1000 to 2500	n=39	5.1 (.6)	2.6 (.3)	25.6 (3.2)	66.7 (8.3)	100% (12.5%)
2501 to 5000	n=44		4.5 (.6)	18.2 (2.6)	77.3 (10.9)	100% (14.1%)
5001 to 10 000 n=81			1.2 (.3)	25.9 (6.7)	72.8 (18.8)	100% (25.9%)
10 001 to 20 000 n=78			9.0 (2.2)	28.2 (7.0)	62.8 (15.7)	100% (24.9%)
>20 000	n=49			12.2 (1.9)	87.8 (13.7)	100% (15.7%)
Column Total	N=313	(1.0)	(4.2)	(22.4)	(72.5)	(100%)

Figures in brackets = percentage of N
Number of missing observations: 18

TABLE 10

"Deans and Heads Foster Importance of Teaching Responsibilities"
Distribution of Responses by Size of Respondent Institution

Size		Low 1-2-3	Confidence Level Moderately Low 4-5	Moderately High 6-7	High 8-9-10	Row Total
<1000	n=22	9.1 (.6)		36.4 (2.6)	54.5 (3.8)	100% (7.0%)
1000 to 2500	n=40	5.0 (.6)	5.0 (.6)	17.5 (2.2)	72.5 (9.3)	100% (12.8%)
2501 to 5000	n=45		6.7 (1.0)	22.2 (3.2)	71.1 (10.2)	100% (14.4%)
5001 to 10 000	n=79		5.1 (1.3)	27.8 (7.0)	67.1 (16.9)	100% (25.2%)
10 001 to 20 000	n=77	2.6 (.6)	3.9 (1.0)	35.1 (8.6)	58.41 (14.4)	100% (24.6%)
>20 000	n=50		10.0 (1.6)	14.0 (2.2)	76.0 (12.1)	100% (16.0%)
Column Total	N=313	(1.9)	(5.4)	(25.9)	(66.8)	(100%)

Figures in brackets = percentage of N
Number of missing observations: 18

of deans and heads fostering the importance of teaching responsibilities. As demonstrated in Table 9, only 62.8% of the 10,000 to 20,000 size rated this item in the "high" confidence range, compared to 87.8% of the over 20,000 size. Similar results can be seen in Table 10, where the 10,000 to 20,000 size group had less confidence than the group from the largest institutions. While the correlations between size and confidence levels are not strong or consistent throughout, there is sufficient evidence to suggest that teaching improvement efforts should take into account institutional characteristics, including size, which may influence policy and program planning and implementation.

The primary interest of the investigators has been to focus on the cumulative data from several countries and to make comparisons from one country or region to another. The centrality of this interest remains after examining the results of the survey by nature of involvement of the respondent in instructional development and by size of the respondent's institution. That said, we are sure that the faculty developer's role and mandate within the institution, as well as the size of the institution constitute important factors in determining instructional development program design in a given context.

Summary and Conclusion

The survey of teaching improvement practices was designed to take the pulse of the international community of faculty developers. The resulting data represent the perspectives of the practitioners on "what works" in the panoply of options within the instructional development enterprise. Our findings do not provide definitive answers, but they determine a starting point for reflection and action in pursuing the overall goal of teaching enhancement in higher education.

According to our respondents, academic deans and department heads can play critical roles in campus efforts to improve the effectiveness of teaching. By fostering the importance of teaching responsibilities, promoting a climate of trust for classroom observation, praising and rewarding good teaching, and facilitating the opportunity for classroom research, deans and heads can exercise their academic leadership to make a significant impact on the quality of teaching in colleges and universities. The place of deans and department heads in the pursuit of teaching enhancement is seen as central by the faculty development respondents in all of the countries included in the study. The implications for those involved in instructional development are far-reaching: a great deal of thought and energy should be devoted to developing approaches which closely involve deans and heads in the institutional instructional development program. Faculty developers should organize workshops for deans and heads, involve them as speakers and workshop facilitators, explain the components and objectives of their programs to them, design programs and services to meet the specific needs of a given department or faculty, and work with them to promote policy changes which improve the status of teaching. With many issues competing for the attention of deans and heads it is quite possible that they overlook the ongoing task of maintaining and improving the quality of teaching. How can the person responsible for faculty development help the academic administrator to pursue a program of teaching enhancement without evoking a negative response? How can department heads and deans prevent the day-to-day requirements of their functions from dominating their calendars to the point that pedagogical concerns seem distant, even trivial, in comparison? There are no easy answers to these questions, but we suspect that both faculty developers and academic administrators do not expend as much energy as warranted by the results of our survey in seeking solutions to the dilemma of too little time to accomplish too many tasks.

Another major finding of our study is that certain employment policies and practices, especially the recognition of teaching as an important factor in tenure and promotion decisions, are thought to have great potential to improve teaching in higher education. The item on the consideration of teaching in tenure and promotion decisions ranked at the top of every national group's list. Once again, the implications are clear for faculty developers and all those in higher education who are concerned about the quality of teaching: resources must be devoted to ensuring that this condition becomes a reality in the institutional setting. It is difficult to modify academic culture, but surely attention to policies, procedures, and programs related to the amelioration of the tenure and promotion experience and its outcomes is essential if proponents of teaching improvement are to further their fundamental objectives and *raison d'être*. The activities of an academic staff development unit or committee for teaching and learning are of limited value if nothing is done to ensure that teaching is held in high regard and is scrutinized in a context which rewards effectiveness with procedures which are fair, equitable, and widely accepted.

Our study shows that teaching improvement specialists are confident that the work of teaching centers will improve instruction. The most promising services are mentoring programs and support for new professors, grants to faculty to devise new approaches to teaching, workshops on teaching methods for targeted groups, expert consultation, and, under certain circumstances, the organization of consultation on course materials among faculty peers. These programs can involve faculty from a wide variety of disciplines in small and large group activities which break down isolation and build community, explore new pedagogical ideas and techniques, and stimulate faculty initiatives to improve teaching in their fields. In mounting programs, those responsible for the development of academic teaching staff must be mindful of the tensions among the needs: 1) to present a wide variety of approaches for the benefit of faculty members; 2) to concentrate energies and resources for maximum impact; and 3) to create a cohesive program linked to current institutional goals, priorities, and concerns.

What is the place of those elements of a campus teaching improvement program which received low levels of support from survey respondents? With the possible exception of invited speakers on trends in higher education (too general to have an impact on teaching), the various teaching improvement practices deserving of close consideration include the mid-ranking funds for faculty to attend conferences on teaching, classroom videotaping for improvement purposes, and the sponsorship of conferences on teaching and learning on campus. And the low-ranking provision of print resources may not bring about immediate changes in the quality of teaching and learning, but teaching improvement specialists should nonetheless promote the value of teaching bulletins, articles, and books. Few significant ideas which are not articulated and defended in print make an impact in the academy; faculty developers and department heads are uniquely positioned to influence the reading agendas of the professoriate.

The very limited confidence in the potential of various summative evaluation practices contrasts sharply with the high confidence expressed for the potential of recognizing the importance of teaching in employment policies and practices. Ideally, according to Murray (1993), summative evaluation and faculty development enjoy a "synergistic relationship" (p. 85). The Canadian professor of psychology advocates two steps "to improve faculty commitment to and performance in teaching… (1) evaluate teaching comprehensively and validly, and (2) incorporate evaluation of teaching into the institutional reward system (summative evaluation)" (p. 85). Adoption of these two steps constitute an "inexpensive and efficient" form of faculty development (p. 86).

Our survey respondents identify the pressing need for institutions to recognize the importance of teaching in personnel decisions, but they don't believe that summative evaluation is an effective strategy to improve teaching. Perhaps our respondents regard greater recognition for teaching effectiveness as a *pre-condition* to embracing summative evaluation practices, whereas in reality, it may be that greater recognition will come only after mechanisms to closely scrutinize teaching are firmly in place. The practical alternative, of course, is to work towards concurrent adoption of widely accepted summative evaluation procedures and personnel policies which give full credit to effective teaching.

In emphasizing the issue of the tangible rewards discussed above, we should not overlook what Hutchings (1993) calls the "intangibles." Higher education professors yearn for "the chance to be a part of a community of teachers, to talk seriously about teaching and learning, to have one's ideas listened to and taken seriously, to get to slow down for a moment and reflect, and to be recognized by peers as contributing to an important larger enterprise" (p. 65). Faculty development programs, at their best, can help deliver elements of all of the aforementioned "intangible rewards" and promote a sense of well-being in the professoriate. What is more, efforts to provide intangible and tangible rewards are perfectly compatible.

This chapter has introduced several teaching improvement practices, including elements of policy and program, with a view to offering some perspective on their relative importance and place in a comprehensive faculty development program. The analysis reveals which practices tend to transcend national borders because they are central to improving quality in almost any higher education setting. The chapters which follow provide more information, more references to theory, and more practical advice for the implementation of a wide range of faculty development strategies. Successful teaching improvement programs in higher education draw on lessons from the literature as well as the advice of experienced practitioners to introduce a richly varied, comprehensive approach to faculty development, an approach which will have a positive impact on teaching and learning outcomes and effect significant change in the dynamics of higher education in the institutional setting.

The teaching improvement practices survey capitalized on the training and experience of practitioners from over 300 higher education institutions in several countries around the world to identify elements of program and policy which *they believe* have an impact on the quality of instruction. Though this information is useful, there remains a pressing need to measure the effectiveness of teaching improvement practices and to disseminate the results in academic conferences and publications. A sustained effort to build a research component into faculty development programs would lead to informed choices for program development and more serious consideration for the intellectual dimension of teaching and the scholarship of teaching. Faculty development specialists are noted for their openness and sense of community. This results in conferences and meetings marked by a refreshing atmosphere of support and mutual understanding. The challenge is to increase the research base in this field while maintaining true collegiality–avoiding the pitfalls of competitive academic and disciplinary jealousies.

The following chapters take up many of the teaching improvements practices which were the object of specific items in the international survey of faculty development practitioners in higher education. Examples include an in-depth discussion of the organization and outcomes of teaching development workshops, a description of the teaching portfolio and its implementation in the institutional setting, and an analysis of faculty development consultation strategies.

Other chapters in the book address matters which were not, *per se*, covered in the international survey, but have great potential for improving instruction. These matters include: programs designed to develop faculty at different stages of their careers; the introduction of specific approaches to teaching and curriculum organization; the transmission of basic teaching and learning concepts for the classroom and the laboratory, and with partnerships to make teaching and learning more effective and more equitable.

The focus of this book is on change at the institutional level, but some chapters also examine major influences and mechanisms which effect change on both the institutional and the national levels. Taken together, the contributed chapters provide the valuable insights of the some 20 expert practitioners into the complex realm of improving teaching in higher education.

REFERENCES

Aleamoni, L.M. (1978). The usefulness of student evaluations in improving college teaching. *Instructional Science, 7*, 95-105.

Aleamoni, L.M. (Ed.). (1987). *New Directions for Teaching and Learning: No. 31. Techniques for evaluating and improving instruction.* San Francisco, CA: Jossey-Bass.

Angelo, T.A. (Ed.). (1991). *New Directions for Teaching and Learning: No. 46. Classroom research: Early lessons from success.* San Francisco, CA: Jossey-Bass.

Angelo, T.A., & Cross, K.P. (1993). *Classroom assessment techniques: A handbook for college teachers* (2nd ed.). San Francisco, CA: Jossey-Bass.

Arreola, R.A., & Aleamoni, L.M. (1990). Practical decisions in developing and operating a faculty evaluation system. In M. Theall & J. Franklin (Eds.), *New Directions for Teaching and Learning: No. 43. Student ratings of instruction: Issues for improving practice* (pp. 37-55). San Francisco, CA: Jossey-Bass.

AAU Sub-Committee on Faculty Development. (1989). *Final report* (unpublished). Halifax, NS: Association of Atlantic Universities (AAU).

Astin, A.W. (1993). *Assessment for excellence: The philosophy and practice of assessment and evaluation in higher education.* Phoenix, AZ: American Council on Education and The Oryx Press.

Bok, Derek. (1986). *Higher education*. Cambridge, MA: Harvard University Press.

Boyer, E.L. (1990). *Scholarship reconsidered: Priorities of the professoriate*. Princeton, NJ: Princeton University Press.

Brooks, G. (1993). *Sabbatical policies in Atlantic universities: Will leave be granted for teaching related projects?* Report to the Association of Atlantic Universities Co-ordinating Committee on Faculty Development. Halifax, NS: Association of Atlantic Universities.

The Carnegie Foundation for the Advancement of Teaching. (1987). *A classification of institutions in higher education*. Princeton, NJ: Carnegie Foundation.

The Carnegie Foundation for the Advancement of Teaching. (1991, May/June). Research-intensive vs. teaching-intensive institutions. *Change*, pp. 23-26.

Centra, J.A. (1993). *Reflective faculty evaluation: Enhancing teaching and determining faculty effectiveness*. San Francisco, CA: Jossey-Bass.

Clark, H.C. (1993). Foreword. In M.C. O'Neil & W.A. Wright, *Recording teaching accomplishment: A Dalhousie guide to the teaching dossier* (4th ed., p. vii). Halifax, NS: Dalhousie University, Office of Instructional Development and Technology.

Cochran, L.H. (1989). *Administrative commitment to teaching*. Cape Girardeau, MO: Step Up.

Cohen, P.A. (1980). Effectiveness of student-rating feedback for improving college instruction: A meta-analysis of findings. *Research in Higher Education,13*(4), 321-341.

Cohen, P.A. (1990). Bringing research into practice. In M. Theall & J. Franklin (Eds.), *New Directions for Teaching and Learning: No. 43. Student ratings of instruction: Issues for improving practice* (pp. 123-132). San Francisco, CA: Jossey-Bass.

Cross, K.P., & Angelo, T.A. (1988). *Classroom assessment techniques: A handbook for faculty*. Ann Arbor, MI: NCRIPTAL.

Diamond, R. (1993-94). Changing priorities in higher education: Promotion and tenure. *Teaching Excellence* [bulletin], *5*(3).

Eble, K. (1990). The degradation of undergraduate education. In J. Jussawalla (Ed.), *New Directions for Teaching and Learning: No. 44. Excellent teaching in a changing academy: Essays in honor of Kenneth Eble* (pp. 11-19). San Francisco, CA: Jossey-Bass.

Erickson, G. (1986). A survey of faculty development practices. *To Improve the Academy, 5*, 182-197.

Fairweather, J.S. (1993). *Teaching, research, and faculty rewards: A summary of the research findings of the faculty profile project*. University Park, PA: National Center on Postsecondary Teaching, Learning, and Assessment.

Franklin, J., & Theall, M. (1990). Communicating student ratings to decision makers: Design for good practice. In M. Theall and J. Franklin (Eds.), *New Directions for Teaching and Learning: No. 43. Student ratings of instruction: Issues for improving practice* (pp. 75-95). San Francisco, CA: Jossey-Bass.

Gil, D.H. (1987). Instructional evaluation as a feedback process. In L.M. Aleamoni (Ed.), *New Directions for Teaching and Learning: No. 31. Techniques for evaluating and improving instruction* (pp. 57-64). San Francisco, CA: Jossey-Bass.

Green, M.F. (1990). Why good teaching needs active leadership. In P. Seldin & Associates, *How administrators can improve teaching: Moving from talk to action in higher education* (pp. 45-62). San Francisco, CA: Jossey-Bass.

Herteis, E.M., & Wright, W.A. (1993). *Learning through writing: A compendium of assignments and techniques* (2nd ed.). Halifax, NS: Dalhousie University, Office of Instructional Development and Technology.

Higher Education Council. (1990, December). *Higher education: The challenges ahead.* National Board of Employment, Education and Training, Australia.

Hutchings, P. (1993). Lessons from AAHE's Teaching Initiative. In Weimer, M. (Ed.). *Faculty as teachers: Taking stock of what we know* (pp. 63-66). University Park, PA: National Center on Postsecondary Teaching, Learning, & Assessment.

Jussawalla, J. (Ed.). (1990). *New Directions for Teaching and Learning: No. 44. Excellent teacing in a changing academy: Essays in honor of Kenneth Eble.* San Francisco, CA: Jossey-Bass.

Kapp, C.A. (1994). Policies, practices and procedures in staff development in higher education: Results of an international survey. *Proceedings of the Twentieth International Conference on Improving University Teaching* (pp. 462-471).

Konrad, A.G. (1983). Faculty development practices in Canadian universities. *The Canadian Journal of Higher Education, 13*(2), 13-25.

Lucas, A.F. (1989a). Editor's notes. *New Directions for Teaching and Learning: No. 37. The department chairperson's role in enhancing college teaching* (pp. 1-3). San Francisco, CA: Jossey-Bass.

Lucas, A.F. (Ed.). (1989b). *New Directions for Teaching and Learning: No. 37. The department chairperson's role in enhancing college teaching.* San Francisco, CA: Jossey-Bass.

Lucas, A.F. (1990). Chairperson interventions for enhancing the quality of teaching in the department. *Proceedings of the Seventh Annual Conference on Academic Chairpersons: Developing Faculty, Students, and Programs, 34,* 390-397.

Lunde, J.P., & Healey, M.M. (1991). *Doing faculty development by committee.* Stillwater, OK: New Forums Press.

Massey, W.F., Wilger, A.K., & Colbeck, C. (1994). Overcoming "hollowed" collegiality. *Change, 26*(4), 10-20.

McKeachie, W.J. (1987). Can evaluating instruction improve teaching? In L.M. Aleamoni (Ed.), *New Directions for Teaching and Learning: No. 31. Techniques for evaluating and improving instruction* (pp. 3-8). San Francisco, CA: Jossey-Bass.

Miller, R.I. (1988). Merit pay in United States postsecondary institutions. *Higher Education, 17*, 219-232.

Moses, I. (1985). The role of head of department in the pursuit of excellence. *Higher Education, 14*, 337-354.

Moses, I. (1987). Educational development units: A cross-cultural perspective. *Higher Education, 16*, 449-479.

Moses, I. (1988). *Academic staff evaluation and development: A university case study.* New York, NY: University of Queensland Press.

Moses, I., & Roe, E. (1989). *HERDSA Green Guide: No. 9. Heading a department: A guide for heads and chairs of departments and schools.* Kensington, NSW, Australia: Higher Education Research and Development Society of Australia.

Murray, H.G. (1993). Summative evaluation and faculty development: A synergistic relationship? In Weimer, M. (Ed.). *Faculty as teachers: Taking stock of what we know* (pp. 85-88). University Park, PA: National Center on Postsecondary Teaching, Learning, and Assessment.

Neill, S.D. (1989, April). No significant relationship between research and teaching, research reveals. *University Affairs*, 18.

Neumann, R. (1992). Perceptions of the teaching-research nexus: A framework for analysis. *Higher Education, 23*, 159-171.

O'Neil, M.C., & Wright, W.A. (1993). *Recording teaching accomplishment: A Dalhousie guide to the teaching dossier* (4th ed.). Halifax, NS: Dalhousie University, Office of Instructional Development and Technology.

Ramsden, P. (1992). *Learning to teach in higher education.* London, UK: Routledge.

Rice, R.E., & Austin, A.E. (1990). Organizational impacts of faculty morale and motivation to teach. In P. Seldin & Associates, *How administrators can improve teaching* (pp. 23-42). San Francisco, CA: Jossey-Bass.

Schulz, R. A. (1988, June). *Possible successful strategies for teaching development offices (TDO's).* Unpublished paper based on a presentation at the Eighth Annual Conference on Teaching and Learning in Higher Education, University of Calgary, Calgary, AB.

Seldin, P., & Associates. (1990). *How administrators can improve teaching: Moving from talk to action in higher education.* San Francisco, CA: Jossey-Bass.

Shackelford, R., Seldin, P., & Annis, L. (1993, Winter). Lessons learned to improve teaching effectiveness. *The Department Chair, 3*(3), 11-13.

Shore, B.M. (1974). Instructional development in Canadian higher education. *The Canadian Journal of Higher Education, 4*, 45-53.

Shore, B.M., Foster, S.F., Knapper, C.K., Nadeau, G.G., Neill, N., Sim, V.W., and with the help of faculty members of the Centre for Teaching and Learning Services, McGill University. (1986). *The teaching dossier* (rev. ed.). Ottawa, ON: Canadian Association of University Teachers.

Smith, B.L., & Smith, D.C. (1993). *The Smith guide to the staff development jungle*. East Sussex, UK: Chatfield Publications.

Smith, S. (1991). *The report of the commission on inquiry on Canadian university education*. Ottawa, ON: Association of Universities and Colleges of Canada.

Stevens, J. J. (1987). Using student ratings to improve instruction. In L.M. Aleamoni (Ed.), *New Directions for Teaching and Learning: No. 31. Techniques for evaluating and improving instruction* (pp. 33-38). San Francisco, CA: Jossey-Bass.

Theall, M., & Franklin, J. (Eds.). (1990). *New Directions for Teaching and Learning: No. 43. Student ratings of instruction: Issues for improving practice*. San Francisco, CA: Jossey-Bass.

Trask, K.A. (1989). The chairperson and teaching. In A.F. Lucas (Ed.), *New Directions for Teaching and Learning: Vol. 37. The department chairperson's role in enhancing college teaching* (pp. 99-107). San Francisco, CA: Jossey-Bass.

Weaver, F.S. (1989). Scholarship and teaching. *Educational Record, 70*(1), 55-58.

Weimer, M. (1988). Reading your way to better teaching. *College Teaching, 36*(2), 48-53.

Weimer, M. (1990). *Improving college teaching: Strategies for developing instructional effectiveness*. San Francisco, CA: Jossey-Bass.

Weimer, M. (Ed.). (1993). *Faculty as teachers: Taking stock of what we know*. University Park, PA: National Center on Postsecondary Teaching, Learning, and Assessment.

Weimer, M., & Lenze, L.F. (1991). Instructional interventions: A review of the literature on efforts to improve instruction. In J. Smart (Ed.), *Higher education: Handbook of theory and research, 7*, 294-333.

Wilfrid Laurier University. (1993a). *Guidelines for mentors*. Waterloo, ON: Wilfred Laurier University, Office of Instructional Development.

Wilfrid Laurier University. (1993b). *WLU new faculty mentor program*. Waterloo, ON: Wilfred Laurier University, Office of Instructional Development.

Wright, W.A. (1993). [Teaching development funds in universities in Canada.] Unpublished raw data. Halifax, NS: Dalhousie University, Office of Instructional Development and Technology.

Wright, W.A., & O'Neil, M.C. (1992). Improving summative student ratings of instruction practices. *The Journal of Staff, Program, & Organization Development*, *10*(2), 75-85.

Wright, W.A., & O'Neil. M.C. (1995). Perspectives on improving teaching in Canadian universities. *The Canadian Journal of Higher Education, xxiv-3*, 26-57.

Wright, W.A., & O'Neil, M.C. (1994). Teaching improvement practices: New perspectives. *To Improve the Academy, 13*, 1-37.

AUTHORS

Alan Wright is the founding Executive Director of the Office of Instructional Development and Technology at Dalhousie University in Halifax, Nova Scotia, Canada, where he is responsible for a comprehensive teaching enhancement program, oversees Instructional Media Services, and holds a cross appointment in Education. Dr. Wright has earned degrees from Mount Allison University (New Brunswick), as well as from McGill University and the Université de Montréal in his native Québec. He has a vast experience in a variety of educational milieux and his current activities in instructional development include writing, speaking at conferences, and presenting faculty workshops in college and university settings.

Carol O'Neil is the Research Coordinator of the Office of Instructional Development and Technology at Dalhousie University in Halifax, Nova Scotia, Canada. She is co-author, with Alan Wright, of Recording Teaching Accomplishment: A Dalhousie Guide to the Teaching Dossier. Her research interests include the evaluation of faculty, student retention, and student experience in higher education, as well as instructional development issues. Her involvement in education extends outside the university and includes work in the areas of adult education and community economic development.

NOTES

[1] The nine categories, as well as an early version of the questionnaire, were devised by Roger Barnsley of St. Thomas University, Graham Skanes of Memorial University of Newfoundland, and Alan Wright of Dalhousie University in 1991. The instrument was first used in June of that year in an instructional development seminar for senior university administrators in the Association of Atlantic Universities (Canada). Several surveys on instructional development practices from the United States and Canada were consulted when drawing up the questionnaire (See especially Erickson, 1986 and Cochran, 1989, as well as AAU Sub-Committee on Faculty Development, 1989, and Schulz, 1988).

[2] The results of the Canadian study and elements of the analysis were reported first in Wright, W.A., & O'Neil, M.C. (1995). Perspectives on improving teaching in Canadian universities. *The Canadian Journal of Higher Education, xxiv-3*, 26-57.

[3] Some of the elements reported below were first discussed in a comparative study of the Canadian and US survey results: Wright, W.A., & O'Neil, M.C. (1994). Teaching improvement practices: New perspectives. *To Improve the Academy, 13*, 1-37.

[4] In 1993, these two organizations merged to become the Staff and Educational Development Association.

[5] The authors wish to acknowledge the assistance of Phil Candy, Queensland University of Technology, and Rod MacKay, University of Canterbury, in compiling this list.

[6] Although our questionnaire deals with the leadership of both deans and heads, the literature reviewed tends to emphasize the role of department heads and chairpersons in improving teaching.

[7] A popular criticism of the perceived dichotomy between research and teaching in higher education relates to the terms commonly used for involvement in these activities, namely "research opportunities" and "teaching loads." The term "fellowship" to describe a teaching development award has, therefore, some appeal.

[8] The Society for Teaching and Learning in Higher Education (STLHE: Canada), the Professional and Organizational Development (POD: US) Network in Higher Education, the Higher Education Research and Development Society of Australasia (HERDSA), and the Staff and Educational Development Association (SEDA: UK) are among the leading groups which organize and sponsor conferences and meetings of this nature in their regions.

[9] Kapp (1994) reviews several definitions of staff or faculty development from the literature in this field. All emphasize the comprehensive nature of the term: faculty development can refer variously to research, teaching, service, and personal growth. Kapp's broad working definition is "All activities, actions, processes and procedures that an organization develops or uses to enhance the performance and the potential of its [faculty]" (p. 463). In this book, faculty/staff development refers essentially to the teaching dimension of the academic's profile.

[10] The guidelines eventually led to the publication of Wright, W.A., & O'Neil, M.C. (1992). Improving summative student ratings of instruction practices. *The Journal of Staff, Program, & Organization Development, 10*(2), 75-85.

2.

Understanding Student Learning: Implications for Instructional Practice

Christopher K. Knapper

Understanding the way students learn is of vital importance to college teach-ers and faculty developers. This chapter reviews relevant research on learning in college settings, including work on learning styles and approaches to studying, paying particular attention to the concepts of deep and surface learning. The chap-ter concludes with some practical suggestions for teachers and developers to en-hance learning and teaching quality.

FACULTY CONCEPTIONS OF TEACHING AND LEARNING

College professors who are critical of faculty development often chal-lenge professionals in the field by asking what information and techniques we can offer that might have a tangible effect on the quality of university teaching. Assuming every university teacher *did* receive some training, would it really make any difference? After all, despite mandatory training for elementary and high school teachers, there is still widespread criticism of the quality of learning in North American schools. This raises an in-triguing question: if you as a faculty developer had the attention of *all* the teachers in your institution for, say, half a day, just what would you tell them? For me the answer is quite simple: I would try to raise the issue of how students learn, beginning by having faculty consider what they know intuitively from half a lifetime of learning themselves.

The act of teaching is, of course, meaningless without a corresponding act of learning. Yet a great irony of much university teaching is that, although professors have themselves excelled as learners, the insights gleaned from this experience are often abandoned as soon as the instructor ascends the classroom podium. Instead of reflecting on their own experience, supplemented by relevant research about effective practices, many faculty base their approach to teaching upon an uncritical adoption of the model that comes most readily to hand–their old professors.

Consequently, it is not surprising that teaching methods have remained largely unchanged since medieval times when lectures predominated largely because of a scarcity of printed books. In other words, a great deal of college teaching is extremely traditional, relying on a didactic model of instruction in which students are seen as "empty vessels" or "blank slates" to be filled up with knowledge (Fox, 1983). While this is clearly not true of all university education (problem-based learning, project work, and other types of individualized, independent learning are obvious exceptions), the predominance of the lecture method is not only conventional wisdom, but has been confirmed by a number of empirical surveys of college teaching methods (Trani, 1979). In addition to being the most popular method among faculty, the lecture is also preferred by a great many students (see Knapper & Cropley, 1991, for a review of relevant research).

Moreover, a good deal of university teaching breaks simple rules that would be obvious to any undergraduate asked to comment on teaching quality. For example, the organization of material is often confused and not made explicit to students; no account is taken of differences in prior knowledge or learning abilities; too much material is presented for comprehension, and so on. These are common criticisms of the lecture method, and knowledge of basic learning principles could certainly be used to improve such presentations. In other cases, depending upon the learning outcomes desired, the lecture method itself may be inappropriate.[1] For example, didactic, passive instruction is largely ineffective if the learning objective involves mastery of a physical or cognitive skill (such as problem-solving or playing tennis). Here, practice and feedback are essential for learning and improvement to take place.

Assessment of student performance is another aspect of college teaching that stands to benefit from a better understanding of student learning. Yet, for some teachers, setting assessment tasks becomes a sort of last-minute afterthought, devised hastily to comply with a deadline for submission of a final exam. It is thus not surprising that much assessment encourages low-level study methods, such as rote learning (Elton, 1982; Milton, 1982). Paradoxically, such learning is not what most college teachers hope to achieve. Surveys of faculty about their desired learning goals consistently reveal an emphasis on critical thinking, analysis, synthesis, and similar abilities (Knapper, 1990).

Other areas where an understanding of learning could profitably inform educational practice include curriculum development and program delivery. For example, the primary strategy for curriculum planning in many academic departments is to ensure that seminal ideas in the discipline are "covered." Yet very few institutions are able to demonstrate that such concepts are indeed useful to graduates in their subsequent lives, or even that they are remembered after leaving college.

The way instruction is delivered involves not just teaching methods, but also organizational arrangements such as the number of courses needed to complete a degree, the number of contact hours in a typical course, and so on. In North America, arrangements are remarkably similar from one institution to another, yet elsewhere (e.g., Australia, Europe) there are quite different approaches. For example, in Britain hours spent in formal lectures have typically been considerably fewer than in the United States, and greater emphasis has been placed upon independent student work. The point here is not to argue merit, but to indicate that choices about such matters are often based more on tradition than on empirical evidence for the type of student learning that will result from different systems.[2]

TRADITIONAL LEARNING RESEARCH AND UNIVERSITY TEACHING

Why are we so poor at understanding learning processes and adjusting our teaching strategies accordingly? Is it simply that faculty are indifferent to students, or uninterested in the way they study and learn? Apparently not, since many instructors have definite and ambitious expectations about the type of learning outcomes they wish to achieve. At the same time, it is probably true that many faculty lack a sophisticated conceptual understanding of how learning takes place in college students. This is hardly surprising. In the first place, most faculty have been trained as researchers in their discipline but have had no background in educational or pedagogical theory. A second reason has to do with the very complexity of human learning. The beguilingly simple term *learning* covers a multitude of different constructs, encompassing memory, comprehension and understanding, acquisition of skills (both physical and intellectual), problem-solving, analysis, and synthesis, as well as attitude formation and change.

A third complication for the practicing teacher is that, while a great deal is known about learning, not very much of the research in this area is of direct help to instructors who wish to enhance the performance of their students. Although learning is perhaps the most prominent topic in all of psychology, many of the studies have been conducted on rats or pigeons in settings far removed from the classroom. Even research that has focused on human learning in real-life situations has often confined itself to the early childhood years–for example, Piaget's seminal work on cognitive development.

This is not to say that traditional learning research has failed to yield any precepts that could serve as a guide to teaching practice. However, the principles concerned are hardly revolutionary. Simply stated, they tell us that *practice* facilitates performance, that *feedback* to the learner (or "knowledge of results") enhances the beneficial effects of practice, and that learning is greatly encouraged when it is *rewarded*.

LEARNING STYLES

One issue frequently mentioned by faculty as a barrier to effective teaching is the difficulty of coping with students of different abilities. In my workshops for college teachers, I sometimes ask participants to think about the last time they set about learning something systematically, and report how they did it. Not surprisingly, I usually find that nearly everyone has undertaken numerous learning tasks, some very complex and others quite mundane. Of particular interest here is that the way faculty report they learn differs considerably from person to person. While some use fairly traditional, formal methods (enrolling in a course, going to the local library), many more seek the advice of knowledgeable friends, or simply learn by trial and error. It seems likely that students too will vary in the way they learn, although of course most college students will have been acculturated by their experiences in school to rely heavily on traditional sources of authority–in particular, teachers and textbooks.

Of the many instruments developed to measure learning styles, perhaps the most well-known are those of Grasha, Kolb, and various adaptations of the Myers-Briggs Type Indicator. (For a good overview of different instruments, see Claxton and Murrell, 1987.) For example, Kolb identifies four learning processes: concrete experience, active experimentation, reflective observation, and abstract conceptualization. Different preferences for these processes allow classification of learners as accommodators, divergers, convergers, and assimilators (Kolb, 1984). The Myers-Briggs Type Indicator (Myers & Myers, 1987) classifies learners in terms of combinations of four different dimensions: extroversion/introversion, thinking/

feeling, sensing/intuiting, and judgment/perception. (For an interesting application with engineering students, see Rosati, Dean, & Rodman, 1988.) The Grasha-Reichman scale, which was developed specifically for students in higher education, uses six dimensions: competitive, collaborative, avoidant, participant, dependent, and independent (Grasha, 1990). There are still other scales with other classification systems–nearly all of them interesting. But, for the practicing teacher, the world of learning styles measurement can be both bewildering and daunting.

North American faculty developers have shown considerable interest in the exploration of learning styles, and they are quite a popular topic for faculty workshops. There is also a good deal of empirical research on learning styles, and data from the different inventories has been collected and summarized for many thousands of students. However, learning styles inventories have a number of limitations as guides to the improvement of teaching and learning. For example, most of the scales lack content validity: although they do distinguish differences among learners, it is not clear that these differences are the most *salient* characteristics of learning–the factors that really matter. Secondly, once a teacher has gathered data about the different learning styles of students in a class, there is the question of what can be done with this information.

There have been attempts to match learning styles and teaching approaches–for example by dividing a large class into sections according to learning style, and having each section taught differently (Rosati, Dean, & Rodman, 1988). However, on the whole, the results of these experiments have been disappointing or inconclusive. In any case, there are formidable logistical obstacles to organizing courses in this way, even if we were confident that inventories are measuring significant aspects of learning. Grasha himself (1990) has recently expressed his "disenchantment with traditional approaches to the study of learning styles" (p. 26), commenting that attempts to use learning style data to guide teaching methods have been only marginally successful. Instead, he now advocates "naturalistic approaches to assessing learning styles grounded in the ongoing experiences of students" (p. 28), which might serve to make faculty think more about their teaching and how they might better meet the needs of different learners in their classes.

Although these comments may seem rather negative, I think that the issue of learning styles is an interesting one, and that the concept–and even the inventories–can prove useful for both developers and instructors. In my own workshops about learning, I try to emphasize the limitations of all the learning styles inventories, pointing out that we cannot be sure that they measure the most important aspects of learning, and that in any case the accuracy of the diagnosis is uncertain for any individual learner. At the same time, having students and teachers measure their learning styles and compare them with others can be a marvellous consciousness-raising exercise. Faculty and students often realize for the first time that the way they learn something is not true for many of their colleagues. The next step is to have faculty reflect about the process and consider whether their teaching could be modified to take account of the considerable individual differences between students in the way they learn.

RECENT RESEARCH ON APPROACHES TO LEARNING

A great deal of the work done on learning styles has been done in the US. A rather different research approach, with European roots, has focused on approaches to studying, with a particular emphasis on the way information is processed and conceptualized.[3] Even more interesting is the fact that we now have some empirical data that shed light on the relationship between different teaching methods and students' approaches to learning.

This research derives from a number of individuals working in different countries–but relying greatly on a cross-fertilization of findings and methods of inquiry. The work is associated with the names of researchers such as Pask, Entwistle, Ramsden, Parlett, and Hounsell in Britain, Biggs in Australia and Hong Kong, Marton and Säljö in Sweden, and to some extent Perry in the US (Biggs & Collis, 1982; Entwistle & Ramsden, 1983; Hounsell, 1990; Marton & Säljö, 1976a, 1976b; Miller & Parlett, 1974; Pask, 1976; Perry, 1970).

They have focused on the "phenomenological" world of the learner, generally in real-life situations. By and large they eschew strict experimental methods (although they are willing to make use of them where appropriate), and adopt what might be termed an "anthropological" approach to the study of learning. In contrast to a great deal of traditional psychological research, which has been preoccupied with learning *outcomes* (often in relation to varying learning conditions manipulated by the experimenter), these researchers have examined the *process* of learning or study, and have identified the different approaches, strategies, or styles that may be adopted by different groups of learners.

Perry (1970) identified three learning orientations, which he termed "absolutist," "relativistic," and an approach characterized by "personal commitment and responsibility," with individuals progressing through each via Piaget-like stages of cognitive development. Pask distinguished between "serialists" and "holists" (or, to use his earlier more evocative term, "stringers" and "lumpers"). Of particular interest here are the classic papers by Marton and Säljö (1976a, 1976b), who first used the terms "deep" and "surface" approaches to learning. Miller and Parlett (1974) categorized learners as "cue-conscious," "cue-seeking," or "cue-deaf," while Entwistle, Hounsell, and Ramsden developed the descriptors "meaning orientation" and "reproducing orientation" (Entwistle & Ramsden, 1983; Hounsell, 1990).

Even for faculty who have never encountered this research, the meaning of the descriptive terms is not hard to divine, and the categories have a certain intuitive appeal to college teachers who have taken the trouble to monitor the way their students study and complete assignments. The commonalities among the different constructs are evident. For example, students with a "meaning orientation" tend to have a "deep learning approach," and so on. Most writers today use the terms *deep* and *surface* as generic descriptors. In contrast to a good deal of research from the US on learning styles (for example, that of Kolb or Grasha), which has tended to argue that no one style is inherently superior to any other, the terms used by the researchers discussed here are unequivocally evaluative. In other words, no bones are made about the superiority of a deep learning, cue seeking, or meaning orientation–at least as far as most university-level work is concerned.[4]

The original work by Marton, Ramsden, and others involved a complex process of interviewing students (and, in some cases, observing them perform learning tasks such as summarizing a passage of prose) to determine whether they adopted deep or surface approaches to learning. However, in the early 1980s, Ramsden developed a scale to measure approaches to studying and student perceptions of the learning environment (Ramsden, 1992). The existence of these instruments, the Approaches to Studying questionnaire and the Course Perceptions questionnaire, made it considerably simpler to gather data from large numbers of students, and this has stimulated empirical investigations into deep and surface learning orientations in many parts of the world–although so far there has been very little interest in the approach in North America. Biggs, too, developed an instrument, the Structure of the Observed Learning Outcome (SOLO) taxonomy (Biggs & Collis, 1982) which also measures learning orientation and has been used in a number of empirical studies.

LEARNING APPROACHES AND TEACHING METHODS

Assuming there is some validity in the constructs of deep and surface learning approaches, and that learners can be reliably distinguished in terms of the way they conceptualize and go about the process of study, what are the implications for teaching practice in universities? In particular, do some teaching styles promote particular learning strategies? Can students change their strategies from less desirable orientations to ones that may be more suited for university-level learning? If so, how can this best be achieved?

There has been a flurry of interest in the question of how existing instruction in higher education affects student learning processes. Two studies can serve as typical examples. In Australia, Watkins and Hattie (1981) carried out an ambitious longitudinal study of 540 university students as they proceeded through their undergraduate programs. They measured approaches to study by a number of different methods, including a questionnaire and personal interviews. The research revealed that students' learning orientations did not become "deeper" (in Marton and Säljö's sense of the word)–a finding that is all the more discouraging in view of the fact that many of the weaker or more disillusioned students had withdrawn from the university before the final measures were taken–meaning that the findings describe only those who "succeeded" in the system. Watkins and Hattie attributed their findings primarily to the examination system which, they concluded, encouraged surface-level learning approaches.

More optimistic conclusions can be drawn from an investigation by Ramsden and Entwistle (1981), who studied some 2,000 students in various British universities. There was no universal pattern of change in learning orientation over time. However, a relationship was discovered between deep learning and "good teaching," "greater freedom in learning," and "avoidance of overloading." Good teachers were defined by Ramsden and Entwistle as instructors who try to understand student difficulties, are ready to give help and advice on study methods, and take care to pitch material at an appropriate level for their students. The authors define "freedom in learning" as allowing students a choice of tasks to complete course requirements, and a choice of learning methods to accomplish these tasks.

Intrigued by these findings, a student and I undertook a small replication in a Canadian university (Bertrand & Knapper, 1991). Participating students were selected from three academic departments that seemed to be quite different in their teaching approaches. The Department of Chemistry did most of its teaching through traditional lectures and labs, and was known for its large class sizes, heavy workloads and fairly rigid assessment methods (for example, multiple-choice exams with very little choice for students). The Department of Environment and Resource Studies was a small academic unit that placed great emphasis on individual and group project work which was closely linked to real-world issues; the department had fairly small class sizes, and students had considerable input into the choice of assessment tasks they undertook. This department was also characterized by a good deal of informal interaction between students and faculty. The third department, Psychology, combined a mixture of teaching approaches, ranging from very large, traditionally taught classes, assessed by objective tests, to much smaller courses that involved a good deal of independent student work.

A total of 183 students participated in the study, all majors or intended majors in the disciplines concerned. Approximately half were in the second year of their programs, and half in their fourth year. All of them completed the Approaches to Studying questionnaire and the Course Perceptions questionnaire. The latter was used as a control measure to ensure that the hypothesized differences in departmental teaching ambience were indeed reflected in the perceptions of students.

Results were remarkably in line with our predictions based upon informal observation. The three departments were seen quite differently by respondents as measured by the Course Perceptions instrument. For example, Chemistry was significantly different from Environment and Resource Studies on the dimensions of "Formal Teaching," "Freedom in Learning," "Good Teaching," "Workload," and "Openness to Students." Scores on these dimensions for Psychology were, as predicted, between the two extremes.

Even more interesting were the scores on the Approaches to Studying questionnaire. Table 1 reports mean scores for two scales: deep learning ("meaning orientation") and surface learning ("reproducing orientation"). It can be seen clearly that, as predicted, students in Environment and Resource Studies were the highest of the three departments on deep learning approach and lowest on surface learning. Chemistry students scored lowest on deep learning approach and, along with Psychology students, had the highest scores on surface learning orientation. With the exception of one cell, Psychology students scored mid-way between the two extremes. This pattern of differences is statistically significant.[5] These results confirm

TABLE 1

Mean scores on the *Approaches to Studying* questionnaire from students in three disciplines

	Chemistry		Psychology		Environment & Resource Studies	
	Year 2 N=35	Year 4 N=31	Year 2 N=37	Year 4 N=36	Year 2 N=23	Year 4 N=21
Deep Learning Approach	14.09	15.65	14.70	15.81	17.39	16.48
Surface Learning Approach	14.63	13.90	14.89	12.47	10.87	10.33

the British findings of Ramsden and Entwistle. Of course, my sample was much smaller, and the research was not a longitudinal study that followed the same group of students over the course of their university programs, as was done by Ramsden and Entwistle and Watkins and Hattie. Another difference is that the earlier research measured learning approaches by interviewing students and observing them perform learning tasks, whereas my own indicators were indirect and based upon student self-perceptions as reported on a standardized questionnaire. However, Ramsden (1983) does cite evidence for correlations between scores on the Approaches to Studying questionnaire and measures derived from more sophisticated observational procedures.

Students in the Australian and British studies on the whole tended to display even greater surface learning orientation as they progressed through their programs, but my own data reveal a modest trend in the other direction: there was a tendency for students in Chemistry and Psychology to display more of a deep learning approach in their fourth year. I think a plausible explanation for the difference has to do with the particular characteristics of the Canadian institution (and perhaps all Canadian universities), whereby third- and fourth-year students tend to encounter smaller class sizes, more challenging assignments, and have greater contact with faculty than do those in first or second year.

SOME PRACTICAL IMPLICATIONS

Although this study, and those of Watkins and Hattie and Ramsden and Entwistle, paint a gloomy picture of much traditional teaching practice with respect to the encouragement of sophisticated approaches to learning, the research is encouraging in the sense that it shows that the way we teach is important, and can guide students away from a surface-type learning orientation and towards deeper approaches. These investigations, along with results from an increasing body of literature by the other researchers mentioned, lead to a number of conclusions about university teaching and its effects on learning.

The first implication is that teaching does indeed have marked effects on study approaches and learning quality and that, in addition to *what* is taught, there are marked influences from the general "learning ambience" in a department, including workload, teaching methods, choice of assessment tasks, opportunity for faculty-student interaction, and similar components of the academic environment. All this should serve to remind us that most learning takes place outside the lecture hall or classroom at times and in places where the students are left to their own devices and adopt their own study methods without recourse to the guiding hand of an instructor. Such learning is often influenced by factors that many teachers may be unaware of–the so-called "hidden curriculum" (Snyder, 1971) whereby students' study methods are determined largely by what they divine as the "demand characteristics" of the course, based upon a heady mixture of student gossip, past examination papers, hints by the professor about what will be on the final, allusive comments on essays and assignments, and similar factors.

In other words, despite what might be said in the course outline, covered in lectures and the textbook, or stated explicitly by the instructor, it is what is on the exam (or what is thought will be there) that largely determines not only the *what* of learning but also the *how* of learning. One implication of the research on learning approaches is that we might do well to make the curriculum a little less hidden by sharing with students our teaching goals and expectations, explaining our choice of teaching methods, and generally making teaching and learning processes far more explicit.

WHERE NEXT?

The argument advanced in this chapter is that learning is the primary purpose of higher education institutions, and hence it is vitally important for faculty developers to understand how learning takes place and how it may be facilitated through different approaches to teaching. Although traditional psychological research on learning offers disappointingly little guidance to practicing college teachers, the recent work of some European and Australian scholars offers considerable promise in understanding how students approach the learning task, and what types of teaching methods serve to encourage more sophisticated (deeper) learning approaches. This research has implications for the way faculty teach and the way faculty developers might encourage more effective instruction.

Suggestions for Teachers

What might the individual instructor do who wishes to encourage the deeper type of "meaning orientation" in learning that is generally claimed to be the aim of most university teaching? From the research discussed, it is possible to derive the following general prescriptions.

Decide what learning is important. Decide first what sort of learning it is important for your students to achieve in your course. Pay particular attention to learning that will be of some value in the long term, after the individual has left the university. Is mastery of facts the main objective? Acquisition of skills? Change of attitude?

Appraise your teaching. Honestly appraise your teaching in order to see how the course activities encourage or discourage the type of learning you hope to foster. Pay most attention to the tasks students must accomplish in the course (as opposed to the content you are transmitting), especially tasks that will be graded on exams or assignments.

Match aims to approaches. It is possible that your aims for the course will primarily involve acquisition of facts–but very unlikely if you are a university teacher. If you are trying to inculcate higher-level skills, then passive learning approaches are almost certainly inadequate, and you will need to think of ways to encourage student activity, whether it be through discussion, extensive individual study outside the classroom, collaborative project work, peer learning, or other methods.

Consider what is taught/what is learned. Remember that what is taught (the course content) is not the same as what is learned (the process involved), and examine what you do in the classroom–and outside–for cues that might contribute to the "hidden curriculum" and a misperception by students of your real learning objectives.

Emphasize the process of learning. If you agree that the process of learning is at least as important as mastering a body of facts, then those processes should be taught explicitly and not taken for granted. This may mean deliberate instruction in such skills as writing essays, effective problem solving, working in groups, conducting independent research for assignments, making use of the library, and so on.

Evaluate time on task. Recognize that most learning takes place outside your purview and without your direct knowledge. There is a difference between "seat time" and learning time. Try to understand how your students study (perhaps by conducting class discussions about important projects, interviewing individual students, or having them keep diaries). Then try to discover how you can influence this process.

Apply research findings to teaching. Research studies discussed above indicate that the best role for a teacher transcends that of a simple transmitter of information. Instead, arrange learning tasks that don't baffle or overwhelm the student, but do provide sufficient challenge to motivate excellent performance and active exploration of alternative methods of learning. If possible, recognize individual differences by allowing students to meet course requirements through choice among alternative tasks and by different learning methods.

Put learning theory into practice. Bear in mind the lessons of conventional learning theory which suggest that a good teacher provides rewards, gives ample feedback on learning progress, and acts as a personal example or role model for effective learning.

Suggestions for Faculty Developers

The bottom line is learning. In Chapter 1, Alan Wright and Carol O'Neil present the results of an international survey of faculty developers. It is interesting to note that very few of the development strategies listed deal directly with the student learning issues discussed in this chapter–although, of course, workshops, grants, and library resources might in some cases focus on learning effectiveness. Of the 36 strategies listed, the most explictly relevant is number 10: "Seminars on understanding student learning," which was ranked no higher than 16th by respondents from the different countries surveyed. In my view, the topic of student learning deserves a much higher profile.

Although developers work primarily with faculty, their primary objective should be to undertake activities that have tangible effects on student learning and on the types of sophisticated (deep) learning and problem solving that have been discussed in this chapter. This does not mean that developers should abandon the traditional activities that appear in the list on Wright and O'Neil's questionnaire–organizing workshops, consulting with faculty on teaching problems, training teaching assistants, and so on. But it does suggest that hard questions should be asked about how such activities enhance the type of learning that research suggests is important. In other words, running a workshop on more efficient information transmission (lecturing) may be counter-productive if all this does is to reinforce inappropriate instructional methods. On the other hand, there is nothing wrong in starting with traditional approaches, improving them as far as possible, and encouraging exploration of alternatives consistent with more effective learning outcomes.

Whatever strategies faculty developers adopt, the research reviewed here suggests that student assessment is a vitally important topic. I have argued that assessment methods probably influence student learning processes and outcomes far more than most other aspects of teaching, such as the way information is presented in lectures. The work of Watkins and Hattie, Ramsden and Entwistle, and others suggests that choice of assessment tasks has a major impact on whether students adopt a deep or surface approach to learning. Hence, whatever teaching improvement strategies we employ as faculty developers, we should constantly remind our colleagues that teaching is not just telling–however well we do it–but also involves the tasks we set for students, the assignments and exams we give, and the way we award grades.

Faculty developers should have a clear conception of what they mean by effective learning. They should be prepared to articulate and defend this viewpoint to the faculty (and students) they serve. There is a danger in our profession of trying to be all things to all people, and while such eclecticism can serve an important purpose in reaching a wide range of faculty, in the long run it may encourage teaching approaches that are not consistent with desirable institutional learning goals. Although faculty spend a large part of their professional lives as teachers, many of our colleagues have never really articulated a "philosophy" of teaching–although, as Fox (1983) has pointed out, they do often have quite firm intuitive notions about their role as teachers and their conceptions of how learning takes place.

Faculty developers, on the other hand, have usually thought deeply about teaching and learning and have developed clear views about effective pedagogy that go beyond intuition and indeed are rooted in a broad range of research findings. But I believe we are shy about saying publicly, voicing what effective teaching and learning comprise, and how instructional methods and organizational structures might be changed to do the job better. For example, how many of our annual reports provide a definition of effective teaching? To what extent do our programs reflect this? Do we present our ideas at appropriate policy-making bodies–senate? the budget review committee? the long-range planning committee?

Virtually every decision a university makes about resource allocations has implications for teaching and learning, but it is surprising how often such decisions are made without a thorough examination of their potential impact on the quality of student learning. If you are fortunate, the senior academic officers of your institution will be aware of such issues. Their work can be enormously helped by informed advice from the faculty development office about appropriate learning goals and how they might be facilitated–or compromised–by institutional policy and resource allocation decisions.

Developers need to become involved with curriculum development. Although we have tended to avoid curriculum as the preserve of the disciplines, *what* is taught has just as much influence as *how* it is taught. Hence, simply concentrating on improving teaching methods will have limited success if the curriculum is outdated, overladen with factual material, introduces topics at inappropriate times, or has overlaps and duplications. Course and program content is inextricably bound with teaching methods and learning goals, so that any attempt to achieve deep learning outcomes must inevitably involve some attention to course and program planning.

Naturally, the discipline-based faculty are the ultimate custodians of such matters, but in many cases they are educational amateurs. We have all been to curriculum planning meetings where decisions were based primarily on disciplinary traditions or faculty subject-matter expertise and topic preferences, with absolutely no consideration of how a program might prepare students for life beyond university. Faculty developers could play an immensely important role in guiding a more rational approach to curriculum development. Indeed, some faculty development offices have had considerable success in making curriculum renewal a central component of their activities–a notable example being the Center for Instructional Development at Syracuse University (US). Successful involvement in curriculum development requires considerable sensitivity, but it can have large payoffs for the institution in effecting change that enhances learning.

Find and publicize examples of effective student learning. Given that much teaching is fairly traditional, there is often considerable resistance from both faculty and students to innovate and change. For example, fostering lifelong learning, where students are encouraged to take on more tasks themselves, will often be seen as threatening to learners and risky for instructors. Why change when everyone accepts the tried and true methods? Certainly, the methods may have been tried, but there is a lot of debate about whether they are true, which is why there is increasing public debate about the effectiveness of higher education, both within the academy and in the wider public domain. (For example, see Wingspread Group on Higher Education, 1993.)

Introducing new teaching methods in a traditional academic environment requires both knowledge (discipline-based and pedagogical) and courage. Faculty developers have the former and can encourage the latter, not only through consultation and moral support, but also by disseminating information about the effectiveness of alternative teaching approaches. To some extent, this is a matter of gathering information from successful innovations elsewhere. Even more persuasive for many cautious colleagues will be demonstration projects that are carefully planned, executed, and evaluated within the home institution.

While it is true that the effectiveness of much traditional university teaching is taken for granted without the carefully marshalled evidence we would expect in discipline-based research, departures from the traditional will be scrutinized closely for evidence that improvements really have been demonstrated. Most faculty developers are familiar with the wide range of innovations that have been used in higher education, and they can play an invaluable role in validating the effectiveness of new approaches introduced by faculty colleagues who are bold enough to try.

REFERENCES

Bertrand, D., & Knapper, C.K. (1991). *Contextual influences on students' approaches to learning in three academic departments.* Unpublished honors thesis, University of Waterloo, ON.

Biggs, J.B., & Collis, K.F. (1982). *Evaluating the quality of learning: The SOLO taxonomy.* New York, NY: Academic Press.

Bligh, D.A. (1972). *What's the use of lectures?* Harmondsworth, UK: Penguin.

Bligh, D.A. (Ed.). (1982). *Professionalism and flexibility in learning.* Guildford, UK: Society for Research into Higher Education.

Claxton, C.S., & Murrell, P.H. (1987). *Learning styles: Implications for improving educational strategies* (ASHE-ERIC Higher Education Report No. 4). College Station, TX: Association for the Study of Higher Education.

Elton, L. (1982). Assessment for learning. In D.A. Bligh (Ed.), *Professionalism and flexibility in learning.* Guildford, UK: Society for Research into Higher Education.

Entwistle, N.J., & Ramsden, P. (1983). *Understanding student learning.* London, UK: Croom Helm.

Fox, D. (1983). Personal theories of teaching. *Studies in Higher Education, 8,* 151-163.

Grasha, T. (1990). Using traditional versus naturalistic approaches to assessing learning styles in college teaching. *Journal on Excellence in College Teaching, 1,* 23-38.

Hounsell, D.J. (1990). Teaching and learning to learn. In I. Moses (Ed.), *Higher education in the late twentieth century: Reflections on a changing system.* Kensington, AUS: Higher Education Research and Development Association of Australasia.

Knapper, C.K. (1990). Lifelong learning and university teaching. In I. Moses (Ed.), *Higher education in the late twentieth century: Reflections on a changing system.* Kensington, AUS: Higher Education Research and Development Association of Australasia.

Knapper, C.K., & Cropley, A.J. (1991). *Lifelong learning and higher education* (2nd ed.). London, UK: Kogan Page.

Kolb, D.A. (1984). *Experiential learning: Experience as the source of learning and development.* Englewood Cliffs, NJ: Prentice-Hall.

Marton, F., & Säljö, R. (1976a). On qualitative differences in learning: I–Outcome and process. *British Journal of Educational Psychology, 46,* 4-11.

Marton, F., & Säljö, R. (1976b). On qualitative differences in learning: II–Outcome as a function of the learner's conception of the task. *British Journal of Educational Psychology, 46,* 115-127.

Miller, C.M.L., & Parlett, M. (1974). *Up to the mark: A study of the examination game.* London, UK: Society for Research into Higher Education.

Milton, O. (1982). *Will that be on the final?* Springfield, IL: Charles C. Thomas.

Myers, P.B., & Myers, K.D. (1987). *Myers-Briggs Type Indicator.* Palo Alto, CA: Consulting Psychologists Press.

Pascarella, E.T., & Terenzini, P.T. (1991). *How college affects students.* San Francisco, CA: Jossey-Bass.

Pask, G. (1976). Styles and strategies of learning. *British Journal of Educational Psychology, 46,* 128-148.

Perry, W.G. (1970). *Forms of intellectual and ethical development in the college years: A scheme.* New York, NY: Holt, Rinehart and Winston.

Ramsden, P. (1992). *Learning to teach in higher education.* London, UK: Routledge.

Ramsden, P. (1983). *The Lancaster approaches to studying and course perceptions questionnaire: Lecturers' handbook.* Oxford, UK: Educational Methods Unit, Oxford Polytechnic.

Ramsden, P., & Entwistle, N.J. (1981). Effects of academic departments on students' approaches to studying. *British Journal of Educational Psychology, 51,* 368-383.

Rosati, P., Dean, R.K., & Rodman, S.M. (1988). A study of the relationship between students' learning styles and instructors' lecture styles. *IEEE Transactions on Education, 31,* 208-212.

Snyder, B.R. (1971). *The hidden curriculum.* New York, NY: Knopf.

Trani, E.P. (1979). *Final report on the project: Helping students become more sophisticated consumers of their own education.* Unpublished manuscript, University of Nebraska, Lincoln.

Watkins, D.A., & Hattie, J. (1981). The learning processes of Australian university students: Investigations of contextual and personological factors. *British Journal of Educational Psychology, 51,* 384-393.

Wingspread Group on Higher Education. (1993). *An American imperative: Higher expectations for higher education.* Racine, WI: Johnson Foundation.

AUTHOR

Christopher Knapper is Director of Instructional Development and Professor of Psychology at Queen's University, in Kingston, Ontario, Canada. He has written widely on various topics, including educational technology, instructional evaluation, lifelong learning, and distance education, and his most recent book is Lifelong Learning and Higher Education (Kogan Page, 1991). Dr. Knapper has given workshops on college teaching and learning in many parts of the world, including Canada, the US, Sweden, Australia, New Zealand, Zimbabwe, Japan, and Korea. Outside higher education, his research interests are in environmental psychology and driving behavior. He is a Fellow of the British Psychological Society and a founder of the Canadian-based Society for Teaching and Learning in Higher Education.

NOTES

[1] Bligh (1972) made a comprehensive survey of research on effectiveness of lectures. Although his review was completed over 20 years ago, his conclusions still stand.

[2] The monumental monograph by Pascarella and Terenzini (1991) analyzed over 2,600 studies in an attempt to understand how different characteristics of higher education institutions affect student learning, cognitive growth, self-concept, values and attitudes, and career success. Among their conclusions are that active learning methods result in greater cognitive development and that "student learning is unambiguously linked to effective teaching" (p. 619).

[3] What, then, is the difference between a learning *style* and a learning *approach*? This is rather a vexed question, since different commentators and researchers use the terms in different ways–or even interchangeably. However, a rough distinction would be to regard learning styles as a set of basic characteristics somewhat akin to personality traits, whereas learning approaches are seen as a type of "mental set" or predisposition, often context-dependent. It is implied that the latter are more amenable to change than the former.

[4] It is tempting to conclude that the different philosophical assumptions underlying the American and European work in this field reflect cultural differences: traditional hierarchical societies versus a society that places great emphasis on egalitarianism, but perhaps this is too fanciful an interpretation.

[5] For the statistically-minded, an analysis of variance indicated a significant main effect for department on each dimension.

3.

Increasing Faculty Understanding of Teaching

Keith Trigwell

This chapter describes how the results of research studies on the conceptions and approaches of university science teachers have been incorporated into academic staff development programs. Faculty awareness of the diversity in teaching among their colleagues in a discipline can trigger conceptual change or development. The academic development activities based on the disciplinary studies enjoy high credibility among faculty members, and the processes are applicable to all discipline areas.

INTRODUCTION

The idea of improving teaching by developing an awareness of variation in teacher thinking, and teacher action consistent with that awareness, forms the core of this chapter. This approach is innovative in focusing not on awareness at the traditional teaching tips or activities level *per se*, but rather on the relation between this level and the thinking-about-teaching level. The origin of this approach lies in research into conceptions (or ways of thinking) of Australian teachers of first-year university science classes.

University science teaching has, for many academic staff at least, been largely a secretive and personal activity. Many teachers are unaware of forms of teaching other than those which they themselves use or to which they have been exposed as students. Research seminars or public lectures are the main forums in which these academic staff expose their "teaching" to their peers. In both cases, the idea of teacher-centered transmission is reinforced.

Science lecturers are aware that there are different strategies, such as questioning, demonstrations, and problem solving, that can be used in teaching. They have also heard that interactive methods, such as group discussions, occur in environments other than laboratories. But to accept and adopt some of these strategies found to encourage the type of university learning that most faculty say they want, some faculty may themselves need to undergo a conceptual change. This is not an easy task. However, without such a change, there may be no improvement. From some perspectives, a number of these strategies make no sense and are impossible for faculty to accept. For example, lecturers who believe teaching is nothing more than information transmission tend to reject the suggestion of establishing group interaction in a lecture theatre of 200 students, saying that it is impossible. From a similar perspective, they may interpret the strategy of questioning as no more than "Did you hear that at the back?", "Do you understand that?" or "Are you with me so far?"

The results of research studies suggest that faculty who do think of teaching from teacher-focused perspectives will be unlikely or unable to accept strategies based on student-focused ideas. The authors of these studies conclude that attempts to improve student learning through the improvement of teaching strategies alone will be very unlikely to succeed (Trigwell, Prosser, & Taylor, 1994).

Teachers must be made aware of the known range of conceptions of teaching; then it may be easier to change *their* conceptions because they now know what it is they can become. This process can also be helped by clarifying the nature of the strategies and interpretations associated with those conceptions. For first-year science teachers, these conceptions and self-reports of approaches have been explored and identified in empirical studies (Prosser, Trigwell, & Taylor, 1994). Other studies of teaching from a number of disciplines report similar conclusions (Dall'Alba, 1991; Samuelowicz & Bain, 1992).

This chapter explores the relations between those conceptions of teaching and teaching practices and outlines how this information is used to improve the learning of science students. It begins with a review of the role of conceptions of learning and how they are used to increase awareness of learning issues for students with a view to improving the quality of learning in universities (see also Knapper in this volume). In the third section, the parallels with the teaching context are developed, especially the idea of teaching as a way of thinking, and relations are shown among the three levels of teaching-related activities (conceptions, planning, and strategies).

The results of research into teachers' conceptions are outlined in the fourth section. The use of this information in faculty development activities is the subject of the final section; it includes a description of some of the materials used (a questionnaire, a series of videos, and extracts from interviews), and examples of how the activities associated with them are organized.

CONCEPTIONS OF LEARNING

The way people think about a phenomenon can be either a limiting or liberating condition. Some conceptions are closer approximations to "accepted wisdom" than others, some conceptions explain observed behavior better than others, and some conceptions are associated with more acceptable practices than others. Conceptions that are not consistent with accepted wisdom or are associated with less acceptable behaviors are normally limiting conceptions.

For many years, the majority of the people that thought about it at all conceived of the sun, the moon, and the planets as revolving around the Earth. This conception allowed them to explain why the sun rose in the east each day, and why the moon followed a similar path. But this conception was not consistent with observations of the motion of the planets or of the stars. This was (and is) a limiting conception. Strategies or predictions based on it may not be accurate or reliable. A feature of these limiting conceptions is that they often contain components which are consistent with more sophisticated conceptions (the moon does revolve around the Earth).

As knowledge increases, conceptions that approximate "accepted wisdom" become more sophisticated and either replace or subsume less sophisticated conceptions. Studies of the conceptions of a phenomenon reported by a group of people consistently show a range of qualitatively different ways of conceiving that phenomenon (Marton, 1981, 1986). Some of these are likely to be more sophisticated than others, and some may be limiting. An example of such a range has been found in a study of the conceptions of learning of adult students (Marton & Säljö, 1976; Säljö, 1979). In summary, this work reported that the replies of adult students, when asked to say what they understood by learning, could be classified into different categories:

1. learning as a quantitative increase in knowledge
2. learning as memorizing
3. learning as the acquisition of facts, methods, etc. which can be retained and used when necessary
4. learning as the abstraction of meaning; and

5. learning as an interpretive process aimed at understanding reality.

Marton, Dall'Alba, and Beaty (1993) identified a sixth conception (learning as changing as a person) in a study which also identified the five conceptions from the earlier work. This sixth conception and Conception 5 (learning as an interpretive process aimed at understanding reality) are sophisticated conceptions and subsume Conceptions 1-4.

Conceptions 1-3 are limiting conceptions. Without the ability to conceive of learning as being more than a quantitative increase in knowledge, or memorizing, students have extreme difficulty in adopting practices that lead to high quality learning. Table 1 shows the results of a study by Marton and Säljö (1976) of the relations between students' conceptions of learning a topic and their self-reported approach to learning that topic. Deep and surface approaches to learning, defined in the chapter by Knapper, are qualitatively different ways in which students approach their learning of a

TABLE 1

Relations between approaches to learning and conceptions of learning

Approach to Learning	Conception of Learning				
	1	2	3	4	5
Deep	0	4	7	11	12
Surface	6	19	8	1	1

task (for example, reading a text or solving a problem). Deep approaches to learning are more likely to lead to high quality learning than surface approaches (van Rossum and Schenk, 1984).

The results suggest that students who conceive of learning as a quantitative increase in knowledge, or as memorizing, are unlikely to adopt a deep approach to learning. Conversely, students who conceive of learning as the abstraction of meaning, or an interpretive process aimed at understanding reality, are more likely to adopt a deep approach to learning of that topic.

Conceptions of Teaching

Relationships similar to those described for student learning have been observed between teachers' conceptions and approaches to teaching (Trigwell & Prosser, 1994). Teachers who describe sophisticated conceptions of teaching and learning are more likely to adopt approaches to teaching which focus on the student and on student learning as the outcome of the teaching process. Limiting conceptions of teaching are therefore likely to prevent teachers from seeing or accepting approaches to teaching which focus on the student.

An example of the influence of limiting teaching conceptions was observed by the author in the development and testing phase of a questionnaire on science teaching methods and intentions (Approaches to Teaching Inventory, Prosser & Trigwell, 1993). Some items in the inventory asked faculty to comment on the extent to which they engage students in learning tasks which are active rather than passive. For example, "We take time out in lectures so that students can discuss, among themselves, the problems they encounter studying the subject." Faculty who, for this context, intend to *transmit information* do not see the value of, or need for, this type of activity, and they responded to this item on the questionnaire by saying that such an activity is not possible in lectures. They went on to say that the inventory was flawed because items such as this were unrealistic. Since all items in the inventory are constructed from quotes made by science teaching staff about what they do in their teaching, these items are clearly *not* unrealistic for some staff.

Limiting conceptions of teaching constitute the greatest barrier to teaching (and learning) improvement. They are likely to prevent successful adoption and application by teachers of processes known to facilitate student learning. An example of this involving buzz groups is described later in this chapter. The teacher who fails to see that learning involves the student making sense of the subject, which could be different from explaining the subject more clearly, is unlikely to adopt processes which focus on the student.

Attempts to change the effectiveness of teaching processes by focusing on what the teacher does may result in improvements in the strategies themselves, but not necessarily in student learning. Improving effectiveness may require a change in thinking and a change in strategy. For example, many science students work from conceptions which hinder the development of their understanding of a subject. Teachers who do not attempt to challenge those conceptions, no matter what strategy they adopt, are not likely to help improve those students' understanding.

To return to the analogy from astronomy introduced in the previous section, such measures which focus on current practice are somewhat akin to improving the resolution of the telescope or spending more time observing, while maintaining the focus on the moon. As long as the focus remains on the moon, a conceptual change to the more sophisticated view of the solar system as we now see it is very unlikely.

The improvement of skills and strategies *within* a conception is described as conceptual development (Prosser et al., in press). The practice adopted in most courses and programs developed for the improvement of university teaching is at the conceptual development level. For teachers with a sophisticated conception of teaching (and learning), this is an appropriate practice at a time when even more sophisticated conceptions are unknown. However, many university teachers do not have sophisticated conceptions, and the processes are doing no more than improving the use of strategies associated with those limiting conceptions. Conceptions of teaching are normally not challenged; such an approach may, in fact, be counter-productive.

In the case of student learning, attempts to improve the learning strategies of students who had limiting conceptions of learning simply increased the efficiency of their surface approaches to learning (Ramsden, Beswick, & Bowden, 1986). Students from anatomy, chemistry, history, psychology, and engineering were invited to attend a regular program throughout the academic year aimed at improving study skills. At the end of the program, those who attended did not alter their deep approaches to learning relative to a group who did not attend, but they did enhance their use of surface approaches, in contrast to the non-attending group, whose use of surface approaches declined.

New teaching-improvement strategies may not be consistent with everyone's teaching ideas. If that is the case, the ideas will be ignored as unrealistic or irrelevant. At worst, they may be misinterpreted, and attempts to apply them may lead to inappropriate teaching practices.

The way to prevent such an outcome is to look at the components of teaching as an integrated whole. Biggs (1993), using a cognitive systems approach, refers to Schön's metaphor of the higher education teaching and learning process as a swamp: "one's framework needs to be able to map the state of the swamp, and not just the anatomy of the alligators" (p. 74). To illustrate the whole (swamp) and its consituent parts, he describes shells of influence on the student.

FIGURE 1

Macro- and constituent micro-systems in tertiary education

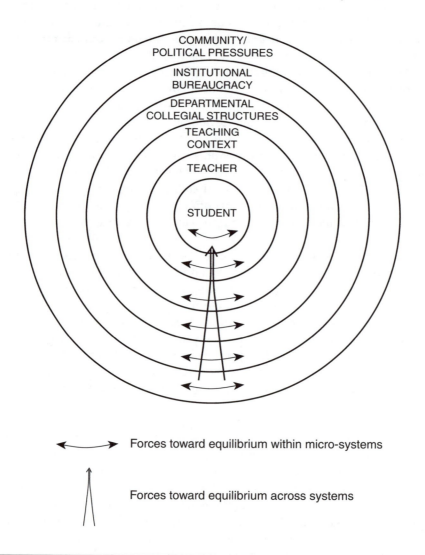

COMMUNITY/
POLITICAL PRESSURES

INSTITUTIONAL
BUREAUCRACY

DEPARTMENTAL
COLLEGIAL STRUCTURES

TEACHING
CONTEXT

TEACHER

STUDENT

Forces toward equilibrium within micro-systems

Forces toward equilibrium across systems

The "teacher" shell described by Biggs can itself be conceived as containing three components within the education "swamp." The components include teacher thinking, planning, and strategies and are closely related (Figure 2). The inner level (nearest the student) is the teacher strategies, or the things that teachers do in their teaching. The second, or middle level, is the planning level which ties together the conceptions and the strategies. The third, or outer level, is the thinking or conceptions level.

FIGURE 2

Levels of influence in the teaching and learning process

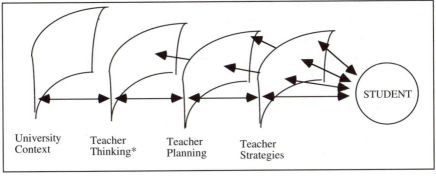

University Context   Teacher Thinking*   Teacher Planning   Teacher Strategies   STUDENT

*Also called the teacher's conception level.

All teaching involves these three components, though at times (for example, in evaluating the quality of teaching) the thinking component is forgotten by the designers of evaluation methods. Teacher strategies are the more visible aspects of teaching, including lecturing skills, the feedback given on assignments, organization and management of tutorials, availability to students for consultation, and the structure of the syllabus. This is the area that has the greatest impact from the students' point of view and is the area where most students are asked for their comments in assessing aspects of teaching. Students may see evidence of planning, but not the planning itself. They are often influenced by teacher thinking, but cannot comment on it. For example, most mature age students have learned to learn for themselves and prefer teaching strategies based on teaching-to-help-students-learn rather than transmission styles. Many express the discomfort of this clash of styles.

While the students may not be able to articulate the influences from these three teaching components, their learning is strongly influenced by all three. This interaction is represented in Figure 2 by the arrows between all levels and the student. At the planning stage, *teacher thinking* drives what the teachers intend to do in the classroom or the laboratory. Some academic development activities address this area through, for example, curriculum planning and development, lecture preparation, and assessment planned in conjunction with the teaching methods. As planning is not visible, it is not addressed as frequently as the strategies level. Second, it is normally addressed only *in conjunction with* the teaching strategies level. That is, planning is done according to what it is that the teacher is going to do. Curriculum design focuses on what has to be covered, and lecture preparation addresses what methods will be used to get the information across. Occasionally, the process includes the student (what influence on student learning will this approach have?), but rarely in courses for university teachers is the planning considered in conjunction with the conception of teaching that drives that planning approach.

The third component is rarely addressed, yet as noted earlier, research suggests that the way teachers think about teaching can be either a limiting or liberating factor in both teaching and in student learning. That a group of teachers will use a range of conceptions of teaching in informing their planning and strategies is no longer in dispute. Some of the results that lead to this conclusion are reported in the next section of this chapter. Yet courses and books on teaching in higher education, with few exceptions, still focus on teaching strategies rather than the thinking or conceptions related to those strategies. When they do, the connections between the two are often time consuming or difficult to demonstrate. Two notable exceptions are the book *Learning to Teach in Higher Education* (Ramsden, 1992), and the video series *Teaching Matters* (McKenzie & Scott, 1994).

Figure 2 also illustrates the broader view of the teaching/learning process by showing the connections between 1) the wider university context, 2) the teachers' thinking, planning, and strategies, and 3) student learning. Such a picture suggests that in different situations (determined by the wider context) the same teachers may think differently (and plan and act differently).

It is the treatment of the improvement of teaching through a focus on the interaction between all three of these teaching components and their integration with the wider context that is the core of this chapter and of the academic development activities described in it.

RESEARCH INTO TEACHERS' CONCEPTIONS

If a focus on the links between the three components of teaching is important, then identification of the different conceptions of teaching is crucial. Also crucial is the definition of conception being used in this analysis. The chapter by Knapper introduces the research on different ways of thinking about teaching. With the possible exception of the teaching metaphors offered by Fox (1983), most of the ways of thinking about teaching parallel the learning styles results also described in the Knapper chapter. These learning or thinking styles are normally considered characteristics of individuals.

The results used in the academic development activities described in this chapter are taken from phenomenographic studies in which conceptions are not hypothesized to reside within individuals, but are relations between individuals and a particular task and context. This is illustrated in Figure 2 by the arrow (all arrows are double headed) at the extreme left of the diagram. Consequently, the conceptions are not stable entities within cognitive structures but are dynamic and depend on the particular context and task in which they are being studied (Marton, 1981, 1986).

It is possible (and has been observed) that a faculty member who works with a conception of teaching at the graduate level, which is described as teaching as facilitation of student learning, may decide that at the college entry level the teaching intention and the related strategy is to transmit information. This may be because the teacher works with a different conception of teaching at the first-year level. For example, this teacher could argue that students need to know the basics first, and those basics should be transmitted to them; or that there is a lot of material to get through, and it has to be transmitted. In a different (graduate) context where the faculty member feels the students already know the basic material, or there is no curriculum content driving the process, the teacher works within a facilitating learning conception. This teacher is capable of working from either conception: the context is a component of the conception.

The range of conceptions of teaching presented in this chapter is derived from a study of teachers of first-year physical science in two Australian universities. Six teachers in each of the chemistry and physics departments of the two universities (24 in all) were individually interviewed about their approaches to teaching and their thinking about teaching and learning. Their teaching covered service courses to engineers, life scientists, nurses, and dentists, as well as courses for chemists and physicists. They held positions from lecturers to professors, they all conducted lectures as part of their teaching, and most were involved in tutorials and / or laboratory teaching.

Each interview was analyzed phenomenographically (Bowden & Walsh, 1994; Dahlgren, 1984). The range of conceptions of science teaching constituted from the interviews is presented in Table 2. Each conception is described more fully in the following paragraphs (Prosser et al., in press).

Each one is a category of description of science teacher thinking. The word *concept* referred to in the categories of description is the science concept being learned, such as force or gravity or atomic structure.

TABLE 2

Conceptions of First-Year Science Teaching

Explanation given in terms of:	Focus of teaching on:		
	Syllabus/text Concepts	Teachers' Conceptions	Students' Conceptions
Teacher:			
transmitting information	A	B	
helping students acquire concepts	C	D	
helping students develop conceptions			E
helping students change conceptions			F

Conception A: Teaching as transmitting concepts of the syllabus

Teachers describing this conception focus on the science concepts detailed in the syllabus or textbook, and see their role as transmitting information about those concepts to their students. The focus is not on how the components of the information are related to each other or on students' prior knowledge of the topic.

Conception B: Teaching as transmitting the teachers' knowledge

Within this conception of teaching, teachers focus on their own structure of knowledge (which may be different from that described in books), but again see their role as transmitting information based upon those conceptions to their students. Similarly, the focus is not on how the components of information are related or on students' prior knowledge of the topic.

Conception C: Teaching as helping students acquire concepts of the syllabus

Within this conception of teaching, as in Conception A, teachers focus on the science concepts as detailed in the textbook or the syllabus, but rather than being transmitters, they see themselves as helping their students acquire those concepts and understand relationships among them. Unlike Conceptions A and B, students' prior knowledge is seen as being important.

Conception D: Teaching as helping students acquire teachers' knowledge

Teachers describing this conception, as with Conception B, focus on their own understanding of science concepts. But like Conception C and unlike Conception B, they see themselves as helping their students acquire those concepts and relations between them. Unlike Conceptions A and B, students' prior knowledge is seen as being important.

Conception E: Teaching as helping students develop conceptions of science

Teachers describing this conception of teaching focus on their students' world views or conceptions of the subject matter rather than their own conceptions or those based on the textbooks. They see their role as helping their students develop their conceptions in terms of further elaboration and extension (conceptual development).

Conception F: Teaching as helping students change conceptions

Teachers describing this conception of teaching again focus on their students' world views or conceptions of the subject matter rather than their own conceptions or those based on the textbooks. They differ from those describing Conception E in seeing teaching as helping students change their conceptions or world views (conceptual change).

Table 2 has been constructed to represent a hierarchy of conceptions similar to the range of conceptions of learning described by Säljö (1979). Conception F would not preclude the transmission of information but would suggest that there is more to teaching than just transmitting information. On the other hand, Conceptions A and B, as described in this context, mean that the transmission of information is the sole aim of teaching, with the differences between the two being in the focus on what is being transmitted. In terms of our current understanding of teaching and learning, Conceptions A and B would be limiting conceptions of teaching, even in the large introductory class.

The range of conceptions of first-year science teaching reported here are derived from one study. Other studies using a similar methodology with different groups of teachers have yielded results which differ in detail but contain the same overall structure. Samuelowicz and Bain (1992) report five qualitatively different conceptions among 13 teachers. The extremes of their categories of description range from imparting information to activity aimed at changing students' conceptions or understanding of the world, and supporting student learning. Dall'Alba (1991) found seven different categories of description ranging from teaching as presenting information to teaching as bringing about conceptual change; while Balla and Martin (1991) report three conceptions: teaching as presenting information, teaching as encouraging active learning, and relating teaching to learning. The common feature of all these studies is that they identify, at one extreme, teachers who think teaching is only about transmission of content, and at the other, teachers who think teaching is about helping students to learn, a part of which may be the transmission of content. Teachers teaching the same topic at the same first-year college level may have quite different ideas about the nature of teaching.

The importance of the differences in this range of conceptions from which teachers work is illustrated by focusing on two examples of the approaches taken by teachers. Both examples–buzz groups and breaks in lectures, and the use of questions in lectures–are concerned with student involvement in the teaching and learning process. The point is that the teaching strategies are used and interpreted differently from the perspective of different conceptions of teaching and learning.

Buzz groups, described by Gibbs, Habeshaw, and Habeshaw (1984) as short sessions in which students are asked to form small groups to discuss a key issue being addressed in a teaching session, are an example of a strategy suggested in teaching tips books. A strategy also advocated in similar books is the incorporation of "rest-times" during lectures to help maintain student interest in and concentration on the lecture by providing a variation in stimulation (Bligh, 1971, p. 50). Buzz groups have also been suggested as a rest-time strategy. Teachers with an information transmission intention may see this advice as a method of varying stimulation, or one to keep students from becoming bored with the lecture. While this is a development, it misses the point of buzz groups which is to help the teacher find out about students' prior knowledge, or for students to become aware of the variation of the conceptions among their peers, or as a way of developing discussion among students. Without a focus on student learning, teachers are unlikely to gain these benefits of the use of buzz groups.

Similarly, the idea of using questions as a teaching strategy looks quite different from the perspective of different conceptions. The following three quotes on the use of questions come from faculty who reported conceptions of teaching in the non-student-focused group (Conceptions A-D).

It isn't always possible because when you are conveying a set of facts then there isn't an opportunity to ask questions other than "What did I just say?"

Oh, when I ask a question it's almost always a rhetorical question. Students [like] to ask a lot of non-rhetorical questions, but I don't like to treat a lecture like a school class where I want someone in the audience to answer this question.

There [are] usually three groups of students in the class. The ones who pick the right answer, the ones who pick the wrong answer, and the ones who don't say anything. I usually say 'who thinks this, who thinks that, and who doesn't think at all?' Quite a few of them admit to not thinking at all.

The next two quotes are from faculty who reported using conceptions E and F, respectively, in their first year teaching.

Yes, I do a lot of questioning. Some of it is directed specifically for an answer there and then or an exploration there and then. One of the things about my questioning is that I'm not necessarily interested in the person who's got the right answer. I notice that people are often reluctant to say anything unless they've got the right answer already, in which case what's the value of that? I'm much more interested in directing the questions and engaging with people where they are exploring, and are prepared to think on the spot.

[I would do a demonstration and] say, 'Look, I'm going to do this. What's going to happen?' And then do it. And what happens is different to what most people are going to guess. So you get them thinking about that and quite often they would get the answer wrong. I then say, 'Hey, that's homework—go and think about that for next time.'

To gain maximum benefit from the vast knowledge now accumulated on effective teaching strategies, teachers' conceptions of teaching must also be addressed. One way of doing so (conceptual change through developing an awareness of the variation) is described in the next section.

A second way, which is not described here in detail, but could be incorporated into the process described in the next section, involves conceptual development. Because of the relation between contexts and conceptions, conceiving of teaching in totally new ways may not always be required for some teachers. Instead, what may be required is the translation of the same (sophisticated) conception from one context to a new context. For example, the teacher referred to earlier as describing the use of different conceptions for graduate versus first-year teaching already works with a sophisticated conception of teaching (in one context). To change this person's approach to teaching at first-year level involves conceptual development rather than conceptual change. It involves the development of an awareness that approaches used to teach graduate students may have applications, relevance and value in the first-year context. Because the idea of facilitating student learning has already been accepted in the graduate context, this move to applying it in the first-year context is likely to be a much easier task than conceptual change.

Improving Teaching

The aims of the academic development activities described in this section are to:

- develop among teaching staff an awareness of the variation in teacher thinking
- generate discussion on conceptions of teaching which are thought to lead to improved student learning
- illustrate, through example on video, the strategies and practices (often thought by staff to be difficult or impossible) that are consistent with these conceptions
- use the comments of students and graduates to support the teaching direction taken by teachers who adopt these practices

These aims are achieved using a variety of materials and methods. Materials include videos, questionnaires, and extracts from interviews with science teaching staff.

Videotapes

The videotapes contain exemplary practice (illustrations of teaching strategies), reflections by the teachers using those practices, and comments from students in the classes of those teachers. In their publication on the production of these materials, McKenzie and Scott (1994) note that the videos were constructed "primarily as a mechanism for dissemination of good practice, and to illuminate the ways of thinking about teaching which underlie good practices in different university contexts" (p. 420). The characteristics of good teaching which have been selected are heavily influenced by the work of Ramsden (1992), but an attempt has been made in the tapes to avoid making the experienced teachers appear to be too 'perfect.' "This has been achieved by including aspects of teaching that didn't go so well and by mediating this with the views of the students and the teacher himself/herself" (p. 420).

The videotapes make explicit the links between four of the components of Figure 2–teacher thinking, teaching strategies, the university context, and the students. The fifth component (planning) is implied in many of the explanations given by faculty for their approaches, and in the organization of the classroom activities.

Questionnaires

As part of the research study (described above) into the way university teachers of first-year science experience their teaching, the Approaches to Teaching Inventory was developed (Prosser & Trigwell, 1993). A shortened version of the inventory is shown in Appendix A. It contains only sub-scales for the extremes of the approaches identified in the interview studies. The shortened inventory is composed of two sub-scales (strategy and intention) for each of the extremes (student-focused strategy and conceptual change intention, and teacher-focused strategy and information transmission intention). Each sub-scale contains four items to which responses are sought on a five-point scale from "this item was only rarely true for me in this topic," to "this item was almost always true for me in this topic."

Extracts from Interviews

The extracts illustrate the range or diversity of the teacher thinking (conceptions) or the described action (approaches) of first-year science teachers (Appendix B). All of the extracts are taken from responses from the science academic staff who participated as subjects in the conceptions of science teaching research referred to earlier.

These materials have been used in a variety of contexts, from singular three-hour workshops for academic staff to parts of year-long programs or award courses for higher education teachers. In all cases, the aim is to challenge and change limiting conceptions and develop the more sophisticated ones.

A typical program has the following format. It begins with the members of the group identifying themselves and their discipline. Because of the relational nature of conceptions, this is an important part of the exercise, and it is usually recorded and maintained for reference during the exercise. The Approaches to Teaching Inventory (Appendix A) is distributed to all participants, and they are asked to complete it for a context in which they teach. They are also asked to circle the question number of any questions which they feel do not apply to their context. The completed questionnaire is set aside for later analysis, but faculty are assured that results for individuals will not be collected or discussed in the session.

In the next phase, participants are given extracts from interviews (Appendix B) to read and are then asked to characterize the differences in the teaching reflected in those extracts. The extracts used are usually the differences in either teacher thinking (conceptions of teaching–interviews 1 and 2) or approaches to teaching (interviews 3 and 4), but not both. These differences are discussed extensively (initially in small groups, then all together) as a non-threatening way of exposing the characteristics of the two extremes. The full range of conceptions (Table 2) or approaches is made available at the end of the discussion.

It is at this point that some academic staff claim that it is not possible to teach large classes with a student-focused approach, or will ask for information on how it is done. This is the key point of the session. Overly optimistic, idealistic, or dogmatic responses alienate those faculty who raise this issue. There are two approaches which have proved successful. The first is to ask other participants to suggest ways in which they go about teaching such classes. Since the range of conceptions and approaches was derived from interviews with actual teaching staff, it is possible that among the group are faculty able to talk about their experiences from such a conception. The second method, usually used after the first, is to show examples of such teaching from the videos. As already noted, the videos contain teachers' explanations of their intention in using the illustrated strategy, thus tying together teacher thinking and action.

To give the participants a view of where they think they fit in the range of teaching approaches found in one study, their responses to the Approaches to Teaching Inventory are analyzed. The first step is to highlight those questions they thought did not fit their context. Listing these on a board leads to and overlaps with the next step of revealing the structure of the inventory. Question numbers from the conceptual change and student-focus end of the range of approaches are sometimes already listed on the board as not being relevant. They are then asked to tally their scores for each of the two dimensions, supplied with the ranges found in other studies using the inventory, and are offered the opportunity to (privately) discuss their results.

To complete the session, the videotapes, and especially the students' comments illustrating their preferred teaching approach, are used to reinforce the ideas of developing student-focused thinking and teaching approaches.

CONCLUSION

This chapter has addressed a component of teaching development which has been largely ignored in academic development. Increasing faculty understanding of teaching, like increasing student understanding of learning, includes the process of finding out about the conceptions currently being used and changing or developing them.

Recent research into conceptions of teaching and learning in higher education has played a major role in increasing faculty understanding of teaching. The results are revealing two new routes to teaching development, both involving an awareness of the diversity of teacher thinking. The first route is a function of the form of the results of that research. In some cases, the categories of description of teaching can be constituted as a hierarchical range. The use of this range and the idea that some conceptions subsume others (and thereby establish a conceptions value system) have been outlined in this chapter. With the use of the integration of teachers' conceptions with their planning and teaching approaches, this academic development method focuses on changing conceptions of teaching.

The second characteristic of the results from this research is that conceptions are considered not to reside within individuals, but are a function of the relation between individuals and a context. This relational nature of conceptions of teaching leads to an alternate route to improving teaching through conceptual development. Because of the relation between contexts and conceptions, conceiving of teaching in new ways (the aim of the first route) may not always be required for some teachers. Conceptual development, which is likely to be a much easier task than conceptual change, may be all that is required.

ACKNOWLEDGMENTS

Many of the ideas and practices included in this chapter were developed in collaboration with Professor Michael Prosser of La Trobe University in Melbourne, Australia. In the research reported, he was a co-Chief Investigator. The research was funded with the support of Australian Research Council grants, and the contributions of research assistants, Jason Kelleher and Philip Taylor are acknowledged.

REFERENCES

Balla, M., & Martin, E. (1991). Conceptions of teaching and implications for learning. *Research and Development in Higher Education, 13,* 298-304.

Biggs, J.B. (1993). From theory to practice: A cognitive systems approach. *Higher Education Research and Development, 12,* 73-85.

Bligh, D.A. (1971). *What's the use of lectures.* Exeter, UK: D.A. and B. Bligh.

Bowden, J., & Walsh, E. (Eds.). (1994). *Phenomenographic research: Variations in method.* Melbourne, Australia: RMIT.

Dall'Alba, G. (1991). Foreshadowing conceptions of teaching. *Research and Development in Higher Education, 13,* 293-297.

Dahlgren, L.O. (1984). Outcomes of learning. In F. Marton, D. Hounsell, & N. Entwistle (Eds.), *The experience of learning* (pp. 19-35). Edinburgh, UK: Scottish Academic Press.

Fox, D. (1983). Personal theories of teaching. *Studies in Higher Education, 8,* 151-163.

Gibbs, G., Habeshaw, S., & Habeshaw, T. (1984). *53 interesting things to do in your lectures.* Bristol, UK: Technical Educational Services.

Marton, F. (1981). Phenomenography: Describing conceptions of the world around us. *Instructional Science, 10,* 177-200.

Marton, F. (1986). Phenomenography: A research approach to investigating different understandings of reality. *Journal of Thought, 21,* 28-49.

Marton, F., Dall'Alba, G., & Beaty, E. (1993). Conceptions of learning. *International Journal of Educational Research, 17*(3), 277-300.

Marton, F., & Säljö, R. (1976). On qualitative differences in learning: 1. Outcome and process. *British Journal of Educational Psychology, 46,* 4-11.

McKenzie, J., & Scott, G. (1994). Teaching matters: Making a video on teaching in higher education. *Research and Development in Higher Education, 16,* 419-424.

Prosser, M., & Trigwell, K. (1993). Development of an approaches to teaching questionnaire. *Research and Development in Higher Education, 15,* 468-473.

Prosser, M., Trigwell, K., & Taylor, P. (1994). A phenomenographic study of academics' conceptions of science learning and teaching. *Journal of Learning and Instruction, 4,* 217-231.

Ramsden, P. (1992). *Learning to teach in higher education.* London, UK: Routledge.

Ramsden, P., Beswick, D., & Bowden, J. (1986). Effects of learning skills interventions on first year university students' learning. *Human Learning, 5,* 151-164.

Säljö, R. (1979). *Learning in the learner's perspective. 1. Some common-sense conceptions.* (Reports from the Department of Education, University of Gothenburg, Sweden).

Samuelowicz, K., & Bain, J.D. (1992). Conceptions of teaching held by teachers. *Higher Education, 24,* 93-112.

Trigwell, K., & Prosser, M. (1994, July). *Relating approaches to teaching to conceptions of teaching.* Paper presented at the Annual Conference of the Higher Education Research and Development Society of Australasia, Canberra.

Trigwell, K., Prosser, M., & Taylor, P. (1994). Qualitative differences in approaches to teaching first year university science. *Higher Education, 27,* 75-84.

van Rossum, E.J., & Schenk, S.M. (1984). The relationship between learning conception, study strategy and learning outcome. *British Journal of Educational Psychology, 54,* 73-83.

Appendix A

Approaches to Teaching Inventory (ATI) (Shortened version)

Respond to each of the following questions by indicating which number on the scale most nearly represents your teaching experience:

1 – This item was only rarely true for me in this topic.

5 – This item was almost always true for me in this topic.

If you feel that a question does not apply to your context, circle the question number.

TEACHER FOCUS

- I design my teaching in this topic with the assumption that most of the students have very little useful knowledge of the subject.
- When I give this topic, I provide the students with only the information they will need to pass the examination.
- In this topic, I concentrate on covering the information that might be available from a good textbook.
- I structure this topic to help students pass the examination.

INFORMATION TRANSMISSION

- I feel it is important that this topic should be completely described in terms of specific objectives relating to what students have to know for examinations.
- I feel it is important to present a lot of facts in lectures so that students know what they have to learn for this topic.
- I feel that I should know the answers to any questions that students may put to me during this topic.

- I think an important reason for giving lectures in this topic is to give students a good set of notes.

STUDENT FOCUS

- I feel it is better for students to generate their own notes rather than always copy mine.
- In my lectures I try to develop a conversation with students about the topics we are studying.
- We take time out in lectures so that the students can discuss among themselves the difficulties that they encounter studying this topic.
- In lectures for this topic I use difficult or undefined examples to provoke debate.

CONCEPTUAL CHANGE

- Formal teaching time is made available for students to discuss their changing understanding of the subject.
- I feel that examinations in this topic should be an opportunity for students to reveal their changed conceptual understanding of the subject.
- I encourage students to restructure their existing knowledge in terms of the new ways of thinking about the subject that they will develop.
- I feel a lot of teaching time in this topic should be used to question students' ideas.

Appendix B

Interview Extracts

CONCEPTIONS OF TEACHING

Interview 1

[L = lecturer; I = interviewer]

I: What do you think teaching is about?

L: Well, I suppose teaching is showing the way, underlining the key ideas which show the way from one idea to the next, and showing how to apply these ideas.

I: When you say showing the way from one idea to the next, what are we talking about there?

L: Oh, I suppose in this particular course, the approach develops very gently from—let's say motion at constant speed in a straight line, accelerated motion in a straight line, accelerated motion in two dimensions and the ideas as they're developed in this textbook and in conventional physics textbooks proceeds in that direction. So you go from one idea to another which is a bit more complicated. So the teacher is showing the way there. But then I suppose when you come to the end of that particular part of the work, you are in a position to show how all these different varieties of motion from the simple to the complicated are embraced in one particular equation or physical principle. So all that's there, presented there in the textbook. You're just underlining key ideas that are there in the textbook.

Interview 2

I: What do you think teaching is about?

L: I suppose I want to make it interesting. Motivating students is a big part of it; doing things that'll get them interested. That ranges from things you do in lectures, through to choosing examples and subject matter that you think students will find interesting. It's encouraging them to work at it. I think on the one-to-one level, with tutorials and labs, there's a lot of encouraging people to do things. And on their own. And one of the conflicts we have in the lab sometimes is students come in expecting to be told exactly what they've got to do in there, and the response is, well what we want you to do is try to work out what you are going to do... I think that's part of teaching: to encourage that independent part.

APPROACHES TO TEACHING

Interview 3

I: What do you do in preparing for lectures?

L: ... So in preparing for an hour lecture I decide what I want the students to get out of this lecture, specifically what I want them to be able to do as a result of this lecture. So that is one of the first parts of planning my list if you like, planning my lecture. I also plan them in a way so that I know the notes that I want the students to get. I'll write my notes in such a way so that the students don't have to decide when to take notes, I tell them to. I'll dictate to them, I have handouts prepared, I have gaps in them that they fill in and I take that decision away from the students about when and how to take notes because I feel it's very important that the session is a learning experience at least and not just a note-taking exercise.

I: When you decide it's a good time for them to take notes, why do you do that?

L: Well, as I say, the session is tightly structured before I go in there. In other words, I like things carefully planned, so that you know, I've made the judgment about when it's time to take down some notes. I make that judgment. I think it's important the students do get a good set of notes. After all, there are exams we expect these students to pass.
They know they don't have to worry about taking it down. They have to worry about listening and concentrating and learning, I hope.

I: When you think that it's a good idea for them to just listen, rather than take notes, what do you think that achieves?

L: Well, learning and understanding, giving them a chance to think about them. The concept, the topic, the skill, under consideration at the moment, rather than just wondering about should I take notes at this stage, what do I need to learn here? Those sort of decisions, they don't worry about them, just try and concentrate and learn and get an understanding of this concept or the skill or whatever.

Interview 4

I: What do you do in lectures?

L: … Another thing I've been doing, and still do, is just have a pretty straightforward quiz, which I find breaks up the middle of a session. I put up an overhead transparency, maybe just a multiple-choice question or two, get the people to respond, put up their hand, to ask for this, that, or the other.

I: I see. All right.

L: And we discuss the answers.

I: What do you hope to achieve by doing those things? Let's look at some. First the buzz sessions. What do you hope to achieve by doing them?

L: Well, getting the students to… think, to be actively involved in what's going on, to think about it themselves. And I think the buzz session technique… is easier than asking individual people to respond to straight questions. People come back and say… things without necessarily having to represent only their own point of view. It is just to get people involved, getting them to think about the topic.

I: Why do you want them to do that?

L: 'Cause I think that's how learning happens. And I think the tradition of lectures is a pretty passive sort of thing, just spraying out information. What I read about research on the subject indicates it's not a terribly good method of transmitting information.

I: Mm. Mm.

L: (pause). I think, more explicitly what I want to achieve with… buzz sessions and the questions and stuff is confronting students with their pre-conceived ideas about the subject which quite often conflict with what we're talking about, the official dogmas as it were… So you've got to bring out that conflict and make the people aware that what they already know may not be what is the official line, as it were.

I: Mm.

L: And I think the buzz sessions and quizzes attempt to do that. I mean, I select questions for those things, which are designed to bring up those conflicts.

AUTHOR

Keith Trigwell is Associate Professor and Director of the Centre for Learning and Teaching at the University of Technology, Sydney, Australia. He began his academic career as a lecturer in Chemistry, and, following a period of six years at the Open University in the UK, developed an interest and career in studying university science teaching and learning. With colleagues, he is a recipient of many national competitive research grants focusing mainly on the phenomenographic ideas of the relations between contexts and teaching and student learning. Student learning also forms the core of a year-long course for faculty taught by the Centre for Learning and Teaching. From 1990 to 1994, Dr. Trigwell was co-editor of the journal Higher Education Research and Development, and a member of the national executive of the Australasian higher education society which publishes the journal.

4.

Preparing Faculty as Tutors in Problem-Based Learning

David Kaufman

Problem-based learning represents a radical departure from the traditional university mainstay of the lecture method. This chapter surveys the research on problem-based learning and describes a multi-stage approach to prepare faculty as tutors for a case-oriented, problem-based curriculum.

INTRODUCTION

This chapter begins with a description of a relatively recent innovation in higher education, referred to as "problem-based learning" (PBL). The PBL approach is described, a rationale is provided, and various roles are outlined for faculty.

The next section provides a detailed discussion of faculty recruitment and faculty development issues. An outline is given of the seven-stage faculty development process used in the undergraduate medical education curriculum at Dalhousie University, Nova Scotia, Canada, and some early evaluation results are presented.

An overview is presented of the relatively limited research conducted on tutoring in PBL and implications are discussed for tutor recruitment and faculty development. Some questions are then proposed for further research in this area.

The chapter concludes with a summary of some lessons learned from the literature and from the experience at Dalhousie University.

OVERVIEW OF PROBLEM-BASED LEARNING

Definition and Background

Various definitions of problem-based learning have appeared in the literature (Barrows & Tamblyn, 1980; Boud, 1985; Boud & Feletti, 1991; Kaufman, 1985). One of the most straightforward formulations was proposed by Barrows & Tamblyn (1980) as "the learning which results from the process of working towards the understanding or resolution of a problem" (p. 1).

There are many variations of the PBL process, but its essential stages may be described generally as follows (Barrows & Tamblyn, 1980). First, the problem is encountered before any preparation or study has occurred and is presented to students as it would be in reality. Students work with the problem in such a way that their abilities to reason and apply knowledge are challenged and evaluated, appropriate to their level of learning. Areas of learning requiring attention are identified and used as a guide to individualized study. The skills and knowledge acquired through the individualized study are applied to the problem, evaluated, and reinforced through discussion. Finally, the learning that has occurred in working on the problem and in individualized study is summarized and integrated into the students' existing knowledge and skills.

Problem-based learning is a relatively recent innovation in higher education. Case Western Reserve in Ohio (US) is usually credited as the first university to use PBL in its curriculum. However, McMaster University in Ontario, Canada is, in fact, the home of the first complete PBL medical school (established in 1969) to prepare future physicians (Neufeld, Woodward, & MacLeod, 1989). Since that time, numerous medical schools have implemented complete or partial PBL curricula (Armstrong, 1991; Des Marchais, 1990; Edwards, 1990; Kantrowicz, Kaufman, Mennin, Fulop, & Guilbert, 1987; Kaufman et al., 1989; Mann & Kaufman, 1994; Schmidt, Dauphinee, & Patel, 1987), and PBL has been introduced in programs or courses in other disciplines (Boud, 1985; Boud & Feletti, 1991). A recent bibliography on PBL (Australian Problem-Based Learning Network) listed more than 300 English-language references in 19 different disciplines as diverse as agriculture, business, engineering, and social work. More than two-thirds of these references are in the health professions. The references listed have a distinctly international flavor, with several countries (North American, European, Australasian and Middle Eastern) represented. Nearly all have been published since 1980. The reason for this widespread interest in PBL stems from the belief that PBL is a viable approach for improving teaching and learning in the academy (Association of American Medical Colleges [AAMC], 1992).

One recently developed PBL program is the undergraduate medical education curriculum at Dalhousie University. My experience in PBL is derived mainly from participation in the planning, design, implementation, and evaluation of this curriculum, as well as from visits to other PBL program sites, attendance at professional conferences, and reading of the literature.

Rationale for PBL

PBL represents a significant departure from the traditional lecture-based approach and radically transforms the roles of teacher and learners. Therefore, one would expect resistance from faculty and many legitimate questions and concerns about the approach's appropriateness and effectiveness (for example, Berkson, 1993).

Several rationales may be advanced in support of PBL (Barrows, 1985; Boud, 1985; Boud & Feletti, 1991; Coles, 1990; Norman & Schmidt, 1992; Schmidt, 1989). These are described briefly in six categories: philosophical, psychological, educational, professional practice, political, and research.

Philosophical. PBL can be justified philosophically on several grounds. It empowers students, since the tutor may become a co-learner in the group, rather than an authority figure. The concept of empowering education has been explored in detail by Shor (1992). Therefore, PBL encourages students to develop responsibility for their own learning, as well as for assisting other members of their group in their learning.

PBL recognizes the multidisciplinary nature of knowledge, since "real-life" problems do not fall within a single discipline. It also maintains a close integration of theoretical and applied knowledge.

Psychological. Learning theory has provided the primary theoretical rationale for PBL (Coles, 1990; Norman & Schmidt, 1992; Schmidt, 1989). Schmidt (1983) proposed an information-processing model to support PBL, according to three learning theory principles:

1. Activation of prior knowledge: Students use knowledge they already possess to understand and structure new information. Students encounter problems which contain new information and therefore are forced to use existing knowledge as a base upon which to build;

2. Encoding specificity: The closer the resemblance between the situation in which something is learned and the situation in which it will be applied, the more likely that transfer of learning will occur. Coles (1990) referred to this as "contextual learning theory." In PBL, students encounter problems based on real situations commonly seen in practice; and

3. Elaboration of knowledge: Information will be better understood and retained if there is opportunity for elaboration. This means that students should examine thoroughly the information from different perspectives, using activities such as discussion, questioning, summarizing, and teaching their peers.

Support for PBL also has been provided by motivation theory. PBL graduates have reported a more stimulating learning environment than have graduates of conventional schools (Norman & Schmidt, 1992). Four motivating factors are present in the PBL process: learners' interest in the subject is aroused and sustained, the instruction is relevant to their personal needs and goals, success is seen by learners as attainable and under their control, and the tasks and rewards are intrinsically satisfying (Keller, 1983).

An effective PBL approach takes these four factors into account. Students are presented with a problem which arouses their curiosity and is relevant to future practice. They quickly learn that, with appropriate self-directed study and group discussions, they are able to acquire the required knowledge to solve the problem. This provides them with a high level of intrinsic satisfaction.

Educational. Problem-based learning incorporates the "Seven Principles for Good Practice in Undergraduate Education" articulated by a task force of higher education experts (Chickering & Gamson, 1991). Good practice: 1) encourages student-faculty contact; 2) encourages cooperation among students; 3) encourages active learning; 4) gives prompt feedback; 5) emphasizes time on task; 6) communicates high expectations; and 7) respects diverse talents and ways of learning.

In a PBL program, students and their tutor develop relationships through frequent and close contact in tutorials. The tutorial process provides a balance between positive interdependence and individual accountability which characterizes cooperative learning (Millis, 1991, see also Millis in this volume). Students in PBL groups engage in active learning (Eison, 1993), involving animated discussions, and they receive continuous and immediate feedback from their peers and tutor. They develop self-directed learning skills through independent study outside tutorials (an average of 30-40 hours per week was reported by Dalhousie first-year medical students). Since PBL emphasizes peer teaching, it communicates to students that their abilities are valued, and that their peers (and tutor) have high expectations. Finally, PBL creates a cooperative team environment in which students work together toward a common goal, regardless of differences in gender, race, ethnicity, interpersonal skills, or learning styles.

Professional practice. The requirements of professional practice, particularly in medicine, have increased rapidly in recent times, and several critical skills are required. The quantity of information has been increasing exponentially and threatens to overwhelm the future professionals, who must learn to retrieve, organize, and manage it. They will need to engage in lifelong, self-directed learning in order to maintain the currency of their knowledge and skills. Their success depends upon their ability to accurately assess the limits of their knowledge, both in their field and in specific situations which they encounter, described as "reflection-in-practice" and "reflection-on-practice" (Schön, 1987). With the increasing complexity of modern life, many unique and new situations present themselves to professionals. Routine procedures or pattern recognition are no longer adequate, and problem-solving skills will be required in future professional life (Jackling, Lewis, Brandt, & Snell, 1990). Also, because many problems are multifaceted, professionals must develop skill in working in teams comprised of individuals from various backgrounds, with differing expertise and personalities. Professionals need to communicate clearly with one another, with their clients, and with the lay public.

PBL has the potential to address each of the above requirements of professional practice. It develops, and often evaluates, students' attainment of the skills necessary to handle these requirements.

Political. Several recent reports by national associations have called for reform in higher education, and the purposes and priorities of university education are being discussed on most campuses. In medical education, several influential reports have been published by the Association of American Medical Colleges (Muller, 1984; AAMC, 1992). Most notably, *Assessing Change in Medical Education: The Road to Implementation* (AAMC, 1992) made recommendations and proposed strategies for significant change in medical education, specifically recommending PBL as a desirable educational strategy.

Research findings. There have been numerous studies on PBL, and three recent papers have summarized the findings from these studies. Norman and Schmidt (1992) reviewed the experimental evidence supporting possible differences in students' learning that can be attributed to PBL. The authors concluded that there is no evidence that PBL curricula result in any improvement in general, content-free problem-solving skills. However, they concluded that PBL may foster increased retention of knowledge and enhance the transfer of concepts to new problems and the integration of basic science concepts with clinical problems in medicine. Further, they concluded that PBL enhances intrinsic interest in the content and appears to enhance and maintain self-directed learning skills.

The two remaining papers report on meta-analyses of the PBL literature. The first was cautious in its conclusions: compared to conventional instruction, the authors found that PBL is more nurturing and enjoyable, and that PBL graduates perform as well, and sometimes better, on clinical and faculty evaluations (Albanese & Mitchell, 1993). Furthermore, faculty tend to enjoy teaching using PBL. However, PBL students in a few instances scored lower on basic sciences exams and viewed themselves as less well-prepared in the basic sciences than their conventionally trained counterparts. Also, PBL graduates tended to engage in backward reasoning rather than the forward reasoning experts use; this means that they tended to work backwards from the possible diagnosis, rather than forward from the signs and symptoms to the possible diagnosis. There also appeared to be gaps in their cognitive knowledge base that could affect practice outcomes. Finally, Albanese and Mitchell concluded that the costs of PBL may slow its implementation in medical schools with class sizes larger than 100 students.

Vernon and Blake (1993) conducted five separate meta-analyses on 35 studies representing 19 institutions. Using standard meta-analytic statistical techniques, they concluded that the value of PBL, compared to conventional curricula, is greater in the areas of students' program evaluations, faculty attitudes, student mood, class attendance, academic process variables (for example, more emphasis on in-depth understanding and self-directed study, less emphasis on rote learning and memorization), and measures of humanism. Other research studies generally have reported positive or similar findings for PBL, compared to conventional curricula (Kaufman et al., 1989; Moore, 1991; Schmidt et al., 1987; Woodward, 1990).

Models of PBL

There have been many different implementations of this basic PBL process, both in curricula and in individual courses (Boud, 1985; Boud & Feletti, 1991). These are described below in five categories: primary purpose, educational setting, case format, student support, and student evaluation.

Primary purpose. PBL may be useful in a number of disciplines and for a variety of purposes, such as stimulating the learning of content and/or the reasoning process in a particular discipline; developing problem-solving skills in a particular domain; and developing an appreciation and understanding of the multiple perspectives possible in "real-life" situations (Christiansen, 1987; Gawley, 1991; Heycox & Bolzan, 1991; Norman, 1989; Shulman, 1992).

More than one of the primary purposes described above may be achieved in a PBL curriculum or course. Other skills also may be enhanced, such as cooperative learning, communication and interpersonal relations, self-directed learning, and self/peer assessment. However, these are secondary purposes for implementing PBL; the primary purpose is usually one of the three listed above.

Educational setting. Wilkerson and Feletti (1991) proposed six educational settings in which PBL can be used: small-group tutorial with a faculty tutor (the most common setting); cooperative learning group (no teacher present); case method teaching (large group discussions); case-based lectures; problem-based labs (not just a "programmed" step-by-step lab assignment); and independent study (e.g., directed study). These options provide a practical solution for schools which lack the support or resources necessary to implement a full PBL curriculum. They permit PBL to be integrated into conventional educational settings. However, their relative benefits with regard to the purposes of PBL may be quite variable.

Case format. There is great variability in the format of cases (or problems) presented to students. Case scenarios can vary significantly in length and detail provided. Various media can be used to present the case. Most cases are print-based, since these are the easiest and least expensive to prepare. However, in medicine there has been increasing development of case simulations presented through the use of video and computer technology and of real and simulated patients (Barrows, 1976; Lyon et al., 1992).

Student support. There is great variability in the support provided to students in PBL situations. These variables relate to the subject matter expertise of the tutor (expert versus non-expert); the degree of structure in discussing and working through the case; the degree to which students are directed in the identification and pursuit of objectives and/or learning issues; and whether students are provided with all the necessary resources or must develop the information retrieval skills required of self-directed learners.

Student evaluation. As in traditional university education, there are many different methods used to evaluate students in the PBL situations. The format may vary and may be more or less consistent with the philosophy and principles of PBL. Students are generally evaluated at two stages: during the tutorial process and at the end of the course or program. Students' tutorial progress is usually rated by the faculty member, but self assessment and peer assessment may also play a role. Students may be evaluated in terms of their knowledge acquisition and their reasoning, co-operative learning, and interpersonal skills. A range of evaluation methods is employed: from written and oral examinations to case study analysis. In some programs, evaluation focuses on tests of recall or knowledge, while others emphasize the testing of higher level cognitive skills, such as the application and integration of knowledge.

It is clear from this discussion that PBL is a general approach which may have many variations. However, as will be seen later, faculty who tutor in such programs can appeal to a PBL philosophy and principles to guide their instructional actions.

TUTOR ROLES AND FUNCTIONS

Faculty can participate in PBL in numerous ways. Most PBL curricula require faculty who can serve in one or more roles, such as case writer, resource expert, lecturer, scientific and computer laboratory monitor, exam writer and/or marker, course coordinator, and committee member. The most frequent and very demanding way to participate in PBL involves serving as a tutor for a group of students, and this is the focus of the rest of this chapter.

Tutor Roles

Several writers have discussed the multiple roles which faculty must play when tutoring in a PBL situation (Barrows, 1988; Grand'Maison & Des Marchais, 1991; Wilkerson & Feletti, 1991). These have been described as parent, professional consultant, confidant, learner, and mediator (Wilkerson & Feletti, 1991). The writers describe each of the roles in detail and explain how they are necessitated by the close relationship formed between students and the tutor, as well as by the dynamics of the group process. They also point out that tutors may still retain their former roles as dispensers of information (to a limited degree) and evaluators. Barrows (1988) has referred to three phases of the tutor's role: modeling, coaching, and fading.

Modeling. This is the initial phase. The tutor questions frequently, ensures that students consider each step in their reasoning, guides students through the case, and ensures that learning issues are generated and recorded. The tutor is modeling the thinking process for his/her students, demonstrating to them the questions that should be asked to deal with the problem or task at hand (Barrows, 1988).

Coaching. At this second stage, the tutor intervenes less frequently, such as when students skip a step in the process, or seem to be floundering or confused. The behaviors "modeled" in the early stages of the group have largely been learned by the students who, as a result, require less help.

Fading. At this stage, the tutor deliberately and progressively withdraws as students become more skilled. Eventually, students are responsible for their own learning, with the tutor serving as a "safety net" for the group. In some situations, advanced students may run their own tutorials without a faculty tutor (DeGrave, Volder, Gijselaers, & Damoiseaux, 1990).

Tutor Functions

Some schools with PBL curricula have checklists which describe in detail the criteria for effective tutoring. These are analogous to the checklists used in most schools to evaluate lecturing. However, these lists may be too detailed for beginning tutors to use and have to be simplified. The functions of the PBL tutor, sometimes referred to as "tasks" (Barrows, 1988), may be described simply according to the following categories.

Navigating. This refers to the tutor's interventions to guide the tutorial group through the steps of the instructional process. As discussed earlier, students simply may need guidance through a discussion of issues in the case. However, in many medical school PBL programs, students work through a structured reasoning process; the Dalhousie University process is shown in Figure 1.

The tutor should ensure that each step in the process is covered rigorously. Also the tutor may need to assist the group in setting its pace, in deciding on the depth of discussion, and in determining when to persevere and when to seek help.

Questioning. This refers to the tutor posing questions which assist students in many ways, such as checking for understanding, assisting in clarifying points made, pushing students to deeper levels of inquiry, raising controversial points, and focusing on important areas missed by students. Questions at various cognitive levels may be asked about the material being studied. However, the best questions are "metacognitive," as they address students' thinking processes (Barrows, 1988). Examples include questions such as, "How do you know that's true?", "How does this new information help you?", and "Can you think of other explanations?"

Facilitating. This refers to the actions taken by the tutor to create and maintain a positive and constructive group process. Much has been written about effective facilitation of small groups, which involves numerous techniques (Bouton & Garth, 1983). Barrows (1988) describes a few of these

Figure 1

Outline of the
Case-Oriented Problem-Stimulated
Learning Process

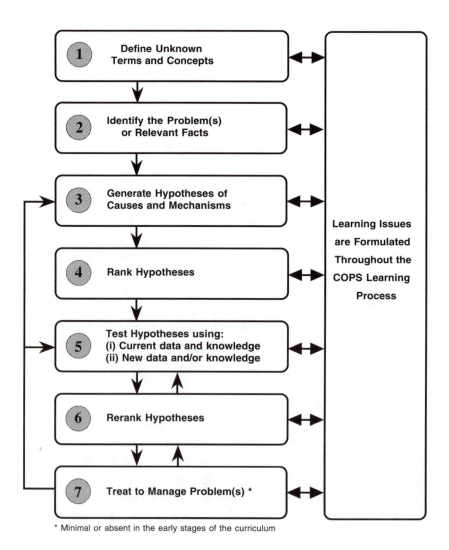

* Minimal or absent in the early stages of the curriculum

as follows: solicit various points of view from group members; check for understanding by group members; encourage full discussion of important issues; avoid being the center of discussion by encouraging students to question one another; deflect questions from students to the tutor back to other students in the group; and discuss the group process regularly with group members.

Diagnosing. This refers to the tutor continually monitoring the educational progress of each student in the group (Barrows, 1988). A tutor who notices early that certain students are having difficulties can assist those students before it is too late. These difficulties can take many forms, such as nonparticipation in the group discussions; faulty reasoning; poor understanding of the material; and inability to locate appropriate information.

The tutor must remain alert to each student in the group and ask probing questions which will help to determine students' current understanding.

RESEARCH ON TUTORING IN PBL

One of the most controversial and important questions in PBL is whether the tutor must be an expert in the content being covered in the cases. This is important from a practical perspective, since many schools do not have enough 'experts' in a particular discipline to provide expert tutors for each tutorial group. Other factors, such as scheduling, also restrict availability of expert tutors. Employing non-expert tutors provides more flexibility in implementing PBL in a small group tutorial format. The necessary expert guidance can then be provided by fewer faculty, who serve as expert resource persons outside of tutorials.

From an educational perspective, some writers have argued that the best tutor is one who is an expert in the process of tutoring, as well as in the content of the case (Barrows, 1988; Schmidt, Van Der Arend, Mous, Kokx, & Boon, 1993). An expert can better ensure that students stay 'on track,' and that misinformation is not transmitted. However, in a new PBL program, where faculty are inexperienced as tutors, the tutor who is a content expert may tend to dominate the tutorial, resulting in a faculty-centered 'seminar,' rather than a student-centered 'tutorial.'

A number of research studies have been conducted to compare the effects of expert versus non-expert tutors on the processes and outcomes of student learning. Although not all studies have found differences between expert and non-expert tutors, the overall results of these studies tend to favor using faculty who are experts in the content, but who also are skilled in the tutoring process. Some researchers have found that content-expert tutoring results in higher student scores on tests and exams (Schmidt et al., 1993; Davis, Nairn, Paine, Anderson, & Oh, 1992). In their study of 336 tutorial groups and more than 1,000 students in a PBL health sciences undergraduate curriculum, Schmidt et al. (1993) found that the effect of subject-matter expertise was strongest in the first curriculum year, which led the authors to suggest that novice students are more dependent on their tutors' expertise than are more advanced students. In contrast, DeGrave, et al. (1990) compared first-year student groups tutored by faculty with other groups tutored by third-year undergraduate students and found no significant differences in the achievement levels of the two groups. Swanson, Stalenhoef-Halling, and Van Der Vleuten (1990) found no relationship between the content expertise of tutors (in medicine, biology, or social science) and students' performance on tests in these areas. However, in this latter case, the format of the tests (true-false) may have failed to capture differences at higher cognitive levels.

Students of content-expert tutors spend more time engaging in self-directed study (Schmidt et al., 1993) and rate their experiences higher (Davis et al., 1992) than do students of non-expert tutors. Johansen, Martenson, and Bircher (1992) found that, where senior students are used as tutors, the more advanced student tutors stimulated greater productivity in the groups than did less experienced student tutors.

Researchers have also investigated the process variables associated with expert and non-expert tutoring. One study which observed the interactions of expert and non-expert tutors and their students in a PBL medical undergraduate curriculum highlights the potential dangers of using content experts as tutors. Silver and Wilkerson (1991) reported that expert tutors more frequently provided direct answers to students' questions while non-experts more often contributed informative or facilitative statements rather than answers. Finally, the authors found expert tutors to be more directive in tutorials and, when the discussion involved a topic within the tutor's area of expertise, fewer students spoke and tutors tended to take over the discussion from students.

Schmidt et al. (1993) discovered that content-experts made more extensive use of their subject matter knowledge to guide students. Eagle, Harasym, and Mandin (1992) found similar results: groups tutored by experts, compared to non-experts, not only generated almost double the number of learning issues per case, but these issues were almost three times more congruent with case objectives. In addition, students in the expert-tutor group reported that they spent almost twice as much time per case in pursuing their learning issues. Two interesting secondary findings were reported. First, a disproportionate number of learning issues generated by groups tutored by non-experts were in the tutor's area of personal expertise. Second, non-expert tutors who had tutored the particular case for a number of years and/or who had taken time to specifically study the details of the case achieved results similar to expert tutors.

In a survey of North American medical schools, Blumberg, Michael, and Zeitz (1990) discovered that the majority of PBL programs provide faculty-generated learning objectives to students to guide learning. The authors assert that a blend of student-generated learning issues and faculty objectives seems to be an effective compromise. In other words, faculty should provide objectives as a guide to learning but should encourage and value learning issues pursued by students. At five of the schools surveyed, students are evaluated on their ability to generate learning issues and to learn effectively from them. Their findings have implications for training tutors to assist students in adequately generating, recording, studying, and reporting appropriate learning issues.

Several studies have examined other tutoring variables. In an interesting qualitative research study, Wilkerson and Maxwell (1988) found that tutors need not be quiet to promote student discussion. They asserted that the amount and type of participation by the tutor are not as important as the pattern of participation. They found that tutors who exhibit behaviors associated with expertise in the tutoring process are more highly rated by students. For example, student-centered tutors build on preceding comments by students. They listen to student discussion through lengthy periods before intervening, and interrupt infrequently. They also tolerate periods of silence that occur when students have nothing to add, are referring to a text, or are thinking. They wait several seconds after asking a question.

Other studies reinforce the importance of tutors using a student-centered approach. Feletti, Doyle, Petrovic, and Sanson-Fisher (1982) surveyed 50 first-year medical students about their perceptions of their 27 tutors. Their results indicated that the most important factor is "caring for students," that is, indicating to students an interest in their progress and concerns. Other findings emphasized the importance of these interpersonal skills in tasks involving interactions among individuals and encouraging students' independent learning. The authors conclude that the tutors are seen to fulfill a leadership role, where their main task is to develop and facilitate the cohesion of the group while caring for individuals. However, the other area rated highly was the tutors' knowledge of the course structure and teaching philosophy. This suggests that the best tutors are those who guide students in self-directed study, but who also recognize when it is necessary to intervene in a more directive way.

These findings reaffirm the principle expounded by Barrows (1988): the ideal situation is to have tutors with expertise both in the case and the tutorial process.

Implications of the Research on Tutoring

The implications from the studies reported are important and may be summarized as follows:

- The ideal tutor is one who is a content expert, as well as an expert in the student-centered tutorial process.
- If tutors are content experts, they can utilize their expertise to assist students. However, tutors should understand clearly the principles of student-directed learning described above and should observe these principles.
- If tutors are not content experts, their students can achieve a level of performance equal to students tutored by content experts, if the following conditions are met: a) the non-expert tutor understands the course goals, case objectives, and issues intended to be covered in the cases; and b) the non-expert tutor talks to other tutors or other faculty members familiar with the case and/or is given a proper 'Tutor Guide' for the case.
- Tutors should be supported through effective faculty development in which the principles and practice of PBL are taught. The two major areas which should be addressed are a) effective tutoring in PBL: navigating, facilitating, questioning, diagnosing, and evaluating; and b) good knowledge of the objectives and issues intended to be covered in the cases.

FACULTY DEVELOPMENT FOR TUTORING IN PBL

Faculty Recruitment

Two approaches have typically been used to recruit faculty to use PBL. These may be characterized as either faculty-initiated, in which faculty self-select, or institution-initiated, in which the institution is faced with the challenge of recruiting faculty to teach in a new PBL curriculum. Both approaches require faculty development initiatives to develop knowledge and skills required in the PBL process.

Recruitment of tutors. This is not a straightforward task and involves a variety of strategies. The Dalhousie University approach has been reported elsewhere in detail (Holmes & Kaufman, 1994), and only the essential highlights are described here. For the first year of the undergraduate medical curriculum (1992-1993), almost 80 tutors from a faculty pool of 317 full-time equivalents and numerous part-time faculty were needed. These individuals already had multiple responsibilities, such as teaching traditional courses, conducting research and publishing, preparing grant applications, running a clinical practice, training clerks and residents in clinical settings, serving on course development teams and committees, and writing cases for the new PBL curriculum.

A variety of strategies was used for recruitment, including:

- Broad consultation with faculty, distribution of a Curriculum Task Force Report to all faculty, and a vote by faculty on adoption of the PBL curriculum
- Faculty visits to other schools with PBL curricula; a two-day pilot tutor training workshop with outside experts; demonstrations of PBL for faculty, using outside experts; and presentations, seminars, and workshops by the Medical Education Unit for Department Heads and faculty
- A newsletter to all faculty—COPS (Case-Oriented Problem-Stimulated) Bulletin—to inform everyone about planning and progress prior to implementation and during the first year
- A report on first tutors' very positive experience in the first unit (Anatomy, eight weeks), with testimonials published in the COPS Bulletin (helping to recruit tutors for later units)
- Encouraging faculty to tutor outside their disciplines, while retaining flexibility of choice when necessary to attract tutors, and allowing faculty to share a longer unit by team-tutoring, with the first tutor conducting the first half, the second tutor conducting the second half
- Providing support to faculty through a strong faculty development process (described below)

Dalhousie University was successful in recruiting the required number of tutors in the first year, using a relatively informal approach. However, in the second year, two years of the preclinical curriculum were implemented, requiring double the number of tutors (about 150 faculty). Therefore, two fundamental changes were made in order to formalize the recruitment process. First, the Dean assigned each department a quota for faculty involvement in tutoring which was proportional to the departmental teaching budget. Equally important, the Faculty's promotion and tenure guidelines were modified to recognize and reward faculty involvement in the PBL curriculum.

Faculty Development

Faculty development in the health professions has evolved and expanded, although teaching skills are still a prominent aspect (Hitchcock, Stritter, & Bland, 1993). Stritter (1983) described faculty development activities using the following three broad categories:

1. Technical Assistance: This involves an educational specialist working with individual tutors in a consultative manner to improve some aspect of the tutorial process. In PBL, this can be achieved through workshops or observation of tutorials by an educational expert or experienced tutor.
2. High Faculty Involvement: This involves faculty colleagues learning with and from one another about tutoring or the tutorial process. This can be achieved through workshops, tutor meetings, and peer observation.
3. Assessment: This involves providing feedback to faculty about the effects of their teaching from evaluations by themselves, their learners, and their colleagues.

Each of these categories has been addressed in the Dalhousie Medical School's seven-stage faculty development process described below. Hitchcock et al. (1993) offered several suggestions to those planning faculty development interventions for their institutions or programs. These are relevant to recruiting and developing PBL tutors and include defining the specific mission, consulting experts and faculty in planning and design, appointing an effective leader, establishing a faculty evaluation process, and changing the institutional reward structure. All of the above suggestions have been incorporated into the Dalhousie recruitment and faculty development process. These suggestions provided guidance in the design of the program, as did our review of other faculty development programs, visits to other medical schools such as McMaster, Harvard, Hawaii, Sherbrooke, and New Mexico, and insights gained from Association of American Medical Colleges' and Association of Canadian Medical Colleges' annual meetings. Knowles' (1980) principles of adult learning also provided useful criteria for the design of our faculty development process. These principles have been elaborated by Carroll (1993) as follows: faculty need to know "why" they should learn something; faculty already possess much experience to be used as a learning resource; faculty will become ready to learn after a "need to know" is experienced; the faculty development program should be task-centered with an emphasis on immediacy and application; and faculty demonstrate a high degree of self-direction and therefore should not all be "forced" to participate in exactly the same way.

Some faculty development programs for tutoring in PBL. Most programs in medicine consist of one or more workshops. For example, in the former Primary Care Curriculum at the University of New Mexico (US), the tutor-training workshop has been conducted over three days. It covers the following topics using brief discussions, information packets, and practice sessions: philosophy of problem-based learning; clinical reasoning process; role of the tutor; evaluation and feedback; conflict management; phases groups go through; techniques of questioning, probing, and facilitating; and use of resources (Lucerno, Jackson, & Galey, 1985).

At the medical school at the University of Limburg in Masstricht, the Netherlands, the tutor-training workshop lasts two days. Sometimes problems from other faculties are used (e.g., Law) in order to put the trainees into a beginner's role. The tutor trainer and peers give feedback to the faculty member practicing the new skills. Videotapes, handouts, observation schemes, and a manual written especially for this workshop are used. Topics are similar to the New Mexico program (Moust, DeGrave, & Gijselaers, 1990).

The Université de Sherbrooke, Québec, Canada, takes a more comprehensive approach to tutor training. Faculty may choose to attend a two-day introductory workshop on educational principles and their application in medical education. This may be followed by a one-year basic training program in medical teaching requiring more than 100 hours of participation. Faculty wishing to tutor in the PBL program must attend a comprehensive three-day workshop in PBL tutoring followed by a one-day per year refresher workshop. The format of this three-day workshop includes theoretical explanations of PBL, small group discussion, individual reading, construction of PBL problems, and experience of the PBL method with a non-medical problem. Participants also practice tutoring medical students using medical problems, and they receive feedback on their performance. The one-day refresher workshop is geared to participants' needs and promotes discussion of tutor tasks and PBL steps as well as new themes, such as how to become a more active tutor (Grand'Maison & Des Marchais, 1991). Similar approaches are used at the McMaster, Harvard, and Bowman Gray Universities' schools of medicine.

These tutor training efforts have several common threads, including 1) provision of information on theory and practice; 2) multiple roles for faculty who serve both as student and tutor in a small group; 3) consideration of various tutor functions such as questioning, facilitating, and evaluating; and 4) provision of feedback to faculty participants. These faculty development efforts all strive to instill in faculty a positive attitude toward PBL, confidence in their ability to serve as tutors, and a shift in focus from a teacher-centered to a student-centered educational philosophy.

Dalhousie University process for preparing tutors. The faculty development principles and programs described above provided the formulation upon which Dalhousie University built its seven-stage process for preparing faculty to tutor in its PBL curriculum. The stages of the process may be described as follows.

1. Orientation Workshop. Prior to this one-and-a-half-day workshop, faculty receive a tutor manual and directions on how to prepare for the workshop. The overall goal is for faculty to gain confidence as novice tutors and to be exposed to a new style of teaching. The first session introduces the participants to the tutoring process and the PBL approach to learning in which a seven-step clinical (or scientific) reasoning process is used to guide group discussion (see figure 1). Faculty play the role of students in a small group simulated tutorial led by one of the tutor trainers serving as a "model" tutor. During the second session, the participants practice being tutors with small groups of student "volunteers" who are paid an honorarium for their participation. These volunteers are recruited from across campus and include a variety of students, e.g., graduate students and undergraduate students interested in medicine. Faculty receive feedback from the tutor trainer, their peers, and the students. They also participate in a discussion and an exercise on student evaluation, and they practice giving feedback on student performance at the end of the day to one of the students in their group. Faculty are very comfortable with the clinical reasoning process because, as one tutor stated, "this is what we do in our work." Evaluations of this workshop by the 150 or so faculty who have participated thus far have been very positive (Holmes & Kaufman, 1994).

2. Orientation Meeting. Each course head, with the help of the Medical Education Unit, organizes a meeting to orient tutors to the unit in advance (three to six weeks prior to the start of the unit). Tutors are introduced to each other, and a schedule is provided of all tutor commitments for the unit. Tutors are provided with some advance copies of the cases and the corresponding tutor guides, and the first case is discussed in detail. Administrative requirements such as student evaluation forms and room assignments are also clarified. Faculty have found these meetings to be essential for all tutors and particularly helpful to non-expert tutors. These sessions have been well attended, highly rated, and have provided an opportunity to address questions and misinformation which still remained about the curriculum.

3. Weekly Tutor Meetings. Tutors meet weekly for less than one hour as a group with the unit head, case writers, and sometimes the resource experts. These meetings provide an important feedback function for the unit head about the case just completed and about other aspects of the week's activities, such as lectures and labs. Tutors are also briefed on the next case. Although these meetings are important, they add an extra hour per week to their already heavy commitment. As noted earlier in this chapter, non-

expert tutors must be well prepared in the case content, objectives, and issues. These meetings helped to fulfill this function.

4. Tutorial Observation. Each tutor is observed at least once, either by a member of the team which offers the Tutor Orientation Workshop or by a colleague. The observer provides informal feedback to the tutor after the session and sometimes discusses his or her observations with the tutorial group if asked by the students. Faculty suggestions for improvement in this process include being observed earlier in their unit to boost confidence, using a checklist to give feedback, and providing feedback to the whole group about their tutorial process. Currently, we have established an informal peer observation network involving experienced tutors who have volunteered to observe and provide feedback to new tutors.

5. Unit Evaluation. The last formal meeting of tutors and unit planners is held at the conclusion of the unit for the purposes of reviewing group performance, assessing the cases and other unit components, and making recommendations for improvement.

6. Tutor Evaluation. Each tutor receives a summary of the results from end-of-unit questionnaires completed by students to evaluate their tutors. A summary of results for the whole class is also provided, so that faculty can compare their individual ratings and comments with the overall results. Data thus far indicates that students and faculty have a high level of agreement on the attributes of a "model" tutor. Both groups used descriptions which mainly fell into two categories: 1)personality/behavior–enthusiastic, friendly, unintimidating, able to smile, respect for students, open to criticism, sense of humor; and 2) group facilitation skills–intervene appropriately, stimulate discussion when necessary, recognize strengths and weaknesses and give feedback, don't talk too much, ask students to summarize regularly, discuss group dynamics with group, be willing to receive feedback from the group, help the group maintain its focus, respect the pace of the group, and pay attention.

In the end-of-unit evaluations completed by the students, the overall ratings indicated that students were very satisfied with their tutors. We wonder if a novelty effect was operating here, as 79% of students in the first unit (Human Body) and about half in the other units rated their tutor as 'outstanding (could serve as a model for other tutors).' However, tutors were rated in each unit after the first as needing improvement on the following three items: facilitating the smooth and effective functioning of the tutorial groups; evaluating, at regular intervals and together with students, how well the group was functioning; and using interventions which were appropriate. Some particularly pointed comments also were made by students about the following aspects of the tutorial process: tutor feedback should emphasize areas which need improvement (i.e., constructive criticism); and some tutors should be less directive. These, and other concerns, will be addressed as tutors and students gain more experience with the COPS process.

7. Continuing Education. In their end-of-year tutor questionnaire, tutors suggested areas for future faculty development. These topics included evaluation of students' tutorial performance, questioning techniques, and facilitation of small groups (particularly how and when to intervene). We followed up with a lunch meeting with tutors in which results from the tutor questionnaire were presented, and faculty discussed their experiences as tutors in small groups. In particular, ideas were exchanged for dealing with difficult situations. These sessions provided faculty tutors with an opportunity to continue their input into the evolution of the curriculum and their own faculty development.

Tutors reported that they spent significant extra time on their teaching and that they spent an average of six hours per week on tutoring-related activities outside tutorials, workshops, and formal meetings. These results indicate that the time commitment for first-time tutors has a "hidden" cost in the hours required. However, 84% of tutors still committed to tutoring in the following academic year, and several volunteered to tutor in more than one unit or to act as a back-up tutor when a colleague was required to be away from the university.

SUMMARY AND CONCLUSIONS

This chapter began by describing problem-based learning, a recent educational innovation in higher education. A rationale for PBL was given, and a variety of possible approaches were discussed. The various assumptions about teaching, as well as tutor roles and functions in PBL, were outlined.

The most commonly employed PBL model (a faculty tutor and small group of students) was the focus of a review of educational research studies of the tutorial process. In particular, the question of the relative effectiveness of content expert tutors versus non-expert tutors was addressed. Several implications for faculty development were drawn from these studies.

The remainder of the chapter reviewed several principles and practices for recruitment and faculty development. The seven-stage faculty development process used in the PBL undergraduate medical curriculum at Dalhousie University was described.

It is clear from the discussion in this chapter that implementing a PBL program presents a relatively complex challenge compared to the traditional lecture-based approach. There are significant benefits to PBL, but there also are some real and perceived barriers. In order to overcome these barriers and meet the challenge, institutional strategies for recruitment of faculty, as well as a significant faculty development effort, are required.

REFERENCES

Albanese, M.A., & Mitchell, S. (1993). Problem-based learning: A review of the literature on its outcomes and implementation issues. *Academic Medicine, 68,* 52-81.

Armstrong, E.G. (1991). A hybrid model of problem-based learning. In D. Boud & G. Feletti (Eds.), *The challenge of problem-based learning* (pp. 137-149). London, UK: Kogan Page.

Association of American Medical Colleges (AAMC). (1992). *Assessing change in medical education: The road to implementation.* Washington, DC: AAMC.

Australian Problem-Based Learning Network Bibliography. Campbelltown, Australia: PROBLARC.

Barrows, H.S. (1976). An evaluation of problem-based learning in small groups utilizing a simulated patient. *Journal of Medical Education, 51*(1), 52-54.

Barrows, H.S. (1985). *How to design a problem-based curriculum.* New York, NY: Springer.

Barrows, H.S. (1988). *The tutorial process.* Springfield, IL: Southern Illinois University School of Medicine.

Barrows, H.S., & Tamblyn, R.W. (1980). *Problem-based learning.* New York, NY: Springer.

Bender, W., Hiemstra, R.J., Scherpbier, A.J.J.J.A., & Zwierstra, R.P. (Eds.). (1990). *Teaching and assessing clinical competence.* Groningen, The Netherlands: Bock Werk.

Berkson, L. (1993, October supplement). Problem-based learning: Have the expectations been met? *Academic Medicine, 68*(10), S79-S88.

Blumberg, P., Michael, J.A., & Zeitz, H. (1990). Roles of student-generated learning issues in problem-based learning. *Teaching and Learning in Medicine, 2*(3), 149-154.

Boud, D. (Ed.). (1985). *Problem-based learning in education for the professions.* Sydney, Australia: Higher Education Research and Development Society of Australasia.

Boud, D., & Feletti, G.I. (Eds.). (1991). *The challenge of problem-based learning.* New York, NY: St. Martin's Press.

Bouton, C., & Garth, R.Y. (Eds.). (1983). *New Directions for Teaching and Learning: No. 14. Learning in groups*. San Francisco, CA: Jossey-Bass.

Carroll, R.G. (1993). Implications of adult education theories for medical school faculty development programmes. *Medical Teacher, 15*, 163-170.

Chickering, A.W., & Gamson, Z.F. (Eds.). (1991). *New Directions for Teaching and Learning: No. 47. Applying the seven principles for good practice in undergraduate education*. San Francisco, CA: Jossey-Bass.

Christiansen, C.R. (1987). *Teaching and the case method*. Boston, MA: Harvard Business School Publishing.

Coles, C.R. (1990). Evaluating the effects curricula have on student learning: Toward a more competent theory for medical education. In Z.M. Nooman, H.G. Schmidt, & E.S. Ezzat (Eds.), *Innovation in medical education: An evaluation of its present status* (pp. 76-87). New York, NY: Springer.

Davis, W.K., Nairn, R., Paine, M.E., Anderson, R.M., & Oh, M.S. (1992). Effects of expert and non-expert facilitators on the small-group process and on student performance. *Academic Medicine, 67*(7), 470-474.

DeGrave, W.S., Volder, M.L., Gijselaers, W.H., & Damoiseaux, V. (1990). Peer teaching and problem-based learning: Tutor characteristics, tutor functioning, group functioning, and student achievement. In Z.M. Nooman, H.G. Schmidt, & E.S. Ezzat (Eds.), *Innovation in medical education: An evaluation of its present status* (pp. 123-134). New York, NY: Springer.

Des Marchais, J. (1990). The involvement of teachers as problem-based learning tutors in the new Sherbrooke programme. *Annals of Community-Oriented Education, 3*, 35-54.

Eagle, C.J., Harasym, P.H., & Mandin, H. (1992). Effects of tutors with case expertise on problem-based learning issues. *Academic Medicine, 67*(7), 465-469.

Edwards, J.C. (1990). The problem-based curriculum at Bowman Gray School of Medicine. *Academic Medicine, 65*(6), 363-364.

Eison, J. (1993). *Active learning: Creating excitement in the classroom*. Workshop handout. Center for Teaching Enhancement, University of South Florida, Tampa, FL.

Feletti, G.I., Doyle, E., Petrovic, A., & Sanson-Fisher, R. (1982). Medical students' evaluation of tutors in a group-learning curriculum. *Medical Education, 16*, 319-325.

Gawley, P. (1991). A problem-based module in mechanical engineering. In Boud, D. & Feletti, G. (Eds.), *The challenge of problem-based learning* (pp. 177-185). London, UK: Kogan Page.

Grand'Maison, P., & Des Marchais, J. (1991). Preparing faculty to teach in a problem-based learning curriculum: The Sherbrooke experience. *Canadian Medical Association Journal, 144*, 557-561.

Heycox, K., & Bolzan, N. (1991). Analyzing problem-based learning in first year social work. In Boud, D. & Feletti, G. (Eds.), *The challenge of problem-based learning* (pp. 186-193). London, UK: Kogan Page.

Hitchcock, M., Stritter, F., & Bland, C. (1993). Faculty development in the health professions: Conclusions and recommendations. *Medical Teacher, 14*, 295-309.

Holmes, D.B., & Kaufman, D. (1994). Tutoring in problem-based learning: A teacher development process. *Medical Education, 28*, 275-283.

Jackling, N., Lewis, J., Brandt, D., & Snell, R. (1990). Problem-solving in the professions. *Higher Education Research and Development, 9*(2), 133-149.

Johansen, M.-L., Martenson, D.F., & Bircher, J. (1992). Students as tutors in problem-based learning: Does it work? *Medical Education, 26*(2), 163-165.

Kantrowicz, M., Kaufman, A., Mennin, S., Fulop, T., & Guilbert, J.J. (1987). *Innovative tracks at established institutions for the education of health personnel: An experimental approach to change relevant to health needs* (Offset Publication No. 101). World Health Organization, Geneva, Switzerland.

Kaufman, A. (Ed.) (1985). *Implementing problem-based medical education: Lessons from successful innovations.* New York, NY: Springer.

Kaufman, A., Mennin, S., Waterman, R., Duben, S., Hansburger, C., Silverblatt, H., Obenshain, S.S., Kantrowicz, M., Becker, T., Samet, J., & Wiese, W. (1989). The New Mexico experiment: Educational innovation and institutional change. *Academic Medicine, 64*(6), 285-294.

Keller, J.M. (1983). Motivational design of instruction. In C.M. Reigeluth (Ed.), *Instructional design theories and models: An overview of their current status* (pp. 383-434). Hillsdale, NJ: Lawrence Erlbaum Associates.

Knowles, M.S. (1980). *The modern practice of adult education: From pedagogy to andragogy* (2nd ed.). New York, NY: Cambridge Books.

Lucas, A.F. (Ed.). (1991). *New Directions for Teaching and Learning: No. 37. The department chairperson's role in enhancing college teaching.* San Francisco, CA: Jossey-Bass.

Lucerno, S.M., Jackson, R., & Galey, W.R. (1985). Tutorial groups in problem-based curriculum. In Kaufman, A. (Ed.), *Implementing problem-based medical education: Lessons from successful innovations* (pp. 45-70). New York, NY: Springer.

Lyon, H.C., Healy, J.C., Bell, J.R., et al. (1992). PlanAlyzer: An interactive computer-assisted problem to teach clinical problem-solving in diagnosing anemia and coronary artery disease. *Academic Medicine, 67*(12), 821-827.

Mann, K.V., & Kaufman, D. (1994). The Dalhousie PBL curriculum: A response to the ACME-TRI Report. Submitted for publication to *Medical Education.*

McGuire, C.H., Foley, R.P., Gerr, A., Richards, R.W., & Ezzat, E.S. (Eds.). *Handbook of health professions education.* San Francisco, CA: Jossey-Bass.

Millis, B.J. (1991). Fulfilling the promise of the 'seven principles' through cooperative learning: An action agenda for the university classroom. *Journal on Excellence in College Teaching, 2,* 139-144.

Moore, G.T. (1991). The effect of compulsory participation of medical students in problem-based learning. *Medical Education, 25,* 140-143.

Moust, J., DeGrave, W., & Gijselaers, W. (1990). The tutor role: A neglected variable in the implementation of problem-based learning. In Z.M. Nooman, G.G. Schmidt, & E.S. Ezzat (Eds.), *Innovation in medical education: An evaluation of its present status* (pp. 135-151). New York, NY: Springer.

Muller, S. (1984). Physicians for the twenty-first century: Report of the project panel on the general professional education of the physician and college preparation for medicine. *Journal of Medical Education, 59,* Part 2.

Neufeld, V.R., Woodward, C.A., & MacLeod, S.M. (1989). The McMaster M.D. program: A case study of renewal in medical education. *Academic Medicine, 64,* 423-432.

Nooman, Z.M., Schmidt, H.G., & Ezzat, E.S. (Eds.). (1990). *Innovation in medical education: An evaluation of its present status.* New York, NY: Springer-Verlag.

Norman, G.R. (1989). Problem solving skills versus problem-based learning. *Cornell Vet, 79*(4), 307-310.

Norman, G.R., & Schmidt, H.G. (1992). The psychological basis of problem-based learning: A review of the evidence. *Academic Medicine, 67*(9), 557-565.

Reigeluth, C.M. (Ed.). (1983). *Instructional design theories and models: An overview of their current status.* Hillsdale, NJ: Lawrence Erlbaum Associates.

Schmidt, H.G. (1983). Problem-based learning: Rationale and description. *Medical Education, 17*(1), 11-16.

Schmidt, H.G. (1989). The rationale behind problem-based learning. In H.G. Schmidt et al. (Eds.), *New directions for medical education: Problem-based learning and community-oriented medical education* (pp. 105-111). New York, NY: Springer-Verlag.

Schmidt, H.G., Dauphinee, W.D., & Patel, V.L. (1987). Comparing the effects of problem-based and conventional curriculum in an international sample. *Journal of Medical Education, 62,* 305-315.

Schmidt, H.G., Lipkin, M., Jr., deVries, M.W., & Greep, J.M. (Eds.). (1989). *New directions for medical education: Problem-based learning and community-oriented medical education.* New York, NY: Springer-Verlag.

Schmidt, H.G., Van Der Arend, A., Moust, J.H.C., Kokx, I., & Boon, L. (1993). Influence of tutors' subject-matter expertise on student effort and achievement in problem-based learning. *Academic Medicine, 68*(10), 784-791.

Schön, D.A. (1987). *Educating the reflective practitioner.* San Francisco, CA: Jossey-Bass.

Shor, I. (1992). *Empowering education.* Chicago, IL: University of Chicago Press.

Shulman, J.H. (Ed.). (1992). *Case methods in teacher education.* New York, NY: Teachers College Press.

Silver, M., & Wilkerson, L. (1991). Effects of tutors with subject expertise on the problem-based tutorial process. *Academic Medicine, 66*(5), 298-300.

Stritter, F.T. (1983). Faculty evaluation and development. In C.H. McGuire et al. (Eds.), *Handbook of health professions education* (pp. 294-318). San Francisco, CA: Jossey-Bass.

Swanson, D.B., Stalenhoef-Halling, B.F., & Van Der Vleuten, C.P.M. (1990). Effects of tutor characteristics on test performance of students in a problem-based curriculum. In W. Bender, R.J. Hiemstra, A.J.J.J.A. Scherpbier, & R.P. Zwierstra (Eds.), *Teaching and assessing clinical competence* (pp. 129-134). Groningen, The Netherlands: Bock Werk.

Tosteson, D.C. (1990). New pathways in general medical education. *The New England Journal of Medicine, 322*(4), 234-238.

Vernon, D.T.A., & Blake, R.L. (1993). Does problem-based learning work? A meta-analysis of evaluative research. *Academic Medicine, 68*(7), 550-563.

Verwijnen, M., Tjaart, I., Snellan, H., et al. (1989). The evaluation system at the Maastricht Medical School. In Schmidt, H.G. et al. (Eds.), *New directions for medical education: Problem-based learning and community-oriented medical education* (pp. 180-195). New York, NY: Springer-Verlag.

Wilkerson, L., & Feletti, G. (1991). Problem-based learning: One approach to increasing student participation. In A.F. Lucas (Ed.), *New Directions for Teaching and Learning: No. 37. The department chairperson's role in enhancing college teaching* (pp. 51-60). San Francisco, CA: Jossey-Bass.

Wilkerson, L., & Maxwell, J. (1988). A qualitative study of initial faculty tutors in a problem-based curriculum. *Journal of Medical Education, 63*, 892-899.

Woodward, C.A. (1990). Monitoring an innovation in medical education: The McMaster experience. In Z.M. Nooman, H.G. Schmidt, & E.S. Ezzat (Eds.), *Innovation in medical education: An evaluation of its present status* (pp. 27-39). New York, NY: Springer.

AUTHOR

David Kaufman has taught at Loyola College (now Concordia University), and Simon Fraser, Saint Mary's, and Dalhousie Universities (Canada), in the faculties of engineering, education, and medicine. He has served as Director of Course Design for the Open Learning Agency (British Columbia's distance education institution), and has been involved in staff training in business, industry, and government settings. Dr. Kaufman has published extensively in the educational literature and has co-edited a book, Distance Education in Canada *(Croom-Helm, 1986). He is currently Director of the Medical Education Unit in Dalhousie's Faculty of Medicine and has been heavily involved, with his colleagues, in transforming the undergraduate medical curriculum from a lecture-based to a problem-based learning approach.*

5.

Introducing Faculty to Cooperative Learning

Barbara J. Millis

Increasingly recognized as a viable teaching approach in higher education, cooperative learning gives faculty active, practical, effective alternatives to lecturing. Cooperative learning is defined as a structured form of group work where students, who are individually assessed, work toward common group goals. This chapter discusses the nature and value of cooperative learning and offers faculty developers, department heads, and other academic leaders some specific guidelines for fostering its use on their own campuses.

INTRODUCTION

Higher education is never static. Issues of quality and accountability and the subsequent close scrutiny of faculty roles and rewards have prompted faculty to re-examine some of their basic academic premises. This reflection has been stimulated by additional forces, such as the assessment movement; the necessity for lifelong learning in a technologically driven, multicultural workplace; the influx into classrooms of non-traditional students; and an increasing awareness that time-worn methods of delivery, such as unrelieved reliance on the lecture, are ineffective for the majority of students. As a result, many faculty seem more open to teaching and learning innovations, and faculty developers now find faculty eager for their services.

Several researchers (Boehm, 1992; Davis, 1993; Johnson, Johnson, & Smith, 1991a, 1991b; McDaniel, 1994) have suggested that a paradigm shift is now occurring in college and university teaching, one predicated on more student-centered, interactive classroom approaches. One such approach is cooperative learning, a structured form of group work where students, who are individually assessed, work toward common group goals. The use of cooperative learning in the classroom is increasing in higher education. Smith, Johnson, and Johnson (1992), after a review of the cooperative learning research, note these four trends:

- Interest in cooperative learning in colleges and universities is growing at an incredible rate.
- Cooperative learning is as or more effective than lecturing in helping student[s] master conceptual material and in helping them develop cooperative skills.
- Cooperative learning is being implemented in a wide range of courses and programs from health sciences and law, to writing and teacher preparation.
- Instructors are applying cooperative learning in a variety of ways–cooperative lecture, base groups, formal task groups, structured controversy discussion groups, jigsaw groups, and computer enhanced courses. (pp. 34-35)

Similarly, Slavin (1993) announced that:

> *After many years in elementary and secondary schools, Cooperative Learning (CL) is finally going to college. Of course, CL has long existed in post-secondary education; study groups, discussion groups, and work groups of various kinds are hardly new... What is new in recent years is that post-secondary professors are beginning to use CL as a major focus of their teaching, and research on such applications in higher education is growing. This is an important and fundamental change. (p. 2)*

Practical corroboration from faculty came at the 1994 meeting of the Lilly-West Conference on College Teaching when participants were asked by Milton Cox to "list some teaching approaches that you think are emerging trends in college teaching." The most frequently cited option was "collaborative and cooperative learning" (Rhem, 1994, p. 12). Cooperative learning, a more structured variation of collaborative learning, offers classroom applications based on sound theory and research.

THE EDUCATIONAL PHILOSOPHY OF COOPERATIVE AND COLLABORATIVE LEARNING

Bruffee (1993) points out that interdependence is well known to current college and university students who participate in sports activities or community projects, who plan parties or protest marches, and who recognize that their future lies in arenas such as government, industry, science, and the professions where teamwork and cooperation are increasingly important. Thus, although faculty may be skeptical about the aura of newness surrounding cooperative learning in higher education, its concepts and approaches have been known and used for decades (Gere, 1987; Goodsell, Mahler, Tinto, Smith, & MacGregor, 1992).

Both Cuseo (1992) and Smith and MacGregor (1992) have written definitively about collaborative learning and cooperative learning. They agree that collaborative learning is the broader term, encompassing, according to Smith and MacGregor (1992):

> *a variety of educational approaches involving joint intellectual effort by students, or students and teachers together. In most collaborative learning situations students are working in groups of two or more, mutually searching for understanding, solutions, or meanings, or creating a product. There is wide variability in collaborative learning activities, but most center on the students' exploration or application of the course material, not simply the teacher's presentation or explication of it. Everyone in the class is participating, working as partners or in small groups. Questions, problems, or the challenge to create something drive the group activity. Learning unfolds in the most public of ways. (p. 10)*

Both agree that cooperative learning is a highly structured subset of collaborative learning. Cuseo (1992) finds cooperative learning to be "the most operationally well-defined and procedurally structured form of collaboration among students ... [and it] has been the most researched and empirically well-documented form of collaborative learning in terms of its positive impact on multiple outcome measures" (p. 3).

As might be expected, cooperative learning and collaborative learning share a common philosophical framework. Underlying both approaches are a respect for students and a belief in their potential for academic success. Thus, as Sapon-Shevin, Ayres, and Duncan (1994) suggest:

> *Cooperative learning... builds upon heterogeneity and formalizes and encourages peer support and connection. All students need to learn and work in environments where their individual strengths*

are recognized and individual needs are addressed. All students
need to learn within a supportive community in order to feel safe
enough to take risks. (p. 46)

Both cooperative learning and collaborative learning share a sense of community. Learning is inherently social. This socio-instructional approach helps students become cognitively involved with content through systematic classroom interactions. An intellectual synergy develops. Furthermore, the ensuing peer relationships can have affective results, such as helping students foster positive relationships. Cooper and Mueck (1990) note: "The most consistent positive findings for cooperative learning . . . have centered on affective or attitudinal change. Outcome measures such as racial / ethnic relations, sex difference relations, self-esteem, and other prosocial outcomes have all been documented in the Cooperative Learning research" (p. 71).

This belief in constructive social interaction leads to a third commonality. Both cooperative and collaborative learning share a belief that learning is an active, constructive process. Myers and Jones (1993) find that such learning "provides opportunities for students to *talk and listen, read, write,* and *reflect* as they approach course content through problem-solving exercises, informal small groups, simulations, case studies, role playing, and other activities–all of which require students to *apply* what they are learning" (p. xi). As a result, learning is not passively absorbed, nor are facts simply added systematically to existing schemata. Students often take new material–including conflicting viewpoints–and integrate, reinterpret, and transform it until new knowledge is forged. Thus, learning is produced, not reproduced. Further, the role of the instructor changes from a deliverer of information to a facilitator of learning. This does not mean that faculty members, who will always remain authorities in the definitive sense, abdicate their responsibility to students; rather, it means that they assume different roles such as that of midwife professors who "assist . . . students in giving birth to their own ideas, in making tacit knowledge explicit and elaborating on it" (Belenky, Clinchy, Goldberger, & Tarule, 1986, p. 217).

THE RESEARCH BASE

Faculty reluctant to consider cooperative learning can be reassured by the fact that the research base for cooperative learning is long-standing and solid. Both the learning outcomes and the social dynamics of cooperative learning have been studied under a number of conditions. Slavin (1989-1990) regards it as "one of the most thoroughly researched of all instructional methods" (p. 52). Similarly, Johnson and Johnson (1994) describe the amount of research conducted over the past 90 years as "staggering" and conclude that:

> *During the past 90 years, more than 600 studies have been con-*
> *ducted by a wide variety of researchers in different decades with*
> *different age subjects, in different subject areas, and in different*
> *environments. We know far more about the efficacy of cooperative*
> *learning than we know about lecturing… or almost any other facet*
> *of education. (p. 38)*

In addition to cooperative learning's positive effect on student achievement, Johnson, Johnson, and Smith (1991b) also find that it significantly affects interpersonal relations:

> *As relationships within the class or college become more positive,*
> *absenteeism decreases and students' commitment to learning, feel-*
> *ing of personal responsibility to complete the assigned work, will-*
> *ingness to take on difficult tasks, motivation and persistence in*
> *working on tasks, satisfaction and morale, willingness to endure*
> *pain and frustration to succeed, willingness to defend the college*
> *against external criticism or attack, willingness to listen to and be*
> *influenced by peers, commitment to peers' success and growth,*
> *and productivity and achievement can be expected to increase.*
> *(p.44)*

Faculty in higher education can feel assured, also, that although much of the research in the last decades has been conducted at the kindergarten through twelfth grade level, its benefits, according to Natasi and Clements (1991), seem to be universal:

> *Cognitive-academic and social-emotional benefits have been re-*
> *ported for students from early elementary through college level,*
> *from diverse ethnic and cultural backgrounds, and having a wide*
> *range of ability levels… Furthermore, cooperative learning has been*
> *used effectively across a wide range of content areas, including*
> *mathematics, reading, language arts, social studies, and science.*
> *(p. 111)*

Similarly, Bossert (1988), after a meta-analysis on the now substantial body of research, concludes that its benefits affect students of all ages, in all content areas, for a wide variety of tasks, including problem solving. Cooper and Mueck (1990) cite some key earlier studies in higher education showing positive achievement gains using cooperative learning approaches conducted by Dansereau (1983), Treisman (1985), and Freirson (1986). On-going research at their campus, California State University Dominguez Hills (US), shows that "the overwhelming majority of the students prefer cooperative learning. Outcome measures such as higher-level thinking skills, interest in subject matter, general class morale, and frequency/quality of interactions with classmates receive particularly favorable ratings" (p. 71). Johnson and Johnson (1993), having completed a meta-analysis of the studies of cooperative learning among college students, offer five reasons to take this research seriously:

1. *CL has a rich history of theory, research, and practice;*
2. *The research on CL has a validity and 'generalizability' rarely found in the education literature;*
3. *CL affects many different instructional outcomes simultaneously;*
4. *Quite a bit is known about the essential components that make CL work;*
5. *Finally, CL creates learning opportunities that do not exist when students work competitively or individually. (p. 17-18)*

Perhaps the most compelling endorsement of cooperative learning in higher education has come from Astin's (1993) comprehensive longitudinal study of the impact of college on undergraduate students. Using samples from 159 baccalaureate granting institutions, Astin investigated 22 outcomes affected by 88 environmental factors to determine influences on students' academic achievement, personal development, and satisfaction with college. He determined that two factors in particular, student-student interaction and student-faculty interaction, carried the largest weights and affected the largest number of general education outcomes. Because of the influence of peers and faculty, he concludes that "how students *approach* general education (and how the faculty actually *deliver* the curriculum) is far more important than the formal curricular content and structure" (p. 425). He unequivocally endorses cooperative learning as a valid and effective pedagogical approach:

> *Under what we have come to call cooperative learning methods, where students work together in small groups, students basically teach each other, and our pedagogical resources are multiplied. Classroom research has consistently shown that cooperative learning approaches produce outcomes that are superior to those obtained through traditional competitive approaches, and it may well be that our findings concerning the power of the peer group offer a possible explanation: cooperative learning may be more potent than traditional methods of pedagogy because it motivates students to become more active and more involved participants in the learning process. This greater involvement could come in at least two different ways. First, students may be motivated to expend more effort if they know their work is going to be scrutinized by peers;*

and second, students may learn course material in greater depth if
they are involved in helping teach it to fellow students. (p. 427)

Light (1990, 1992) supports Astin's findings, particularly in the preface
to the *Harvard Assessment Seminars: Second Report*, when he concludes, "All
the specific findings point to, and illustrate, one main idea. It is that students who get the most out of college, who grow the most academically,
and who are the happiest, organize their time to include interpersonal activities with faculty members, or with fellow students, built around substantive, academic work" (p. 6). As Cooper (1993) points out in a review,
the efficacy of small groups is the overriding finding that dominates both
Harvard reports.

Because of these conclusive findings, the focus of recent cooperative
learning research has shifted from comparisons of cooperative learning
approaches with non-cooperative instructional strategies, such as competitive and individualistic ones, toward more sophisticated studies of the specific conditions that result in measurable instructional outcomes (Brown &
Palincsar, 1989; Cohen, 1994).

Faculty interested in an overview of the cooperative learning research
base should consult Johnson and Johnson (1989); Johnson, Johnson, and
Smith (1991b), particularly chapter three; Cooper et al. (1990); and the cooperative learning special interest group (SIG) of the American Educational
Research Association.

THE CHARACTERISTICS OF COOPERATIVE LEARNING

As a subset of collaborative learning, cooperative learning has some
distinct characteristics. Cooper (1990) concludes that the two most important of these are interdependence and individual accountability and responsibility.

Positive Interdependence

By helping one another, students discover that all group members benefit. Instructors can create these "win-win" situations through careful planning. For example, they can establish mutual goals for students placed in
permanent groups, such as reaching consensus on a problem's solution.
They can offer mutual rewards, such as additional points for a team whose
coaching of one another for ongoing quizzes has resulted in an overall group
improvement. They can encourage students to assume mutually dependent roles within a learning team, such as leader, spokesperson, or recorder,
which are rotated frequently to be certain that everyone has an opportunity for participation and leadership development. Perhaps most impor-

tant, they can offer structured tasks that allow students to work together constructively—much as they do or will do in the workplace—on meaningful, real-world tasks.

Individual Accountability

Even though students may coach one another in learning teams, students cannot coast on the achievements of others; they must be responsible for their own learning. Hence, most instructors assess student learning much as they always have, on the basis of individual quizzes and tests. If group projects are required, instructors must determine—often through peer and individual self-assessment—the relative value of each student's contribution.

Appropriate Grouping

Appropriate grouping is also essential. Students are placed in small groups of ideally no more than six members. Groups of four, sometimes called *quads*, are effective because they are usually inclusive (trios sometimes result in an odd-person-out dynamic). They can function meaningfully despite an occasional absence and lend themselves well to pair work. Quads are small enough to allow equitable participation, but large enough to contain the diverse talents useful for problem solving.

Most practitioners use instructor-selected groups to ensure heterogeneity, modelling workplace realities. Each group should contain members of varying abilities and attributes to strengthen problem solving. To ensure varying perspectives, students can be arranged by many characteristics, such as ethnicity, gender, age, or declared major. For example, in a literature class, particularly one on special interest topics such as children's literature or science fiction, distributing English majors among the groups is effective; in an accounting course, faculty members might want to establish heterogeneity through students' intended emphasis (cost, tax, financial, or auditing). Such groups, sometimes called *learning teams*, are usually either permanent, remaining together throughout a semester, or semi-permanent, reconfiguring at the mid-semester point. Over time, such groups typically become both cohesive and supportive. Initially, to help students accept what may be new classroom practices, faculty members should explain the rationale both for group work and for the teacher-assigned group composition. They should also address student concerns arising from previous negative experiences with group work less structured than cooperative learning.

Two further attributes of cooperative learning–social skills and group processing or monitoring–help faculty and students avoid pitfalls, such as unproductive group members, and help foster the successful functioning of groups.

Interpersonal and Group Skills

Social skills in a cooperative learning setting go beyond mere courtesy to include listening actively, paraphrasing accurately, questioning skillfully, and providing feedback constructively. Such skills should be modeled and reinforced by the instructor. Both faculty and students share the responsibility for creating positive environments where students discover and provide both cognitive and motivational support. The team effort allows them to experience and value a variety of thinking patterns and problem solving approaches. Within the comparative safety of the group, they can respond to different beliefs, ideas, and attitudes. Students' thinking can grow and develop when they are asked, in constructive ways, to clarify, elaborate, or justify their own ideas.

Group Monitoring or Processing

Because social skills are essential to student learning, groups must be carefully monitored and encouraged to conduct their own processing activities to ensure that the environments remain positive and conducive to learning. Group roles can contribute to the monitoring effort. Group leaders should be responsible for keeping the teams on task and for making certain that everyone has an opportunity to contribute equitably. They should allow no unfair criticism of a member's contribution to the group. Additionally, the instructor must be actively involved in the classroom activities, moving from group to group to be certain that each is indeed on task and that all members are encouraged to participate. By circulating among the groups, faculty members can determine and influence the degree of learning and pinpoint potential pitfalls that might lead to dysfunctional groups. By listening to student interactions, they can identify areas of confusion and benefit from hearing their lecture content or the textbook material "translated" by students for their classmates.

In a cooperative classroom, the instructor is a facilitator and a manager in addition to being a dispenser of knowledge. Few instructors ever forgo lecturing altogether, but by including cooperative learning activities, they expand their areas of influence and dissolve what Finkel and Monk (1983) have dubbed "The Atlas Complex," a mind-set of instructor-student expectations that results in teachers bearing all responsibility for the success of a class. If, for example, instructors observe inappropriate behavior as they are moving among the learning teams, instead of immediately intervening, they can take the leader aside and suggest that he or she address the problem. Monitoring can be done more formally, also, by the use of classroom assessment techniques such as "Quality Circles" or "One-Minute Papers" (Angelo & Cross, 1993). For example, faculty can ask students to record on index cards their responses to questions such as "How well did your group work today?"; "What could help the group work more smoothly during the next class session?" It is useful to have students discuss their responses within the team as a way of identifying and resolving problems. Faculty members can also collect the cards for later review. Having students keep learning logs, more typically called journals, also gives instructors valuable insights into group processes, particularly if questions are focused on classroom dynamics, learning outcomes, and specific classroom activities.

SELECTED COOPERATIVE LEARNING ACTIVITIES

As emphasized earlier, a cooperative learning classroom is predicated on an underlying belief in the potential of all students to succeed. It also operates on the assumption that such success is fostered by student-to-student interactions in carefully monitored permanent or semi-permanent student learning teams. Day-to-day classroom functions, however, are carried out or operationalized by specific *structures*. Structures are essentially content-free procedures, such as a brainstorming technique called *Roundtable*, which can be used in virtually any discipline for a variety of purposes. When content is added to a structure it becomes a specific classroom activity. For example, the Roundtable structure can be used in a composition class to generate possible topics for a classification paper or in a political science class to challenge students to identify the ethical issues facing Congress. When a series of activities are linked, they become a lesson or unit plan. Some of the most commonly used structures in higher education are discussed below.

Think-Pair-Share

In this activity, developed by Frank Lyman (1981), the instructor poses a question, preferably one demanding analysis, evaluation, or synthesis, and gives students 30 seconds or more to think through an appropriate response (Think). This time can also be spent writing the response. Students then turn to partners and share their responses, thus allowing time for both rehearsal and immediate feedback on their ideas (Pair). During the third and last stage, student responses can be shared within learning teams, with larger groups, or with the entire class during a follow-up discussion (Share). The caliber of discussion is enhanced by this technique since, too often, the extroverts with the quickest hand reflexes are called on when an instructor poses a question to the entire class. In addition, all students have an opportunity to learn by reflection and by verbalization. Think-Pair-Share, like most other cooperative learning structures, capitalizes on the principle of simultaneity (Kagan, 1992, p. 4:5-7). Many students (50% in Think-Pair-Share) are actively vocalizing ideas at a given moment, whereas in a more traditional classroom, only the lecturer is active, or the one student at a time who is responding to the lecturer's question.

Three-Step Interview

Common as an ice-breaker or a team-building exercise, this structure, developed by Kagan (1989), also helps students reinforce and internalize important concept-related information based on lectures or textbook material. It can be used to share ideas such as hypotheses or reactions to a film or article. Some faculty have used it successfully as a modified role-playing activity, having students interview one another while assuming the roles of historical characters. The interview questions, focused on content material and having no right or wrong solutions, are usually posed by the instructor. In a Three-Step Interview, one student interviews another within specified time limits (Step one). The two then reverse roles and conduct the interview again (Step two). In a learning team composed of two pairs, the students then share the highlights of the information or insights gleaned from the paired interview (Step three). This structure also results in the formation of new learning quads which may then move on to other team-related activities. An extra question can be added for pairs working more rapidly than others, an "extension" or "sponge" recommended for many cooperative learning activities. This structure reinforces listening and probing skills, helps students process and rehearse information, and results in shared insights.

Roundtable

In this brainstorming technique, which has no clear origin, students in a learning team write in turn on a single pad of paper, expressing their ideas aloud as they write. As the tablet circulates, more and more information is added until various aspects of a topic are explored. This activity builds positive interdependence among team members because of the shared writing surface, but more importantly, it builds team cohesion and reinforces the power of teamwork because students see in action the value of multiple viewpoints and ideas.

Structured Problem Solving

Members of learning teams, usually composed of four individuals, count off: 1, 2, 3, and 4. The teacher poses a question or problem requiring higher-order thinking skills. Sponges or extensions with additional content-related problems or activities are particularly important here for teams working faster than others. Students discuss the question or solve the problem, making certain that every group member can summarize the group's discussion or can explain the problem. The instructor calls a specific number and the designated team members (1, 2, 3, or 4) respond as group spokespersons. To avoid repetition, faculty members will usually ask for responses from only three to six groups. The desired learning will already have occurred. In this activity, students benefit from the verbalization, from the opportunity to exchange differing perspectives, and from the peer coaching that helps high and low achievers, alike. Less class time is wasted on inappropriate responses, and the principle of simultaneity is operative because at any given time 25% of the students are vocal within their groups. Students become actively involved with the material and, since no one knows which number the teacher will call, each has a vested interest in being able to articulate the appropriate response. Those chosen randomly as spokespersons–frequently students who do not volunteer during a whole-class discussion–feel far less threatened giving a team, rather than an individual, answer. Students can retain this number for use in other activities, such as *Jigsaw*. Some faculty members prefer the use of playing cards because the teams then have an immediate identity (Aces, Jacks, Queens, and Kings) and the individual members are identified by the suit of the cards (hearts, clubs, diamonds, and spades).

Jigsaw

In this complex cooperative learning structure, originally described by Aronson, Stephan, Sikes, Blaney, and Snapp (1978), the faculty member divides an assignment or topic into different parts. The number of parts should coincide with the number of students in the learning teams (often designated as "home" teams in this activity). Working with representatives from the other groups, each team member will become an expert on one of the different parts. Students can volunteer or they can be assigned to an expert team based on the numbers or suits assigned in the activity above. In a literature class, for instance, each team member might take a different character in a novel for an in-depth analysis. Accounting faculty can break down a complex transaction so that each student grapples with a single portion. Expert teams with members from each home team then work together on a two-tier assignment: they must master their portion of the material and they must discover the best way to help others in their home team learn it. Because groups larger than six become unwieldy, in large classes several expert teams can work on the same piece of the jigsaw. All expert students then reassemble in their home learning teams where they teach the other group members. This structure capitalizes on the value of peer teaching.

Send/Pass-a-Problem

This structure is particularly effective for problem solving. Its exact source is unknown, but the Howard County Maryland Staff Development Center developed a version of it inspired by Kagan's (1989) high-consensus-oriented Send-a-Problem structure using rotating flashcards for content review. The starting point is a list of problems or issues, which can be selected by the teacher or generated by students through an activity such as a Roundtable. Each team identifies the particular problem or issue upon which they wish to focus initially and records the choice on the front of a folder or envelope. Each team selects a different problem. The teams then brainstorm effective solutions for these problems and write them down. At a predetermined time, their notes are placed in the folder or envelope and forwarded to another team. The members of the second team, without looking at the ideas already generated, compile their own list. This second set of ideas is forwarded to a third team which now looks at the suggestions provided from the other teams, adds its own, and then decides on the two most effective solutions. Besides encouraging collaborative higher-order thinking skills, this structure results in student evaluative judgments, the highest cognitive level in Bloom's well-known taxonomy. Reports to the whole group occur as time permits and can take many forms, including written reports when the material is relatively complex. Some faculty members use this structure for examination review sessions by putting typical exam questions in folders for group problem solving.

Dyadic Essay Confrontation (DEC)

Developed by Sherman (1991), this structure enables faculty members to "front load" learning by making certain that students work independently outside class to master assigned material. Students then extend and validate their individual study through an in-class writing or thinking cooperative learning exercise. Students read assigned material, such as a textbook chapter, and prepare an essay question. They come to class with their essay question on one sheet of paper, along with a second sheet of paper on which they have written the essay question and their carefully thought-out response. Randomly paired students exchange questions, spending about 20 minutes writing a closed-book answer to their partner's essay question. The two then read, compare, and discuss the four answers, looking in particular for the differences between the in-depth responses prepared before class and the spontaneously generated in-class responses. This structure promotes critical thinking by requiring students to confront differing ideas, offers writing-to-learn opportunities, and provides solid and immediate feedback to students about their intellectual responses to discipline-specific material.

Bridging the Gap Between Theory and Research and Classroom Applications

Many faculty members, especially those in large research institutions, may be skeptical of what they regard as pedagogical fads or may be nettled by what Rhem (1992) characterizes as the style of cooperative learning: the unfamiliar, immature sounding jargon such as "think-pair-share" or the non-traditional classroom activities where student voices replace the lecture. Before undertaking even incremental changes, faculty rightly insist on concrete, persuasive information on practical, easy-to-implement, research-based instructional activities. Pintrich (1988) suggests that there is a gap between research on learning and cognition and a need for "directly applicable information relevant to... classroom practice" (p. 72). Bridging this gap between theory and research and the classroom applications that are predicated on them can be the greatest service provided by a faculty developer.

Naturally, no one wants a faculty development program to be associated with a single model of classroom practice. To maintain integrity, faculty development offerings must meet the needs (sometimes unarticulated) of the constituents, which include students, faculty members, teaching assistants, and institutional administrators committed to academic excellence. There must be no suggestion that faculty will be force fed a single model of teaching enhancement. For a number of reasons, however, cooperative learning should be shared with virtually all individuals associated with teaching. Cooperative learning is an important pedagogy not only because of its significant, growing research base but also because of its classroom base, which is eclectic, practical, and relevant.

Eclectic

One of the most positive features of cooperative learning is its versatility. As Neil Davidson pointed out in his keynote address at the 1990 conference of the International Society for the Study of Cooperation in Education, it is compatible with virtually every known pedagogical movement. For example, many of the structures are uniquely suited to strengthen students' writing and critical thinking skills, thus furthering the aims of writing and thinking across the curriculum movements (Millis, 1994b; Davidson and Worsham, 1992; McKeachie, 1988). Dyadic Essay Confrontation, for example, is highly effective in this regard (Millis, Cottell, & Sherman, 1993).

Perhaps more important, many effective learning strategies can be used under the philosophical umbrella of cooperative learning. For example, many of the classroom assessment techniques advocated by Angelo and Cross (1993) dovetail nicely with the group processing and monitoring aspects of cooperative learning (Cottell, 1991). Cooperative learning techniques can be used to fulfill all of the "Seven Principles for Good Practice in Undergraduate Education" advocated by a prestigious group of educators (Millis, 1991) and even Total Quality Management (TQM) principles (Millis, 1993). It is flexible enough to be used with technology (Hooper, 1992) and with case studies (Millis, 1994a). It also fits very well with adult learning practices (Millis, Davidson, & Cottell, 1994).

Practical

Too often, faculty members exposed to exciting pedagogical theories, often during a workshop, find that the ideas and inspiration vaporize over time with the press of other demands. Those exposed to cooperative learning rationale and structures, and given some time to reflect on their own discipline-specific applications, have a solid basis for implementation. Structures such as Think-Pair-Share or Send/Pass-a-Problem provide a specific, step-by-step framework for implementation, giving faculty members extremely focused classroom applications, not just abstractions.

Because of their easy application, the structures can virtually guarantee faculty willingness to experiment, but they alone are not enough. Faculty should also learn classroom management techniques to build confidence and ensure success. For example, faculty should be exposed to the concept of a quiet signal–often a raised hand, sometimes augmented by an audio signal such as a bell–to recapture students' attention when they are working in groups. They should also feel comfortable using sponges or extension activities for groups who complete a given task before the specified time frame, thereby potentially risking off-task behavior.

Another practical aspect of cooperative learning lies in the incremental nature of its implementation. Faculty developers almost invariably encourage faculty to take risks with their teaching methods, but they don't want them to become so ambitious that they set themselves–and their students–up for failure by attempting too much too soon. The key turning point in a cooperative classroom lies in the formation of permanent or semi-permanent learning teams. Johnson, Johnson, and Smith (1991a, 1991b) call these "formal" groups and distinguish them from short-term "informal" groups used for brief activities. Until faculty are ready to make the major commitment toward permanent or semi-permanent learning teams, they can begin with a few low-risk structures such as Think-Pair-Share or Roundtable. As they experience success, they can move toward the more complex structures such as Jigsaw and Send-a-Problem that require learning teams.

Relevant

Cooperative learning is uniquely suited for the variety of students entering academia. Its underlying philosophy, which is based on talent development, is compatible with the new teaching and learning realities. The increasing numbers of women and minorities are bringing to the higher education classroom different educational needs and different approaches to learning. Furthermore, an increasing number of students are studying part-time, balancing academic demands with vocational and family commitments. To meet these teaching challenges, faculty members must muster all the known pedagogical ammunition. Many of these non-traditional students are pragmatists who need "learn-by-doing" activities to supplement the theory that most college and university professors bring to the classroom (Schroeder, 1993). Cooperative learning activities offer faculty an opportunity to supplement lectures and other pedagogical approaches. Thus, various learning styles are addressed.

Cooperative learning is relevant in yet another way. Learning to work in groups helps prepare students for the current work force in at least three important ways:

- The workplace is becoming more team-oriented. In a globally connected society, competition may still be the norm in some sectors, but it is not acceptable within most forward-looking organizations where cooperative teamwork, quality circles, and total quality management practices are increasingly common.
- The work force is becoming more diverse. Students who have learned to work with others and to value others' contributions will be more prepared to function in the multicultural workplace.
- With fast-paced technological change and increasing international trade and communications, individuals must continually upgrade their skills and enlarge their knowledge base.

As Ventimiglia (1994) suggests, "The two skills we will all need to be successful in the workforce 2000–neither of which is taught as the content of a course or from a textbook–are the ability to work together cooperatively and the ability to be a life-long learner" (p. 6).

PROFESSIONAL DEVELOPMENT

Faculty developers well versed in a broad range of cooperative learning approaches will be better able to meet the diverse requirements of their faculty constituents. Familiarity with a variety of cooperative learning applications and techniques will enable faculty developers to assist professors in selecting the most appropriate ways to incorporate this teaching method into their classes. Faculty developers can undertake a number of professional development activities in order to learn more about cooperative learning theory and practice.

Take Workshops

Faculty developers should take workshops, if possible, from leaders in the movement and from fellow faculty developers who have practical experience with cooperative learning. Such faculty developers often assume an eclectic approach, drawing the best ideas from all schools of cooperative learning and from what is known about effective teaching and learning in general.

Join Organizations and Networks

Faculty developers should consider joining the International Society for the Study of Cooperation in Education (Box 1582, Santa Cruz, CA 95061-1582, USA: 1994 individual memberships, $30 US) and its local chapters such as the MidAtlantic Society for the Study of Cooperation in Education. Most importantly, they should join the Cooperative Learning in Higher Education Network (HFA-B316, California State University Dominguez Hills, 1000 E. Victoria Street, Carson, CA 90747, USA). All of these organizations produce newsletters or journals filled with solid cooperative learning teaching ideas.

Read, Reflect, and Teach, if Possible

Many books and articles are available now on cooperative learning techniques in higher education and more are coming every day. Faculty developers should place cooperative learning in the broader context of good practice in teaching and learning, looking for connections to other trends and initiatives, such as Angelo and Cross's (1993) classroom assessment techniques, Chickering and Gamson's (1987) "Seven Principles," and even TQM. Nothing, though, is more convincing than informed practice. Faculty developers who use cooperative learning techniques in their own classrooms will experience the power of structured group work and will also learn how to overcome the occasional problems that occur. Their credibility with faculty will clearly be enhanced with direct experience.

WORKING WITH FACULTY MEMBERS

Develop a Resource Library

Faculty, too, need opportunities to read and reflect. Many teaching centers maintain resource libraries, drawing from a wide variety of sources. These libraries should contain the cooperative learning resources that enable faculty to read, reflect, and implement cooperative learning strategies. A key newsletter is *Cooperative Learning and College Teaching* (New Forums Press, Inc., P.O. Box 876, Stillwater, OK 74076, USA: 1994 subscriptions, $30 US.) Faculty developers interested in promoting cooperative learning often make available to faculty specific articles or even "how-to" packets designed to increase their familiarity with and confidence in cooperative learning.

Learn to Translate and Adapt Material Developed at the K-12 Level

Much effective material on cooperative learning is targeted toward elementary and secondary school teachers. This fact should not deter resourceful faculty developers who can make it useful and appropriate to faculty in higher education. Materials can be rewritten to avoid terminology that might be unfamiliar to college and university faculty.

Help Faculty Understand the Theory and Research That Informs Practice

Weimer (1992) feels that faculty development efforts can be undermined by a failure to ensure that faculty have a firm grasp of the principles which underlie the pedagogy:

> *Teaching is a highly complex, idiosyncratic, dynamic process. To convey the impression that it is nothing more than a bag of tricks, that getting students involved in a class is no more than knowing 22 participation strategies, belies the inherent complexity of the teaching phenomenon… To improve instruction by technique alone is to oversimplify and underestimate the complexity of teaching and the process of improving it. And when we oversimplify, we devalue. (pp. 18-19)*

Cooperative learning certainly is not a "quick fix." Its solid theoretical and research base can be shared with faculty, as needed. Murray (1994) makes the case that teachers need this global perspective if they are to be knowledgeable, versatile practitioners.

Encourage Reflective Experimentation

As indicated, cooperative learning structures and strategies can be introduced gradually as teachers gain in knowledge, experience, and commitment. Faculty developers can support these careful ventures in a number of ways, including offering to visit or videotape classes. Perhaps most important, however, is putting would-be experimenters in touch with other faculty who are successfully using cooperative learning techniques.

Form Support Groups Across Campus

The Cooperative Learning Users Group (CLUG) at California State University, Dominguez Hills (US), a model which has been replicated on other campuses, encourages faculty to share experiences and to provide support for one another's efforts in the cooperative classroom. Problems can be solved, successes celebrated, and new ideas generated through faculty collaboration that extends beyond the classroom. Such support groups typically are interdisciplinary, allowing faculty to experience the stimulating cross-fertilization of ideas that occurs beyond departmental boundaries. Smith, Johnson, and Johnson (1992) observe that "[c]hange is hard and typically does not occur without a group of colleagues who care and provide support and encouragement for one another. The research support for cooperation among faculty is just as strong as that for cooperation among students" (p. 36).

Encourage Faculty to Visit Cooperative Classrooms

Few faculty experienced positive group work during their undergraduate days. Many, in fact, may have been disillusioned by their experiences with loosely structured, ineffective group work where the over-achievers completed often ill-defined tasks. Role models for effective classroom implementations are essential. As Ekroth (1990) notes, "Observing classes taught effectively in alternate ways or talking with instructors who approach teaching differently can stimulate creative changes in one's teaching. Modelling provides one of the most effective means of learning new behavior styles" (p. 2).

Get Chairpersons Involved

This is sound advice for faculty developers regardless of the aim they wish to further. Faculty loyalty lies with their disciplines, and the reward structures at most colleges and universities are channeled through the department. Chairpersons' endorsement of and support for cooperative learning can be an important catalyst in promoting its implementation. For example, in 1993, the accounting firm, Deloitte and Touche, invited selected faculty from across the nation to a five-day cooperative learning workshop with the specific goal of strengthening teaching and learning within the discipline of accounting. Many of these faculty returned to their departments where, with the support of their chairs, they gave presentations to departmental colleagues.

Look for Ways to Connect Cooperative Learning with Other Campus Initiatives

Faculty developers convinced of the efficacy of cooperative learning will find opportunities to integrate its principles and practices with other campus initiatives. For example, the University of Maryland University College received a grant from the Pew Charitable Foundations, enabling the institution to establish a complex Diverse Students Project. As the Assistant Dean of Faculty Development, I conducted a series of cooperative learning workshops for the faculty involved with the project to help them excel in multicultural classrooms. In collaboration with the Director of the Effective Writing Program, I also coordinated a workshop on the use of cooperative learning methods in building writing and critical thinking skills. Cooperative learning techniques can be effectively modelled in workshops for faculty teaching distance education courses and using technology in the classroom or computer lab.

ORGANIZING WORKSHOPS

As the international faculty development survey described in the opening chapter indicates, workshops are considered an effective means of helping faculty enhance their teaching effectiveness. Workshops are widely used by faculty developers because they are easy to organize; they provide practical, interactive, hands-on experiences which prepare faculty to try new techniques in their classrooms; and they are usually fairly cost effective. The following advice, based on extensive experience, can also help faculty developers plan and provide effective cooperative learning workshops.

Screen Print Materials and Facilitators Carefully

Faculty developers, who almost invariably have limited resources, must ensure that workshops are of high quality and are cost effective. Usually, they tap two resources: in-house cooperative learning practitioners and outside consultants. Campus practitioners who testify to the value of cooperative learning and who model effective practices can be extremely effective. Besides having credibility with their peers, they are also available for further consultation. Carefully chosen presenters from outside the institution can also be very effective. Workshops using outside presenters often create interest and stimulate enthusiasm for follow-up activities, and outsiders with national reputations sometimes catch the attention of skeptical faculty members. Additionally, they can provide an important connection to other campuses and practitioners. In both cases, faculty developers should be certain that the workshop presenters effectively present and model cooperative learning practices.

To identify external consultants, faculty developers should seek advice from others who have used presenters. The Professional and Organizational Development Network in Higher Education (POD:US), the Society for Teaching and Learning in Higher Education (STLHE:Canada), the Staff and Educational Development Association (SEDA:UK), and the Higher Education Research and Development Society of Australasia (HERDSA:Aus), can provide helpful information.

Provide Handouts for Pre- and Post-Workshop Reading

Having faculty read beforehand some cooperative learning material can set the stage for the workshop. Often it can be sent ahead with their registration confirmations. Selections should be brief, perhaps a single article calculated to whet the appetite rather than to overwhelm workshop registrants. Reinforce the interest and enthusiasm generated by a workshop through carefully designed follow-up handouts which can expand upon information gleaned from workshops. Such handouts also conserve workshop time. Presenters will not need to lecture on cooperative learning's extensive research base, for instance, if the handout packet provides relevant articles.

Reinforce Cooperative Learning Activities

Faculty developers committed to cooperative learning can find many ways to introduce the concepts and practices to their faculty. Offering a series of workshops provides a way to help faculty build on skills learned previously. They can offer workshops such as "Enhancing Student Thinking Skills Through Structured Small Group Work" or "Creating Cooperation in a Multicultural Classroom." All these efforts can emphasize the critical tenets of cooperative learning which distinguish it from collaborative learning, specifically positive interdependence and individual accountability, and offer activities for immediate classroom application. While general workshops are effective, discipline-specific cooperative learning sessions are particularly effective because of immediate faculty interest and opportunities for application.

Be Certain that Workshop Presenters Provide Action-Oriented, Experiential Activities

No one can lecture effectively about cooperative learning. Encourage presenters not to waste workshop time with lengthy documentation of the extensive cooperative learning research base. Faculty can read about it if they are skeptical; the evidence is readily available. Presenters should use credible resources such as Astin (1993) and then move on to the activities themselves. Faculty actually have to experience the structured activities before they understand the principles and the classroom applications. Encourage presenters to build in time for reflection and the opportunity to develop specific classroom applications.

Workshop presenters must model positive cooperative learning classroom behaviors. They should, for example, actively monitor groups, commenting, paraphrasing, and reinforcing positive behavior. Comments, such as "Tom very effectively asked Mary probing questions" or "Alice did a fine job of summarizing Richard's cooperative learning efforts in a large lecture class" also build rapport between the presenter and the participants.

CONCLUSION

Cooperative learning's efficacy is well documented. Faculty developers can play an essential role in increasing faculty confidence in this important movement by helping faculty to understand the theoretical and research basis for cooperative learning and by helping them to implement a cooperative approach, in ways that suit the individuals, their students, and their institutions. Such innovations should not be considered radical. Rather, they should be placed in the context of what it means to be a professor in a complex, changing world headed for the 21st century. Nevin, Smith, and Udvari-Solner (1994) clearly articulate this new professionalism:

> Professors who practice cooperative learning often find themselves collecting rich data sources: student anecdotes, increased class averages, and changes in the quality as well as the quantity of student products. If this data is published, professors integrate two of the four forms of scholarship promoted by Boyer (1990)–the scholarship of teaching and the scholarship of integration. This type of balanced academic life may be the hallmark of professors who actualize the new paradigm of college teaching. (p. 126)

Given the solid theoretical and research base upon which cooperative learning rests and the testimonials of committed practitioners in all disciplines, faculty members can be confident that they are embracing a pedagogy that will pay enormous dividends in student academic achievement and affective development.

REFERENCES

Anderson, A.S. (Ed.). (1981). *Mainstreaming digest.* College Park, MD: University of Maryland College of Education.

Angelo, T.A. (Ed.). (1991). *New Directions for Teaching and Learning: No. 46. Classroom research: Early lessons for success.* San Francisco, CA: Jossey-Bass.

Angelo, T.A., & Cross, K.P. (1993). *Classroom assessment techniques: A handbook for college teachers* (2nd ed.). San Francisco, CA: Jossey-Bass.

Aronson, E., Stephan, C., Sikes, J., Blaney, N., & Snapp, M. (1978). *The jigsaw classroom.* Beverly Hills, CA: Sage.

Astin, A.W. (1993). *What matters in college: Four critical years revisited.* San Francisco, CA: Jossey-Bass.

Belenky, M.F., Clinchy, B.M., Goldberger, N.R., & Tarule, J.M. (1986). *Women's ways of knowing: The development of self, voice, and mind.* New York, NY: Basic Books.

Boehm, L. (1992). In wake of crisis: Reclaiming the heart of teaching and learning. In T.J. Frecka (Ed.), *Critical thinking, interactive learning and technology: Reaching for excellence in business education* (pp. 24-40). Chicago, IL: Arthur Andersen Foundation.

Bossert, S.T. (1988). Cooperative activities in the classroom. *Review of Educational Research, 15,* 225-250.

Bouton, C., & Garth, R.T. (Eds.). (1983). *New Directions for Teaching and Learning: No. 14. Learning in groups.* San Francisco, CA: Jossey-Bass.

Boyer, E. (1990). *Scholarship reconsidered.* Lawrenceville, NJ: Princeton University Press.

Brown, A.L., & Palincsar, A.S. (1989). Guided, cooperative learning and individual knowledge acquisition. In L.B. Resnick (Ed.), *Knowing, learning, and instruction: Essays in honor of Robert Glaser* (pp. 393-451). Hillsdale, NJ: Lawrence Erlbaum Associates.

Bruffee, K.A. (1993). *Collaborative learning: Higher education, interdependence, and the authority of knowledge.* Baltimore, MD: The Johns Hopkins University Press.

Chickering, A.W., & Gamson, A.F. (1987). *Seven principles for good practice in undergraduate education.* Racine, WI: The Johnson Foundation/Wingspread. [Available by contacting the Seven Principles Resources Center, P.O. Box 5838, Winona State University, Winona, MN 55987-5838; (507) 457-5020]

Cohen, E.G. (1994). Restructuring the classroom: Conditions for productive small groups. *Review of Educational Research, 64,* 1-35.

Cooper, J. (1990, May). Cooperative learning and college teaching: Tips from the trenches. *The Teaching Professor,* pp. 1-2.

Cooper, J. (1993). Review of the Harvard assessment seminars. *Cooperative Learning: The Magazine for Cooperation in Higher Education, 13*(30), 46-47.

Cooper, J., & Mueck, R. (1990). Student involvement in learning: Cooperative learning and college instruction. *Journal on Excellence in College Teaching, 1,* 68-76.

Cooper, J., Prescott, S., Cook, L., Smith, L., Mueck, R., & Cuseo, J. (1990). *Cooperative learning and college instruction.* Long Beach, CA: The California State University Foundation.

Cottell, P.G., Jr. (1991). Classroom assessment in accounting: Assessing for learning. In T.A. Angelo (Ed.), *New Directions for Teaching and Learning: No. 46. Classroom research: Early lessons for success* (pp. 43-54). San Francisco, CA: Jossey-Bass.

Cuseo, J. (1992, Winter). Collaborative & cooperative learning in higher education: A proposed taxonomy. *Cooperative Learning and College Teaching, 2*(2), 2-4.

Dansereau, D.F. (1983). *Cooperative learning: Impact on acquisition of knowledge and skills* (Report No. 341). Abilene, TX: U.S. Army Research Institute for the Behavioral and Social Sciences. [ERIC Document Reproduction Service No. ED 243 088]

Davidson, N., & Worsham, T. (Eds). (1992). *Enhancing thinking through cooperative learning.* New York, NY: Teachers College Press.

Davis, J.R. (1993). *Better teaching, more learning.* Phoenix, AZ: The Oryx Press.

Ekroth, L. (1990, Winter/Spring). Why professors don't change. In L. Ekroth (Ed.), *Teaching Excellence: Toward the Best in the Academy.* Stillwater, OK: Professional and Organizational Development Network in Higher Education.

Ekroth, L. (Ed.). (1990, Winter/Spring) *Teaching excellence: Toward the best in the academy.* Stillwater, OK: Professional and Organizational Development Network in Higher Education.

Finkel, D.L., & Monk, G.S. (1983). Teachers and learning groups: Dissolution of the Atlas complex. In C. Bouton & R.Y. Garth (Eds.), *New Directions for Teaching and Learning: No. 14. Learning in groups* (pp. 83-97). San Francisco, CA: Jossey-Bass.

Frecka, T.J. (Ed.). (1992). *Critical thinking, interactive learning and technology: Reaching for excellence in business education.* Chicago, IL: Arthur Andersen Foundation.

Frierson, H. (1986). Two intervention methods: Effects on groups of predominantly black nursing students' board scores. *Journal of Research and Development in Education, 19,* 18-23.

Gere, A.R. (1987). *Writing groups: History, theory, and implications*. Carbondale, IL: Southern Illinois University Press.

Goodsell. A., Mahler, M., Tinto, V., Smith, B.L., & MacGregor, J. (Eds). (1992). *Collaborative learning: A sourcebook for higher education*. University Park, PA: National Center on Postsecondary Teaching, Learning, and Assessment.

Hooper, S. (1992). Cooperative learning and computer-based instruction. *Educational Technology Research & Development, 40*(3), 21-38.

Johnson, D.W., & Johnson, R.T. (1989). *Cooperation and competition: Theory and research*. Edina, MN: Interaction Book Company.

Johnson, D.W., & Johnson, R.T. (1993, Spring). What we know about cooperative learning at the college level. *Cooperative Learning: The Magazine for Cooperation in Higher Education, 13*(3), 17-18.

Johnson, D.W., Johnson, R.T., & Smith, K.A. (1991a). *Active learning: Cooperation in the college classroom*. Edina, MN: Interaction Book Company.

Johnson, D.W., Johnson, R.T., & Smith, K.A. (1991b). *Cooperative learning: Increasing college faculty instructional productivity* (ASHE-ERIC Higher Education Report No. 4). Washington, DC: The George Washington University School of Education and Human Development.

Johnson, R.T., & Johnson, D.W. (1994). An overview of cooperative learning. In J.S. Thousand, R.A. Villa, & A.I. Nevin (Eds.), *Creativity and collaborative learning: A practical guide to empowering students and teachers* (pp. 31-44). Baltimore, MD: Paul H. Brookes Publishing.

Kagan, S. (1989). *Cooperative learning* (1st ed.). San Juan Capistrano, CA: Resources for Teachers.

Kagan, S. (1992). *Cooperative learning* (2nd ed.). San Juan Capistrano, CA: Resources for Teachers.

Light, R.J. (1990). *The Harvard assessment seminars: First report*. Cambridge, MA: Harvard University Press.

Light, R.J. (1992). *The Harvard assessment seminars: Second report*. Cambridge, MA: Harvard University Press.

Lyman, F. (1981). The responsive classroom discussion. In A.S. Anderson (Ed.), *Mainstreaming digest*. College Park, MD: University of Maryland College of Education.

McDaniel, T.R. (1994, Winter). College classrooms of the future: Megatrends to paradigm shifts. *College Teaching, 1*(42), 27-31.

McKeachie, W.J. (1988, September). Teaching thinking. *Update, 2*(1), i.

McKeachie, W.J., Pintrich, P.R., Lin, Y., & Smith, D.A. (1986). *Teaching and learning in the college classroom: A review of the research literature.* Ann Arbor, MI: The University of Michigan.

Millis, B.J. (1991). Fulfilling the promise of the "Seven Principles" through cooperative learning: An action agenda for the university classroom. *Journal on Excellence in College Teaching, 2,* 139-144.

Millis, B.J. (1993). Creating a TQM classroom through cooperative learning. *To Improve the Academy, 12,* 147-161.

Millis, B.J. (1994a). Conducting cooperative cases. *To Improve the Academy, 13,* 309-328.

Millis, B.J. (1994b). Increasing thinking through cooperative writing. *Cooperative Learning and College Teaching, 4*(3), 7-9

Millis, B.J., Cottell, P.G., Jr., & Sherman, L. (1993, Spring). Stacking the DEC to promote critical thinking: Applications in three disciplines. *Cooperative Learning and College Teaching, 3*(3), 12-14.

Millis, B.J., Davidson, N., & Cottell, P.G., Jr. (1994). Enhancing adult critical thinking skills through cooperative learning. In J.D. Sinnott (Ed.), *Interdisciplinary handbook of adult lifespan learning* (pp. 270-281). Westport, CT: Greenwood Press.

Murray, F.B. (1994). Why understanding the theoretical basis of cooperative learning enhances teaching success. In J.S. Thousand, R.A. Villa, & A.I. Nevin (Eds.), *Creativity and collaborative learning: A practical guide to empowering students and teachers* (pp. 3-11). Baltimore, MD: Paul H. Brookes Publishing.

Myers, C., & Jones, T.B. (1993). *Promoting active learning: Strategies for the college classroom.* San Francisco, CA: Jossey-Bass.

Natasi, B.K., & Clements, D.H. (1991). Research on cooperative learning: Implications for practice. *School Psychology Review, 20*(1), 110-131.

Nevin, A.I., Smith, K., & Udvari-Solner, A. (1994). Cooperative group learning and higher education. In J.S. Thousand, R.A. Villa, & A.I. Nevin (Eds.), *Creativity and collaborative learning: A practical guide to empowering students and teachers* (pp. 115-127). Baltimore, MD: Paul H. Brookes Publishing.

Pintrich, P. (1988). Student learning and college teaching. In R.E. Young & K.E. Eble (Eds.), *New Directions for Teaching and Learning: No. 33. College teaching and learning: Preparing for new commitments* (pp. 71-86). San Francisco, CA: Jossey-Bass.

Resnick, L.B. (Ed.). (1989). *Knowing, learning, and instruction: Essays in honor of Robert Glaser.* Hillsdale, NJ: Lawrence Erlbaum Associates.

Rhem, J. (1992). Getting past the doorman. *The National Teaching & Learning Forum, 2*(1), 4.

Rhem, J. (1994). Conference report: Emerging trends in college teaching for the 21st century. *The National Teaching & Learning Forum, 3*(4), 12.

Sapon-Shevin, M., Ayres, B.J., & Duncan, J. (1994). Cooperative learning and inclusion. In J.S. Thousand, R.A. Villa, & A.I. Nevin (Eds.), *Creativity and collaborative learning: A practical guide to empowering students and teachers* (pp. 45-58). Baltimore, MD: Paul H. Brookes Publishing.

Schroeder, C.C. (1993, September/October). New students–new learning styles. *Change: The Magazine of Higher Learning,* pp. 21-26.

Sherman, L.W. (1991, April). *Cooperative learning in post secondary education: Implications from social psychology for active learning experiences.* Paper presented at the American Educational Research Association Annual Conference, Chicago, IL.

Sinnott, J.D. (Ed.). (1994). *Interdisciplinary handbook of adult lifespan learning.* Westport, CT: Greenwood Press.

Slavin, R.E. (1989-1990). Research in cooperative learning: Consensus and controversy. *Educational Leadership, 47*(4), 52-55.

Slavin, R.E. (1993). What can post-secondary cooperative learning learn from elementary and secondary research? *Cooperative Learning and College Teaching, 4*(1), 2-3.

Smith, B.L., & MacGregor, J.T. (1992). What is collaborative learning? In A. Goodsell, M. Mahler, V. Tinto, B.L. Smith, & J. MacGregor (Eds.), *Collaborative learning: A sourcebook for higher education* (pp. 9-22). University Park, PA: National Center on Postsecondary Teaching, Learning, and Assessment.

Smith, K.A., Johnson, D.W., & Johnson, R.T. (1992). Cooperative learning and positive change in higher education. In A. Goodsell, M. Mahler, V. Tinto, B.L. Smith, & J. MacGregor, (Eds.), *Collaborative learning: A sourcebook for higher education* (pp. 34-36). University Park, PA: National Center on Postsecondary Teaching, Learning, and Assessment.

Thousand, J.S., Villa, R.A., & Nevin, A.I. (Eds.). (1994). *Creativity and collaborative learning: A practical guide to empowering students and teachers.* Baltimore, MD: Paul H. Brookes.

Treisman, U. (1985). A study of the mathematics performance of black students at the University of California, Berkeley [Doctoral dissertation, University of California, Berkeley, 1986]. *Dissertation Abstracts International, 47,* 1641A.

Ventimiglia, L.M. (1994, Winter). Cooperative learning at the college level. *Thought & Action: The NEA Almanac of Higher Education, 9*(2), 5-30.

Weimer, M. (1992). Improving higher education: Issues and perspectives on teaching and learning. *To Improve the Academy, 11,* 13-23.

Young, R.E., & Eble, K.E. (Eds.). (1988). *New Directions for Teaching and Learning: No. 33. College teaching and learning: Preparing for new commitments.* San Francisco, CA: Jossey-Bass.

AUTHOR

Barbara Millis is Assistant Dean for Faculty Development, University of Maryland University College (US). She frequently offers workshops at professional conferences (American Association for Higher Education, Lilly Conference on College Teaching, Council of Independent Colleges) and for various colleges and universities. Dr. Millis' publications include a book on cooperative learning and accounting, and articles on cooperative learning, classroom observations (she directed a FIPSE Project on that topic), the teaching portfolio, adjunct faculty, mentoring, Total Quality Management (TQM), and syllabus construction. Her PhD is from Florida State University.

6.

Improving Laboratory Teaching

Elizabeth Hazel

Laboratory work is the hallmark of education in science and technology based fields. Student laboratories are a costly resource yet their educational potential is often not fully realized in practice. It is timely that their design and delivery and the forms of student assessment used be examined critically for their contribution to high quality student learning. This chapter discusses strategies to introduce faculty to improved design, delivery, and assessment in laboratory teaching.

THE POTENTIAL OF STUDENT LABORATORIES

What is the educational potential of student laboratories? Central to the rationale for the student science laboratory is the notion of socialization into a scientific discipline or appreciation of the ways in which scientists work. There may also be the assumptions that the laboratory provides an opportunity to learn generalized systematic ways of thinking which should transfer to other disciplines and levels, and that laboratory instruction should result in a more comprehensive view of science, including not only the orderliness of its interpretations of nature, but also the tentativeness of its theories and models (Anderson, 1976).

There is much agreement in the literature on the following range of goals for laboratory work:

1. Learning scientific information and concepts
2. Participating in the construction of scientific knowledge, understanding the interplay of theory and methodology

3. Understanding the processes of scientific enquiry and appreciating and emulating the role of scientists in enquiry
   - observing and measuring
   - seeing a problem and seeking ways to solve it
   - interpreting data and formulating generalizations
   - building, testing, and revising a theoretical model
4. Developing scientific imagination and creativity
5. Learning manipulative and technical skills and the use of equipment
6. Developing relevant professional values, attitudes, and interests
7. Developing an orientation to the social, historical, and philosophical aspects of science
8. Appreciating the application of scientific knowledge and methods
9. Developing literature skills
10. Learning how to communicate verbally and orally
11. Learning to work cooperatively with colleagues, developing teamwork

Is the potential of laboratories fulfilled? By no means always, according to reviews of the literature (e.g., Boud, Dunn, & Hegarty-Hazel, 1989). The following problems have been highlighted:

- Many of the goals are not exclusive to the laboratory and may be attained more efficiently elsewhere.
- Laboratory programs, and especially their assessment, may emphasize low-level goals at the expense of higher-level goals and may encourage students to concentrate on methodology without an understanding of the interplay of theory and methodology.
- Assessment often fails to provide evidence of whether goals are attained or not and it may be possible for students to do well in a course without even attending a laboratory.
- Many laboratory classes have too many, too diffuse aims and it would be better to do a few things well.
- Students often find labs tedious and boring and do not take them seriously.

Laboratory classes can provide educationally worthwhile and personally fulfilling experiences for students and they can also be a waste of time and money and a negative educational experience for students:

> ...*the beauty of Saturday morning when it melted! That I'd got a fluctuation big enough to cause melting. I'd worked through the*

maths behind the fluctuation terms and I'd got an answer, and it was right. There's a beauty behind it all—there's a reason.

The good thing was that we were able to work on our own when we wanted to and the supervisor only came in when we were in difficulty. So most of the time we were working on our own and we felt a sense of achievement really.

...the experiment—it's the thought of being there for five hours at a time and when you come out you don't feel you've done anything. It's also the thing that thousands of undergraduates have done it before—it's so stereotyped you could almost use a tape recorder instead of a person... all right, you've got to build up from basics, but surely you must feel inside that you're doing something useful, because if you're not, what's the point of it? In my mind it leads to a lot of apathy. (Bliss, 1990, p. 387-394)

These are from the 'good' and 'bad' stories found in comprehensive studies of students in first-, second- and third-year laboratories (Bliss, 1990; Bliss & Ogborn, 1977). The good stories came mostly from students undertaking work of an investigative nature, especially projects in third year. Projects represented a real challenge, students felt fully involved and often experienced a sense of responsibility, independence, and achievement. Bad stories were common, especially prevalent amongst first- and second-year students and when students were engaged in traditional controlled exercises in their laboratory classes. Striking features of the stories were the disengagement or alienation of the students, their feelings of anxiety and insecurity, and limited experience of success in the laboratory setting.

The purpose of the following sections is to explore ways in which course designers can try to increase the incidence of students having good educational experiences in the laboratory.

A WAY OF REFLECTING ON STUDENT LABORATORY EXERCISES

There are several major alternatives for presenting student laboratory work, and they differ greatly in purpose and degrees of student autonomy. In order of decreasing teacher control and increasing student autonomy, these are controlled exercises, experimental investigations, and project work.

The differences can be recognized using a simple but sound scheme which analyzes the level of openness for scientific enquiry in different laboratory exercises (adapted from Herron, 1971; Boud et al., 1989):

Type of laboratory	Level of enquiry	Definition of level			
		Aim	Material	Method	Answer
Demonstrations	0	Given	Given	Given	Given
Controlled exercises	1	Given	Given	Given	Open
Structured investigations	2	Given	Given all or part	Part given or open	Open
Unstructured investigations	3	Given	Open	Open	Open
Projects	4	Open	Open	Open	Open

This scheme which uses familiar descriptions of laboratories and clarifies the dimension of student autonomy will be used throughout the following sections. It is one which has proved of value in faculty development work directed to changing the profile of student exercises (Boud et al., 1989; Hegarty-Hazel & Cheary, 1993).

Current appreciation of good practice in university education emphasizes development of the self-directed and lifelong learner. Faculty development programs need ways of making this concrete in individual courses and individual laboratory programs, ways of designing new programs which are student centered and which foster students' deep engagement with the discipline and, more commonly, ways of modifying existing programs. In most cases, new or modified programs need to be educationally innovative whilst operating within the traditional resource structure.

I would argue for decreasing the traditional reliance on controlled exercises and increasing the use of investigations and projects which can be scientifically worthwhile, interesting, and motivating for students, and are likely to foster deep approaches to learning in the laboratory (Boud et al., 1989; Hegarty-Hazel, 1990a; Ramsden, 1992). Investigations and projects run true to the nature of scientific disciplines and, with experience, can be well managed in undergraduate laboratories (Klopfer, 1990; Layton, 1990). The following sections address the improvement of each kind of these student laboratory exercises.

IMPROVING THE DESIGN AND DELIVERY OF LABORATORY TEACHING

Controlled Exercises

These are activities which are wholly designed by the teacher and are often thought of as verification exercises. They can be completed by a student within a short timespan, typically one or two laboratory periods. There is a known outcome and if students follow the instructions, they should arrive at that outcome (more or less). Controlled exercises are often thought to be valuable in the early stages of a course where the emphasis may be on using a skill or technique with accuracy, making observations, transforming data, and drawing conclusions. Research on life in university classrooms shows that during controlled exercises, students are focused on following instructions, carrying out manipulations and discussions with low-level questions and answers, whilst teachers may be taking a supervisory role (Hegarty-Hazel, 1990b).

Steps in conducting a controlled exercise, each of which could be the focus of faculty development programs, are:

- Define the objectives of the exercise and communicate this to students
- Identify reading material to be given to the students before the class
- Provide a detailed account of the procedure to be followed by students
- Identify and provide all the laboratory materials and equipment
- Specify the observations that have to be made
- Describe the nature of the report required for assessment purposes
(adapted from Newble & Cannon, 1991, p. 61)

A key point for faculty development is recognition that controlled exercises cannot meet all of the educational objectives for the laboratory shown at the beginning of this chapter. They are notably unsuitable for embodying the spirit of enquiry. Traditional controlled exercises have often been expected to carry a large range of objectives and have been found wanting. In a development setting, faculty can identify the objectives of each exercise, map the range of objectives over a whole program and then streamline so that each controlled exercise has only one or a few objectives and the program covers a suitable range.

Advantages of controlled exercises. Potentially, the best qualities of controlled exercises are that they may be elegant and ingenious, each one a microcosm of the art of experimentation (Ogborn, 1977). They can provide introductory experience with the materials and processes of a discipline, equipment, apparatus, organisms, and chemicals, as appropriate. In many disciplines, the whole procedure has become very well honed. Teachers who wish to use controlled exercises with their students can often locate suitable experiments in laboratory manuals from their own student days, in commercial texts, or in discipline-specific education journals. For faculty, a major appeal of using controlled exercises is the ease of finding them and the charm of their predictability. They can be used from year to year with minimum fuss.

Disadvantages of controlled exercises. A major disadvantage is that students often do not like controlled exercises very much, finding them dull and tedious. Students may not be very sympathetic towards the elegance of exercises nor regard their lab work as a microcosm of experimentation. They can find the pre-lab work a meaningless ritual, the introductory talks boring ('the great glaze-off,' as one student described it to me recently), and the controlled exercises as lacking personal satisfaction or connection to their world. Results and reports from students in previous years are often readily available and there is the temptation for the task of writing up to become one of 'faking good' the results.

Female students and controlled exercises. The "potted" nature of the enterprise, the lack of motivational context, especially the lack of demonstrated social relevance, and the emphasis on an imposed analytical process are thought to play a role in making controlled exercises less attractive to female students in the laboratory than to male students (Mallow, 1981; Novak, 1990), part of the process whereby women may 'tune in, turn off, drop out,' especially in the physical sciences (Rigden & Tobias, 1991; Tobias, 1990). As well, differences in maturity are likely to be relevant, at least at the first-year level. Research suggests that female students who opt for science are more mature than their male counterparts and are less likely to enjoy the certainty of structured work, preferring problem solving and enquiry.

Improving controlled exercises. Simplifying controlled exercises so that students can do a few things well would do much to improve the value of the laboratory experience. Looking at the range of agreed goals shown earlier in this chapter, #1, #2, #5 to do with knowledge and technical skills could perhaps be met in controlled exercises. To have lab work illustrate or verify requires that students make the link with earlier parts of a subject. This will not happen as a matter of course—at the very least this requires explicit directions by the teacher and attention to timetabling. It is easiest for students to make links when the relevant lectures and tutorials or assignments are closely integrated with the laboratories. It is most difficult for students when the laboratory program has no apparent connection with any other sector of a course, as in the "circus" or rotating arrangements common in the physical sciences.

Students can learn technical skills or the use of equipment in more engaging ways than mere recipe following. Students could, for example, be presented with a wide range of experimental setups and be asked to discuss the kinds of information which could be expected from each of the setups and the limitations of each. They could be asked to imagine uses for equipment, techniques, or setups in applied settings, such as medicine or agriculture or engineering, in ways which would meet goals #4 on scientific imagination and creativity and #8 on the application of scientific knowledge and methods.

Improvements have been made in the motivational context by tapping students' interests or providing choice. Improvements from enhancing learner activity have been made by encouraging reflective processes or by introducing an element of student planning (doing this whilst retaining teacher control requires some ingenuity). Improvements in student interaction have been achieved by specifically providing a discussion or tutorial phase to the lab, providing well-structured, prompt questions or challenges. Improving the students' knowledge base requires attention to the sequencing of coursework. Here, one might turn to accounts of cycles of laboratory work moving from more prescribed to less (for example, where Venkatachelam & Rudolph, 1974, had cycles moving from what they termed cookbook to creative chemistry in the laboratory).

Experimental Investigations

This term is used to cover a wide variety of teaching methods which foster deep approaches to study by encouraging students to take personal initiative in the performance of the exercise. This might range from experimental design, choice of variables for investigation, choice of materials or methods, choice of methods of data analysis, through to choice of the problem for investigation. The investigation would usually be limited in time and scope and would not qualify as a project. Thus, it might be an extension of a controlled exercise which appealed to the student, or a variation of a well-known theme or method. Experimental investigations can be more or less structured—and often this means shorter or longer. Research on life in university classrooms shows that students are focused on their roles as designer, planner, and organizer, as well as on carrying out an experiment, and on discussions with higher-level questions and answers, whilst teachers may take the role of challenger and questioner, and support the student investigation by helping find materials and get organized (Hegarty-Hazel, 1990b).

Steps in conducting a student investigation, each of which could be the focus of faculty development programs, are:

- Define the objectives of the exercise
- Identify a series of problems which incorporate the subject area of interest
- Devise a series of research questions of a limited nature (e.g., 'What is the effect of changing pH and temperature on the growth characteristics of the bacteria provided?')
- Provide or suggest background resource materials
- Provide the range of equipment and materials necessary to solve the set problem tasks
- Describe the nature of the report required for assessment purposes

(Newble & Cannon, 1991, pp. 62-63)

Structured investigations retain teacher control of materials or methods whilst giving students an opportunity for enquiry. Unstructured investigations retain teacher control of the aim but allow students to plan the materials and methods. In practice, experienced teachers can do much to anticipate students' needs in the laboratory and avoid situations where unforeseen or unreasonable demands are placed on the technical support system.

Advantages of investigations. The first is the opportunity to allow students to practice skills of scientific enquiry, such as planning part or all of an experiment, whilst the second is the provision of a good motivational context. The two are linked: planning requires students to invest some personal initiative, and a sense of ownership and initiative is likely to be motivating. In the laboratory setting, it would seem that independent learning, project work, and experimental investigations share the qualities of independence and student motivation, but with decreasing freedom for independent learning.

Interviews with students show that they are very aware of the freedom for independence and of its effects on their motivation: the key to running successful investigations with junior students is not to throw them in from the deep end but to help them proceed from an adequate base of knowledge and skills. The idea of learning cycles is well described in the literature (e.g., Atkin & Karplus, 1963) and is further discussed in Boud et al. (1989).

Disadvantages of investigations. Why are controlled exercises retained as traditional fare? When do the disadvantages of investigations outweigh the advantages? Costenson and Lawson (1986) interviewed teachers and proffered a list of the top 10 teacher perceptions which have prevented the introduction of enquiry-oriented curricula into junior courses, or have resulted in this type of curriculum being discarded. Any faculty member introducing an investigative approach in undergraduate laboratory work might take note of which of these views they have heard expressed by colleagues.

1. Requires too much time and energy
2. Too slow
3. Required reading is too difficult
4. Risk is too high
5. Tracking—only the best students can cope
6. Student immaturity
7. Teaching habits are too ingrained
8. Sequential material is a management problem
9. Teacher discomfort with perceived loss of control
10. Too expensive

The issues at the heart of this worry list should be addressed in any staff development programs upon introduction of a new course. Sometimes such views are based more on perceived threat, prejudice, or conservatism than rationality and evidence. Sometimes, faculty have tried a move in the direction of investigations and found it a risky venture—things can go wrong technically, teachers can be underprepared and students can feel lost. A course designer or reviser must take care in the introduction of new investigations—for a university teacher, it is necessary to prepare yourself, your students, and your colleagues for their new roles in an enquiry-oriented program.

Project Work

Projects are major pieces of work which are intended to simulate elements of real-life research and development activities. It is usually necessary to devote significant periods of time to projects, likely to be from a few weeks to a semester or even one or two years of an undergraduate course. Project strategies are devised whereby students can apply prior knowledge to new problems, and, in doing so, to integrate various manual, technical, and enquiry skills in one coherent activity. Important characteristics are that the research problem must be a new one (where the student's experimental work and results could be seen as a genuine attempt to contribute to scientific knowledge) and that the student carries out the work in a research setting where there would be access to research supervisors or team leaders (in an apprenticeship role, with a potential mentor). One

key finding of research on life in university laboratories is that the more
the student work is like a project, the more students know what they are
doing and enjoy the experience (Bliss, 1990; Hegarty-Hazel, 1990b).

An approach to the task of supervising a project is outlined below. Each
of the steps, but especially the first and last, could be the focus of faculty
development exercises for supervisors.

- Meet with the student and agree on the objectives of the exercise
  and the problem to be researched.
- Work out a schedule of work covering the period during which
  the project is to be conducted, with provisional deadlines for
  completion of each stage (e.g., a literature review; hypothesis
  generation and experimental design; experimental work; data
  analysis; and report).
- Arrange a regular meeting time with the student to check
  progress (remember the task is to guide, not direct).
- Assist the students to prepare the final report or to give the
  seminar presentation by means of critical discussion and practice.
  (Newble & Cannon, 1991, p. 64)

Advantages of projects. Historically, participation in research projects
was the common mode of students working in science courses, but concerns of cost and convenience gradually led to the reservation of research
projects for postgraduate students and the use of controlled exercises for
undergraduates. However, since the mid-1970s, there has been a widespread
return to the use of projects with undergraduates. This seems to be a recognition of the need for students to be involved in intrinsically interesting,
personally involving activities which are true to the nature of a science
discipline (Bliss, 1990; Bliss & Ogborn, 1977; Dowdeswell & Harris, 1979;
Ogborn, 1977).

Benefits of project work are many. The learning is individualized and
students are likely to find their project a unique experience. Students are
encouraged to accept responsibility for a piece of work and to build up
some commitment to the scientific endeavor; they get the satisfaction of
working on a sustained task and the opportunity to enhance their oral and
written communication skills.

Disadvantages of projects and improving them. Conceptually, the disadvantages of projects are few—they seem ideally suited to students enhancing their technical, enquiry, and many other skills within a holistic
experience. Practically, projects can be risky. The initial choice of a problem
may be misguided, practical problems can result in overruns of time, energy, and cost, and the supervisory relationships may not work well. In
short, with the scale of project work, there is great need for careful plan-

ning by staff to ensure that the experience is a worthwhile one for each student. Special attention has been paid to the issues of care in organization and fairness in assessment and these issues have been explored by Dowdeswell and Harris (1979), Harris and Smith (1983), and Boud et al. (1989).

IMPROVING STUDENT LEARNING IN THE LABORATORY

Fostering Student Autonomy and Self-Direction

There is a great deal of interest at present in the notion of preparing students for lifelong learning and, allied with this, increasing self-direction and autonomy in learning. Most studies of graduates and employers show very high value for these goals so that evaluating one's own work may share a top place in the list with problem solving. It is argued that self-teaching is the natural state for adults—and that almost all of adult learning, taken over a lifespan, is done this way. University students are adults, or in transition to adulthood, so it follows that the university experience should be one emphasizing self-direction. University teaching should help improve the student's abilities and capacities to be a student.

By designing a laboratory program so students encounter teaching of several types across the continuum, from teacher-controlled exercises to more student-controlled exercises, much can be done to foster self-direction. However, one cannot assume that students will immediately want autonomy or that they will be willing or able to transfer their capabilities for control from one setting to another. Candy (1991) has a good account of the emotional issues which are involved and what teachers need to do to support the student's move across the continuum. He discusses issues such as individual differences in the acceptance of learner control (for example, preferences for directed instruction and learned helplessness), and the sense of personal control (for example, providing the opportunity to exert control, making learning an object of reflection, and situating learning in real-life contexts). A useful focus for faculty development would be to find ways of helping students take on responsibility for their learning in the laboratory—perhaps by increasing the diagnostic value of student record keeping and assessment. This would both help students with 'How am I going?' and help teachers know their students better, especially those at risk.

Strategies for Improving 'Studenting'

The laboratory can provide a setting, some would say the best setting, for students to reflect on their learning. Two major parts of fostering self-direction in learning by students in laboratories are developing skills for

self-directed learning and facilitating independent mastery of subject matter. In traditional laboratory manuals, the most common approach is to ask
some questions or set a problem extending the experiment. There is no
evidence that these are successful unless special attempts have been made
to draft questions asking students to reflect on their learning (Do I fully
understand this? Do I understand enough to justify stopping? What do I
have to do to achieve full understanding? Is it worth doing?) (Baird, 1990).

Two techniques which have proved successful in fostering reflection in
the laboratory are concept maps and Vee maps. Both have been discussed
in detail by Novak (1990) in an exploration of the interplay of theory and
methodology in the laboratory.

Concept mapping. With this technique, students map out their understanding of a scientific concept in a diagrammatic way to show the mean-
ings and relationships. Concepts are linked by scientific propositions which
describe the relationships. Research studies show many valuable qualities
of concept maps. Students of all ages can learn to use them successfully
and the ability to produce good concept maps is related to deep approaches
to study (Hegarty-Hazel & Prosser, 1991a, 1991b). Students like doing the
maps and mapping has a positive effect on both their learning and attitudes to science. Students who use concept mapping in the laboratory are
likely to have a good idea of what they are doing and may be expected to
be less prone to blindly 'following a recipe.'

Vee maps. These provide a diagrammatic representation of students'
understanding of the interplay of the theory and methodology behind the
events which occur in an experiment. They were designed to sharpen students' thinking about the "telling question," the key concepts, the methods of enquiry used, and the conclusions as knowledge claims and value
claims. For convenience, the heuristic is arranged in Vee form to prompt
questions about relationships. Research studies have found that Vee maps
can be used successfully by secondary-school students and university students, and that students using Vee maps have better understanding of their
laboratory experiments, more positive attitudes, and more of a constructivist
view of knowledge (Novak, 1990). Although Vee maps look a bit odd and
may be regarded with initial suspicion, students usually like them and find
them useful.

Reflective journals. A more general approach to enhancing students'
knowledge and control of their learning would be to have them keep reflective journals (Boud, Keogh, & Walker, 1985) and these have been a key
part of several recent projects aimed at improving the quality of students'
learning (Gibbs, 1992). These would be simply a diary or log where entries
could be made for each lab exercise and project, or at regular time inter-

vals. Candy (1991) cautioned that a high degree of self discipline and critical reflectivity is required to report on one's own learning as it unfolds, but he commended reflective journals for tracking thoughts and emotions more closely than in *post hoc* reconstructions. In some settings, it may be found that keeping a reflective journal without prompts may be a difficult task for junior students. However, this will likely change when more secondary-school students have experience with journal keeping. Teachers can provide prompts in the form of questions or cues or show examples of reflective journals kept in a variety of different styles.

ASSESSMENT OF STUDENTS' LABORATORY WORK

Provision of Worthwhile Assessment in the Laboratory

The provision of meaningful assessment which fosters valuable student learning is one of the chief educational challenges in the higher education of our era. Regular indiscriminate assessment of laboratory work is a notorious burden for teaching staff, as well as students, and it is doubtful whether it serves a useful purpose for either diagnosis or certification. The improvement of assessment so that it "counts" in the laboratory for both students and staff is an issue for faculty development.

Looking at the broad perspective of student assessment and the values of academic institutions, Boud (1990) makes a strong link between learning and assessment and argues that many assessment practices are incompatible with the goals of independence, thoughtfulness, and critical analysis. Boud et al. (1989) highlight the special issues for the laboratory. These authors see the following challenges to university teachers:

1. Low priority has been given to the provision of assessment for diagnosis (formative assessment) because of convenience. Rather, high priority should be given because of the influence of good quality feedback on improving the quality of student learning. Diagnostic feedback, which is readily accepted by students, is timely, specific, direct, and touches only matters which are within the student's control. Time and energy can be saved by streamlining the process using stylized feedback schemes on lab work, teamwork, and reporting in the lab.

2. Students are assessed on those matters on which it is easy to assess them, and this leads to an over-emphasis on memory and lower-level skills, such as technical ability in the laboratory. If students perceive performance of technical skills or recall of procedures to be rewarded before all else, they will emphasize

those. Yet, if they see investigations or problem solving emphasized, they will tend to practice enquiry skills or solving problems.

3. Assessment encourages students to focus on those topics which are assessed, at the expense of those which are not. Where laboratory work may take a great deal of students' time but receive a very low proportion of the marks in a subject overall, students may take the message that lab work is unimportant or that the skills of the experimentalist are less valued than those of the theoretician. Students may decline to turn up for lab sessions or may be tempted to copy results and reports to save work.

4. Successful students seek cues from teachers to enable them to identify what is important for formal assessment purposes. Addressing this issue means identifying the relationship between important objectives and assessment—ascertaining that what is important is what is assessed. Teachers could provide cues to students in a formal way by showing what constitutes exemplary lab work or exemplary lab reports.

5. Assessment tasks are set which encourage a narrow, instrumental approach to learning that emphasizes the reproduction of what is presented, at the expense of critical thinking, deep understanding, and independent activity. In the lab, this might mean setting the performance of a project or its report as the main item of assessment and reducing the practice of assessing reports on each lab exercise.

6. Unilateral assessment, in which staff decide on the aims and objectives, the assessment tasks, the criteria for judgment, and the final outcomes for the process, has other intrinsic consequences and limitations. In particular, it can obstruct the attainment of one of the common goals of higher education—that students should take responsibility for their own learning. There is a variety of ways in which student laboratory work can be assessed by teachers. Although the literature suggests there has been limited experience with self assessment and peer assessment, these could have advantages in cost saving as well as building for autonomy. (adapted from Boud, 1990, pp. 102-104, and Boud et al., 1989, pp.79-106)

Assessment Techniques

There are many techniques for assessing students' work in the laboratory and choice amongst them will depend on the objectives of the work. Providing there are clear statements of the course objectives and clear indication of which objectives should be met in students' lab work, then assessment can be directly linked to criteria. In practice, good laboratory assessments can both test important educational objectives and contribute to grading (Boud et al., 1989).

Criterion-referenced testing can be used successfully in the laboratory with a range of objectives, including laboratory knowledge and comprehension, observing and measuring, recognizing problems, devising ways to investigate problems or enquire, interpreting, drawing conclusions from data gathered, and communicating (Boud et al., 1989; Klopfer, 1971). For any objective, there would usually be a choice of testing methods, some of which are illustrated in the following section.

Practical tests allow direct testing of a student's ability to perform laboratory tasks under practical examination conditions and have a definite place where laboratory work helps students meet professional standards or is part of a competency-based program. With adequate practice and preparation, students can do practical tests in an environment that is both realistic and supportive.

Observing and measuring are aspects of scientific enquiry for which practical tests are essential. However, skills of interpretation and skills of problem identification and investigation can also be tested in a practical situation. These objectives can be tested under examination conditions by presenting students with phenomena to observe and/or with experiments, partly done by the teacher, for which students might take measurements, interpret results, make the next decision, or carry out the next action.

Observations are essentially similar to practical tests, but they are usually conducted as part of normal work, not under examination conditions. Teachers are asked to observe a student's performance in carrying out techniques or manipulations in the laboratory. The great advantage of observation is that it is, by definition, direct. Any alternative method when such objectives are important would be a surrogate, measuring by inference.

A reliable observation scheme can be constructed easily as long as the criteria to be assessed are clearly agreed and a checklist of behavior can be developed. Assessing students' performance by impressionistic marking is not likely to be very helpful.

Observers must develop lists of criteria for assessment of laboratory skills. In each setting, it is necessary to determine the standards to be met. Some skills may be considered essential and are best assessed with mastery standards, looking for near 100% performance. These can easily be organized into a barrier examination whereby students are not permitted to continue to the final examination until they have shown satisfactory performance on the mastery skills examination. In this case, opportunities for feedback and re-testing have to be provided.

Written tests are often used inappropriately in laboratory settings. If performance is required for a profession or for successful participation in a later course, a written test is no guarantee of standards. However, useful written tests could concern knowledge of laboratory equipment. Tests could make use of photographs or diagrams of equipment. Students could be asked to read scales and determine measurements, to select correct settings, or to choose suitable conditions for operation. They could examine an illustration and decide whether a piece of equipment has been set up correctly. Other common uses for written tests include making calculations, error analysis, preparing graphs, and other data manipulation techniques.

Design posters. In recent years, presentation of posters has become a regular feature of conferences in most areas of science and technology. These can be used for assessment of parts of students' laboratory work and, at the same time, introduce the idea of conference presentations. Design of experimental investigations is one of the most important parts of laboratory work, and posters are a good way for individual students or groups to display their designs. Posters can be very appropriately assessed by student peers in emulation of the conference situation, as well as by faculty or as a self assessment.

Written and oral reports are probably the most conventional forms of assessment of students' laboratory work. Reporting mirrors an important activity for scientists and plays a useful role in building an appreciation of the ways in which scientists work and in the socialization of students. The main cautions needed are to realize that both are indirect techniques and both are *post hoc* reconstructions (the same is often said of scientific publications, but in the students' case, presents a need for checking what did actually transpire in the classes). Other cautions include the need to protect against bias on grounds of gender and to be aware that it has sometimes been found that the factor most highly correlated with high grades in reports is neatness.

INTRODUCING CHANGE IN LABORATORY PROGRAMS

Many laboratory programs are characterized far more by stability than by change. What makes an innovation successful? A new or changed laboratory program should foster improved student learning in a way which reflects the university mission and the department's special contribution to teaching and research. As with innovations in other areas of university provision, the new program should be demonstrably superior to the practice it replaces (Moses, 1988). The organization and its authorities should provide power and resources to support the innovation. There should be ongoing evaluation of the program and the course coordinator would often be in a good position to identify areas where change is needed. Someone has to take responsibility for introducing the new or changed program and for steering its impact on any related or follow-up courses. Because departmental leaders, such as the head and coordinator of undergraduate programs, are in strong positions to take initiating or responsible roles, their support is invaluable.

Sudden innovations are seldom acceptable. The following suggestions are for the gradual introduction of innovations in laboratory programs and for supportive faculty development programs.

FACULTY DEVELOPMENT AND SUPPORTING INNOVATIONS IN LABORATORY PROGRAMS

Supporting Innovators

Academic leaders can foster the innovator role amongst faculty by valuing and rewarding innovation and avoiding situations where an innovation is marginalized. In my experience, the best ways to demonstrate changes in the academic climate include: inviting innovators to show their work to other departments within the university; encouraging them to document their work for presentation at conferences and publish in the journal literature; valuing their educational development, teaching, and scholarship when they present a case for tenure or promotion; and supporting their role as leaders in internal or externally-funded teaching development projects.

Faculty development can play a valuable role in supporting innovations in both teaching and program design in the laboratory. Faculty retreats, workshops, or seminars could be used to help build a supportive environment where academic staff can be introduced to new ideas in laboratory teaching. One approach which has been used with success has been to observe exemplary teachers in the laboratory or on videotape. At the University of Technology, Sydney (AUS), a videotape has been made with vignettes of innovative teaching in practical settings and it has been useful for faculty to see others in their own laboratory teaching contexts and be able to discuss ideas which could be adopted (and those which could not). Complementary micro-teaching sessions enable faculty and teaching assistants to review their own teaching styles in the laboratory and to try out new approaches which may be needed as part of a new program.

Faculty retreats, workshops, or seminars can also be used to help build an environment rich in ideas which faculty could use in innovative program design. Development sessions could be used to help faculty use the science journal literature to provide ideas for student investigations and research projects. Scientists from local research institutes could be invited to provide ideas or material on their current investigations which could be used in student projects. The networking strategies used by faculty could be enhanced in development sessions to strengthening links with a wide range of contemporary scientists, finding ways for such professionals to interact with students as well as teachers in the laboratory.

Building Department Commitment to Change

Most of the faculty development strategies which have proved useful in building department commitment involve engaging the academic expertise of a range of faculty across a department. For example, ask several colleagues to evaluate old and new laboratory exercises for their difficulty, level of enquiry, types of science processes represented, coherence of the theory, and methodology. It could be done in a workshop setting or by circulation of analyses. Other and complementary strategies are to encourage colleagues to contribute to a new program one exercise, or one sequence, based on their research, consulting, or other scholarly interests, and to invite them to be involved in trials of the new program, acting as teachers, students, or observers. More general approaches to building support would be circulating literature, inviting speakers, organizing a faculty development retreat about the aims and methods of a new program, sponsoring academic staff development programs on fostering high quality student learning in the laboratory.

Offering quality programs requires cooperation between faculty and a variety of university staff who might include professional technical staff, workshop staff, and printers, as well as administrators. It can greatly enhance the smooth running of laboratory classes, and especially the introduction of change, to form quality teams to look at ways of adopting new roles or more flexible approaches to organizing and supplying student materials; ways of estimating how much new equipment, materials, or other resources will be required; and how much could be done by modification of existing resources or in visits to alternative facilities. The team can also be the focus for deciding how to find resources for an innovation, where to pitch development applications, how to approach the institution, government, or private foundation for support of an innovation.

Supporting the Students' Growth in Autonomy

Improving the quality of students' learning in the laboratory requires direct attention to the students as well as to faculty development on teaching and course design. To succeed, an innovation should be carefully matched to students' needs and should provide support in areas where students may lack experience.

In a program of faculty development, the issue is how can faculty support students so that they are able to participate in and succeed in a new or revised laboratory program. If a laboratory program is to place greater emphasis on developing students' autonomy as learners, faculty could seek ways of sequencing the exercises so that there is gradual building from student dependence on the teacher for design and control to greater independence in laboratory investigations—if students are thrown in at the deep end it can be a distressing experience for all concerned. If a program is to emphasize scientific enquiry, problem solving, or issues-based learning, faculty need to explore ways of making these matters explicit to students as well as whatever may be implicit in the new program design.

Ideas can be introduced or practiced in the setting of faculty development—not only ways to implement the ideas, but monitoring and giving feedback. Thus, a faculty development program on the use of reflective journals in the lab could include simulations where faculty work with students' reflections, finding ways of giving students high quality feedback.

Improving the Design of Laboratory Exercises

Where faculty are designing new laboratory exercises, a development program might focus on the issues of design and delivery: defining objectives of the exercises and communicating these to students, identifying problems for investigation, devising research questions, identifying resources needed, and designing appropriate assessment. More often, faculty are in the situation of modifying existing exercises. Issues for faculty development might include clarifying the objectives and structure of exercises so they address a few aspects well, modifying controlled exercises to be used as investigations, running projects at the undergraduate level, and dealing with increased student enrollments.

In my 20 or so years of faculty development work on student laboratories in the biological and physical sciences, I have found that a consistently valuable way for teachers to get started on design or revision of a program is to learn to use the analysis scheme described earlier in this chapter for looking at the level of openness for scientific enquiry in each of the exercises to be undertaken by students. The scheme can be used as a content analysis, where level of enquiry is assigned on the basis of the written instructions which are supplied to students for each exercise, or in a laboratory manual. It can be applied to all or a sample of the current exercises. Faculty who see the profile of their student exercises shown in this manner can readily decide whether it meets their expectations and can define the direction of any changes needed in a new or revised program.

One approach is for an expert panel to grade all the exercises and present the results to a faculty curriculum committee for a decision on the profile. Another approach, which seems to have greater potential for commitment to curriculum change and to faculty development, is to involve a wide range of teachers by having a few faculty members analyze the same set of exercises.

Developing Teachers' Good Practice in the Laboratory

Being aware of these attributes can encourage laboratory teachers to be more critical of their approach and to identify aspects they may wish to change. Changing awareness and providing a supportive environment in which teachers can practice new or changed behaviors are areas which can be well dealt with in a faculty development program.

Some desirable attributes of the laboratory teacher are (adapted from both general and specific sources in Horobin, Williams, & Anderson, 1992, p. 33; Newble & Cannon, 1991, p. 58; Ramsden, 1992, p. 89):

Sharing enthusiasm and making laboratory work an enjoyable experience for students. Finding ways for love of the subject to come across to students, helping make the students' work relevant, interesting, stimulating, and challenging. Being friendly, helpful, and available to the students. Using humor and other techniques for fostering an enjoyable, relaxed, and non-stressful atmosphere in the laboratory. Being a good role model for students.

Showing expertise. Being on top of the subject matter, being well prepared for the lab, being familiar with the ideas of the subject, the design of experiments, the use of equipment. Making it clear what has to be done and understood and why; making clear explanations about the ideas, material, and activities; using assessment methods which are valid and reliable; and giving students prompt and high quality feedback on their work.

Respecting students. Demonstrating respect for each student as a person; valuing diversity; demonstrating a positive attitude and teaching free of discrimination or stereotyping of students because of gender or ethnicity; and monitoring student groupings in the lab and the nature of classroom interactions to bring out the best in each student.

Fostering student independence and growth. Supporting students warmly when they are in high challenge situations; encouraging active participation by students; and avoiding having them stand around in an observational capacity in the lab.

Enhancing student learning. Emphasizing critical thinking, problem-solving, aspects of scientific enquiry, and other intellectual activities which require the students to think. Encouraging students to focus on the integration of the practical exercises with the learning of material taught in other components of the course. Encouraging students to have a lively understanding of the interplay of theory and methodology in the laboratory.

Meeting students where they are in their learning. Supervising students closely enough to recognize those having difficulties with the concepts on which the laboratory exercises are based. Showing encouragement and empathy. Giving students positive feedback and encouraging them to note their own achievements. Providing adequate opportunities for students to practice their skills and to receive precise feedback.

CONCLUSION

Ubiquitous though they may be in science settings, laboratories are an under-examined resource. Discipline-specific accounts are needed of high quality student learning and assessment in different laboratory settings. What aspects of course design and teaching foster students' appreciation of the work of scientists and development as scientists? What aspects of course design and teaching foster students' autonomy as learners and their commitment to lifelong learning? What characterizes good practice in laboratory teaching for science majors in their major field and that for students from another field or in a service course? Which aspects of faculty development are discipline specific?

Course designers should seek ways of lifting the level of challenge and enquiry of student exercises and ways of obtaining profiles of student learning in the laboratory. Rather than bald numerical scores typically based on a global assessment of laboratory reports, assessment should be linked to explicit objectives for a course. How has the laboratory program enhanced students' scientific imagination and creativity, their practical skills, their understanding of the interplay of theory and methodology, their enquiry skills, their teamwork, communication (or other) skills? How does the assessment foster students' deep engagement with the discipline? How is the laboratory program overall contributing to the profile of graduates and to the department's mission?

Academic leaders and faculty developers should seek ways of making student laboratories an object of both support and scrutiny. What is being done to support faculty in their roles as innovators, designers and teachers, to develop teaching assistants in the academic role, to develop students as autonomous and reflective learners in the laboratory? What evidence is there that high quality student learning is fostered in the laboratory setting? In what ways can laboratory resources be enhanced? Are there parts or all of a laboratory program which could be replaced by the use of kits, videotape, computer assisted learning, interactive multimedia packages or private study?

What is being suggested here is the serious examination of a precious and under-exploited resource for student learning—the science laboratory.

REFERENCES

Anderson, O.R. (1976). *The experience of science: A new perspective for laboratory teaching.* New York, NY: Teachers College Press.

Atkin, J.M., & Karplus, R. (1963). Discovery or invention? *Science Teacher, 29,* 45-51.

Baird, J.R. (1990). Metacognition, purposeful enquiry and conceptual change. In E. Hegarty-Hazel (Ed.), *The student laboratory and the science curriculum* (pp. 183-200). London, UK: Routledge.

Bliss, J. (1990). Student reactions to undergraduate science: Laboratory and project work. In E. Hegarty-Hazel (Ed.), *The student laboratory and the science curriculum* (pp. 383-396). London, UK: Routledge.

Bliss, J., & Ogborn, J. (1977). *Student reactions to undergraduate science .* London, UK: Heinemann.

Bloom, B.S., Hastings, J.T., & Madaus, G.F. (Eds.). (1971). *Handbook of formative and summative evaluation of student learning.* New York, NY: McGraw Hill.

Boud, D. (1990). Assessment and the promotion of academic values. *Studies in Higher Education, 15,* 101-111.

Boud, D., Dunn, J., & Hegarty-Hazel, E. (1989). *Teaching in laboratories.* Guildford, UK: Open University Press.

Boud, D., Keogh, R., & Walker, D. (Eds.) (1985). *Reflection: Turning experience into learning.* London, UK: Kogan Page.

Candy, P.C. (1991). *Self-direction for lifelong learning: A comprehensive guide to theory and practice.* San Francisco, CA: Jossey-Bass.

Costenson, K., & Lawson, A.E. (1986). Why isn't inquiry used in more classrooms? *The American Biology Teacher, 48,* 150-158.

Dowdeswell, W.H., & Harris, N.D.C. (1979). Project work in university science. In D. McNally (Ed.), *Learning strategies in university science* (pp. 203-240). University College Cardiff Press: ICSU Committee on the Teaching of Science.

Gibbs, G. (1992). *Improving the quality of student learning*. Bristol, UK: Technical and Education Services.

Harris, N.D.C., & Smith, B. (1983). Undergraduate project work. *Assessment and Evaluation in Higher Education, 8,* 280-288.

Hegarty-Hazel, E. (Ed.) (1990a). *The student laboratory and the science curriculum.* London, UK: Routledge.

Hegarty-Hazel, E. (1990b). Life in science laboratory classrooms at tertiary level. In E. Hegarty-Hazel (Ed.), *The student laboratory and the science curriculum* (pp. 357-382). London, UK: Routledge.

Hegarty-Hazel, E., & Cheary, R. (1993). Curriculum reform in physical science programs. *Research and Development in Higher Education, 15,* 426-433.

Hegarty-Hazel, E., & Prosser, M. (1991a). Relationship between students' conceptual knowledge and study strategies. Part II Student learning in Biology. *International Journal of Science Education, 13,* 421-429.

Hegarty-Hazel, E., & Prosser, M. (1991b). Relationship between students' conceptual knowledge and study strategies. Part I Student learning in Physics. *International Journal of Science Education, 13,* 303-312.

Herron, M.D. (1971). The nature of scientific enquiry. *School Review, 79,* 171-212.

Horobin, R. & Williams, M., with Anderson, B. (1992). Active learning in practical classes. Module 6. In Cryer, P. (Ed.), *Effective learning and teaching in higher education.* Sheffield, UK: CVCP Universities' Staff Development and Training Unit.

Klopfer, L.E. (1971). Evaluation of learning in science. In B.S. Bloom, J.T. Hastings, & G.F. Madaus (Eds.), *Handbook of formative and summative evaluation of student learning.* New York, NY: McGraw Hill.

Klopfer, L.E. (1990). Learning scientific enquiry in the student laboratory. In E. Hegarty-Hazel (Ed.), *The student laboratory and the science curriculum* (pp. 95-118). London, UK: Routledge.

Layton, D. (1990). Student laboratory practice and the history and philosophy of science. In E. Hegarty-Hazel (Ed.), *The student laboratory and the science curriculum* (pp. 37-59). London, UK: Routledge.

Mallow, J.V. (1981). *Science anxiety: Fear of science and how to overcome it.* New York, NY: Van Nostrand Reinhold.

McNally, D. (Ed.). (1979). *Learning strategies in university science.* University College Cardiff Press: ICSU Committee on the Teaching of Science.

Moses, I. (1988). *Academic staff evaluation and development: A university case study*. St Lucia, AUS: University of Queensland Press.

Newble, D., & Cannon, R. (1991). *A handbook for teachers in universities and colleges: A guide to improving teaching methods* (rev. ed.). London, UK: Kogan Page.

Novak, J.D. (1990). The interplay of theory and methodology. In E. Hegarty-Hazel (Ed.), *The student laboratory and the science curriculum* (pp. 60-74). London, UK: Routledge.

Ogborn, J.M. (Ed.). (1977). *Practical work in undergraduate science*. London, UK: Heinemann.

Ramsden, P. (1992). *Learning to teach in higher education*. London, UK: Routledge.

Rigden, J.S., & Tobias, S. (1991). Tune in, turn off, drop out. *The Sciences, 31*(1), 16-20.

Tobias, S. (1990). They're not dumb. They're different. *Change, 22*(4), 11-30.

Venkatachelam, C., & Rudolph, R.W., (1974). Cookbook versus creative chemistry. *Journal of Chemical Education, 51*, 479-482.

READING LIST

Books

Boud, D., Dunn, J., & Hegarty-Hazel, E. (1986, 1989 rev. ed.). *Teaching in laboratories*. Guildford, UK: SRHE and NFER–Nelson/Open University.

Hegarty-Hazel, E. (1990). *The student laboratory and the science curriculum*. London, UK: Routledge.

Ogborn, J.M. (Ed.). (1977). *Practical work in undergraduate science*. London, UK: Heinemann.

Guides

Gibbs, G. (1989). Practical and laboratory teaching. Module 4. In Gibbs, G. (Ed.), *Certificate in teaching in higher education by Open Learning* (pp. 1-40). Oxford, UK: Oxford Centre for Staff Development.

Horobin, R., & Williams, M., & Anderson, B. (1992). Active learning in practical classes. Module 6. In Cryer, P. (Ed.), *Effective learning and teaching in higher education* (pp. 1-68). Sheffield, UK: CVCP Universities' Staff Development and Training Unit.

Chapters

Brown, G., & Atkins, M. (1988). Effective laboratory teaching. Chapter 5 (pp. 91-114) in*Effective teaching in higher education*. London, UK: Methuen/Routledge.

Newble, D., & Cannon, R. (1991). Teaching practical and laboratory classes. Chapter 4 (pp. 57-69) in *A handbook for teachers in universities and colleges: A guide to improving teaching methods* (rev. ed.). New York, NY: Kogan Page.

AUTHOR

Elizabeth Hazel is Associate Professor in the Centre for Learning and Teaching at the University of Technology, Sydney, Australia. A biological scientist by background, she has longstanding interests in both science and science education which are reflected in her choice of doctoral studies on the role of the laboratory in students' learning in science and in her many publications. She is an author and editor of two major international books on the student laboratory and the science curriculum. Dr. Hazel has been the director of a variety of projects on learning in science and on the recruitment and retention of women as students and scientist, as well as gender and students' perceptions of learning in the science laboratory.

7.

From Shaping Performances to Dynamic Interaction: The Quiet Revolution in Teaching Improvement Programs

Richard G. Tiberius

Programs for improving teaching and learning have changed dramatically over the last few decades. The techniques and strategies have become more individualized, more sensitive to context, and more interactive, and developers' use of these methods has also evolved. Students and teachers have a larger, more active role in their own development, and developers tend to be more eclectic in their selection of methods.

INTRODUCTION

There is a quiet revolution taking place in the design of programs for teaching improvement. I used the word "quiet" in my title because the new programs have not announced themselves with great fanfare. In the 1970s, we had improvement programs based on student questionnaires, on practice with feedback, on video playback, and on individualized consulting. The programs we have today still fit into these categories. The occasional traveler in the land of teaching improvement may get the false impression that nothing changes. But a more focused and historical examination of programs reveals important developments. Indeed, I used the word "revolution" in my title because both the aims and the process of teaching improvement programs have changed remarkably in the last few decades.

The aim of traditional teaching improvement programs was to equip teachers with a set of generic teaching skills and performances. The teacher who possessed such skills could presumably "go forth and teach" *anyone* under *any* circumstances. Although the instructional development community still considers generic skills to be important—particularly for beginning teachers—programs are now being designed to address specific teaching problems and particular contexts. Perhaps even more dramatic are the attempts to help teachers acquire the communication and relationship skills needed to continually enhance their own teaching in dynamic response to changing conditions.

The *process* of teaching improvement is evolving, too. Traditional programs demonstrated and explained model performances and shaped weak ones (those that did not conform to the model) by means of practice with corrective feedback. Increasingly, programs are being designed that improve teaching not only by correcting performances, but also by discovering and enhancing strengths in the teachers. Teachers are being given more choice in how they will improve and more responsibility for the process of their own development. Moreover, the burden of responsibility for educational development is shifting from one that is the teachers' alone to one that is shared between teachers and students. The traditional focus on teacher performance is shifting to a focus on the teacher *and* the learner, their relationship, and their context.

This chapter examines five different types of teaching improvement programs from the point of view of this trend toward individualization, situational specificity, and a more dynamic and interactive process. The purpose is to demonstrate the exciting developments that have taken place in these programs over the last few decades; to provide an organizational framework for colleagues who find the vast array of contemporary programs confusing; to shed some light on why some programs might fail while others, that seem so similar, succeed; and, finally, to suggest ways in which faculty developers and instructional leaders can capitalize on the refined forms of these programs when planning teaching and learning activities in their own settings.

EVALUATION-GENERATED IMPROVEMENT: STUDENT QUESTIONNAIRES

The most common type of teaching improvement program is based on student ratings of teaching, and the use of student ratings is increasing in universities and colleges across North America. Essentially, the method consists of gathering feedback from students and presenting it to the teacher. A number of reviews of the literature have shown feedback from student ratings to be reliable and to have a positive effect on teaching (Centra, 1982; Menges & Brinko, 1986). However, the effectiveness of such evaluative feedback in improving teaching is based on a number of assumptions: feedback must bring some information to the teacher that he or she does not already have, the teacher must *value* the new information, must have the *motivation* to want to do something about it, and, finally, must know *how* to change (Centra, 1993).

Early evaluation-driven programs frequently violated most, if not all, of these assumptions, with the consequence that they enjoyed mixed success. Teachers, who were too busy to make up questionnaires tailored to their own situations, bought or borrowed "standard" questionnaires from other institutions. One of the inherent problems of standard questionnaires is that they often fail to address the specific issues that are troubling one's teaching. And even when they do, the way the items are expressed may not be the same as the way they are experienced by students and may not be phrased in the language of the students. Consequently, the information was seldom newsworthy. Moreover, students saw the questionnaires as scarcely relevant to their real learning situation; their motivation to complete them fell, and so did the validity of their responses (since too few students filled them out to provide a sufficient basis for generalization to the class).

The history of student ratings feedback is one of continuous invention of devices to make them more context sensitive, more specific, more helpful to individual teachers, and to give teachers and students a greater degree of control and responsibility over the process. A brief description of some of the main innovations is instructive.

Item Content

Early evaluation forms focused on teacher characteristics. For decades, virtually all of the commercially available rating forms included essentially the same list of teacher characteristics—effective communication skills, rapport, knowledge of the subject, organization, enthusiasm, fairness, and ability to stimulate self-learning and thinking. This high level of consistency resulted from a consensus based on many studies directed at identifying the primary teacher behaviors associated with effective teaching (e.g., Wotruba and Wright, 1975).

Today, many rating forms have expanded their item content beyond teacher characteristics to include other components of the teaching-learning situation, such as laboratories, assignments, textbooks, media, exams, and the contributions of teaching assistants. Such items enable evaluators and teachers to understand the extent to which these other components of the course are perceived to be successful (see The Student Instructional Report, 1989; Instructor and Course Evaluation System, Student Instructional Rating System, 1982).

Some rating forms (e.g., IDEA, 1988) contain student self-ratings of their study habits, including the amount of time and effort they put into the course, their interest in the course, and so on. Such items enable teachers to learn about aspects of their students' lives that may profoundly affect their learning. For example, the interpretation of student ratings of a teacher might change if it came to light that students really were not studying the material because of competing pressures.

Finally, some rating forms include items designed to measure the degree to which the *objectives* of the course *are achieved*. Such items are too specific for standard forms since they refer to the specific objectives of a particular course and teacher. Commercially available forms get around this limitation by offering a menu of possible objectives from which teachers can choose (e.g., IDEA, 1988).

The Specificity of Items

Rating systems that are aimed at improving teaching must elicit responses that are specific enough to give the teachers sufficient understanding of the problems to form a plan of improvement. Yet early forms typically contained items describing teacher characteristics, such as fairness, and items describing general performance, such as "speaking skills." (A noteworthy exception was the University of Massachusetts' "Teaching Assessment by Students"—TABS—which consisted of behaviorally specific items, such as "The instructor's explanation of the work expected from each student"). Although there is no conclusive evidence as yet to substantiate the superiority of behaviorally specific items for teaching improvement, a strong case has been made in their favor (see Murray, 1987).

Student Response Options

Traditional rating forms gave students an opportunity to indicate the degree to which they agreed with a brief description of some characteristic of a teacher or component of a course. The characteristic was always written in the positive sense, for example, "The teacher gives clear explanations." Even when the concern was a negative one, the item was worded in the positive sense, for example, "The amount of work covered in the course is reasonable." The requirement to respond only by indicating degree of agreement is quite constraining. A simple agreement response mode did not allow students to express the view that the teacher does give clear explanations, but not very often. The agreement response mode was designed for items that described characteristics about teachers, the old teaching-as-performance metaphor again. The IDEA system (1988), in contrast, requires students to indicate the *frequency of occurrence* of a particular characteristic or behavior rather than agreement with it. Such items allowed students to indicate that their teacher gives clear explanations "hardly ever," "occasionally," "sometimes," "frequently," and "almost always."

Another interesting response option was developed at the University of Iowa. The form asked students how *helpful* each of these aspects of the course *are to your learning*. The beauty of this response mode is that it enables the student to judge the relative value to their learning of various components of the course which is not the same as judging the quality of each component. For example, the tutorials may have been clear and well organized but still may not have contributed much to learning in the course.

The expansion of student response options enables the evaluator to focus more specifically on the precise aspect of teaching that is under examination. If the evaluator wants to know how strongly the student holds a particular perception, then "degree of agreement" might be the response mode of choice; if the evaluator wants to know how frequently a behavior has occurred, then "frequency of occurrence" might be the response mode of choice; and if the evaluator wants to know the impact of a particular aspect of the course on learning then the "degree of helpfulness to your learning" might be the response mode of choice. Years ago, these fine distinctions were blurred when discussing the results of a typical evaluation focused on teaching characteristics. If a teacher was rated high in "communication skills," we assumed a host of specific behaviors and assumed all sorts of beneficial effects on learning.

Choice of Items

Standard questionnaires contained items that were fixed. When such items were perceived as irrelevant to a particular course, they bored both teachers and students; teachers tended to pay less attention to the feedback, and students became less conscientious about completing the forms. The Measurement and Research Center at Purdue University (US) developed one of the first widely used rating systems which allowed substantial choice of items. The system, called CAFETERIA (1980) is commercially available. From a catalogue of 200 items, each instructor selects 35 which best fit her or his individual course requirements and purposes. The teacher records the items by catalog number on a special request form and mails the form to the processing center. At the center, a tailored rating instrument is generated, by computer, from the teacher's own choices. Today, there are several flexible student rating evaluation systems. James Kulik's (1987) "Instructor-Designed Questionnaires," or IDQ is one which provides a pool of over 900 items out of which the teacher can select up to 35 to compose an individualized questionnaire. The result is an efficient, highly relevant questionnaire that delivers precisely what each teacher really needs to know without annoying students with irrelevant items.

Instructor-Written Items

Even item banks as large as 900 items may not provide all the questions that teachers would like to ask. Therefore, popular ratings systems have been designed to allow instructors to write in items themselves, like the instrument "Students' Evaluation of Educational Quality" (SEEQ, 1991). The number of spaces provided for write-in questions varies from just a few to over 20. Although teacher-written items provide teachers with the opportunity to add very specific items, there is a drawback. Most teachers benefit from a menu from which to select since they can seldom define all of the dimensions that are relevant to their teaching. Since the questions in the item banks have been tested, simply selecting from the list eliminates the difficulty teachers have wording the questions unambiguously.

Teacher-Generated Rating Forms

Perhaps the most individualized and context-specific form of student rating is the teacher-generated rating form. Although it gives control of the process to the teacher, designing a comprehensive rating form and standardizing it requires more specialized skills and time than most teachers have available. Teachers are urged to buy, borrow, or adapt an existing rating form. On the other hand, these caveats do not apply to *brief* teacher-generated evaluation forms, such as the so-called "mini-forms" advocated by Patricia Cross and Tom Angelo (1988). Cross and Angelo recommend using only three to five questions which can be administered in less than ten or 15 minutes at the end of the class. The purpose of the mini-forms is to gather limited, *focused* data. For example, a teacher may ask whether her examples were helpful and whether she used a sufficient number of them. Students would respond on a five-point scale with anchor points clearly identified by a phrase such as "more examples would be redundant" on one pole and "more examples are necessary" on the other. Another teacher may choose to ask whether his examples are *simple* enough or *brief* enough rather than *clear* enough.

The mini-forms are not intended to provide a comprehensive, end-of-class survey of the entire course. They are spot checks. Indeed, Cross and Angelo recommend that they be administered at regular intervals, such as a quarter and half-way through the course. Since they are written by teachers, the questions can be worded to take into consideration the specific context and thus provide a better basis for improvement of teaching.

Moreover, Cross and Angelo emphasize the importance of completing the feedback loop by describing to the class both a summary of the results and the specific actions that the teacher will take in response to the feedback. This public disclosure of the process is very important to student morale. It shows students that the teacher respects their views and cares enough about them to change her or his teaching to accommodate them. The authors recommend that teachers ask questions about only those things that they can change, and then promise more modest changes than they think they can achieve so that they do not have to disappoint the students. Since teacher-generated rating forms are more intimate and personal than standard rating forms, they provide an occasion for building rapport with students. The entire process—the gathering of feedback, disclosure to the class of the plan for change, implementation of the changes, and subsequent re-evaluation—can take place several times during a semester. The result is a continual readjustment of the implicit contract between teacher and students, a dynamic interchange that is the basis of cooperative action.

PRACTICE WITH FEEDBACK

Practice with feedback has always been the quintessential approach to skills-training. In the days when the teaching improvement field was dominated by a concept of teaching as a set of skills, practice with feedback was one of the most popular approaches. Historically, the most widely used of these approaches, particularly in elementary and high school education, was micro-teaching.

Micro-Teaching

The original micro-teaching program, as described by its designers Dwight Allen and Kevin Ryan (1969), was a training device that focused on the classroom in microcosm, a highly simplified version of the classroom environment. It allowed the teacher to demonstrate one teaching skill at a time and immediately afterward receive constructive feedback from a sample of real students. The theory behind micro-teaching was that teaching could be broken down into a number of specific component skills which could be isolated and practiced separately. The interesting feature, from the point of view of the theme of this chapter, was that the teachers did not choose the skills to be practiced. The skills—seven of them—were selected by the program designers and were explained in handouts. The program attempted to shape teachers to fit a pre-conceived, ideal performance model.

If the specific set of teaching performances offered by the program happened to be ones that the teacher needed to practice, then her or his time might have been well spent. But, given the hundreds of possible teaching behaviors, it is unlikely that any teacher would receive training in the set of skills that were most relevant for her or his particular situation. Moreover, the training was limited to performance—what the teacher does—rather than the effect it has on learning; as a result, it failed to encourage teachers to pay attention to subtle aspects of their teaching that were not obviously manifested in behavior, such as the teacher-student relationship, that might have profound consequences for the quality of learning in their courses (Bergquist & Phillips, 1975). And since it focused on *shaping performances* through *corrective* feedback exclusively, the process did not identify and enhance the teacher's individual strengths. Finally, the teaching episodes were too short to enable the teachers to practice some of the more subtle aspects of teaching, such as creating an accepting class climate.

Micro-teaching only began to penetrate universities and colleges a decade later when it evolved into a more flexible and more context-specific form. The many contemporary variations of the basic "teach, analyze and re-teach" format developed by Allen and Ryan deviate from the original in significant ways. Indeed, Bergquist and Phillips (1975) have given the new programs a different name—"The teaching laboratory"—although most professionals in the field continue to refer to the modified approaches as "micro-teaching" used in a broader sense than it was used in the original program.

The Teaching Laboratory

The teaching laboratory is a more flexible and individualized outgrowth of micro-teaching. Typically, a small group of faculty gather in a circle. They take turns enacting a brief teaching sequence that each has chosen. Teachers are encouraged to practice sequences with which they have had difficulty in the past. All but one of the other faculty temporarily take on the role of the learner. The teacher explains to the other participants what kind of learner role they should enact so that they will provide a realistic context for her or his teaching episode. For example, a teacher might ask participants to take the role of first-year students attending their first lecture of the year, who are slow at settling down. The one participant—a different one each round—who does not take a learner role, becomes the "consultant" for that round. It is the consultant's job to guide the discussion so that it remains relevant and constructive and to ensure that the teacher speaks first. The roles of teacher and consultant rotate around the entire group so that, after a few hours, every member has had a chance to practice teaching and consulting once and to enact the role of student several times.

By allowing them to choose the skill that they want to practice, the teaching laboratory enabled teachers to channel their efforts to the precise behaviors with which they were having difficulty and gave them more control of their own improvement efforts. Also, the outcomes of the teaching laboratory extended beyond skill training. By engaging teachers in role-reversal (teachers taking the role of students), teachers gained insight into the perceptions and emotions of their own students. I recall, in teaching laboratory sessions that I have run, listening to teachers describe how antagonized they felt by certain styles of teaching demonstrated by their colleagues. Their negative, even hostile, reactions made them look with more understanding at similar behaviors in their own students. Moreover, as Bergquist and Phillips (1975) point out, learning how to give feedback in a constructive manner is also an important learning experience for faculty. Finally, collaborating with a group of teachers instead of working in isolation has its own benefits—teachers are comforted by the realization that other teachers have similar problems and teachers form friendships with colleagues who share an interest in teaching.

On the other hand, the teaching laboratory shares some of the limitations of micro-teaching. It focuses on those obvious teacher performances that can be demonstrated in a group and allows only short teaching episodes. In addition, some of the most important contextual variables of teaching are excluded by substituting faculty for students. In my experience in medical education, faculty peers knew too much medicine to act like first-year medical students. Indeed, even the students themselves sometimes do not respond in a laboratory situation as they do in the actual classroom setting. One remedy for this limitation is to reintroduce students into the teaching laboratory when indicated, that is, to use both faculty and students, with students acting as themselves and faculty acting as observers. In fact, modifications such as this are in wide use.

A more radical remedy to the limitations of the teaching laboratory is to take the "practice with feedback" format into the classroom itself. The "classroom research" approach has done just that, generating a high level of excitement since the late 1980s.

Classroom Research

Classroom research, as it is described by Cross and Angelo (1988), is a process of involving teachers in the formal study of teaching and learning.

The approach is also a powerful teaching improvement technique. Indeed, it is probably the most highly individualized, context-specific program utilizing "practice with feedback" that has ever been developed. Cross and Angelo's (1988) "Handbook for Faculty," provides teachers with a wide range of assessment techniques to collect feedback on how students learn and how they respond to various teaching approaches. All of the techniques are used directly in the classroom.

Perhaps the most impressive aspect of the handbook is the enormous range of techniques—30 individual techniques and many variations—which enable the teacher to gather feedback from students on a wide range of dimensions. By selecting an appropriate set of techniques, a teacher can get feedback on practically any aspect of her or his teaching or any student outcome. Although the handbook on classroom research goes beyond the traditional assessment of teaching performances, faculty who are interested in traditional performance assessment will find eight techniques. These are further sub-divided into techniques for measuring students' perceptions of *teaching methods* and students' perceptions of *course materials*. In addition, the handbook also offers techniques designed to measure students' *academic skills* and *intellect* and students' *attention to and awareness of their own learning processes*. Within each of these categories, the techniques are further sub-divided. Under the category "Techniques for Assessing Academic Skills and Intellectual Development," one finds techniques aimed at assessing students' subject matter mastery, critical thinking, and creative thinking. Under the category "Student Self-assessment," one finds techniques aimed at assessing students' awareness of their learning styles and preferences and their learning skills.

The wide array of techniques available expands teachers' awareness to a broad range of dimensions of teaching and learning. By contrast, teachers engaged in a teaching laboratory exercise are constrained by the limits of their knowledge of the dimensions of teaching and learning. They often do not know what is important to ask students.

Some of the techniques require little preparation and can be used on the spur of the moment, providing teachers with tools for continual response to changing conditions in the classroom. Many of the techniques require active engagement of the learners in the process, increasing the learners' level of responsibility for the improvement of teaching. Finally, the techniques are not limited to correction of poor performances; they raise awareness of good ones as well. For example, one instrument asks students to write brief, focused profiles of a teacher whose values, skills, and actions they greatly admire.

Computer Network

Classroom research techniques are not without their limitations. For example the handbook is not domain specific; it is aimed at teachers of history and physics alike, even though there may be important differences in how these subjects are taught. Cross and Angelo recommend "a computer network through which teachers in various disciplines, such as math..., can share domain-specific teaching and assessment techniques with math teachers across the country" (p. 6). Indeed, the Professional and Organizational Development Network in Higher Education's computer network is beginning to serve this function. Although the network is not designed to separate subscribers by their discipline, in practice it often works that way. When I asked the members of the network for help with a problem in medical education, those who responded were other educators working in health sciences settings. The Society for Teaching and Learning in Higher Education (STLHE), the Higher Education Research and Development Society of Australasia (HERDSA), and the Staff and Educational Development Association (SEDA) have also established computer networks to facilitate discussion of teaching and learning issues[1].

Video Playback

The use of video playback in training was called "self-confrontation" in the 1970s. Advocates of this approach attributed almost magical powers to the viewing of the videotape itself, as if the truth about a teacher somehow jumped out of the screen. The motivating force for change was assumed to be discrepancy reduction. After teachers compared their own conception of their teaching with the "truth," they were expected to make corrections automatically. According to Fuller and Manning, (1973), who reviewed the early literature, the optimism of the practitioners using videotape in their programs was not justified by the outcomes of the research: "What is hoped is that teachers will correct what they are doing wrong and improve what they are doing right. As we have seen, the probability is low that this will result from current average practice" (p. 508). Indeed, the consensus was that video playback by itself, without other components, often produced fear, disturbance, and anxiety, without improvement. Videotape can communicate powerful messages about aspects of the teachers' work that are perceived by others but not by the teachers themselves. Teachers may fear that the facilitator is "one up" on them for having knowledge about them that they do not have. They may feel foolish and embarrassed (Fuller & Manning, 1973). On the other hand, so-called "self-confrontative" video feedback did appear to solve two of the more difficult problems of the developer—it motivated student-teachers, and it put the responsibility for learning in their own hands.

The typical video playback situation involved student teachers who watched one or more videotapes of their teaching, sometimes alone and sometimes in the presence of a facilitator. In early uses of videotape, teachers often viewed their tapes by themselves. The rationale for this practice was that teachers would see themselves as performers and would correct poor performances if given an opportunity to witness them. Unfortunately, the teacher's feelings were left out of this formulation. Most teachers, in fact, focused on their personal appearance and idiosyncrasies rather than on their teaching behaviors and the reactions of their students. And many who were not young, good-looking, and self-confident were devastated by their physical appearance, verbal or physical tics, and characteristics of voice. Teachers who had a good opinion of themselves, who were open to change, who were intelligent, and were relatively well satisfied with their performance were the most likely to benefit from self-confrontation. For the many who failed to meet these criteria, the program was not helpful unless modified. Trained facilitators could reduce the negative consequences of viewing videotapes by encouraging the teacher to focus on behaviors that could be changed and to manage their own feedback, by deliberately selecting discrepancies that were surmountable or by focusing the teacher on one aspect of teaching at a time (Fuller & Manning, 1973). From early programs, we have learned the benefit of facilitators who have, in the language used in the helping skills literature, CARE: Communicated Authenticity, positive Regard for the other, and Empathy (Carkhuff, 1969).

Contemporary programs have incorporated many of Fuller and Manning's recommendations. David Taylor-Way, for example, uses videotape, not merely to display physical characteristics and teaching performances, but as a recall stimulus that encourages teachers to develop their own concepts and principles and to build a deeper understanding of teaching (Taylor-Way & Brinko, 1989). His objective is to use videotape to facilitate reflective practice (see Schön, 1987) in teachers by encouraging them to articulate their thoughts and feelings and how these affect their teaching.

The teacher watches the videotape with a remote control in hand and is instructed to stop it whenever she or he thinks or feels something is worth sharing. The teacher takes control of the process, and the tape becomes a stimulus for self-reflection. Teachers are discouraged from identifying "good" or "bad" behaviors. Instead, they define issues that they would like to address. The initial focus is on understanding the behavior and helping the teacher develop a framework for thinking about teaching. The facilitator asks the teacher to try to discern patterns or regularities which the facilitator then gives a name, such as "warming up" or "summarizing."

In an exciting variation of this method, Professor Taylor-Way (1987) used students to help teachers analyze their videotapes. The two perspectives lead to different interpretations of the tape, with teachers often surprised to find, for example, that taped segments of the class that they deemed tedious and slow were seen by the students as clear and organized. Taped segments that teachers perceived as showing themselves "on a roll" were sometimes recalled by students as a time when they were lost.

Another contemporary program designer with extensive experience in video playback is Larry Quinsland. He uses a split-screen technique, enabling the viewer to see simultaneous images of both teacher and students (Quinsland, 1987). Such an arrangement is ideal for comparing teachers' goals and actual student behavior. At a workshop that I attended, Dr. Quinsland showed a clip of a teacher who was trying to maintain attention while his students were passing one another notes or sleeping in the back of the hall. His program is organized so that the teacher can control the process. He provides the teacher with a 74-item teaching skills inventory. Teachers are asked initially to check every item that interests them and to make a final selection of five items on which they wish to concentrate their efforts. Teachers are taped once per week throughout the course to provide evidence of improvement on the selected dimensions. In order to avoid a possible stigma attached to participating in a program that could be regarded as "remedial," even master teachers are required by the college to engage in the process.

INDIVIDUALIZED CONSULTATION

Without doubt the most individualized and context-specific approach to improvement of classroom teaching is individualized consultation. The consultation process is described by Bergquist and Phillips (1977) as "a systematic, confidential, structured exchange of ideas, perceptions and suggestions between a faculty development consultant… and an individual faculty member, the purpose of which is to identify and improve teaching strengths and weaknesses" (p. 69). The typical process includes four stages: gathering information about the instructor's teaching, analyzing that information, developing and implementing strategies for improvement, and evaluating the impact of those strategies through the collection and analysis of new information. Ideally, the entire process can be completed within one semester of teaching, and this basic plan can be modified in any number of ways to suit individual teachers and situations.

The Massachusetts Clinic to Improve University Teaching

The first individualized consultation program to become widely known, the Clinic to Improve University Teaching at the University of Massachusetts (US), was developed in the early 1970s. The consultant gathered information from interviews with the teacher, from direct classroom observations, from videotapes of the classroom teaching, and from questionnaires administered to both teacher and students. The questionnaire was composed of 50 statements describing specific teaching skills and behaviors. Respondents were asked to indicate on a five-point scale the extent to which they felt their instructor needed improvement. Teachers completed this questionnaire twice, once to indicate their opinions about their own teaching and another time to predict student responses. All of this data, far too much to discuss in a single session, was studied by the consultant, focusing on each teachers' most important strengths and weaknesses. Particular attention was paid to comparisons between the different sources of information. It was assumed that accurately predicting student satisfaction would reassure the teacher, accurately predicting dissatisfaction would motivate the teacher to change, and inaccurately predicting student opinions would motivate the teacher to explore the discrepancy further. After the data was understood, the faculty member and the consultant generated improvement strategies. The strategies were selected for their accommodation to the instructor's specific needs and willingness to change and to the availability of needed resources.

One could hardly imagine a more individualized approach to teaching improvement, nor a more comprehensive one. The fact that its popularity has waned may be due to the time-consuming nature of the process during this period of shrinking resources. It is not surprising that the individualized consulting approaches that are gaining popularity require considerably less faculty and consultant time. But there is more to the new developments than economy. They give students greater responsibility to define the issues, concepts, ideas, and even the language that will be used in the consulting process. Note that, although the Massachusetts Clinic draws from both student and teacher responses to the questionnaire, the questionnaire itself is a standardized instrument designed by consultants. The new programs, described below, use various techniques to stimulate a high level of teacher and student involvement, including direct dialogue between teachers and students and among teachers.

Moreover, in early individualized consulting programs, the consultant was a professional educator who usually mediated between teacher and student. As mediators, consultants are supposed to facilitate communication between students and teachers but they do this at the price of displacing teachers from direct contact with students. It happened to me. I realized, after consulting for many years, that teachers were beginning to view me as the "teaching guru." I could be relied upon to explain what students were *really* thinking. It was true that I was in touch with students, but the reason was not some mystic psychic power, out of reach to ordinary faculty. It was simply that I had conducted dozens of feedback groups each year. I was constantly in conversation with students about teaching. In order to avoid becoming a barrier to face-to-face dialogue, my colleagues and I developed a consulting procedure that attempted to put the teacher closer to the action, to give the teacher the direct experiences with students and peers that had been so valuable to me as a consultant. The program, called *Alliances for Change*, uses peer coaching to give the teacher a consulting experience. It includes direct, face-to-face interaction between teachers and students. Another program, called *Partners in Learning*, uses peer consultation to accomplish similar goals. Both of these programs are described below. Since "focus group" interviews are used in all of these procedures, I will briefly explain the role of focus groups in contemporary teaching improvement programs.

Focus Group Interviews

The use of focus group interviews has expanded dramatically over the last 50 years. The typical focus group is a structured or unstructured interview that lasts an hour or two and includes six to 12 members (Stewart & Shamdasani, 1990; Patton, 1990). The interviewer may choose an unstructured format in order to determine students' perceptions about a teacher or course, and a structured format to seek responses to specific questions. The key to the success of the focus group is the encouragement of a lively discussion among students with little interference by the interviewer. The interviewer guides the discussion so that each issue that is raised is discussed by everyone. He or she asks students to explain differences of opinion. This technique is especially valuable when one needs to uncover what is really important to students; to generate a rich elaboration of an issue; to flesh out issues with anecdotes stated in the colorful vernacular of the students; to clarify subtle aspects of teaching and learning, such as issues concerned with the teaching-learning relationship; and to reconcile subtle differences of opinion. Because unstructured discussion groups are particularly free from the constraints inherent in the vocabulary and conceptual framework of the interview, students are able to phrase questions in their own words.

Small Group Instructional Diagnosis

Small group instructional diagnosis (known by its acronym SGID) creates a series of focus groups right in the classroom (Clark & Bekey, 1979; Clark, 1982). A facilitator, who has previously become acquainted with the teacher's style, asks the class to divide into groups of about five and to select a recorder and a spokesperson. The groups are asked to discuss what they like about the course, what they think should be improved, and what suggestions they have for bringing about improvements. After ten minutes, the facilitator asks each spokesperson to report one response to each of the questions. Responses are written on the board. These comments are copied down by the facilitator and discussed later with the teacher. At the next class, the teacher uses the first ten minutes to clarify and summarize students' comments.

The SGID procedure draws the entire class into the dynamics of teaching improvement because of the high level of student involvement. The process can profoundly enhance attitudes toward the teacher and the learners' sense of responsibility and commitment to the improvement process, even before any changes are made in the teaching. Positive attitudes in students are manifested by the common observation that learners typically continue to make helpful suggestions long after the SGID process has ended.

SGID allows the critical issues to be defined by the students themselves. After discussion among their peers, they choose what they consider to be the most important strengths, weaknesses, and recommendations for improvement. Moreover, SGID provides several opportunities for two-way communication that corrects errors of misinterpretation. Students are able to clarify the issues by talking among themselves; the facilitator can ask students questions about an issue in order to gain an understanding of the context of the students' suggestions; and, during the subsequent session, when the teacher clarifies the ideas, they have another opportunity to pinpoint the issues.

Alliances for Change

Alliances for Change (Tiberius, Sackin, Janzen, & Preece, 1993) is a teaching improvement program that I have developed with colleagues in the Ontario (Canada) higher education system. The premises underlying this method are quite different from those underlying the Massachusetts Clinic described above. The broad agenda of *Alliances* is to enhance understanding between teachers and students, to help them become more collaborative, and to encourage a view of teaching and learning as a process of dialogue rather than as a transmission of information. The central feature of *Alliances* is a face-to-face conversation between teachers and small groups of students. Indeed, the procedure is designed primarily to provide the conditions under which teachers and students can discuss teaching improvement directly, with minimal anxiety and defensiveness.

In our experience, in addition to helping teachers in specific ways, such as enhancing their strengths and reducing weaknesses, *Alliances* has had a powerful effect on teacher and student perceptions and attitudes. It has been designed to uncover subtle dimensions of teaching, particularly those involved with the teacher-student relationship.

After a workshop at which the procedure is explained, teachers are invited to form pairs. Each partner visits the other's class once and conducts a focus group with a random sample of students drawn from that class. After writing brief summaries of the information gathered from their focus groups, the two partners exchange summaries and talk about their students' perceptions and opinions. A second group of students is then drawn from each class. This group differs from the first in a number of important ways. It is not selected by the partner, nor is it selected randomly. Instead, the teacher asks for volunteers to read the comments that the first group has generated so that they may help the teacher interpret the comments and generate responses. This second group is called *The Conversation Group*, and its format is specifically designed to maximize free expression. The members are encouraged to speak in the third person, about the issues that "they" (other students) have raised. The teacher has had time to preview the agenda, and engagement is completely voluntary.

Another distinctive feature of *Alliances* is its emphasis on the amplifying, as well as corrective, use of feedback: helpful behaviors are enhanced and supported in addition to unhelpful behaviors being corrected. For example, feedback to the teacher can enhance the collaborative relationship, especially if it lets the teacher know what students are thinking and feeling conveyed in their own words (Endo and Harpel, 1982; Tiberius et. al., 1989).

Partners in Learning

Partners in Learning was developed under the guidance of the late Joseph Katz (Finkelstein & Smith, 1992; Katz & Henry, 1988) as a state-wide development program for New Jersey (US). The premises underlying this method are similar to those of *Alliances*. The ultimate goal of the program is not enhancement of teaching skills but enhancement of the communication between faculty and students and among faculty. The assumption is that once the communication is enhanced, once teachers and students are communicating to one another on a regular basis, specific teaching problems will be solved automatically. The process of teaching and learning is conceptualized as a dialogue. The objective is to transform teachers and students from the antagonists that they frequently are into active collaborators.

The program arranges partnerships among pairs of teachers for the purpose of helping one another. Each partner sits in the other's class frequently (typically every second week) throughout the semester. They interview one another and one another's students. The aim of these interviews is to build intimacy between partners and to reduce tension about the observation process. The teacher typically interviews three of his or her's partner's students somewhere between three and five times during the semester. The topics of these interviews extend beyond teaching and learning to include the family, home environment, employment, background, and even social life of students.

The process helps teachers to learn in several ways: from their observations of different teaching styles and discussions with students they learn specific lessons about teaching; from observation of others they pick up techniques they might try in their own classrooms; from discussion with students they gain an understanding of the perceptions and thoughts of students. Lively interaction with others who care about teaching rejuvenates them and helps to reduce their sense of isolation and stress. Finally, the wide-ranging interviews provide teachers with a sense for the context within which students live and learn (Finkelstein & Smith, 1992).

Teachers also learn from one another. At monthly meetings with all the participants in the program, problems of individual participants are raised, and the advice of the group is solicited. Another approach taken at these meetings is taking turns around the group with each participant commenting from her or his own experience interviewing or observing (Finkelstein & Smith, 1992). Finally, all participants write a reflective essay on their experience with the process. These essays are discussed by members of the group. The writing consolidates learning and helps teachers reflect on their learning.

READING ABOUT TEACHING

Judging by the number of publications directed at teachers, reading about teaching is surely a popular means of enhancing one's teaching. However, until recently, formal programs have not been built around reading. Reading can encourage teachers, through personal stories and exhortations, about the importance and virtues of teaching and can provide teachers with alternative teaching strategies that have been known to work, the so-called "tips for teaching approach."

General Tips for Teachers

One of the earliest works in this field, so popular that it has towered above others for decades, is Wilbert McKeachie's *Teaching Tips: A Guidebook for the Beginning College Teacher*. It began from a set of notes that Professor McKeachie used in a course for new teachers in the early 1950s. It is now in its ninth edition. I would recommend it for every new teacher. I remember years ago agreeing with a fellow developer who said that there was little new ground left in the field for new faculty developers like ourselves since everything had already been covered by McKeachie. But the ensuing years have seen hundreds of titles published, many of which are widely read and highly valued. What do they have to contribute? The answer is, by and large, that they appeal to increasingly defined contexts and content.

Domain Specificity

For one thing McKeachie's book is not *domain* specific. It treats the math teacher and biology teacher alike. The literature serving special subject areas is growing rapidly. There are journals for teachers of biology, engineering, nursing, English, dental education, psychology, and so on. I counted 17 of them in a brief stroll through our library. In the field of medical education with which I am most familiar, since I am based in a medical faculty, there is an enormous literature. One might expect the medical education literature to include specialized articles directed at clinical bedside teaching. And it does (e.g., Douglas, Hosokawa, & Lawler, 1988; Foley & Smilansky, 1980; Schwenk & Whitman, 1987; Westberg & Jason, 1993). But there are also books on *lecturing* in medical education (e.g., Whitman, 1982) and on *small group discussion* in medical education (e.g., Whitman & Schwenk, 1983). These latter books serve to interpret the general literature for medical teachers, using less educational jargon and relating the concepts and strategies to familiar ones in medicine. They also apply the lessons from the general literature to the special situations that medical teachers may encounter. The contextualization has even become sub-divided within the subject of medicine. There are books on medical teaching directed at particular *disciplines* of medicine, such as family medicine (e.g., Fabb, Heffernan, Phillips, & Stone, 1976; Golden, Carlson, & Hagen, 1982).

Situational Specificity—Newsletters

Books like McKeachie's provide readers with general advice for typical situations. They draw on experimental research that was designed to generalize. Any of the recommendations in such books can be counter-indicated in a particular situation: the application of the rule depends on what happened, what will happen after, and in a particular context. I recall a situation in which a faculty member, who was coordinating the teaching for his department, asked me whether a panel discussion was better than a lecture. I told him that I was not aware of any study comparing panel discussions with lectures. When he explained the context further to me, it became clear that the literature comparing lecture with panel discussion was irrelevant to his situation. It became clear that his department should use the panel discussion—or anything but a lecture—in his particular situation. They were teaching three lectures in a row to a large class of medical undergraduates and were wondering if they should break up the sequence with a panel discussion! Their question could not be answered independent of the specific situation.

Articles written by faculty or about specific problems constitute a more contextually specific form of reading than texts on teaching since such articles are usually confined to local newsletters published by the institutions primarily for internal circulation. We have seen a proliferation of such newsletters in the last few decades. Some of these are circulated to other institutions. Some that have come across my desk recently are: "Teaching News," newsletter of the Educational Development Advisory Committee, University of Birmingham (UK); Learning and Teaching Centre "Correspondence," University of Victoria (Canada); "Pedagogue: Perspectives on Health Sciences Education," by the Program for Educational Development, McMaster University (Canada); "Teaching & Learning at the University of Hawaii at Manoa" (US), published by the Office of Faculty Development and Academic Support; and "Newsletter: College Teaching Counts," published by the New Jersey Institute for Collegiate Teaching and Learning (US). Teachers who regularly browse through such publications will occasionally encounter an article at the precise moment that they are ready to benefit from it.

Perhaps *institutional* specificity is a sub-species of situational specificity. There may be little difference between the way math teachers ought to teach at two different universities. But it could make a great deal of difference to the motivation of a math teacher at Northern University if she reads ideas about teaching math written by a colleague rather than by someone outside her institution. We believe that our colleagues are more appreciative than outsiders of the context in which we work, the pressures, the types of students. Local readings, emanating from one's backyard and largely consumed there, are not only cast in language and settings that are familiar to the readers but also radiate a sense of optimism—*we can do it here*. The University of Colorado at Boulder (US) fulfills the need for institutionally specific reading by means of a collection called *Compendium of Ideas for Teaching Practice*, which is generated by the faculty themselves (Shea,

1990). *Learning Through Writing* (Herteis & Wright, 1993) and *University Teaching and Learning* (Wright & Herteis, 1993) are Canadian versions of the same idea, that is, collected tips and advice, generated and consumed internally. Doubtless there are others.

Thematic Specificity

Perhaps the most highly individualized type of reading a faculty member could seek is reading that is specific to her or his peculiar situation: teaching communication skills in an engineering school, the challenge of ethnic diversity in large classes, medical education for native people, and so on. The number of teachers in one institution who seek help in one of these areas may be too small to warrant publication even in local newsletters. Here is the situation that calls for a "guided reading" or "teaching circle" approach in which a faculty developer or other facilitator leads discussion of articles on teaching, but the orientation of the group is in the members' control. If they have a general interest in teaching, they can choose a wide range of articles to read; but if they are interested in ethnic diversity, they can choose their readings accordingly. In Canada such teaching circles are used widely, for example at McGill and Dalhousie Universities and the University of Saskatchewan.

But the teachers may need the answer too quickly to wait until they can organize a reading circle on the topic. Here again is the place for networking on the computer. I continue to be fascinated with the willingness and the speed with which subscribers to networks respond to requests for specific help. It is also surprising to learn how much information is "out there" on a subject that you thought you faced alone.

FINAL COMMENTS

Teaching is increasingly viewed as a process of helping learners rather than as a performance aimed at sending well-articulated messages. Learning is increasingly viewed as a process of constructing meaning through an active process of engagement with the material, rather than as a passive absorption of information. The consequences of these changes to our conceptions of teaching and learning have had a profound impact on the design of instructional development programs in the last few decades. Teaching is no longer viewed simply as explaining things clearly to students, and teacher development is no longer viewed simply as helping teachers explain things clearly to students. In order to help teachers facilitate what is now viewed as the active process of learning, faculty development programs must help teachers establish and maintain continual interaction with learners. Such interaction must not be an occasional response to poor ratings, but a regular part of the teaching and learning process. The programs reviewed in this chapter are getting better at helping teachers move in this direction.

Faculty developers, department heads, and academic leaders can play an important role in creating and maintaining dynamic interaction between teachers and learners through wise selection and implementation of faculty development programs. Although I do not feel comfortable recommending a set of criteria for educational development programs, I do believe that there are lessons to be drawn from the directions toward which the approaches to teaching improvement are evolving. Programs that are consistent with current conceptions of teaching and learning would tend to have the following features: the program will consider the specific characteristics of individual teachers, their strengths, weaknesses, personal styles and preferences; the program will be sensitive to the particular context of the teaching, including institutional and social setting, physical surroundings, and subject matter; the program will utilize information gathered from multiple sources—teacher, students, and trained observers; the program will be on-going and developmental rather than a one-shot affair; the program will involve the faculty, and even the learners, in its planning stages; the program will focus, at least in part, on building a collaborative relationship between the teacher and the learners and on enhancing the quality of communication between the teacher and learners; and the program will include an aspect of support for teachers, both collegial and institutional.

There is a final emerging feature of faculty development efforts that was not illustrated here because it lies outside the program categories that I defined, yet it embraces all of them. The feature that I am describing is the increasing tendency, particularly among the most experienced developers, to extract strategies and techniques from a number of different programs in order to suit the individual needs of the teacher, and further, to continually modify those to accommodate the local context. In writing this chapter, I chose to trace the history of separate educational development streams (or approaches) to make it easier for those outside the field to appreciate the wide spectrum of strategies that are available and changes that have taken place. But to an experienced developer my organization may make the program categories appear more rigid than they are. In fact, experienced developers do not slavishly follow set programs. They jump from stream to stream, fishing out the most useful, appropriate strategies for each situation. They are inventing, modifying, and borrowing to suit the situation. While working with one teacher, an experienced developer might choose to visit a class, use videotape, and then conduct a focus group to collect student feedback. While working with another teacher, the same developer might use a student questionnaire, administer a student learning styles inventory like the Kolb model (1976) and use micro-teaching.

This eclecticism is supported by increasing professionalization of developers and growth of resources. A few decades ago, educational development was carried out by part-time faculty who had little literature to support their efforts and no organizations specifically devoted to the field. Today, educational developers are more likely to be full-time or part-timers with a major commitment to development. And they are supported by a host of journals, books, special societies and networks. The occasional travelers to the land of teaching improvement to whom I referred at the beginning of this chapter will find a new, exciting world out there.

REFERENCES

Allen, D., & Ryan, R. (1969). *Microteaching*. Reading, MA: Addison-Wesley.

Bergquist, W.H., & Phillips, S.R. (1975). *A handbook for faculty development*. Washington, DC: The Council for the Advancement of Small Colleges.

Bergquist, W.H., & Phillips, S.R. (1977). *A handbook for faculty development, Vol II*. Washington, DC: The Council for the Advancement of Small Colleges.

CAFETERIA. (1980). Purdue University, West Lafayette, IN.

Carkhuff, R.R. (1969). *Helping in human relations: A primer for lay and professional teachers, Vols. I & II*. New York, NY: Holt, Rinehart, & Winston.

Centra, J.A. (1982). *Determining faculty effectiveness*. San Francisco, CA: Jossey-Bass.

Centra, J.A. (1993). *Reflective faculty evaluation: Enhancing teaching and determining faculty effectiveness*. San Francisco, CA: Jossey-Bass.

Clark, D.J., & Bekey, J. (1979). Use of small groups in instructional evaluation. *POD Quarterly, 1*(2), 86-95.

Clark, D.J. (1982). The history of SGID development. *SGID Newsletter, 1*(1), 1-4.

Cross, K.P., & Angelo, T.A. (1988). *Classroom assessment techniques: A handbook for faculty*. East Lansing, MI: National Center for Research to Improve Postsecondary Teaching and Learning.

Douglas, K.C., Hosokawa, M.C., & Lawler, F.H. (1988). *A practical guide to clinical teaching in medicine*. New York, NY: Springer.

Endo, J., & Harpel, R.L. (1982). The effect of student-faculty interaction on students' educational outcomes. *Research in Higher Education, 16*, 115-135.

Fabb, W.E., Heffernan, M.W., Phillips, W.A., & Stone, P. (1976). *Focus on learning in family practice*. Melbourne, Australia: Royal Australian College of General Practitioners.

Finkelstein, M., & Smith, M.J. (1992). *Partners in learning.* South Orange, NJ: New Jersey Institute for Collegiate Teaching and Learning, Seton Hall University.

Foley, R.P., & Smilansky, J. (1980). *Teaching techniques: A handbook for health professionals.* New York, NY: McGraw-Hill.

Fuller, F.F., & Manning, B.A. (1973). Self-confrontation reviewed: A conceptualization for video playback in teacher education. *Review of Educational Research, 43*(4), 469-528.

Globe and Mail (1993, November 3). Geneticists map out the diet of a lifetime. p.A13.

Golden, A. S., Carlson, D. G., & Hagen, J. L. (Eds.) (1982). *The art of teaching primary care.* Springer Series on Medical Education, 3. New York, NY: Springer.

Herteis, E.M., & Wright, W.A. (1993). *Learning through writing: A compendium of assignments and techniques* (2nd ed.). Halifax, NS: Office of Instructional Development and Technology, Dalhousie University.

Instructional Development and Effectiveness Assessment (IDEA) System. (1988). Center for Faculty Evaluation and Development, Kansas State University, Manhattan, KS.

Instructor and Course Evaluation System (ICES). (1993). University of Illinois, Urbana, IL.

Katz, J., & Henry, M. (1988). *Turning professors into teachers: A new approach to faculty development and student learning.* New York, NY: ACE/Macmillan.

Kolb, D.A. (1976). *The learning style inventory technical manual.* Boston, MA: McBer and Company.

Kulik, J.A. (1987). *Instructor designed questionnaire.* Unpublished. University of Michigan, Center for Teaching and Learning, Ann Arbor, MI.

McKeachie, W.J. (1994). *Teaching tips: A guidebook for the beginning college teacher.* (9th ed.). Lexington, MA: D.C. Heath.

Menges, R.J., & Brinko, K.T. (1986, April). *Effects of student evaluation feedback: A meta-analysis of higher education research.* Paper presented at the meeting of the American Educational Research Association, San Francisco, CA.

Murray, H.G. (1987). Acquiring student feedback that improves instruction. In M. G. Weimer (Ed.), *Teaching large classes well* (pp. 85-96). San Francisco, CA: Jossey-Bass.

Patton, M.Q. (1990). *Qualitative evaluation and research methods* (2nd ed.). Newbury Park, CA: Sage.

Quinsland, L. (1987, October). *A unique videotape feedback technique and microteaching with new teaching faculty: A blending of two worlds.* Workshop presented at the

Annual meeting of the Professional and Organizational Development Network in Higher Education, Kerville, TX.

Schön, D.A. (1987). *Educating the reflective practitioner*. San Francisco, CA: Jossey-Bass.

Schwenk, T.L., & Whitman, N. (1987). *The physician as teacher*. Baltimore, MD: Williams and Wilkins.

Shea, M.A. (1990). *Compendium of good ideas on teaching and learning*. Boulder, CO: Faculty Teaching Excellence Program, University of Colorado at Boulder.

Student Instructional Rating System (SIRS). (1982). Michigan State University, East Lansing, MI.

Student Instructional Report (SIR). (1989). Educational Testing Service, Princeton, NJ.

Students' Evaluation of Educational Quality (SEEQ). (1991). University of Western Sidney, Campbelltown, NSW, Australia.

Stewart, D.W., & Shamdasani, P.N. (1990). *Focus groups: Theory and practice*. Newbury Park, CA: Sage.

Taylor-Way, D. (1987, October). *Using videotape in faculty consultation*. Workshop presented at the Annual meeting of the Professional and Organizational Development Network in Higher Education, Kerville, TX.

Taylor-Way, D., & Brinko, K.T. (1989). Using video recall for improving professional competency in instructional consultation. In S. Kahn et al., *To Improve the Academy, 8,* 141-156.

Tiberius, R.G., Sackin, H.D., Janzen, K.R., & Preece, M. (1993). Alliances for change: A procedure for improving teaching through conversations with learners and partnerships with colleagues. *The Journal of Staff, Program, & Organization Development, 11*(1), 11-23.

Tiberius, R.G., Sackin, H.D., Slingerland, J.M., Jubas, K., Bell, M., & Matlow, A. (1989). The influence of evaluative feedback on the improvement of clinical teaching. *The Journal of Higher Education, 60*(6), 665-681.

Westberg, J., & Jason, H. (1993). *Collaborative clinical education: The foundation of effective health care*. New York, NY: Springer.

Whitman, N.A. (1982). *There is no gene for good teaching: A handbook on lecturing for medical teachers*. Salt Lake City, UT: University of Utah, Department of Family and Community Medicine.

Whitman, N.A., & Schwenk, T.L. (1983). *A handbook for group discussion leaders: Alternatives to lecturing medical students to death*. Salt Lake City, UT: University of Utah, Department of Family and Community Medicine

Wotruba, T.R., & Wright, P.L. (1975). How to develop a teacher rating instrument: A research approach. *The Journal of Higher Education, 46*(6), 653-663.

Wright, W.A., & Herteis, E.M. (1993). *University teaching and learning: An instructional resource guide for teaching assistants at Dalhousie University* (2nd ed.). Halifax, NS: Dalhousie Univeristy, Office of Instructional Development and Technology.

AUTHOR

Richard Tiberius holds a PhD in Applied Psychology from the Ontario Institute for Studies in Education, at the University of Toronto, Canada. He works as an educational consultant for the Department of Psychiatry and for the Faculty of Medicine at the University of Toronto, collaborating with faculty in the design of faculty development programs and educational research. He has worked for a wide range of university and community college faculties. His scholarly work and consulting practice focus on improvement of the teaching and learning process. Dr. Tiberius has written numerous journal articles and book chapters in US, Canadian, and British journals, and has conducted workshops and lectured both in North America and Europe. He is the author of a popular book entitled Small Group Teaching: A Trouble-Shooting Guide *and a sequel to it for teachers of large groups.*

NOTES

[1] To subscribe to the POD network, send the message *subscribe POD your name* to listserv@lists.acs.ohio-state.edu

To subscribe to the STLHE network, send the message *sub STLHE-L your name* to listserv@unb.ca

To subscribe to the HERDSA network, send the message *subscribe HERDSA your name* to listproc@listproc.anu.edu.au

To subscribe to the SEDA network, send the message *subscribe staff-development your name* to mailbase@mailbase.ac.uk

8.

Faculty Development Workshops and Institutes

James Eison
Ellen Stevens

Workshops a few hours in duration and intensive workshops or institutes lasting up to two weeks constitute popular means of faculty development. This chapter surveys both discipline-based and multi-disciplinary events and outlines organizational strategies designed to maximize the impact and effectiveness of the events.

INTRODUCTION

Given the widespread use of workshops throughout higher education and a growing interest in the value of longer and more intensive faculty development institutes,[1] no text on successful faculty development practices would be complete without an examination of the following five questions: (1) Why are workshops and institutes useful faculty development practices? (2) What does the literature say about workshops and institutes? (3) How are workshops and institutes best conceptualized and designed? (4) How can workshop and institute participation and impact be maximized? and (5) How can workshop and institute effectiveness be demonstrated? This chapter examines and highlights the published workshop and institute literature in these areas. In addition, two brief, illustrative case studies based upon our first-hand experiences are reported. The first is a three-hour workshop developed initially by Jim Eison and Alan Wright and subsequently modified to encourage faculty at the University of South Florida, US (USF) to create teaching portfolios. The second is an intensive ten-day summer institute designed to help USF faculty use active learning strategies in their undergraduate classes.

WHY ARE WORKSHOPS AND INSTITUTES USEFUL FACULTY DEVELOPMENT PRACTICES?

Among the many types of faculty development activities, rationale for the use of workshops and institutes is found in many sources. For example, Eble (1972) observed that the PhD degree is considered an adequate license to teach; on most university campuses, this observation is as true today as it was over 20 years ago. Though doctoral training in one's discipline may involve four or more years of intense scholarly study in the classroom, library, and research laboratory or studio, far too many faculty learn to teach largely by trial-and-error and on-the-job training, with little or no supervision (Wentzel, 1987). Whether guided by faculty-led teaching enhancement committees or by a faculty development professional, the work of introducing faculty to the knowledge and skills needed to teach effectively in higher education rests on the shoulders of relatively few individuals. Therefore, program planners attempt to maximize their impact by sponsoring group rather than individual activities (Levinson-Rose & Menges, 1981; Weimer & Lenze, 1991). In short, skillfully facilitated workshops and institutes provide a relatively time-efficient and cost-effective method of introducing faculty to the art, craft, and science of effective college and university teaching.

Further, workshops and institutes ideally model and explicitly demonstrate principles and practices of instructional excellence, such as active learning, that faculty participants will modify and employ in their own classrooms (Eison, Janzow, & Bonwell, 1990). For example, Frederick (1987), summarizing the views of many, noted that, "Nearly all learning theorists, faculty development consultants, and reports on higher education recommend... interactive, participatory student involvement for learning that affects cognitive and affective growth" (p. 45). Yet, the lecture method prevails throughout higher education, in part because few faculty experienced active learning as college students (Bonwell & Eison, 1991).

In their evaluation of 24 faculty development programs supported by the Bush Foundation in the US, Eble and McKeachie (1986) noted yet another important benefit of workshops and institutes: "One of the crucial needs of faculty as they grow older is [to avoid] becoming isolated as individuals or among their age cohort" (p. 19). Group activities (e.g., work-shops and institutes) are important in "bringing people of different ages, ranks, and disciplines together. Developing teaching that would rise above the merely competent needs the perspectives of both young and old" (p. 19). Workshops and institutes can help reduce a sense of professional iso-lation commonly reported among faculty employed at larger institutions while providing a structured learning opportunity for faculty from across the disciplines to think and talk about their teaching.

Last, but certainly not least, workshops and institutes can help estab-lish and promote a campus culture that encourages and visibly supports ongoing faculty and administrative efforts to promote teaching excellence (Cochran, 1989; Weimer, 1990).

WHAT DOES THE LITERATURE SAY ABOUT WORKSHOPS AND INSTITUTES?

A search through published faculty development literature[2] suggests that surprisingly little has been written about workshop or institute design.

More common among published journal articles are accounts describ-ing specific faculty development workshops or institutes for audiences, such as new or junior faculty (Eison, 1989; Noonan, 1980; Renegar, Sum-mary, Bonwell, & Eison, 1987) and new faculty developers (Brinko, Tiberius, Atkins, & Greene, 1992). Published descriptions can also be found of topi-cal workshops, such as training teaching consultants (Kerwin & Rhoads, 1993), developing multicultural awareness among faculty (Cooper & Chattergy, 1993; Wadsworth, 1992), improving lectures (Paulsen, 1992), and improving faculty members' scholarly and/or grants writing (Lucas & Harrington, 1990). It is important to note that countless faculty develop-ment workshops are conducted on college and university campuses each year. Most recently, a survey of faculty development activities on 94 cam-puses in the US (Hellyer & Boschman, 1993) reported that 93% offered work-shops and discussions. Faculty development workshops have even been described as "the main staple in the instructional improver's cupboard" (Weimer & Lenze, 1991, p. 298). The majority of these are never reported in the published literature; consequently, their strengths, limitations, and impact, along with any lessons learned by the workshop facilitators, re-grettably have not contributed to current knowledge about workshops and institutes.

In Chapter 1 of this volume, Wright and O'Neil report survey data from 331 faculty developers in the United States, Canada, United Kingdom, and Australasia who used a ten-point scale to rate 36 teaching-improvement practices in terms of their confidence in each activity's "potential to improve the quality of teaching in your university or college." Though the terms *faculty development workshops* and *institutes* were not included on this survey, several closely related types of faculty development activities were identified. Three noteworthy findings can be gleaned from the results. Approximately 50% of the respondents rated their confidence in "workshops on teaching methods for targeted groups (e.g., new faculty, graduate teaching assistants, etc.)" with high ratings of 8, 9, or 10 (i.e., most confident); less that 3% of the respondents rated these events with low ratings of 1, 2, or 3 (i.e., least confident). In response to a related survey item, approximately 32% of the respondents rated their confidence in "conferences on teaching and learning conducted on campus and open to faculty from all disciplines" with ratings of 8, 9, or 10; approximately 5% of the respondents rated these events with a 1, 2, or 3. And finally, less than 10% rated the activity of having "speakers on issues or trends in higher education (e.g., competency testing, liberal education)" highly, while approximately 24% gave the activity ratings of 1, 2, or 3. To summarize, therefore, faculty developers believe that the greatest potential for improving the quality of teaching lies in workshops for targeted groups and conferences on teaching and learning open to faculty from all disciplines.

Menges (1980) observed that, "Workshops and seminars are probably the most frequently conducted but least carefully evaluated instructional development activity." Many agree with this observation (e.g., Lacey, 1988; Levinson-Rose & Menges, 1981; Weimer, 1990; Weimer & Lenze, 1991), suggesting that there is still much that remains to be done in terms of assessing and demonstrating workshop impact. This issue will be explored at greater length later in this chapter.

How are Workshops and Institutes Best Conceptualized and Designed?

A long list of specific issues can be organized into three basic categories that must be addressed, regardless of program type: *who* is the group? *What* will the group learn? *How* will the group learn? These questions provide a useful heuristic for conceptualizing and designing workshops and institutes. In practice, the process of designing instruction is iterative and dynamic; a change in one decision will influence changes in previous and subsequent decisions.

Who will comprise the group? Cognitive scientists advise that students learn best when new information is presented within the framework of their existing knowledge (Weinstein & Meyer, 1991). In other words, instructors should help students connect new information to what they already know; for example, connections can be made by selecting analogies, metaphors, text materials, and assignments that incorporate participants' experiences. Likewise, program facilitators can maximize workshop or institute effectiveness by seeking knowledge about participants' backgrounds prior to the beginning of the program. Unfortunately, this goal is difficult to achieve in most workshop settings; the facilitator generally does not have an opportunity to learn much about the workshop participants prior to the workshop and the time-limited workshop schedule seldom provides adequate opportunity for extended participant introductions. At best, workshops involving 20 to 30 participants can begin with brief personal introductions. Facilitators of workshops involving groups of 30 to 200 faculty members, on the other hand, might begin with a 20-minute opening activity that stimulates participants to reflect privately upon a question related directly to the workshop topic. Participants then share their understandings with a partner or within a small group, and possibly in the large group. Workshop facilitators can learn much about their group by attending carefully to the responses shared during this type of workshop opening. While this information would not result in last minute program changes, the facilitator could use it to personalize comments, questions, or examples during the session.

Facilitators of institutes, however, can learn a great deal about the interests, needs, and experiences of the group members by requiring all applicants to provide this type of introductory background information in their initial application for participation in the institute. In addition, facilitators can direct greater attention to issues of group membership during the opening activities of institutes than is possible in short-term workshops.

Topical workshops and institutes on teaching-related themes that transcend specific disciplinary contexts can bring together faculty representing different departments, colleges, and, in some cases, campuses. On many campuses, a well-designed and timely announcement of such programs is sufficient to attract participation from faculty of all ranks—from professors to graduate teaching assistants. For example, an introductory workshop on using cooperative learning strategies could easily be offered in a manner that would interest and engage faculty from accounting, biology, English, mathematics, nursing, and psychology. This mix of different disciplines and backgrounds can provide a richness of experience and information that enhances group activities. When including both faculty and teaching assistants, facilitators should be mindful that faculty and TAs might be reluctant to participate fully in the presence of the other. Knowledge of institutional cultures, appropriate climate setting exercises, and judicious assignments to groups might ameliorate potentially problematic situations.

Faculty development workshops and institutes that invite interdisciplinary participation are more likely to result in greater gender balance among participants. Fewer female voices might be predicted in discipline-specific programs in business, engineering, math, or science. Similarly, faculty demographics in the US suggest that non-European American faculty tend to teach more often in some disciplines than others. Interdisciplinary meetings, therefore, provide an increased likelihood of hearing and benefitting from the diversity of viewpoints and experiences found in the larger academic population.

Discipline-specific programs, on the other hand, have their own unique advantages. Faculty participants in such programs are more likely to know one another; therefore, less time will be needed for rapport-building activities. Faculty participants from a single department or closely related disciplines are more likely to share common concerns about the teaching of their subject matter and about the instructional challenges faced by their colleagues. From a program planner's or facilitator's standpoint, a homogeneous participant population makes it easier to focus program time on discipline-specific issues and individual participant's concerns. Discipline-based workshops also facilitate the transfer of learning: a departmental group which has learned and adopted new instructional strategies can subsequently influence departmental colleagues to learn about and implement the new approaches to teaching. Written resources (e.g., bibliographies) that are uniquely applicable to the participants' discipline area can also be provided.

What will be learned? This question refers to both program goals and content. One of the first decisions that must be made in workshop or institute planning involves identifying specific program goals. Planning decisions about specific program goals will help determine the necessary program length and format, as well as guide the subsequent selection of alternative instructional strategies to be employed in the program. For example, a half-day workshop cannot have program goals of the same breadth and depth as those of a five-day institute.

A short workshop provides opportunities to accomplish several different types of important faculty development goals. First, according to faculty participants at USF's afternoon workshops, these sessions bring colleagues together to exchange ideas, insights, and experiences about teaching. Most report that these workshops provide faculty with the primary opportunity to engage in intellectual conversations about their teaching. Departmental meetings, the most frequent occasion that prompts faculty to convene, focus most often on "housekeeping" issues rather than on the exchange of ideas and experiences about teaching. During departmental meetings, it is not unusual to observe faculty engage in other "work" (e.g., reading mail or grading papers) and to exit the meeting promptly after one hour. In contrast, three-hour faculty development workshops are described as intellectually stimulating and personally satisfying. Faculty report learning new ideas from colleagues in other academic disciplines; they also enjoy hearing others share stories that mirror their own experiences. Providing the opportunity for faculty to talk with colleagues from across campus about teaching is in itself a worthy workshop goal.

Another common faculty development workshop goal is to help introduce participants to a body of knowledge with which they are unfamiliar, or to provide an introductory opportunity for participants to become actively involved in acquiring new teaching skills. Because workshop length is always limited, a facilitator's goals and anticipated outcomes should also be limited. For example, in a 90-minute workshop entitled "Improving Classroom Tests," a facilitator might choose to synthesize research demonstrating the powerful effect that classroom tests have upon student learning and focus on the components of a skillfully planned and developed test. Focusing solely on these two concepts would meet the planning goal of introducing new knowledge. In addition to these two concepts, a three-hour workshop with the same title could provide participants with an opportunity to expand their understanding of recommended classroom testing practices and build their skills by critiquing sample test items and possibly even creating a few test items of their own. In short, when planning a workshop, faculty developers must simultaneously identify program goals and time constraints; as the allotted workshop time is increased, expectations for workshop outcomes can be expanded. Regardless of workshop length, providing carefully selected written resources to guide and assist participants' further study at the program's end has the potential to extend the workshop's impact beyond the time participants share as a group.

Two other types of workshop goals, important to the creation of a visible and significant faculty development program, should be mentioned. First, workshops and their accompanying brochures or advertisements focus campus attention on educational topics of local and national concern (e.g., increasing student diversity, assessing educational outcomes, using active learning strategies in large classes). Thus, some level of increased faculty awareness can be expected to occur when members of a campus community read a carefully crafted workshop announcement. Second, the better a workshop is designed and delivered, the more likely it is that participants will request follow-up activities or additional information about effective teaching as well as recommend subsequent workshops to colleagues.

Institutes are longer than workshops and can consequently address a variety of additional program goals not easily accomplished in workshops. For example, one institute goal might be the creation of a feeling of close camaraderie and cohesiveness among faculty participants. A highly cohesive group will participate in structured activities in ways that facilitate learning both for individuals and among group members. Structuring extensive and intensive interactions with partners or teams can provide the foundation upon which group cohesiveness is built.

Extended time together creates opportunities to achieve additional institute goals. Instead of limiting one's goals to providing a brief overview or introduction to a topic, instructional activities can be expanded and more fully developed; increased depth and breadth of subject matter coverage are more likely to be achieved. Knowledge and skills build upon each other with increased opportunity for practice and feedback. Once again, using "Improving Classroom Tests" as an illustrative example, the added time means that several alternative types of test questions can be critically examined and evaluated. After each test type is presented, institute participants could create and critique items for their courses. Complete exams or small test banks may be produced during an institute.

Participants in USF's summer institutes, which have ranged in duration from two weeks to six weeks in duration, have suggested that having another week or month to read and assimilate all the instructional resource materials provided would greatly enhance their learning. Within the institute format, it is both possible and desirable to set aside designated blocks of time for participants to read and reflect upon the ideas contained in both the institute sessions and the resource materials. Institute impact is maximized when facilitators state how participants are to use these time blocks and hold participants accountable for this time in some fashion. For example, an institute requirement may be that faculty participants apply their new knowledge to course preparation or modification by submitting a written product, such as a new course syllabus or activity plan, by the institute's conclusion.

Faculty often react to the institute setting in much the same manner as students in the classroom. One commonly observes faculty members who become conversation dominators; others quickly retire to a corner of the room; some participants come to morning sessions chronically late; and others will be seen completing homework assignments hastily at the beginning of a session. This approximation of the classroom suggests yet another important and reasonable expectation for institutes—focusing time and attention on group dynamics and classroom processes. Processing interactions among faculty participants, and between the participants and the facilitators, in "real time" provides an authentic opportunity for exploration of effective instructional strategies for similar situations in the class-room. Furthermore, this "time-out procedure" is an effective way to step back from the content of the moment and discuss specific instructional strategies in detail. Just as many students focus primarily on knowledge acquisition, faculty may miss important instructional structures demonstrated during lively and fast-paced institute sessions. Institute facilitators can enhance participants' learning by calling overt attention to these connections between instructional process and institute content.

In terms of how faculty development workshops and institutes are facilitated most effectively, Geis and Smith (1989) have argued cogently that "teaching improvement and faculty development activities might attract more participants and have a greater effect if developers used an adult learning model in carrying out their work with clients" (p. 155).[3] Unfortunately, workshop facilitators at countless professional conferences and campus-based faculty development programs often employ a traditional "teaching is telling" model of instruction. Our extensive experiences as both participants and presenters, however, have convinced us that faculty development programs are most powerful when program leaders "practice what they teach" about instructional effectiveness and demonstrate the use of active learning strategies in their programs. For an extended treatment of how workshop and institute facilitators can employ alternative active learning strategies in faculty development programs, and 22 specific suggestions to help facilitators ensure success when using active learning strategies, see Eison, Janzow, and Bonwell (1990). (See also Appendix B for the 22 suggestions.)

How Can Workshop and Institute Participation and Impact be Maximized?

Both personal conversations with previous institute participants and post-institute evaluations support the belief that institutes are more effective than one-time workshops at initiating substantive change in teaching behaviors. Learning and information-processing theories support this observation, in part, because institutes provide greater opportunities to reinforce and extend learning. While the published literature does not address this issue directly, one could reasonably predict that workshops are more common than institutes. If institutes have greater instructional potential but workshops are more common, it is important to consider how practitioners can maximize the impact of shorter workshop programs. A focus on post-workshop activities designed to enhance and support change would seem not only logical but essential. Suggestions for such activities are presented in two broad categories—communiqués and events.

Communiqués

One of the easiest ways to establish continued contact with workshop participants is to send them additional reading material pertinent to the workshop topic after the program. When possible, keep records of individual participant's expressed interests during the program and forward post-workshop readings related to these interest areas. Though this requires both organization and effort, the impact of such personalization on individual faculty can be significant.

Workshops that involve participants actively have greater potential for continuation than more formal lecture presentations. Encouraging "small-group activities" is a useful way to stimulate involvement by all participants in a time-limited workshop. Often due to time constraints, some groups will not have an opportunity to share the product of their small group discussions with members of the larger group. Limited group sharing during the program with the circulation of post-workshop summaries of participants' group work and other written activities (e.g., idea lists produced during brainstorming activities, two-minute papers) allows each participant and small group to share ideas. These post-workshop communiqués can stimulate additional reflection and can help foster the development of a learning community among participants.

Individual institutions are using local area networks with electronic bulletin boards to facilitate communication among faculty. Developing an electronic bulletin board to promote ongoing faculty discussions about workshop topics can enhance communication among teaching scholars and ultimately involve faculty who did not attend the workshop.

Yet another strategy to extend workshop impact is to solicit and publish papers authored by participants willing to share their teaching insights and experiences with colleagues on campus (e.g., Shea, 1987). Turning teaching insights into publications provides faculty with a method of demonstrating their teaching scholarship (Stevens & Eison, 1994) and expands workshop influence beyond the initial participants.

Events

Scheduling events that bring workshop participants back together is another way to enhance program impact by providing an opportunity for renewing acquaintances and creating a conducive atmosphere for professional networking. These events can be social or can involve a continuation of the original learning experience. For example, participant pairs can meet at a specified later date to discuss their experiences using the ideas introduced at the workshop. Alternatively, discussion or book groups can be organized for all participants.

In addition, program "graduates" can become faculty development ambassadors. Recent workshop participants often enjoy sharing their success stories with colleagues. We have found, for example, that recruiting enthusiastic and talented "graduates" of previous programs to facilitate subsequent programs has an impressive impact on the facilitator and participants alike. Browne and Keeley (1988) advise that post-workshop follow-up activities are especially important when an off-campus consultant serves as the workshop facilitator.

How Can Workshop and Institute Effectiveness be Demonstrated?

Assessing the impact of a program is complicated by the fact that conceptions vary about what constitutes a successful workshop or institute. Most frequently, a participant questionnaire at the program's conclusion is the primary evidence collected to document program success. These questionnaires provide evidence of program quality in much the same fashion as a well-designed student rating of course and instructor form provides one type of evidence of instructional quality (i.e., quality as assessed by the "consumers" of instruction). Measures of participant satisfaction which employ rating scale items or solicit participants' responses to open-ended questions, or both, provide faculty developers with very important and useful evidence to demonstrate program effectiveness. When a significant proportion of workshop or institute participants report that a faculty development program introduced them to new ideas, perspectives, and information, or that they intend to try some of the instructional approaches in their own classes, the program should be judged effective: it has helped these participants become more reflective and knowledgeable about their teaching practices. When a series of individual faculty development workshops and institutes produces a consistent pattern of favorable reactions from faculty participants, such evidence is viewed on many campuses as sufficient to justify program costs.

Perceptions of effectiveness are key to program success; satisfied faculty attend subsequent programs and encourage colleagues to participate. Collecting information about pleasing and displeasing program aspects provides useful suggestions for program refinement or redesign. This data is not difficult to obtain as most experienced facilitators can attest; faculty can be quite vocal in sharing their displeasure with a poorly planned or conducted program. Faculty developers can minimize legitimate complaints and maximize effectiveness through careful workshop planning.

Even so, measures of participant satisfaction do not provide sufficient or direct evidence that a faculty development program has stimulated instructional improvement leading to enhanced student learning—an often stated goal of many programs. Alternative forms of post-program evaluation such as interviews with faculty and students, detailed examinations of course materials, and analysis of personal or videotaped classroom observations would provide more convincing evidence of documented change. Regretfully, one finds little evidence reported in the published literature that this type of data is collected to assess program impact (Weimer & Lenze, 1991).

Several distinguished authors have asserted that assessing the impact and outcomes of workshops and institutes is important to both the profession and our institutions (Menges, 1980; Weimer & Lenze, 1991). The necessary investment of time, energy, and human resources make this task difficult to accomplish. Conducting large-scale programs of participant interviews or conducting direct classroom observations is daunting and may be impossible, particularly for one-person or committee-led faculty development programs. Nonetheless, assessment is crucial for the continued improvement of faculty development programs.

One's specific assessment goals will suggest whether immediate or delayed assessment strategies are needed. If the goal is to document long-term instructional change, both types of assessment are necessary. Used alone, no one strategy is sufficient for a comprehensive assessment; triangulating (i.e., using a combination of several assessment approaches) would produce an evaluation in which one might have greater confidence. The following case studies demonstrate how thoughtful planning, careful goal setting, varying learning activities, and assessing outcomes can result in workshops and institutes which benefit participants and faculty developers alike.

Case Study One: A Three-Hour Workshop

Workshop rationale. From 1991 to 1992, use of the teaching portfolio approach to document and evaluate teaching was introduced on the USF campus by the Center for Teaching Enhancement (CTE) as an idea worthy of discussion rather than as a call for immediate implementation.[4]

Alan Wright, Executive Director of the Office of Instructional Development and Technology at Dalhousie University, Canada, and the CTE's Director, Jim Eison, designed and delivered a half-day workshop entitled "Creating a Teaching Portfolio." The program was offered twice and was attended by approximately 50 faculty. Growing faculty interest in the teaching portfolio concept, prompted by the introduction of a new teaching award program, has encouraged the CTE to offer the "Creating a Teaching Portfolio" workshop on 12 different occasions since Fall, 1993. To date, over 225 additional faculty members and graduate teaching assistants have completed this program, now facilitated by Jim Eison and Ellen Stevens.

Strategies employed to maximize workshop impact. To generate participant interest in this relatively new concept, the workshop announcement described the "Creating a Teaching Portfolio" program as follows:

Creating a teaching portfolio is an especially effective way for faculty and graduate teaching assistants to become more reflective about their teaching and more skillful in documenting their teaching accomplishments to others. As a result, faculty on an ever-increasing number of campuses have prepared teaching portfolios to guide their instructional improvement efforts and to strengthen their applications for employment, tenure, promotion, or teaching awards. Participants in this interactive workshop will examine how portfolios are best conceptualized, planned, written, and revised.

The three primary workshop goals of this three-hour workshop are as follows: (1) Participants learn how teaching portfolios can be used to document and enhance teaching effectiveness, (2) Participants formulate a personal teaching portfolio plan, and (3) Participants receive written resources for use in portfolio preparation. The program was designed to provide a conceptual overview, short yet practical, hands-on writing opportunities, and materials to assist participants' efforts to later prepare portfolios on their own personal timetable. In terms of how the workshops are conducted, faculty must pre-register. Once the three-hour program begins, facilitators involve participants in completing several short activities (e.g., reading, working in pairs or in groups, questioning, and discussing). At the conclusion of the program, participants receive personalized "Certificates of Participation" that could be included in a teaching portfolio as evidence of their individual continuing efforts to improve their instructional effectiveness.

Workshop evaluation procedures and/or outcomes measures. Participants complete a short workshop evaluation form consisting of several traditional five-point Likert rating scale items as well as providing a written response to an "open-ended" question.

They are asked to complete the following sentence: "The workshop did a (an) _____ job of describing how a teaching portfolio can be used to document and enhance teaching." Fifty-seven percent of the 171 participants who attended one of the first ten workshops responded "Excellent" and 32% responded "Very Good." Similarly, in response to the sentence, "In summary, the workshop did a (an) _____ job of describing why teaching portfolios are especially useful and how teaching portfolios are best prepared," 58% of the participants responded "Excellent" and 33% responded "Very Good."

Responses to the open-ended evaluation question asking participants to "Comment on any aspect of today's workshop (e.g., content, usefulness, facilitation) and to offer suggestions for future activities on teaching portfolios" included statements such as:

- Very good workshop. Within the allocated time, the presentation of material was both substantive and, I believe, quite helpful in my efforts to prepare my own portfolio. Thanks.
- The workshop was thorough and effective. It provided stimulation and the exchange of ideas. I especially appreciate the distribution of written resources so that I don't have to try to hunt down information about the subject when I would have no idea where to look for the best sources or even which ones would be the most helpful.
- I came to the workshop with no idea of what was involved. You have made it much clearer to me—helped me start focusing my thoughts by presenting a good "sense" of the basic idea.
- I am continually impressed with the resourcefulness and creativity of these workshops on teaching effectiveness. They are stimulating and always offer a challenge for innovative thoughts and methods.
- Excellent presentation but I must do my homework to see how well I have learned.

Conclusions. As seen readily in these remarks, participants reported consistently favorable reactions to this program. Most importantly, these remarks support the conclusion that the explicit workshop goals—introducing the teaching portfolio as a teaching enhancement document, providing limited practice in creating a personal portfolio plan, and providing additional resources—were accomplished. The pre-registration and attendance data indicate that our implicit goal of reaching faculty from different disciplines, backgrounds, and ranks was also achieved. This case illustrates a workshop designed to appeal to a wide audience, that incorporated realistic and time-appropriate goals, encouraged active participation, and employed useful assessment procedures.

Case Study Two: A Ten-Day Summer Institute

Institute rationale. The need to employ teaching strategies that involve and engage students in active learning throughout higher education has been well documented (e.g., Bonwell and Eison, 1991). Unfortunately, more traditional "teaching is telling" instructional methodologies prevail in the university. The discrepancy between how faculty should teach and how they do teach was viewed as both real and distressing. To address this concern, the CTE at USF has designed and conducted five intensive ten-day summer institutes for faculty entitled "Involving Students: Using Active Learning Strategies in University Classes." To date, over 125 faculty have participated.

Strategies employed to maximize institute impact. To help ensure a high level of participant motivation, faculty members interested in participating in the institute were required to submit a letter of application describing why they wanted to attend and how they hoped to benefit from this program; the name of one course that they would focus on during the program; and their teaching assignment, including the number of undergraduate students served and the number of graduate teaching assistants supervised. A recommendation from their department chairperson was also required. To help maximize the sharing of perspectives and classroom experiences during the institute, participants were selected from the applicant pool to ensure group diversity in terms of race, gender, and academic discipline, as well as level of university teaching experience. Last, but certainly not least, to create an uninterrupted, intensive institute experience, the program was offered during a two-week period in the summer when faculty were generally not in the classroom or on contract. Participants were paid a $1,500 (US) honorarium provided through a grant from the State of Florida Higher Education System.[5]

Helping participants meet and exchange teaching experiences with faculty colleagues from across campus was an important part of the opening session and all subsequent activities. In addition, a variety of active learning strategies were demonstrated and modeled on the first day as participants explored such issues as (a) What is active learning and why is it important? (b) What obstacles commonly prevent faculty from using active learning strategies? and (c) How can these obstacles be overcome? On subsequent days, participants learned practical and research-based strategies, such as creating a classroom climate that supports active-learning approaches; enhancing traditional lectures; using writing to enhance students' comprehension and retention of course subject matter; designing cooperative learning experiences; and addressing difficult issues of testing and grading in active-learning classroom environments. To further enhance participants' knowledge and pedagogic skills after the institute, an extensive *Resource Book* containing session notes and activities, article reprints, and annotated bibliographies was prepared. In addition, participants each received four texts (one at the beginning of the institute, one during the second week, and two at the end of the institute).[6]

Structured follow-up activities were an integral part of the institute. For example, following each institute, to help "spread the word" across campus, the CTE requested that the appropriate chairpersons and deans encourage participants to describe their experiences with colleagues at departmental and college meetings. A significant number of the participants have reported that they were invited to do so; many were thrilled with the positive reactions they received from their colleagues as a result of their presentations. To stimulate continued interaction and collaboration among participants, social reunions and additional instructional skill-building workshops were conducted (e.g., "Teaching Students to Think Critically" and "Recognizing and Responding to Learning Style Differences"). To encourage further reflection on the use of active learning strategies in their classes, participants were invited to prepare manuscripts for a forthcoming CTE monograph entitled *Active Learning: From Theory to Classroom Application* and to develop conference presentations for discipline-based regional or national meetings.

Institute evaluation procedures and outcomes measures. To evaluate the institute's effectiveness and to demonstrate possible outcomes, five sources of data were collected and examined (Eison, 1992): (1) participants' written evaluation of the program, (2) participant interviews conducted four months after the institute, (3) participants' attendance at follow-up workshops and reunions, (4) participants' contributions to *Active Learning: From Theory to Classroom Application*, and (5) participants' scholarly presentations at conferences.

Each participant completed an anonymous written evaluation of the program consisting of several sentence completion items during the final institute session. A complete summary of the results was prepared; illustrative examples are noted below.

When completing the sentence, "My expectations for this program have ...," participants typically reported that their expectations had been met or surpassed. Statements described the institute as "the most intellectually exciting experience in years" and that "it not only explained different teaching techniques, but it presented the participants with a whole new way of thinking about the educational process and their role in it."

Because the institute was designed to provide an opportunity for faculty to meet and share ideas with colleagues, the second item asked respondents to comment on their colleagues. Responses indicated that participants viewed each other as valuable resources and that all actively sought ways to help one another benefit from the program. Members commented on how openly colleagues discussed personal experiences and how the mutual respect promoted friendships that could last a lifetime. When asked to comment on the facilitators, the majority of the responses expressed appreciation for the way the facilitators modeled active learning and practiced what they taught.

Throughout the sessions, participants were challenged to identify ways particular active learning strategies might be used in their classes. Many wrote of a new sense of rejuvenation and renewed excitement for teaching. Some described how they previously felt "burned out" on teaching and saw no way out before the workshop. Now they felt refreshed and more secure in trying new techniques.

When asked to describe the long-term benefits of the institute, the participants related a sense of renewed excitement about teaching. They anticipated fewer bored students and an increased amount of productive learning. Another significant benefit noted was that the institute made the participants more sensitive to students' individual differences (e.g., personality, gender, ethnicity, and culture) beyond differences in intellectual ability.

The last evaluation item asked participants to note additional comments. Two participants' views were as follows:

> *I was genuinely surprised and pleased that the University would offer me concrete assistance in my teaching instead of merely expecting excellent teaching along with publications, creativity, service, etc. Thanks!*

> *This workshop has been the single most effective learning experience I have ever had in all my education. I am not exaggerating…*

To assess the long-term impact of the initial two institutes, a graduate student who served as a participant observer during the programs conducted individual interviews with 36 participants approximately four months after the institutes. These hour-long confidential sessions explored ways the institute influenced participants' teaching during the subsequent semester, how effective these changes have been, what additional follow-up activities might be planned, and how subsequent programs might be improved. The interviews clearly suggest that a majority of participants made educationally significant changes in their teaching methods. For example, 21 of 36 faculty (i.e., 58%) reported an increased use of class discussion as opposed to "standard lectures;" 20 of these 21 participants (i.e., 95%) reported seeing positive results from the discussions (e.g., students were more attentive and had higher energy levels in class). In addition, 21 of 36 participants (i.e., 58%) reported using group projects with similarly positive results. Other frequently mentioned instructional changes included (1) increased awareness of the important role of creating a positive classroom climate upon the teaching and learning process; (2) modification of lecture techniques to stimulate students' metacognitive involvement with the presentation (e.g., providing two-minute pauses or using the "think-pair-share" cooperative learning strategy); (3) improvement in one's questioning strategies to promote increased class participation and higher-order thinking; and (4) increased use of short in-class writing activities to enhance comprehension, retention, and group discussions. While evaluation of this kind requires an investment of time by the participants and funding for the graduate student assistant, documenting the long-term impact of institutes is essential to weighing their merits and planning for future events.

Social reunions and additional instructional skill-building workshops conducted as follow-up activities to the summer institutes were not especially well attended given faculty members' busy schedules during the school year. Twenty of the 42 participants in the initial two institutes did, however, submit manuscripts for *Active Learning: From Theory to Classroom Application*. And, since the institute began, at least five participants are known to have presented papers on their classroom use of active learning strategies at discipline-based regional and national conferences; the institute facilitators have similarly made three presentations at national conferences.

Conclusions. As in every teaching and learning context, the ten-day summer institute described above was different for each faculty participant. Further, not all enjoyed and/or benefitted equally from the physically tiring and intellectually exhausting experience. Converging evidence from the five different sources of data, however, suggests that the institute did indeed have a powerful and lasting impact on most participants.

This case illustrates issues related to the conceptualization, impact, and assessment of institutes. The application procedure ensured a diverse group of participants and provided relevant background information that guided the facilitators in designing sessions that maximized faculty's efforts to learn, reflect upon, and practice new ideas about teaching. The CTE's ongoing communication with these faculty included an invitation to contribute manuscripts to a monograph and encouragement to share what they had learned with colleagues. The evaluations, both immediate and delayed, demonstrated the overall achievement of the institute's goals. In addition to the direct instructional benefits experienced by the thousands of students taught annually by the 125 faculty participants, the summer institutes have helped the CTE identify a large and growing cadre of faculty supporters committed to focusing greater attention campus wide towards teaching excellence.

What Conclusions can be Drawn About Faculty Development Workshops and Institutes?

Over 20 years ago, Freedman and Sanford (1973) commented sadly that, "Perhaps the clearest evidence that teaching undergraduates is not a true profession is the fact that professors, when they talk shop, almost never discuss their teaching" (p. 11). There is increasing evidence in the literature of higher education that this statement is less true on many campuses in 1994 and that workshops and institutes are used widely by faculty developers to stimulate and structure faculty conversations about teaching. Skillfully planned and implemented workshops and institutes provide an efficient and cost-effective opportunity to introduce faculty to the art, craft, science, and research on effective teaching. Further, such events enable facilitators to model and demonstrate effective instructional practices while similarly providing participants with opportunities to share with and learn from faculty colleagues teaching in other disciplines. Participants' evaluations of both the teaching portfolio workshop and the active learning summer institutes conducted at the University of South Florida suggest that such goals can be achieved with consistency. Conversations with faculty development professionals at national and regional conferences in the US indicate clearly that these findings are not unique; campus-based workshop and institute success stories abound, though they seldom appear in the published literature of the profession.

As described previously, productive conversations about teaching can be organized for large interdisciplinary groups or small discipline-based units; program structures can range from a 90-minute workshop to a ten-day summer institute or semester-long study group. Imperative to proper program planning is careful analysis of who the anticipated participants will be, what an appropriate set of program goals might be, and how the facilitator or facilitators will model instructional excellence when conducting the program. Though no simple formula offers guaranteed workshop or institute success, Browne and Keeley (1988) have astutely reminded faculty developers that, "A workshop often produces an adrenaline surge. . . After the workshop, participants ordinarily return to their busy schedules and comfortable habits" (p. 100). Because we all recognize this pattern, it is essential that instructional development workshops be seen as a foundation on which faculty must build. Follow-up communiqués and events help extend significantly the impact and life of a successful workshop or institute.

Last, but certainly not least, program quality can be improved and the literature in faculty development enhanced by attending carefully to the assessment of program impact and publishing both workshop and institute success stories, as well as publishing the equally informative stories of lessons learned when program difficulties occur.

REFERENCES

Bonwell, C.C., & Eison, J.A. (1991). *Active learning: Creating excitement in the classroom* (ASHE-ERIC Higher Education Reports No. 1). Washington, DC: The George Washington University, School of Education and Human Development.

Brinko, K.T., Tiberius, R.G., Atkins, S.S., & Greene, J.A. (1992). Reflections on teaching courses in faculty development: Three case studies. *To Improve the Academy, 11,* 217-232.

Browne, M.N., & Keeley, S.M. (1988). Successful instructional development workshops. *College Teaching, 36*(3), 98-101.

Cochran, L.H. (1989). *ACT: Administrative commitment to teaching.* Cape Girardeau, MO: Step Up.

Cooper, J.E., & Chattergy, V. (1993). Developing faculty multicultural awareness: An examination of life roles and their cultural components. *To Improve the Academy, 12,* 81-96.

Eble, K. (1972). *Professors as teachers.* San Francisco, CA: Jossey-Bass.

Eble, K.E., & McKeachie, W.J. (1986). *Improving undergraduate education through faculty development.* San Francisco, CA: Jossey-Bass.

Eison, J. (1989). Mandatory teaching effectiveness workshops for new faculty: What a difference three years make. *The Journal of Staff, Program, & Organization Development, 7*(2), 59-66.

Eison, J. (1992, October). *Involving students: Using active learning strategies in university classes.* A paper presented at the 1992 POD National Conference, Wesley Chapel, FL.

Eison, J., & Hill, H.H. (1990). Creating workshops for new faculty. *The Journal of Staff, Program, & Organization Development, 8*(4), 223-234.

Eison, J., Janzow, F., & Bonwell, C. (1990). Active learning in faculty development workshops: Or, practicing what we teach. *The Journal of Staff, Program, & Organization Development, 8*(2), 81-99.

Erickson, G. (1986). A survey of faculty development practices. *To Improve the Academy, 5,* 182-196.

Frederick, P.J. (1987). Student involvement: Active learning in large classes. In M. Weimer (Ed.), *New Directions for Teaching and Learning: No. 32. Teaching large classes well* (pp. 45-56). San Francisco, CA: Jossey-Bass.

Freedman, M. (Ed.). (1973). *New Directions for Higher Education: No. 1. Facilitating faculty development.* San Francisco, CA: Jossey-Bass.

Freedman M., & Sanford, N. (1973). The faculty member yesterday and today. In M. Freedman (Ed.), *New Directions for Higher Education: No. 1. Facilitating faculty development.* San Francisco, CA: Jossey-Bass.

Geis, G.L., & Smith, R.A. (1989). If professors are adults. *The Journal of Staff, Program & Organization Development, 7*(4), 155-163.

Hellyer, S., & Boschmann, E. (1993). Faculty development programs: A perspective. *To Improve the Academy, 12,* 217-224.

Hilsen, L., & Wadsworth, E. (1988). Staging successful workshops. In E. Wadsworth (Ed.), *A handbook for new practitioners* (pp. 45-52). Stillwater, OK: Professional and Organizational Development Network in Higher Education.

Jones, W.F. (1988). Leading experiential workshops. In E. Wadsworth (Ed.), *A handbook for new practitioners* (pp. 65-72). Stillwater, OK: Professional and Organizational Development Network in Higher Education.

Kerwin, M.A., & Rhoads, J. (1993). The teaching consultants' workshop. *To Improve the Academy, 12,* 69-78.

Lacey, P.A. (1988). Faculty development and the future of college teaching. In R.E. Young & K.E. Eble (Eds.), *New Directions for Teaching and Learning: No. 33. College teaching and learning: Preparing for new commitments* (pp. 57-89). San Francisco, CA: Jossey-Bass.

Levinson-Rose, J., & Menges, R.J. (1981). Improving college teaching: A critical review of research. *Review of Educational Research, 51*(3), 403-434.

Lucas, R.A., & Harrington, M.K. (1990). Workshops on writing blocks increase proposal development. *To Improve the Academy, 9,* 129-146.

Menges, R.J. (1980). Teaching improvement strategies: How effective are they? *Current Issues in Higher Education, 1,* 25-31.

Menges, R.J., & Svinicki, M.D. (Eds.). (1991). *New Directions for Teaching and Learning: No. 45. College teaching: From theory to practice.* San Francisco, CA: Jossey-Bass.

Nelson, W.C., & Siegel, M.E. (Eds.). (1980). *Effective approaches to faculty development.* Washington, DC: Association of American Colleges.

Noonan, J.F. (1980). An institute on teaching and learning for new faculty. In W.C. Nelson & M.E. Siegel (Eds.), *Effective approaches to faculty development* (pp. 49-56). Washington, DC: Association of American Colleges.

Paulsen, M.B. (1992). Building motivation and cognition research into workshops on lecturing. *To Improve the Academy, 11*, 241-252.

Renegar, S., Summary, B., Bonwell, C., & Eison, J. (1987, Fall). Mandatory teaching effectiveness workshops for new faculty: Lessons learned the hard way. *The Journal of Staff, Program, & Organization Development, 5*(3), 114-118.

Shea, M.A. (1987). *On teaching*. Boulder, CO: Faculty Teaching Excellence Program, University of Colorado.

Sork, T.J. (1984). The workshop as a unique instructional format. In T.J. Sork (Ed.), *New Directions for Continuing Education: No. 22. Designing and implementing effective workshops* (pp. 3-10). San Francisco, CA: Jossey-Bass.

Stevens, E., & Eison, J. (1994). *Transforming teaching insights and experiences into scholarly publications*. Unpublished manuscript. University of South Florida, Center for Teaching Enhancement, Tampa, FL.

Wadsworth, E. (Ed.). (1988). *A handbook for new practitioners*. Stillwater, OK: Professional and Organizational Development Network in Higher Education.

Wadsworth, E.C. (1992). Inclusive teaching: A workshop on cultural diversity. *To Improve the Academy, 11*, 233-240.

Weimer, M. (Ed.). (1987). *New Directions for Teaching and Learning: No. 32. Teaching large classes well*. San Francisco, CA: Jossey-Bass.

Weimer, M. (1990). *Improving college teaching*. San Francisco, CA: Jossey-Bass.

Weimer, M., & Lenze, L.F. (1991). Instructional interventions: A review of the literature on efforts to improve instruction. *Higher Education: Handbook of Theory and Research, 7*, 294-333.

Weinstein, C.F., & Meyer, D.K. (1991). Cognitive learning strategies and college teaching. In R.J. Menges & M.D. Svinicki (Eds.), *New Directions for Teaching and Learning: No. 45. College teaching: From theory to practice*. San Francisco, CA: Jossey-Bass.

Wentzel, H.K. (1987, Spring). Seminars in college teaching: An approach to faculty development. *College Teaching, 35*(2), 70-71.

Young, R.E., & Eble, K.E. (Eds.). (1988). *New Directions for Teaching and Learning: No. 33. College teaching and learning: Preparing for new commitments*. San Francisco, CA: Jossey-Bass.

Appendix A

"Involving Students: Using Active Learning Strategies in University Classes"

ANNUAL FACULTY INSTITUTE

Assumptions

- We share a common commitment to teaching excellence
- We can all learn from each other's experiences
- We believe that the use of active learning strategies is appropriate to all disciplines; the appropriateness of particular active learning strategies to individual disciplines will vary
- We believe that the challenge is to choose the most suitable active learning strategies for accomplishing specific course goals

Goals

- To examine current thinking and research on teaching and learning in university classes
- To demonstrate several alternatives to traditional lecture-based instruction
- To assist participants in developing materials and techniques to more actively involve students in their classes
- To enable participants to exchange classroom ideas and experiences with colleagues
- To provide resources which further encourage participants' instructional improvement efforts
- To support participants' efforts to share their use of active learning strategies with colleagues in their disciplines

Schedule

The workshop participants will meet in Room 1138 in the SVC Annex Building. We will begin promptly at 8:30 and will break for lunch at noon. We will reconvene at 1:30 and will end by 4:30.

Thursday, July 22: The morning will begin with a workshop preview and overview. Then, to help establish a clear context for later activities, Chuck Bonwell and Jim Eison will facilitate an examination of such fundamental questions as: (1) What is active learning?; (2) Why is active learning important?; (3) What obstacles commonly limit the use of active learning strategies?; and (4) How can these obstacles be overcome?

Friday, July 23: Beginning with undoubtedly the most familiar instructional approach, Chuck and the group will examine ways to increase student involvement during lecture presentations. Research suggests that many of today's undergraduates have come to expect that during class teachers will primarily talk and students will primarily listen; faculty efforts to alter this student expectation frequently result in confusion and/or resistance. For this reason, the group will also focus on strategies that can be used to create a different type of classroom participation.

Monday, July 26: Most faculty agree that skillful questioning is central to good teaching. While asking a question may appear to be a rather simple and straightforward act, it is, in fact, an extremely complex instructional endeavor. Research has shown, for example, that in the typical classroom many faculty questions go unanswered and a very high percentage of student responses come from a very small percentage of students. Further, the way in which classroom questions are framed has been shown to influence the level and type of student thinking which results. This session, led by Marsha Vanderford, will review the different types of questions which faculty may ask and examine how one's specific instructional goals might influence the kind of questions used. During this session, participants will also begin to develop different types of course-specific questions.

Group projects and presentations are another commonly used type of active learning strategy which we will examine experientially in this workshop. In the afternoon session, we will describe a group project which participants will engage in during this two-week period. The first two tasks we will complete are the identification of topic areas for group work and the formation of project teams.

Tuesday, July 27: Effective classroom discussions help students learn to think critically and creatively as well as to synthesize and evaluate information. In this session, Jim and the group will explore alternative approaches to stimulate lively and productive classroom discussions and address discussion facilitation problems that faculty commonly experience.

Project teams will have an opportunity to meet and formulate an initial work plan (i.e., from 1:30 to 2:30).

Cooperative learning strategies have been used successfully in K–12 classrooms for many years; the instructional benefits of these techniques in university classes have more recently been demonstrated. Our second afternoon segment (i.e., from 2:45 to 4:30) will examine the use of cooperative learning in university settings and provide practical suggestions for implementing cooperative learning approaches across disciplines.

Wednesday, July 28: In addition to students participating during class discussions, oral presentations are another exciting active learning alternative. This session, facilitated by Marsha, will examine strategies faculty can use to enhance students' listening skills and to reduce students' fears of public speaking. Sample assignments designed to enhance students' speaking skills and approaches for providing feedback on student presentations will be explored.

In the afternoon, participants can do library work, group work, or individual reading and reflection.

Thursday, July 29: Approximately 15 years ago, a national "writing across the curriculum" movement demonstrated clearly that writing could be used successfully to promote student thinking and learning across disciplines. Since then, much has been learned about designing writing assignments effectively; Jim will use these lessons learned to help focus and structure our morning session.

Project teams will meet from 11:00 to 2:00. Each group is encouraged to decide where to dine collectively for lunch.

From 2:15 to 4:30, workshop participants will examine ways to evaluate students' written work efficiently.

Friday, July 30: Project teams will meet from 8:30 to 10:15. During part of this period, the groups will provide progress reports describing their plans for Wednesday's presentations to one of the three workshop facilitators.

Experienced faculty know that recent years have seen dramatic increases in student diversity on campus. This fact has powerful implications for all who care about increasing student involvement and enhancing student access. Starting at 10:30, and continuing in the afternoon, Marsha and the participants will examine ways inclusive teaching can be used to reduce inequities commonly observed in college and university classrooms.

Monday, August 2: Ellen Stevens will demonstrate "case method instruction" and the participants will critically examine elements of effective case method teaching. Participants will then have a chance to explore ways case method writing might be adapted to their own discipline and courses.

Project teams will meet from 2:30 to 4:30 to complete their final preparations for Wednesday's presentations.

Tuesday, August 3: The regular use of active learning strategies in the classroom can create special challenges for faculty when assessing student work and evaluating achievement. For this reason, Jim and the participants will spend the morning exploring practical issues and concerns regarding the evaluation of student performance in active learning classrooms.

During the afternoon session, Marsha will facilitate a large group "trouble shooting" discussion of ways to avoid or remedy problems commonly associated with student group work. This discussion will be drawn from both the research literature and the participants' shared workshop experiences.

Wednesday, August 4: Each project team will share the outcomes of their team efforts with the group. In addition to a final workshop closing activity, participants will evaluate the program's effectiveness and discuss workshop follow-up activities for the coming year.

Appendix B

Guidelines for Presenters

The following suggestions have been designed to help workshop facilitators ensure success when using active learning strategies.

When Planning the Workshop

Have clear and specific objectives for each activity. As with any teaching-learning process, the identification of unambiguous objectives may be the single most important step towards ensuring success. To model excellent teaching, faculty developers must begin by communicating clearly their intended learning objectives; these objectives then become the sextant which guides the development of instructional activities and serves as the standard against which success can be measured.

Choose an active learning strategy most appropriate for each workshop objective. The benefits of clearly stated objectives are diminished if not followed by the careful selection of activities to support them. For example, brainstorming can help generate a long list of creative ideas; short writing assignments can help set the stage for lively large group discussions; role playing activities, however, are best tried only after a climate of trust has been firmly established in the group and when a "live demonstration" is needed to achieve a workshop objective.

Employ variety in your choice of active learning strategies. As with all learning situations, the repeated use of one strategy quickly becomes monotonous and boring. Remember that variety is the spice of life; it is what successful workshops are made of.

Have confidence in the participants' ability to contribute productively. Do not underestimate the talents and creativity of your colleagues. Faculty participants typically bring extensive teaching experience with them to workshops. Inform the group that you recognize their expertise and will rely upon their experience and creativity to help accomplish the workshop's objectives.

Design carefully the written materials that will be used in the workshop. Produce an ample supply of attractive and well-organized materials for participants. A little extra effort in making nicely duplicated workshop handouts and readable overhead transparencies can make the difference between a professional and amateurish presentation. Part of a careful approach to material preparation involves ensuring that each item focuses directly on a stated workshop objective.

Allow adequate time in your plans for the group to complete each activity. Tempus fugit—and almost always faster than the time you've allowed for each activity. Faculty typically underestimate the amount of time required by learners to complete assigned tasks; consequently, we often try to accomplish too much in the time available for the program. Once your workshop objectives have been determined and your activities chosen, estimate a generous amount of time for each activity and then allow participants ten to 20 percent more time.

Plan strategies to deal with potential problems. Before the workshop, anticipate the types of potential schedule and activity problems which could arise. By thinking through how these problems can best be approached should they arise, you minimize the chance that problems—even small ones—will disrupt or redirect the workshop. Advance contingency planning can, in fact, help you turn problems into opportunities.

Anticipate how you can deal with difficult participants (e.g., the "conversation monopolizer," the "it-can't-be-done" person, the "group clown"). One all-too-frequent problem in active learning groups is the difficult participant. To reduce the impact of these distracting personalities, practice strategies that can redirect their comments and which enable you to use their behavior to achieve workshop objectives.

In pre-workshop publicity, advise participants that active involvement is expected. Do not surprise your participants with your intentions. Further, you can prevent a wide variety of problems from occurring if individuals who are uncomfortable with active learning approaches decline to attend the program.

If possible and appropriate, provide participants with a pre-workshop activity. One way to lay the foundation for a successful active learning workshop is to send a short active learning assignment to participants several days in advance of the program. This permits participants to prepare for the workshop and to arrive with a strong sense of what the workshop's objectives will be. This approach also permits the workshop facilitator to spend more workshop time on activities which can be completed only in the group setting.

During the Workshop

Arrange furniture to encourage participant interaction. The physical setting of a room can have a significant influence on the level and type of group interaction that follows. Careful thought about how the workshop environment can best be arranged to stimulate participant interaction will pay significant learning dividends. And, of course, be prepared to rearrange the room as needed.

Begin by having participants introduce themselves. Actively involving the participants from the outset by developing an activity in which they introduce themselves to one another can help establish group rapport and a sense of trust.

Communicate often your expectations regarding active participant involvement. Few things are more important than elucidating your objectives to the workshop participants. If you want participants to complete activities effectively and efficiently, they must understand why and what you expect. Ambiguity of purpose can be the downfall of useful activities such as brainstorming and role-playing. And, of course, communicate clearly your other program objectives to the group.

Seek the groups' feedback to determine if they share your objectives. Be willing to modify your original objectives if necessary. Although you may not want to permit the participants to completely redirect the workshop's focus, it is generally helpful to provide them with the opportunity to choose among several objectives which can be used to accomplish the workshop's overall purpose.

Be sensitive to differences in participants' preferred styles of learning. By carefully providing a wide variety of learning activities, you increase the likelihood of having something for everyone. For example, introverts might favor short writing activities and sharing their responses with one partner while extroverts might favor group brainstorming and role-playing activities.

Be flexible and don't be afraid to be spontaneous. Many great successes have occurred when unexpected events redirect one's teaching in an unplanned way. When such events arise, be prepared to quickly assess how the group members can best be used to achieve your objectives. Do not consider such events as unpleasant intrusions into a well-organized plan; instead, be an opportunist and look for new ways to achieve success.

Develop strategies to monitor and control time. Because active learning strategies often require considerable time, and because the workshop leader typically exercises less direct control over the group's progress, plan convenient and polite ways to change the pace of the group's activities or to bring an activity to a close.

Know when to move on or to change pace. Become sensitive to the group's energy level and pace. Allow each activity to begin slowly, climb to a peak of interest and enthusiasm, and then provide an appropriate closing.

Take care of the participants' personal needs throughout the workshop. Remember that a workshop is a social event. Prepare an atmosphere and schedule which maximizes participants' comfort. Control the room temperature, provide healthful refreshments, identify for participants the location of restrooms, and, of course, provide sufficient breaks for rest and informal interaction.

Solicit participant feedback to help improve future workshops. As with good classroom instruction, a good workshop should provide participants with an opportunity to evaluate the workshop and the effectiveness of your leadership. Invite participants to tell you in an honest and candid fashion what went well and to suggest improvements for future programs.

After the Workshop

Provide materials to stimulate further reading and study following the workshop. Participants will want to know more about the program's topic than time will allow. It is wise, therefore, to develop an annotated bibliography and/or other printed resources to guide their efforts. This will increase the likelihood that participants will continue to think about, and benefit from, the program.

If appropriate and desirable, provide follow-up activities to the workshop. With campus-based programs led by local facilitators, it is often quite possible to organize follow-up activities. Such programs can enhance greatly participants' skill-building efforts.

[Adapted from Eison, J., Janzow, F., & Bonwell, C. (1990). Active learning in faculty development workshops: Or, practicing what we teach. *The Journal of Staff, Program, & Organization Development, 8*(2), 81-99.]

AUTHORS

James Eison, founding director of the Center for Teaching Enhancement at the University of South Florida (US), has made teaching and learning in higher education the focus of his professional career. He has conducted ten extensive faculty development institutes at USF, published over 30 articles, conducted faculty development workshops on over 50 campuses, and delivered an even greater number of conference presentations. Dr. Eison is coauthor, along with Charles Bonwell, of Active Learning: Creating Excitement in the Classroom *(1991, ASHE-ERIC).*

Ellen Stevens served as USF's Center for Teaching Enhancement Assistant Director in 1993 and 1994. She is currently an Assistant Professor of Education at the University of Colorado at Denver (US). Dr. Stevens earned her doctorate in educational psychology from Stanford University. She has conducted research in the area of teaching and learning and has published articles in such prominent journals as The Journal of Higher Education *and* Review of Higher Education.

NOTES

[1] The use of the term *workshop* in this chapter will be consistent with the description provided by Sork (1984): "… *workshop* refers to a relatively short-term, intensive, problem-focused learning experience that actively involves participants in the identification and analysis of problems and with the development and evaluation of solutions" (p. 5). The term *institute* refers to a longer and more intensive faculty development experience (i.e. lasting several days or weeks) for an intact group of participants.

[2] The literature examined included, for example, *Successful Instructional Development Workshops* (Browne & Keeley, 1986); *Making Workshops Work* (Davis & Young, 1983); *Creating Workshops for New Faculty* (Eison & Hill, 1990); *Staging Successful Workshops* (Hilsen & Wadsworth, 1988); and *Leading Experiential Workshops* (Jones, 1988).

[3] In fact, much of what is proposed as "good practice" in faculty development parallels the tenets of adult learning. See Brookfield, S.D. (1988). *Understanding and facilitating adult learning.* San Francisco, CA: Jossey-Bass, for a useful and interesting overview of the adult learning literature.

[4] The teaching portfolio was an important topic in "Promoting Teaching Excellence: Six Modest Ways Department Chairpersons Can Help," a workshop presented at a retreat attended by department chairpersons and senior academic administrators. Further, the USF Undergraduate Teaching Evaluation Task Force also discussed articles on the portfolio approach and, in its report to the Provost, described the teaching portfolio as a promising method of documenting teaching competence. In addition, two prominent teaching portfolio proponents, Peter Seldin and Linda Annis (See Chapter 9 in this volume), made presentations on the topic to department chairpersons and deans.

[5] The state grant funded two workshops during the first summer of operation. The University of South Florida has funded this program each summer since.

[6] Participants received:

Bonwell, C.C., & Eison, J.A. (1991). *Active learning: Creating excitement in the classroom* (ASHE-ERIC Higher Education Reports No. 1). Washington, DC: The George Washington University, School of Education and Human Development.

Lowman, J. (1984). *Mastering the techniques of teaching*. San Francisco, CA: Jossey-Bass.

Moss, A., & Holder, C. (1988). *Improving student writing: A guidebook for faculty in all disciplines*. Pomona, CA: California State Polytechnic University.

Tiberius, R.G. (1990). *Small group teaching: A trouble-shooting guide*. Toronto, ON: OISE Press.

Although the books are meant to stimulate interest in reading more about teaching, both during the workshop period and beyond, the authors do not know if the participants draw on the texts to make changes in their teaching.

9.

Using the Teaching Portfolio to Improve Instruction

Peter Seldin
Linda F. Annis
John Zubizarreta

This chapter focuses on the teaching portfolio as a key strategy for improving instruction. It describes the concept (what it is, how it works, what might be included), highlights how portfolios lead to strengthened classroom performance, and concludes with answers to common questions and concerns about portfolio development.

INTRODUCTION

An important and welcome change is taking place on college and university campuses: teaching is being taken more seriously. Countless institutions are examining their commitment to teaching and exploring ways to improve and reward it. The movement to take teaching seriously has become a groundswell across the United States, enlisting boards of trustees, parents and students, state legislatures, financial donors, academic administrators, and faculty members to scrutinize more carefully the classroom performance of each professor.

Factual information on teaching performance is often skimpy at best. As Seldin (1993) points out, typical professors have little solid evidence about what they do in the classroom and how well they do it. Yet, in the

237

absence of factual information on teaching, how can teaching be evaluated? How can it be rewarded? How can it be improved? Is there a way for colleges and universities to respond to the movement to take teaching seriously and at the same time to the pressures to provide factual information on teaching so it can be rewarded and improved? The answer is "yes." A solution can be found by turning to the teaching portfolio, the best way we know to address both the complexity and individuality of teaching.

The portfolio approach is experiencing explosive growth. An estimated 500 institutions in the United States and Canada are experimenting with or substantively using portfolios, a stunning jump from the estimated ten employing such documents in 1990. Significantly, portfolio programs are operating on campuses everywhere. Many kinds of institutions—public and private, independent, state and church-related, community colleges and professional schools—are involved, and they are in every geographic region of the United States and Canada. Among the current institutions vitally involved with portfolios are Dalhousie University (Nova Scotia), University of Toronto (Ontario), Miami-Dade Community College (Florida), Murray State University (Kentucky), Columbia College (South Carolina), St. Norbert College (Wisconsin), and the United States Military Academy (New York).

WHAT IS A TEACHING PORTFOLIO?

A portfolio is a factual description of a professor's teaching strengths and achievements, including documents and materials that collectively suggest the scope and quality of teaching performance. The portfolio is to teaching what lists of publications, honors, and grants are to research and scholarship, adding the special benefit of providing a foundation for authentic improvement. At bottom, the portfolio does what no other form of evaluation can do: it displays and documents teaching in specific ways consistent with particular disciplinary pedagogies and institutional missions while offering the professor a genuine base for teaching enhancement.

The portfolio is *not* an exhaustive compilation of all the documents and materials that bear on teaching performance. Rather, it presents *selected* information on teaching and solid evidence of effectiveness. Just as statements in a *curriculum vitae* should be supported by convincing evidence (such as published papers of actual research data), so claims in the teaching portfolio should be substantiated by firm empirical evidence.

A word of caution: all college professors have seen poor student work dressed in fancy covers. The teaching portfolio is not an ornamental exterior but a careful, thoughtful gathering of documents and materials that judiciously and honestly reflect a professor's teaching effectiveness.

For what purposes might professors prepare teaching portfolios? They might do so in order to gather and present hard evidence and specific data about teaching competency for purposes of tenure and promotion decisions. Or they might do so in order to provide the needed structure for self-reflection about which areas of teaching performance need improvement. Significantly, the purpose for which the portfolio is used determines what is included and how it is arranged.

Seldin's *Successful Use of Teaching Portfolios* (1993) includes detailed information on using portfolios for personnel decisions. This chapter, however, consistent with other contributions in the volume, focuses exclusively on the use of portfolios for the purpose of improving teaching performance.

MENTORS AND THE VALUE OF COLLABORATION

In theory, a teaching portfolio can be prepared by a professor working alone; however, such isolation has limited prospects for improving classroom teaching. The reason, according to Seldin (1993), is that a portfolio prepared by an instructor working alone does not include the collegial support and specific suggestions and resources needed in a program of teaching improvement. In practice, we find that the portfolio is best prepared not by the professor working alone but rather in consultation with others. A department chair, a faculty colleague, or a teaching improvement specialist can discuss with professors key questions such as why they are preparing portfolios, which areas of the teaching-learning process they expect to examine, and what kinds of information they plan to collect. Some may argue that the contents of the portfolio will be colored by second-party assistance and therefore be less useful because the portfolio represents "coached" performance. But we believe that portfolio development *should* involve interaction and mentoring in the same way that a doctoral dissertation reflects both the efforts of the candidate and the advice of the mentor.

Portfolio mentors must have wide knowledge of current instruments and procedures used to document teaching performance. Faculty development specialists are especially well qualified for the role because they are trained in multiple approaches to and techniques of demonstrating teaching effectiveness; they can also provide valuable suggestions and resources as well as important support during portfolio preparation. Edgerton, Hutchings, and Quinlan concur regarding the merit of collaboration. They conclude that since teaching "tends to be a private, solitary activity, collaboratively-designed portfolios are an antidote to this isolation and a way to promote collegial exchange focused on... teaching" (1991, p. 51).

PREPARING A PORTFOLIO

No single strategy dominates in preparing a teaching portfolio: the document is a highly personalized product, like a fingerprint, and no two are alike. The items chosen depend, to some degree, on whether the portfolio is prepared for purposes of improvement or personnel decisions and on a professor's particular teaching situation. This explains why varying importance is assigned to some items by different instructors. Some professors discuss an item at length, while others address the same item in a sentence or two, or even omit it. Each portfolio is a unique, individualized document shaped by purpose; special needs; institutional culture; and particular philosophy, methods, and style.

The following is *not* a list of items a professor must include (Shore et al., 1986). Rather, it is a list of the components that turn up in portfolios more frequently than others.

The Products of Good Teaching

- Student scores on pre- and post-course exams
- Examples of graded student essays, showing excellent, average, and poor work
- A record of students who succeed in advanced study in the field
- Student publications or conference presentations on course-related work
- Testimonials from employers or students about the professor's influence on career choice

Material from Oneself

- Description of steps taken to improve one's teaching, including changes resulting from self-evaluation, reading journals on teaching one's discipline, participating in instructional development programs
- Statement of teaching responsibilities, including course titles, numbers, enrollments, and a brief description of the way each course is taught
- Instructional innovations and evaluation of their effectiveness
- Representative course syllabi detailing course content and objectives, teaching methods, readings, and homework assignments
- A personal statement describing detailed teaching goals for the next five years

Material from Others

- Student course or teaching evaluation data on diagnostic questions
- Statements from colleagues who have observed the professor in the classroom or who have systematically reviewed the instructor's teaching materials, including course syllabi, assignments, graded tests and essays
- Documentation of teaching development activity through the campus center for teaching and learning
- Statements from colleagues at other institutions on how well students have been prepared for graduate study
- Invitations to present a paper at a conference on teaching one's discipline or requests from outside agencies or community groups to offer a teaching-related workshop

These are the most commonly selected items, but they are not the only ones that appear in valid, well-developed portfolios. Some professors choose a different mix that best profiles their special teaching efforts.

How much information is needed to represent a professor's teaching performance fairly and completely? Experience suggests that a succinct document of six to eight pages (double spaced) plus supporting appendix materials is sufficient for most instructors. (Some institutions put a ceiling on the number of pages they permit in order to prevent data overkill.) Keep in mind that the portfolio does not grow indefinitely. It is a living document that changes over time: new items are added; others are removed.

A TYPICAL TABLE OF CONTENTS

A table of contents identifies the major headings of the portfolio. When the purpose of the portfolio is to improve teaching, a typical table of contents might look like this:

TEACHING PORTFOLIO

Faculty Member's Name
Department/School
Institution
Date

Table of Contents
1. Teaching Responsibilities
2. Statement of Teaching Philosophy

3. Methods and Strategies
4. Description of Course Materials: Syllabi, Assignments, Handouts
5. Efforts to Improve Teaching:
   Conferences/Workshops Attended, Curricular
   Revisions, Experiments in Pedagogy and Methodology
6. Student Ratings on Diagnostic Questions
7. Teaching Goals: Short- and Long-Term
8. Appendices

One element of such a table which may go unnoticed is the date, an item important to any portfolio written especially for teaching enhancement. A date helps the faculty member establish a base line from which to measure actual development in teaching performance. A professor's growth can be gauged by the degree to which the portfolio demonstrates instructional improvement resulting from the teacher's revaluation of philosophy, methods, materials, evaluative instruments, and goals. The portfolio, therefore, becomes one of the professor's most vital tools for authentic improvement.

IMPROVING TEACHING PERFORMANCE

Just as students need feedback to correct errors, professors need factual and philosophical data to improve teaching and performance. Feedback from a range of sources can set the stage for change. The portfolio is a particularly effective tool for instructional improvement because it is grounded in discipline-based pedagogy. That is, the focus is on teaching a particular subject to a particular group of students at a particular point in time.

The preparation of a teaching portfolio also serves to provide the stimulus and structure for self-reflection about areas of teaching that need improvement. The process of selecting and organizing material for a portfolio often results in thinking about teaching in new ways. This process is likely to lead to improved classroom performance. We firmly believe that teaching improvement should be the primary purpose of portfolio development, with use for personnel decisions occurring only occasionally.

More specifically, as Seldin and Annis (1990) point out, the process of collecting the documents and materials that comprise the teaching portfolio encourages the professor to:

- reconsider teaching activities
- rethink teaching strategies and priorities
- plan for the future

Hutchings agrees and states that "as a result, [portfolios] capture the uniqueness of each individual's teaching in a way that few other methods can" (1992, p. 7).

TEACHING PORTFOLIOS, TEACHING IMPROVEMENT, AND THE INDIVIDUAL PROFESSOR

Teaching improvement requires information that can help identify strengths and problems. Because no one formula exists for a portfolio used for teaching improvement, faculty members preparing portfolios focus on what they believe is important in teaching and then secure supportive *evidence*. Once the professor focuses on clear documentation of good teaching, the extraneous, unsupported claims fade away, and teaching problems and opportunities for improvement become clear.

For example, in the following reflective statements, one of the present chapter's authors discovered three major benefits of preparing a teaching portfolio in the area of educational psychology:

1. I Became Clearer About My Teaching Role Within the Department.

Despite teaching in my department for more than 20 years, I had *never* formally described in writing my teaching role. Once I prepared my portfolio, I became clearer on where I have focused my efforts and was able to think sharply about my teaching goals and plans. This exercise taught me that over the years my teaching and research interests have shifted from teaching developmental psychology courses to teaching courses emphasizing teaching and learning. Since that time, I have discussed my discoveries with my department chair, and my teaching assignments are now more reflective of my new emphases. For example, currently I supervise doctoral students who teach sections of a course that I designed on student learning.

2. The Process Helped Me Focus on the Necessity of Documenting the Products of Student Learning.

This is the most troublesome area for many faculty to document in their portfolios. Even people in educational psychology are not immune to the common difficulty of being unable to *document* the effects of teaching on student learning. Preparing a portfolio highlighted the problem for me. Since that time, I have instituted pre- and post-testing of students in all sections of the student learning course I supervise. Recently, I did extensive assessment research on the impact of this course on students, and I now have solid evidence to document its impact on student study behavior.

3. I was Better Able to Formulate Teaching Improvement Goals.

Once I charted in my portfolio what I *was* doing in my teaching, the gaps then became obvious. Consequently, I have both immediate and long-term goals for improvement. For instance, after preparing my portfolio, I realized that I had little or no group work or collaborative learning activities in my classes. Because of exposure to such techniques in my reading and from professional presentations I had attended, I became aware of the value of group learning and wanted to integrate collaborative methods into my classes. Thus, I began with the goal of including at least one group activity in every class I teach. I am convinced that student learning has increased as a result. In fact, I am now planning to make the value of collaboration the next aspect of student learning that I document in future revisions of my portfolio.

How Preparing Portfolios Provides Opportunities for Faculty Development Centers

Current research on teaching enhancement strongly supports the use of teaching portfolios as an important element of faculty development. Seldin (1993) states, "Experience on campus after campus suggests that if the professor is motivated to improve, knows how to improve, or where to go for help, improvement is quite likely" (p. 10). Blackburn and Pitney echo the sentiment:

> We believe a portfolio system would accomplish the goal of continuous faculty growth and development, the realization of the individual's full potential. We believe that the portfolio process fits the conclusions from the research literature and college and university norms, values, structures, and practices. (1988, p. 32)

As faculty members begin to prepare their portfolios, gaps often appear in their ability to provide *evidence* of good teaching in the three basic areas of documentation; thus, an opportunity arises for faculty development centers to offer services to assist in improving professors' ability to document good teaching. The opportunity is, in educational terminology, a very "teachable" moment and an excellent chance for faculty development centers to demonstrate the value of their services.

As noted above, items included in the portfolio commonly fall into the following categories: products of good teaching, material from others, and material from oneself. Ways faculty developers can assist faculty members in generating and compiling evidence in these three basic areas include:

Products of Good Teaching

1. Work with faculty to plan a way to pre-test their students at the beginning of the course on specific aspects of learning and then to retest them at the end of the course. Such information provides concrete evidence of how students have changed as a result of the course. Since faculty often do not have such data currently available, they sometimes must describe their plans to gather the information as a short-term goal in their portfolios.

2. Encourage faculty members to include in the appendix of their portfolios various drafts of student papers with instructor comments and then successive, improved versions of student work. In the narrative body of the portfolio, formative analysis of such student products can complement the appendix material and provide the impetus for detailed change and improvement.

3. Suggest that faculty assign students to produce "Learning Journals" of the kind Humphries and Kramp (1992) discuss. Students are asked to describe where they were initially in their learning in a class and then to detail and assess their growth through responses to various class activities as the class progresses.

Materials from Self

1. Consult with the faculty member regarding various teaching methodologies. Provide resources and models of different teaching philosophies in order to assist the professor in writing a description of teaching philosophy, objectives, and strategies.

2. Provide classroom observation services so that the faculty developer can help the professor prepare a personal assessment of teaching-related activities. The faculty developer can also consult with the teacher in making curricular revisions which can then be described in the portfolio.

3. Work with the faculty member in planning and writing a conference presentation or journal article describing unique teaching ideas to colleagues.

Material from Others

1. Provide videotaping services so the professor can include a full-period videotape of himself or herself teaching a class. An alternative tape might consist of selected segments of various class periods to try to capture the instructor's different methods and levels of performance. Such tapes can be used by a faculty developer as the focus of a process of mentoring and formative evaluation.

2. Develop a mechanism for obtaining student course evaluations and then provide a consulting service so faculty can analyze their evaluations with a faculty developer and plan strategies for improvement.

3. Help faculty with methods of classroom assessment and research for determining student reactions to teachers and teaching methods (Cross & Angelo, 1988). Examples include the one-minute paper and the mid-course review.

Faculty developers often comment that professors who prepare portfolios frequently discover good ideas for improving teaching. The portfolio process is an opportunity for faculty development centers to provide the services, expertise, and encouragement faculty need to put their own good ideas into actual practice.

At the beginning of the teaching portfolio movement, Hart (1989) prophetically stated, "If faculty are to be motivated to change or modify their teaching to improve learning, the portfolio approach may represent an important step in discovering the conditions and circumstances that will facilitate the process" (p. 3). Enhancing student learning is, of course, the motivation behind our advocating the use of teaching portfolios. As a result of our experiences as faculty developers, portfolio mentors, and writers of our own teaching portfolios, we contend that commitment to the use of portfolios results in improved teaching. The ultimate beneficiaries are our students.

COMMON QUESTIONS ABOUT PORTFOLIOS FOR IMPROVEMENT

The teaching portfolio is a boon for faculty committed to improvement because it connects the benefits of deliberate reflection and written analysis with the necessary validation of empirical evidence—a combination that inspires critical insight into teaching philosophy, methods, and outcomes and that leads to real change, especially with the valuable help of a mentor. The most important motives for a faculty member to engage in the process of writing a portfolio are enhancement and revitalization of teaching effectiveness. Hence, the following questions reflect the typical concerns faculty may have during the process of developing a portfolio for the purpose of improvement. The questions raise issues of value, rationale, strategy, motivation, implementation, style, structure, and cost—crucial, productive dialogue that focuses on the unique challenges and rewards of portfolios written to enrich the quality of teaching.

1. If one is a competent teacher already, why use valuable time writing a lengthy, exhaustive teaching portfolio instead of working on scholarly publications?

The portfolio is not a complete history of teaching that includes every minute detail of a faculty member's career as an instructor. Rather, it is a selective profile of teaching accomplishments and goals. In a portfolio written for improvement, items are chosen because they highlight an instructor's range of responsibilities and *possibilities*. Selective discussion of a professor's pedagogical values, strategic successes, opportunities for refined approaches, representative materials, evaluations, and goals points toward future inquiry and action that promote better teaching. Selectivity means fair and generous representation in an honest and reflective profile, not culled and biased information which deludes no one, especially not the professor whose aim is to cultivate teaching. Watkins quotes professors who complain, "A lot of faculty members already have enough to do. They won't want to bother with a portfolio" (1990, p. A17). Yet, faculty spend countless hours writing and documenting research as part of their calling and responsibilities. The quality time spent on a portfolio is not time away from worthwhile research projects, for it is doubtful any professor could complete a creditable professional journal article in the time it takes to produce a valuable portfolio with the help of a trained mentor. The sensible selectivity of a portfolio allows a teacher to spend a manageable few hours to enhance the quality of teaching and redress the balance of teaching and research.

2. What is the guarantee that a portfolio is not comprised of culled and biased information, that it does not circumvent poor teaching, subverting genuine improvement?

The answer to this suspicion is the same as for a *curriculum vitae*. Since the portfolio is an evidence-based document, all information in the narrative must be substantiated in the appendix. If, for example, a *curriculum vitae* lists scores of stellar research accomplishments and publications, the faculty member must be ready to produce actual, empirical evidence in the form of letters, awards, offprints. Similarly, if an instructor claims in a portfolio that student evaluations rate the teacher's high scholarly expectations as outstanding, then rating forms in an appendix must demonstrate excellence in the particular area of performance. If evidence does not corroborate the claim, then the professor knows vividly where improvement is needed. Additionally, a sound portfolio clearly integrates all areas of concern (materials from oneself and others and products of student learning) and offers a *coherent* teaching profile in which all parts support the whole.

For instance, not only will student evaluations bolster the claim of high scholarly expectations but comments from peers and superiors will, too; the statement of philosophy will reflect an emphasis on scholarship in teaching; methods and materials will reveal a focus on scholarship perhaps through descriptions of bibliographies included in syllabi or through library assignments incorporated into weekly activities; and goals will underline the scholarly integrity of the faculty member, suggesting plans to earn a teaching Fulbright or fellowship or to assist students in writing for publication. The key point is that a portfolio cannot hide poor instruction or augment mediocre teaching because in such cases the evidence of excellence simply is not present. Consequently, all efforts toward improvement are grounded genuinely in clearly identified, specific areas. Initiatives for development are focused and precise for effective action.

3. Improvement strongly depends upon risk and experimentation. Can portfolios help teachers improve performance by encouraging experimentation?

Portfolios provide a vehicle for change and development through continual inquiry and analysis. The portfolio does not side step occasional poor performance. After all, few teachers are perfect, and, in fact, the best teachers are daring and experimental, making them more susceptible to flop from time to time. The question is how such teachers continue to maintain overall excellence. The answer is probably that outstanding educators know the value of assessment and change based on experience. Improvement is their constant aim. If institutions state as a specific criterion for evaluation of outstanding teaching the imperatives of innovation, change, and improvement, then the professor's inclusion of a failed classroom endeavor, a singular weak evaluation, or an anomalous unsuccessful course is not a shortcoming but a sign of confidence and competence. The professor's risks will be congruent with institutional priorities, and the portfolio may be the arena in which the teacher turns weaknesses into strengths.

4. Does a gifted writer have a distinct advantage because of developed communication skills?

First, we must remember that a teacher may write a portfolio for purposes other than trying to convince someone else (a personnel committee or award granting agency, for instance) of teaching performance. A portfolio driven by personal mandates for improvement needs no external approval of its style. But since the portfolio is best written in collaboration with a mentor who assists the instructor in discovering and highlighting teaching accomplishments, in developing a clear and effective way of communicating teaching effort, and in identifying improvement opportunities, then most faculty may be assured that most portfolios are honest, useful documents that make the difficult work of mapping out a program for teaching development focused and detailed. And the bottom line, after all, is that no degree of communication savvy or style can make up for the realities of teaching performance as clearly demonstrated through the assessment component of a portfolio. Style is no substitute for real evidence of improvement.

5. How does one maintain the integrity of a portfolio written for enhancement purposes only?

If a portfolio is written for the express purpose of teaching improvement, its scope and content will shift from a wide case for teaching accomplishment and a catalogue of summative evaluation and assessment materials to a narrow, intensive investigation of a particular strategy or a single course. Such a shift reflects an interest in formative discoveries that may lead to philosophical reconsiderations, curricular changes, revision of materials, or new goals for novel experiments. The portfolio, then, is not an apology for teaching or an argument for promotion or tenure; rather, it is an opportunity to reflect upon what has worked in a particular class or in a special teaching enterprise, what has not, and what detailed plans the instructor has to improve the quality of instruction. Some faculty choose to write a short portfolio for each class taught, perhaps selectively highlighting the scope of responsibilities for courses from introductory to advanced, undergraduate to graduate, general education to major levels. In an article describing an AAHE-funded experiment at Ball State University (US), Watkins reports that, although portfolios appear extremely useful for evaluation and salary decisions, the "primary value of a portfolio may lie in self-improvement." Faculty at the institution say that the "process of creating the collection of materials forces them to think seriously about their teaching goals and strategies" (1990, p. A16). Writing portfolios for teaching enhancement stimulates creativity, self-conscious process, and critical scrutiny of why, what, and how we teach. As Seldin says in Watkins' piece, "[P]ortfolios provide a structure for self-improvement efforts," lending value and integrity to the process itself (1990, p. A15).

6. Can the portfolio be used for valid assessment or improvement? Isn't the portfolio really a subjective document?

Faculty who ask such questions have not engaged in one of the most invigorating, rewarding, and crucial activities of writing a portfolio: the collaborative effort between the instructor and a mentor who helps steer the direction of the portfolio to meet the needs of assessment or improvement. Collaboration—especially if the mentor is an outside consultant, a departmental chair, or a peer outside the discipline—insures a fresh, vital, critical perspective that encourages cohesion between the portfolio's narrative and appendices, a connectedness that is important in pinpointing exact areas of development. Virtually all literature on portfolios urges faculty to enlist the creative and supportive help of a mentor in preparing portfolios. For example, in *Teaching Excellence*, a bulletin offprint of the Professional and Organizational Development Network in Higher Education, Seldin and Annis (1991-92) argue from experience that a portfolio "is best prepared in consultation with others. A department chair, a colleague or a faculty development specialist... can discuss with the professor key questions: Which areas of the teaching-learning process are to be examined? What kinds of information [should be collected]? How is the information to be analyzed and presented?" (See also Bird, 1989; Edgerton et al., 1991; Seldin, 1991, 1993; Shore et al., 1986; O'Neil & Wright, 1991; Watkins, 1990). An effective mentor does not assist the instructor in producing or, worse, fabricating subjective, effusive, culled information. Instead, a trained mentor flushes out objective information that is already evident or readily discovered in a teacher's work. An effective mentor's primary role is to help a colleague improve instruction both by referring to authentic products of good teaching which he or she already has, and by identifying areas where the colleague could further develop. Collaboration, then, is a pivotal dimension of the portfolio development process: it counters subjectivity and links the portfolio to objective criteria of excellence that set the parameters for improvement.

7. If the role of the mentor—in addition to a clear, institutional statement of teaching excellence and a balance between narration and evidence—is critical to objectivity and to improvement, then how can an institution manage the cost of workshops and consultations when faculty development money already is scarce? Where does an institution find its mentors?

Writing in isolation does not produce quality portfolios; collaboration is essential; mentors are indispensable. Once faculty have been taught initially about the portfolio and coached by trained mentors, and once faculty are invested in the portfolio concept, a core group may emerge as experienced leaders who can help others in developing useful portfolios. A faculty development administrator may facilitate the process by providing opportunities for in-house workshops; by scheduling appointments between initiates and mentors; by educating faculty, staff, and top-level administrators about portfolios; and by setting aside a library of reading materials, forms, and models related to the portfolio. Eventually, such mentoring and improvement efforts may reach all faculty devoted to strengthening teaching. The cost is nominal; the payoff is better teaching; the ultimate winners are students.

8. The portfolio concept is undoubtedly useful to junior faculty, but why would senior faculty write one?

All faculty stand to benefit from writing a portfolio. In schools where post-tenure review is required, portfolios may play a major role in describing and documenting a professor's ongoing commitment to teaching improvement and professional integrity. Portfolios may also become instrumental in determining salary increases, merit rewards, grants, fellowships, endowed chairs, teaching awards, release time. But teaching improvement is the primary motive for engaging in the reflection and documentation that comprise a valuable portfolio. Thus, senior faculty have written portfolios in order to sharpen their skills in a particular course or to set the stage for radical experimentation. Distinguished teachers with long, impressive careers have written portfolios to leave as legacies within their departments. Such documents will help junior faculty learn intricate details about teaching certain courses, about forging a successful teaching career in the discipline, about what works or doesn't in this or that course, about opportunities for teaching enhancement in the department, or about the student culture in the institution.

9. How important are student learning outcomes in a portfolio, and is there any evidence to suggest that portfolios enhance outcomes?

The products of student learning are an integral component of a valid, complete portfolio. Without the inclusion of the products of good teaching, the reliability of a portfolio, its capacity to address the rigorous demands of assessment, and its efficacy as an agent of change and improvement are seriously impaired. Good teaching is reflected in good outcomes. The impact of teaching on students' progress may be demonstrated by evidence such as student projects, field reports, successful practicums, essays in draft form with instructor's comments, pre- and post-testing, coached student presentations at conferences, student publications, documentation of students' success in higher level courses or post-graduate careers. No extensive studies exist to prove that portfolios strengthen student outcomes, but a portfolio raises a professor's awareness of the importance of products and of what kinds of outcomes to develop for more effective teaching and for a stronger portfolio; such reflection and strategy can improve products as a consequence of the portfolio's processes of discovery, description, documentation, and planning.

10. How different is the portfolio from other methods or programs of development that support teaching improvement?

In the sense that the portfolio goes far beyond the narrow scope of a list of courses taught, limited emphasis on student ratings, a few solicited comments from peers, and perhaps a department chair's brief, routine year-end summary, it is a thoroughly innovative and effective way to describe and document teaching achievement and to lay the groundwork for substantive improvement because it requires careful and detailed written reflection tied to evidence. While other means of collecting quantitative data may be equally serviceable for assessment purposes, the portfolio is more than a filing system. With its focus on improvement through reflective writing, and because of its development within a framework of formative collaboration, the portfolio extends past ordinary instruments of teaching assessment and enhancement usually tied to quantitative, summative information. Portfolios make improvement imminent in a way that rating forms, assessment charts, systematized evaluations, and even development money cannot.

The portfolio is not the only means of describing and documenting teaching effort, but it is the only instrument that simultaneously serves two key purposes: it evaluates performance in a framework of description and evidence, and it improves teaching through the processes of reflective writing and methodical self-scrutiny. In writing a portfolio, a faculty member feels empowered to think about teaching, a seemingly obvious, elemental but vital component of improvement. The portfolio's process of written reflection invokes the power of both personal and public narration to make the often unrecognized dimensions of teaching visible and understood by the self and by a community of readers. The instructor also learns the value of collaboration as opposed to self-serving competition in defining responsibilities, discussing values and methods, providing substantive supportive information, and delineating goals. In becoming a thoughtful practitioner, the faculty member becomes more intentional in generating actual products of good teaching, making students the real beneficiaries of the work that goes into a teaching portfolio.

Finally, the portfolio stands to change the way teaching is not only defined and assessed but valued in the academy, reclaiming the significance of teaching in faculty roles, encouraging continual re-examination of disciplinary pedagogy and teaching methodology, and promoting real evidence of vital improvement.

REFERENCES

Bird, T. (1989). The schoolteacher's portfolio. In L. Darling-Hammond & J. Millman (Eds.), *Handbook on the evaluation of elementary and secondary schoolteachers.* Newbury Park, CA: Sage.

Blackburn, R. T., & Pitney, J. A. (1988). *Performance appraisal for faculty: Implications for higher education* (Tech. Rep. No. 88-D-00210). Ann Arbor, MI: University of Michigan, National Center for Research to Improve Postsecondary Teaching and Learning.

Cross, K. P., & Angelo, T. A. (1988). *Classroom assessment techniques: A handbook for faculty.* Ann Arbor, MI: University of Michigan, National Center for Research to Improve Postsecondary Teaching and Learning.

Edgerton, R., Hutchings, P., & Quinlan, K. (1991). *The teaching portfolio: Capturing the scholarship in teaching.* Washington, DC: American Association for Higher Education.

Hart, K. (1989). Faculty performance appraisal: A recommendation for growth and change. *Accent on improving college teaching and learning.* Ann Arbor, MI: University of Michigan, National Center on Research to Improve Postsecondary Teaching and Learning.

Humphries, W.L., & Kramp, M.K. (1992). *Narrative self-assessment and reflective learners and teachers.* Knoxville, TN: University of Tennessee, Learning Research Center.

Hutchings, P. (1992, Spring). And gladly teach: The changing world of faculty work. *Virginia Commonwealth Teaching, 7,* pp. 2-5.

O'Neil, M.C., & Wright, W.A. (1991). *Recording teaching accomplishment: A Dalhousie guide to the teaching dossier.* Halifax, NS: Dalhousie University, Office of Instructional Development and Technology.

Seldin, P. (1991). *The teaching portfolio: A practical guide to improved performance and promotion/tenure decisions.* Bolton, MA: Anker.

Seldin, P., & Annis, L.F. (1990). The teaching portfolio. *The Journal of Staff, Program & Organization Development, 8,* 197-201.

Seldin, P., & Annis, L.F. (1991-92). The teaching portfolio. *Teaching Excellence: Toward the Best in the Academy, 3*(2). Publication of the Professional and Organizational Development Network in Higher Education.

Seldin, P., & Associates. (1993). *Successful use of teaching portfolios*. Bolton, MA: Anker.

Shore, B.M., Foster, S.F., Knapper, C.K., Nadeau, G.G., Neill, N., Sim, V.W., and with the help of faculty members of the Centre for Teaching and Learning Services, McGill University. (1986). *The teaching dossier* (rev. ed.). Ottawa, ON: Canadian Association of University Teachers.

Watkins, B.T. (1990, May 16). New technique tested to evaluate college teaching. *The Chronicle of Higher Education*, pp. A15-17.

AUTHORS

Peter Seldin is Distinguished Professor of Management, Pace University, Pleasantville, New York (US). A specialist in the evaluation and development of faculty performance and the teaching portfolio, he has conducted seminars for faculty and administrators around the world. Dr. Seldin's well-received books include Successful Use of Teaching Portfolios (1993), The Teaching Portfolio (1991), Evaluating and Developing Administrative Performance (1988), and Changing Practices in Faculty Evaluation (1984).

Linda Annis is Professor of Educational Psychology, Ball State University, Muncie, Indiana, (US) where she has taught since 1969. From 1986 to 1991, she was the founding Director of the Center for Teaching and Learning at Ball State University. Dr. Annis is the author of two books, numerous articles, and has made many presentations in the areas of learning, study techniques, and faculty development. She has been involved in writing, in speaking, and in providing workshops at various institutions on the topic of teaching portfolios and teaching improvement.

Recognized for exemplary teaching by the American Association for Higher Education, the South Atlantic Association of Departments of English, the Methodist Board of Higher Education, the South Carolina Commission on Higher Education, Columbia College, and by the Carnegie Foundation as CASE Professor of the Year (1994) for South Carolina, John Zubizarreta earned his doctorate at the University of South Carolina (US). In addition to publications in modern American and comparative literatures, he has written variously on pedagogy, collaborative scholarship, and teaching portfolios, and has mentored faculty across the United States on developing portfolios. Dr. Zubizarreta is a Professor of English and Director of Honors at Columbia College.

10.

Preparing the Faculty of the Future to Teach

Laurie Richlin

Graduate school is the proper training ground for the professoriate of the future. Successful preparatory programs use research on the development of teaching assistants to design programs to match training to instructional needs, build a core of campus-wide programs while facilitating departmental training efforts, and provide documentation of successful improvement of teaching. Training also must take into account the changing academy, particularly the increasing diversity of students and growing use of technology in the classroom.

THE CHALLENGE

Preparing future faculty to be excellent teachers as well as scholars is one of the important challenges faced by graduate education programs. This chapter discusses the long history of attempts (successful and unsuccessful) to enhance the teaching abilities of new faculty. These attempts have ranged from wholesale reform, notably the Doctor of Arts degree, to the currently most widespread, the teaching assistantship. Review of these programs demonstrates that some methods of working with teaching assistants (TAs) are more effective than others. The chapter concludes with recommendations concerning how graduate education should address the issue of adequately preparing professors-to-be for their roles, particularly through the improvement of TA training for teaching.

IDENTITY AND SOCIALIZATION

The decision to enter the professoriate usually occurs later than for most other careers, often not until students have completed much of their graduate work. Only 20% of the faculty interviewed in a US study indicated that they knew they wanted an academic career prior to coming to college (Sorcinelli, 1986). Although the majority know during childhood or undergraduate years what subjects they want to pursue, they often do not see a direct path to college teaching. Sorcinelli found that there were, therefore, *two* career decision points: one for the discipline and a second, later one, for the academy.

The impression of what a professor's work is like, gained during the undergraduate years, and the resulting decision to become a graduate student play a significant part in the process of recruiting faculty. Bess (1978) surveyed 236 students intending to pursue graduate studies at one US university and compared the characteristics of the 87 who aspired to be faculty with the characteristics of a faculty group. The results show that the aspirants and faculty are so similar that graduate school probably is not needed to socialize the newcomers. Students anticipate the "values and orientations which [would] be required of them as faculty members." Because "grades and achievements in the cognitive domain tend to be emphasized, [and] evocative teaching skills are downplayed or missed" (p. 312), graduate students are unprepared to regard the development of teaching abilities as an important element of their graduate experience. The resulting shock to new professors—that most of their time in the vast majority of institutions will be devoted to teaching activities and advising students—is unfair, both to the new faculty member and to the employing institution.

As noted above, graduate students with an interest in research self-select to attend graduate school. King (1967) stated that, while it "did not bother" him that graduate schools have no programs to prepare college teachers, he was upset that graduate students were "indoctrinated against undergraduate education" (p. 96). Katz (1976) agreed, arguing that "socialization in graduate school does more than just neglect teaching, it conditions students to belittle it" (p. 118). Students who begin by wanting to teach, "have it socialized out of them" in a society where becoming anything but a researcher is failure (Katz & Hartnett, 1976, p. 273). Merriam (1986) said much the same thing: "[T]he graduate research training programs, from which most university professors come, too often develop contempt for undergraduate teaching" (p. 108).

As a result of their research-focused selection process, graduate schools have been "recruiting the 'wrong' people for the professoriate—people who can't teach well and, in fact, would rather not teach at all" (Bess, 1990, p.

20). Because their subjects came easily to them, those who have earned high grades in a field may, without concerted effort, be the least likely to be able to design lessons and teach the required, lower level, undergraduate courses to which they are likely to be assigned early in their careers.

It would seem, then, that successful faculty development efforts to improve teaching must focus first and foremost on finding scholars who are interested in teaching. Next, graduate education should be expanded to encourage graduate students' interest in teaching by providing opportunities not only to teach, but also to learn pedagogical theory and practice. By encouraging the scholarship of teaching, discussed later in this chapter, universities can bring to bear on teaching improvement the same curiosity and energy graduate students have traditionally reserved for their research.

MODELS AND STRUCTURES

This section addresses the rationale for preparing future faculty to teach during their graduate education. It also provides an historical overview of methods that have been used by graduate programs to train their students to teach and discusses current models of teaching assistant programs.

Preparation to Teach During Graduate Education

While there are two points in an academic career where education for college or university teaching might start—as part of the graduate program or for newly hired faculty—there are at least three important reasons why the best time is during the graduate experience. First, graduate students have less ego involvement in personal teaching ability at that time. Introducing teaching theories and methods to active faculty is hampered by the misperception that the "craft of teaching" is not a topic for discussion.

Second, intervention should occur as early as possible in the academic career. A study by Syracuse University (Diamond & Gray, 1987) reported that 75% of the graduate teaching assistants surveyed across the nation planned to teach in colleges or universities when they completed their degrees. The number of graduate students planning to teach was over 50% in every field except architecture, communications, and law. In science and mathematics, the figure was 67%; in education, 79%; and in social sciences, 97%. The National Center for Educational Statistics reported that 57% of all PhDs were working in academe in 1985 (Bowen & Schuster, 1986).

Although the main preparatory institution for the professoriate is the graduate school, a national survey in the US reported that the development of future faculty is a relatively unimportant objective of teaching assistant programs (Sell, 1987). As far back as 1949, a conference report on graduate education stated, "[the] college teacher is the only high level professional who enters upon a career with neither the prerequisite trial of competence nor experience in the use of tools of [the] profession" (in Wise, 1967, p. 77). Almost half a century later, the situation remains virtually the same. Boehrer and Sarkisian noted in 1985 that, "Unlike doctors and many other professionals, most college teachers practice on their clients without benefit of formal training" (p. 15).

The third reason for selecting graduate school as the site for educating about teaching is the impact graduate students' abilities have on undergraduate education. They teach a significant proportion of lower-level courses at major research institutions. For instance, at the University of California, Berkeley and Davis campuses (US), teaching assistants teach about 30% of the undergraduate classes (McMillen, 1986; State of California, 1987). Another study showed that 45% of classes and recitation groups in leading mathematics departments in the US are taught by TAs or part-timers (McMillen, 1986). Richlin (1987) surveyed the largest (in terms of number of doctorates awarded) graduate departments of chemistry, psychology, and education in the United States and found that 91 of 97 departments used doctoral students as teachers of undergraduates, and that over half of the TAs taught more than 50 students.

At Canadian universities, more than half (55%) of the TAs in the humanities or social sciences are graders, while 35% lead discussions, 2% teach in classrooms, 2% teach in laboratories, and 7% have other assignments. In science and engineering, 59% lead laboratories, 29% grade, 5% lead discussions, and 7% have other assignments (Piccinin, Farquharson, & Mihu, 1993, p. 109). Diamond and Gray (1987) found that in US universities, TAs report having multiple responsibilities, the most common being grading (97% of the TAs), office hours (94%), preparing tests (72%), leading class discussions (71%), conducting review sessions (69%), lecturing (60%), advising/counseling (59%), and supervising laboratories (49%) (p. 43). It is obvious that in both the US and Canada, graduate students are providing a significant amount of undergraduate instruction.

It therefore is incumbent upon the graduate education system in each institution and faculty members in individual graduate programs to consider carefully their responsibility for preparing the next generation of faculty. The various models for training graduate students to teach which have been tried, with more or less success, should be evaluated before being adapted to a new situation.

The Rationale for Teaching Assistantships

In the 1940s, Hollis (1945) acknowledged complaints from employers about the narrow focus of doctoral students. In a 1957 survey of graduate deans, graduate faculties, recent PhD recipients, college presidents, and industrial employers, respondents said that the master's degree had lost status and would not suffice as the "acceptable degree for college teachers." They said that the "best chance for revising the traditional graduate program to produce an undergraduate teacher for the smaller liberal arts colleges lies in introducing a new intermediate degree with a (not *the*) doctoral title" (Berelson, 1960, p. 228).

A major attempt to answer the complaints about teaching in the universities in the 1960s came from the Carnegie Corporation, which designed and funded a Doctor of Arts (DA) degree, planned to be "less research-oriented than the PhD, but more subject-oriented than the EdD" (Glazer, 1989, p. 2, 1993; see also Gaff & Wilson, 1971). Between 1967 and 1976, Carnegie provided $4.7 million in planning grants and fellowships to 36 colleges and universities in the US to develop DA programs (Dressel, 1982, Glazer, 1993). Unfortunately, the DA was, as one English DA program director noted, "a noble experiment at the wrong time" (Glazer, 1993, p. 22). The expected great need for college teachers never materialized and, without the market rationale, the traditional programs were perpetuated and the DA was "never assimilated into the academic mainstream" (Glazer, 1989, p. 16). Both training and hiring institutions generally preferred that there be a flexible PhD program that could accommodate a broader definition of scholarship to prepare future faculty (see, for example, Stakgold, in Jackson, 1990).

Complaints about undergraduate teaching in the 1960s, which led to the creation of the Doctor of Arts programs, also had an impact on PhD programs. The most widespread and useful response was to institute programs to improve the skills of the graduate students hired to teach undergraduate courses in their departments. From the institution's point of view, there are three reasons for teaching assistantships: meeting the need for undergraduate instructors, providing funding for graduate students to attend graduate school, and (much less a priority) preparing the faculty of the future to teach. Graduate assistantships are the primary means for funding graduate education (Malaney, 1987). Although the primary benefit of teaching assistantships to the university is financial—both because of the low resulting cost for instruction and the financial support provided to graduate students—it also releases faculty from undergraduate teaching so that they can devote more time to their research (Jaros, 1987). Jaros states, "the teaching assistant system is one of the best devices ever created for the facilitation of faculty research" (p. 371).

There is continuing tension between the views that a TAship is an "apprenticeship to a lifelong career" and that it is strictly financial aid (Boehrer & Sarkisian, 1985, p. 7; see also Allen & Rueter, 1990). Some observers believe that the educational content of graduate programs should be reassessed to eliminate rigidity and overspecialization by giving "increased attention to the training of potential teachers" (Bowen & Sosa, 1989, p. 175). However, they continue to see the TA experience as potentially detrimental because "the main purposes of graduate education can be subverted if students are asked to teach too many hours per year or for too many years" (p. 174). And, as leading academics have recognized for decades, "the training of graduate students as teachers will be less than it should be. . . until a department is willing and able to break the connection between economic necessity and the employment of graduate students" (Eble, 1971, pp.27-28).

The increasing pressure to assure quality instruction for the undergraduates being taught by graduate assistants has resulted in the implementation of some type of teacher training program for TAs at almost all US universities.

The Growth of TA Development Programs

Student uprisings in the US during the 1960s stung the universities with criticism of undergraduate instruction. As a result, several efforts were funded to modify the TAship: the Danforth Foundation gave grants for teaching internships at Washington University and Yale; some Woodrow Wilson internships allowed masters graduates to assume one-year appointments as undergraduate instructors; and Antioch College sponsored nine internships of one year each for instructors to teach half time prior to going on to full-time positions at other institutions (Wise, 1967). These programs were not continued as the PhD "glut" placed more emphasis on research training. More recently, however, there has been a resurgence in support for university teacher training. During the 1980s, the US Department of Education Fund for the Improvement of Postsecondary Education (FIPSE) supported the development of TA programs at a number of universities. Advertisements for teaching fellowships for graduate students in current issues of the *Chronicle of Higher Education* indicate increasing opportunities for prospective new faculty to acquire instructional skills and experience.

Most reports on programs were originally limited to a local situation, covered little more than a semester or a year, were without sound theoretical or research rationale, and could not be generalized. In 1980, Carroll's analysis of empirical studies of teaching assistant training programs brought together what had been reported at that time by individual programs: significant positive differences were reported in the knowledge, attitudes, and behavior of those TAs who participated in training program.

Several large surveys of teaching assistants in North America (Davis, 1987a, 1987b; Diamond & Gray, 1987; Ervin & Muyskens, 1982; Piccinin et al., 1993) found that TAs faced on-going problems in terms of the selection and evaluation criteria for their positions, their training and supervision, and time and funding constraints.

Diamond and Gray (1987) surveyed TAs at eight US universities. Of the 1,357 respondents, 25% of women TAs and 16% of men TAs reported having a problem finding enough time to meet their teaching responsibilities (p. 60), with some reporting working almost twice the contracted 20 hours (p. 29). In comparison, Piccinin et al. (1993) found that, in Canadian universities, TAs typically work ten to 12 hours a week (p. 112). One in five TAs in the US study reported inadequate support and supervision, although this varied considerably from department to department and even from supervisor to supervisor; more problems were reported in arts and sciences departments than in professional schools (Diamond & Gray, 1987, p. 60). In Canada, 76% of the universities reported having training for their TAs (28% of the programs were mandatory), and one-half have a specific person or unit responsible for TA training (Piccinin et al., 1993, p. 114). However, only 21% of the Canadian universities reported evaluating the teaching of their TAs (p. 114).

In the US, there has been increasing attention paid to TA programs, particularly through four biannual conferences where TAs, TA development staff, and administrators have worked on connecting practice with theory: 1987 in Columbus, Ohio (see Chism, 1987); 1989 in Seattle, Washington (see Nyquist, Abbott, Wulff, & Sprague, 1991); 1991 in Austin, Texas (see Lewis, 1993); and 1993 in Chicago, Illinois. Analysis shows that sessions at the first conference dealt with how to establish TA programs and deal with administrative issues, while topics at subsequent meetings have emphasized "teaching skills, instructional strategies, and research into teaching effectiveness practices... This change in emphasis suggests that a large number of campuses have their training programs in place and are moving toward providing more advanced programs that consider the scholarship of teaching as it applies to TA development" (Ronkowski, 1993, p.82).

Teaching Assistant Development

As TAs gain teaching experience, they begin their socialization into the professional role of teacher-scholar. Sprague and Nyquist (1989) suggest three phases in the development of the TA role: *Senior Learners, Colleagues in Training,* and *Junior Colleagues.* Graduate students are selected to be TAs because they are "expert students" (*Senior Learners*), and they usually identify more with their students than with the faculty (Sprague & Nyquist, 1989). These beginning TAs lack expert knowledge of the subject matter, the learning process, and the university system. In this stage of role socialization, TAs begin to separate from the former role of student and begin to adopt the new one of teacher, based on interactions with their mentors and the demands of their assignments (Ronkowski, 1993).

TAs become *Colleagues in Training* during the transition stage. At this point in their development, TAs "become more concerned about their lack of teaching skills. Their confidence as teachers advances... [and] the sense of professional identity starts to emerge... They begin to adapt teaching methods to their own personal styles and to figure out unique solutions to novel problems" (Sprague & Nyquist, 1989, p. 44). In the *Junior Colleagues* stage, TAs begin to see themselves as colleagues with existing faculty in terms of both research and teaching.

TABLE 1

Prototype of Responses to Areas of Teaching Concern at Different Developmental Levels

(Used by permission: M. Svinicki, T. Sullivan, M. Greer, and M. Diaz, 1989.)

	PRESTAGE 1	STAGE 1	STAGE 2	STAGE 3
AREAS OF CONCERN	I'm not really a teacher. OR I will be the perfect teacher.	Can I do it right? Am I good enough to pull it off?	I'm orchestrating student learning.	Teaching is a partnership with the students, both individually & as a group.
SENSE OF SELF IN RELATIONSHIP TO STUDENTS	No identity as teacher, unrealistic view of role, no relationship.	Performance, adequacy, student as listener/ receiver.	Effect on student.	Improvement, partnership.
CONTENT/ COURSE PLANNING	Imposed from outside.	Content is primary, most important thing.	Student grasp of content, motivation of students.	Content is secondary, meta concerns: seeing beyond the requirements, taking a more critical eye toward evaluative content.

	PRESTAGE 1	STAGE 1	STAGE 2	STAGE 3
STUDENTS	Idealized or unknown.	Irrelevant, the opposition.	Performing animals, reflection of instructor.	Partners, primary importance.
EVALUATION/ MONITORING PROGRESS	Don't think about it.	Clueless.	I have to fix it. Why do students rate my teaching this way?	Selectivity, discrimination, ability to perceive what does/doesn't come from oneself.
METHODS	Alternatives exist?	Basic competency, learn to do with focus on me.	Reevaluate teaching to cause certain effects on students, learning to do it.	Choosing among methods, expertise.
COMMUNI- CATION/ PRESEN- TATION SKILLS	Do I know enough to say anything?	Getting answer right, Can I do it? Performance anxiety.	Will students understand? Judging my communication by its effect on students.	Remove self from center of communication, communication or message becomes central.
AUTHORITY/ DISCIPLINE	None.	Concerned with, uncomfortable with exercising.	Recognize need for asserting authority to get the job done.	Comfortable, non-issue, one simply is authoritative.
CAREER CONCERNS	Financing, keeping balance between studies & TA duties, knowing job requirements.	Time management, keeping up to date.	Is it worth it? Appropriate relations between faculty & students. Is this what I want?	

Table 1, developed by Svinicki, Sullivan, Greer, and Diaz (1989), is a prototype developmental scheme based on instructors' responses to areas of teaching concern. It shows the level of commitment to teaching and perceptions of self at different stages. They have identified a pre-stage, during which the new teachers are dualistic, either denying that they are real teachers or working hard to be "perfect." At stage 1, teachers are overpreparers, focused on content, but suffering from "performance anxiety." By stage 2, they are looking outward, at their students, whom they attempt to direct through manipulation. Finally, at stage 3, they see themselves as partners with their students.

Ronkowski (1993) identified nine categories of TA concerns, which she divided into the three stages based on Fuller's concerns model (Fuller & Brown, 1975). She found that the majority of TA concerns, regardless of amount of teaching experience, were at the *survival* level: adequacy of self as instructor and leader. She notes that:

> *This preponderance of survival concerns may result from the common practice of assigning TAs to courses they have not taught before in order to give them a range of course experience. This may result in variety but not depth of teaching experience. Because of the cyclical nature of developmental concerns, each time one teaches or assists in a new course, survival level concerns re-emerge. (Ronkowski, 1993, p. 83)*

Understanding the stages of TA development can provide guidance to faculty development professionals, administrators, and departmental faculty for planning training programs, assigning courses, supervising TA work, and providing career mentoring. Designing activities to help TAs move through the stages in each "area of concern" shown on Table 1 is an important strategy for assuring that new faculty are ready to assume their teaching duties when they are hired.

The Structure of TA Programs

There are many structural decisions to make when designing a training program for teaching assistants, including where it will be located in the institution, whether it will take place prior to or during the first term of teaching, whether it will be mandatory or voluntary, and what methods will be used for training (Andrews, 1985a, 1985b, 1985c, 1987; Andrews et al., 1985; Loeher, 1987; Parrett, 1987; Smock & Menges, 1985; Stokely, 1985; Weimer, Svinicki, & Bauer, 1989; see also Section III in Nyquist et al., 1991).

Location in institution. Because it will determine the focus of the instruction the TA receives about teaching, the most important decision to be made in designing a program is whether it will be based in a department or a centralized unit. A national survey found 48% of programs in the US were provided by the institution, 15% by the school, and 31% by a department (Diamond & Gray, 1987). In most cases, universities have a mixture of program types. The benefits of centralized programs include providing the same opportunity for training for all TAs; uniform training on institutional policies, such as sexual harassment and intellectual integrity; and the opportunity for TAs to work with experts in university teaching (Andrews, 1987; Hiiemae, Lambert, & Hayes, 1991; Rudge, 1991). On the other hand, departmental programs can "be closely coordinated to the substantive issues and disciplinary knowledge that is central to a given department" (Andrews, 1987, p. 109). Many institutions attempt to solve the dilemma by encouraging individual departments to run specialized training sessions in addition to the campus-wide programs. An innovative approach was developed at the University of California, Riverside, where experienced teaching assistants, employed by the graduate division, provided university-wide seminars for TAs grouped into four interdisciplinary clusters: laboratory sciences, mathematical problem-solving disciplines, social sciences and humanities, and foreign languages. This approach is particularly welcomed by departments lacking the resources to provide specialized programs for their TAs (Frongia, 1994).

Timing and content. Constantinides (1987) developed a typology of programs for international teaching assistants (ITAs) that is equally useful in describing all TA development programs. The schema, based on the length of the program and its timing, is described in more detail by Smith, Byrd, Nelson, Barrett, and Constantinides (1992). Programs are categorized as *orientation* or *training* on one axis and *pre-term* (sometimes called "pre-teach") or *concurrent* on another. Orientations include material on policies and procedures which acquaint the TA with the institution, but are not meant to include any training on teaching strategies. Orientations, which usually last from six to 40 hours (one to five days), can occur before the first term of teaching—with or without a follow-up session—or concurrent with the first term of teaching (Smith et al., 1992). In contrast, training programs concentrate on pedagogical matters and are classified as either pre-term, if held during a non-academic term (usually the summer), or concurrent, if they take place during an academic term.

The two most significant problems associated with the various types of orientation and training are the cost of the program (often including housing and board as well as staff and facility time) and the availability of the TAs for training. Often, graduate students do not arrive on campus until very shortly before classes begin; this is particularly difficult to change for international TAs who are dependent on government documents and funding. The main reason students are unable to come to campus until the term begins is that they need to maximize their summer earnings to pay for their schooling. If students are required to begin their work as TAs more than a week before the term, provision should be made to compensate them for their time. Some schools have done this by beginning the TA appointment earlier (thus increasing the length of employment) and spreading the payments over a longer time. In any case, if students are required to participate in pre-term training for their TAships, they should receive that information when they are notified of their appointment.

The primary benefit of conducting orientation and training prior to the beginning of term is that new TAs are better prepared for their teaching duties. The primary drawback, besides the issue of resources, is that until they are actually in the classroom, TAs do not have an opportunity to use what they learn. Schön (1983, 1987) introduced the concept of "reflective practitioner" as one who acts more like a researcher trying to model a system than an expert being modeled (1983, pp. 35-36). This "knowing-in-action" faces the "paradox of learning a really new competence," wherein "a student cannot at first understand what he needs to learn, can learn it only by educating himself, and can educate himself only by beginning to do what he does not understand" (1983, p. 83). This observation certainly applies to learning to teach. The best TA programs provide an active learning experience where the TAs are able to bring their actual teaching experiences to the training program for reflection, diagnosis, and suggestions.

An ideal program would include a graduated set of experiences designed to combine both theory and practice in university teaching: a pre-term orientation and at least one term working with a mentor professor including observing and discussing the professor's class. These are followed by a period of teaching under the supervision of the mentor prior to taking on independent responsibility for class design, pedagogical strategies, testing, and grading. Unfortunately, most institutions cannot afford to have TAs on payroll without teaching responsibilities, and most professors do not have the experience or time to mentor TAs in such an intensive fashion.

Requirement. TA training activities can be required or optional. A mandatory program can lay the groundwork of adequate knowledge and resources for the work of all TAs. Mandatory programs are also economical, easier to plan, and easier to evaluate. Optional programs attract those TAs already interested in improving their teaching. Only 65% of the TAs responding to a major US study reported attending any programs offered on their campuses (Diamond & Gray, 1987). Seventy-six percent of institutions responding to a Canadian study indicated they provided TA training, but only 28% of the programs were mandatory (Piccinin et al., 1993).

International teaching assistant considerations. Special consideration must also be given to designing orientations and training for international teaching assistants (ITAs), many of whom arrive at the institution directly from their native countries. There has been phenomenal growth in the percentage of foreign-born graduate students enrolled in science programs at US universities. Concerns about the performance of ITAs in teaching US undergraduates were well-publicized during the 1970s and 1980s. Over 20 states have responded by passing legislation requiring universities to assess ITAs' language skills before they are allowed to teach. However, the Canadian survey reports that only 12% of responding institutions have any form of special training for international TAs (Piccinin et al., 1993).

Most university programs for preparing ITAs for the classroom have focused on increasing their ability to speak clearly the language of instruction, with some preparation for understanding the local college culture. *Crossing Pedagogical Oceans: International Teaching Assistants in U.S. Undergraduate Education* (Smith et al., 1992) provides excellent reviews of research on training relating to pronunciation, effective teaching, training programs, tasks ITAs perform, and their concerns.

NEW APPROACHES

Changing Faculty Scholarship and the Future Faculty

The Carnegie Foundation for the Advancement of Teaching attempted to broaden our conception of academic roles by moving beyond the simplistic "research vs. teaching" debate to a discussion of the multidimensional aspects of scholarship. In *Scholarship Reconsidered: Priorities of the Professoriate*, Boyer (1990) proposed four interrelated components: "the scholarship of *discovery*; the scholarship of *integration*; the scholarship of *application*; and the scholarship of *teaching*" (p. 16). Boyer emphasized that implementing the new scholarships will depend on broadening graduate study to prepare the "new generation of scholars" for the task. Rather than a "two-track approach" such as the Doctor of Arts degree, Boyer recommended that teacher training be incorporated into all graduate preparation. He stated that, "Teaching assistant programs, perhaps more than any other, are crucial in the preparation of future teachers" (p. 71). Freyburg and Ponarin (1993) pointed out that if we redefine "scholar" to include both the research and teaching roles, it will be necessary to reverse the "specific structures of graduate programs [that] encourage an identity shift among TAs which has negative effects on their teaching" (p. 146).

To be considered scholarly, teaching must be understood as an intellectual activity (Cross, 1990a, 1990b). Arrowsmith (1967) stated that "so long as the teacher is viewed as merely a diffuser of knowledge or a higher popularizer, his position will necessarily be a modest and even menial one... For if the teacher stands to the scholar as the pianist to the composer, there can be no question of parity" (p. 57). He pointed out that, "Our entire educational enterprise is in fact founded upon the wholly false premise that *at some prior stage* the essential educational work has been done" (p. 60).

Rice (1990) identified three important elements of teaching: *synoptic capacity, pedagogical content knowledge,* and *knowledge about student meaning making*. These aspects of scholarly teaching can be loosely defined by noting the higher level knowledge and skills involved in each.

Synoptic capacity involves drawing together various areas of an academic discipline and placing concepts in the larger context of the discipline. This includes acknowledging the interaction of the disciplinary context with the personal context of the learner.

Pedagogical content knowledge, first identified by Shulman (1987) is knowledge about the interaction between learning processes and academic content. It requires expertise in designing examples, analogies, metaphors, and simulations to help students integrate new knowledge into their existing schemata.

Meaning making recognizes the diversity of student learning characteristics through understanding general learning principles. It focuses, in particular, on the stages of student cognitive development, such as those developed by Perry (1970) and Belenky, Clinchy, Goldberger, and Tarule (1986). According to Ronkowski (1993),

> *the teaching/learning process can be viewed as a complex interaction between the instructor, student, and content. Each element [described by Rice] can then be explored in terms of this description... Experienced scholars proficient in these elements of teaching may or may not be able to articulate their scholarship. Yet, articulation is needed if graduate students in training as future faculty are to value teaching as scholarship and if the next generation of faculty is to build on the current scholarship of teaching. When a profession is practiced without reliance on theoretical models and researched principles, the professionals become* bricoleurs, *do-it-yourselfers (Hatton, 1989). It is the way in which bricoleurs approach their work that distinguishes them from the true professional, the scholar. Among other traits, a bricoleur uses existing tools and techniques to solve problems rather than designing new, specific strategies for specific task situations. Bricoleurs use strategies and skills based on previous experience rather than using theory as the foundation for practice. They do*

not add to their instructional repertoires except by luck or chance, further distinguishing them from scholars who extend their professional techniques, skills, and materials through the careful use of principles and theoretical frameworks. Few faculty are bricoleurs when practicing their scholarships of integration, discovery, and practice; however, with little time left to devote to classes and students, faculty are unfortunately often bricoleurs when it comes to their teaching. Because teaching has not been recognized as a form of scholarship, accompanied by appropriate rewards and resources, faculty have traditionally practiced the teaching profession as bricoleurs and inadvertently transmitted this to their graduate students. (pp. 80-81)

As Ronkowski goes on to point out, teaching is becoming more of an intellectual endeavor through articles in refereed journals, such as the *Journal on Excellence in College Teaching,* and discussion at national meetings, such as the Lilly Conferences on College Teaching (US) and those sponsored by the Society for Teaching and Learning in Higher Education (Canada). Faculty are beginning to take the scholarship of teaching as seriously as the other scholarships and provide dynamic role models for their graduate students who will soon be colleagues. A recognition is emerging of the importance of socializing doctoral level graduate students into the role of college faculty and into the scholarship of teaching (Boyer, 1990; Richlin, 1993; Ronkowski, 1993). In order to clearly demonstrate institutional commitment to change, tenure and review processes must give greater value to teaching (Diamond & Adam, 1993; Pister, 1991).

Employment Practices

Recruitment and hiring practices. The current attention to undergraduate education gives graduate programs an unprecedented opportunity to select and prepare individuals interested in becoming teacher-scholars. The recruitment of enough high-quality graduate students suitable to be college teachers depends on finding teaching-oriented students who are not predisposed to narrow, disciplinary investigation (Katz & Hartnett, 1976). As stated by the vice-president of a non-doctorate granting university, "Often we recruit new faculty members as if we were Harvard [University]. Seldom do we consciously try to seek out faculty members who want to be at the institutions we represent… This, in turn, often means that there is no sense of pride for either their institution or their role in it" (in Boyer, 1990, p. 61). Unfortunately, when selecting candidates for admission to a PhD program, most doctoral programs have not yet begun to select students who would be good college teachers. When asked in a recent US survey if potential university teaching ability or interest was considered in the graduate student admission process, department chairs' comments included: "Not a criterion at admissions"; "Not even taken into account"; "We don't select on that basis;" and "Why should we select future teachers?" (Richlin, 1991).

Documenting ability: The teaching portfolio. The professional portfolio is a useful method of reporting and reflecting on scholarly work for graduate students as well as for faculty. During the early graduate school years, the portfolio can be used to "stimulate the collection of scholarly artifacts pertaining to teaching and research; promote reflection about initial teaching and other professional experiences; and encourage discussions about professional activities with faculty mentors." In late graduate school, the portfolio can "stimulate thinking about a philosophy of teaching and a future research agenda" as well as "assist in the academic job hunt" (Froh, Gray, & Lambert, 1993, p. 105).

The portfolio can encourage discussion between advanced graduate students and their mentors about the best institutional fit for their first professional appointment, as well as what areas of their work need special attention. For the hiring institution, the portfolio can provide a richer description of the applicant's teaching. According to Froh et al, search committees are requesting prospective faculty to submit brief portfolios along with their *curricula vitae*, followed by more detailed dossiers for finalists.

Preparation of the teaching portfolio should be nurtured from the beginning of the appointment of TAs. Developing and reworking the teaching philosophy statement and assembling teaching documents encourages TAs to reflect on their progress, aiding them to move through the developmental stages. At the University of Pittsburgh's New TA Orientation, TAs are given a list of items to save during their teaching careers for possible inclusion in a portfolio. Workshops are presented every year on creating the portfolio, and the main project in the course for advanced TAs is assembling a portfolio for job applications.

More information on the use of the teaching portfolio can be found in the chapter by Seldin, Annis, and Zubizarreta.

Preparing for demonstration of teaching scholarship. As they approach the completion of their degree requirements and begin the search for an academic appointment, TAs can benefit from assistance in preparing to teach at least one class as part of an on-campus interview. The guest class provides the applicant with an opportunity to demonstrate his or her teaching abilities. Successfully preparing a guest class calls upon well-developed skills in class planning, understanding students' development, and matching methodology to the content and situation. Careful consideration of these aspects through TA development programs and constructing teaching portfolios will prepare TAs for this important aspect of job search, as well as aid in their success as faculty members.

Recommendations for Designing Programs

Consider the academy of the future. Programs to prepare the faculty of tomorrow to teach should consider changes occurring in the culture of the academy itself: rapidly expanding knowledge, increasing use of technology in the classroom, and the increasing diversity of the undergraduate student population. To succeed as teachers, new faculty must be prepared to adapt to the learning needs of their students, the changing curriculum, and the new methodologies for teaching. Cox and Richlin (1993), in their analysis of journal articles and conference presentations, note that "emerging trends in college teaching reflect a growing realization and acceptance by faculty of the complexity of college teaching and learning." They recommend classifying the trends as changes in the communication process: preparation for the academy of the future needs to involve an understanding of the "population, paths, levels, methods, and assessment involved in teaching and learning" (p. 2). It is no longer enough to teach new professors only to lecture (or even to conduct discussions) and then grade how well students do on pencil-and-paper tests. Faculty and students will communicate through increasingly complex paths, including electronic networks, classroom assessment techniques, and continuous quality improvement teams. It is particularly important for graduate students to understand how to teach for diversity because, as TAs, they teach undergraduates during the critical first years in college; they work more closely with students in small group settings (such as labs); they are in touch with differences in learning styles reflected in student work when they grade papers and tests; and because "many of them will be the faculty of the future" (Chism, 1993, pp. 269-270). See also the chapter in this volume on implementing programs on teaching for diversity, by Chism and Pruitt.

Researchers have analyzed the results of programs for improving how TAs work with student diversity (Border & Chism, 1992; Chism, Cano, & Pruitt, 1989; Green, 1988). Groups considered "nontraditional" include ethnic minorities, returning adults, students with disabilities, women students, and gay and lesbian students. To work with these nontraditional students, the researchers recommend that programs for TAs be designed to communicate the following principles: treat each student as an individual, prevent discrimination in the classroom, encourage full classroom participation, include in curriculum the accomplishments of nontraditional groups, reexamine assumptions about the discipline itself, and create a classroom climate that welcomes discussion of sensitive issues (Chism et al., 1989).

Success in teaching all students will require more than knowledge of one's discipline. Faculty will need to understand diverse learning styles, learn about the culture of nontraditional groups (including women and ethnic minorities), and be willing to investigate the biases in their instructional materials and themselves. It is the responsibility of graduate programs to provide the training necessary to prepare TAs to become successful faculty in the academy of the future.

Match the training to the needs. Research on TA development supports using a developmental model for introduction of TAs to their teaching roles. Information about TA developmental stages can be put to very practical use. Understanding the changes inherent in the TA role and in TA concerns can guide faculty in choosing appropriate supervisory approaches to use with TAs at the various stages of development. Awareness of concerns at each stage can help faculty sequence content of TA training orientations and seminars. It is important to balance the need for depth of experience, gained through teaching a class more than once, with the need to be able to tell a prospective employer that one has taught a variety of courses. Beginning TAs need support and feedback—from students, other TAs, and supervisors. More experienced TAs can collaborate with faculty to design courses. And advanced TAs can train and mentor new TAs. Building these opportunities into the TA program sequence will provide the impetus for TAs' growth as instructors. A particularly ambitious program in this regard is the Future Professoriate Project (FPP) at Syracuse University (US) (Lambert, 1993).

The FPP has three components: Faculty Teaching Mentors seminars, Teaching Associate appointments, and a Certificate in University Teaching. The seminars are led by faculty from across the university who are trained as mentors at a three-day summer conference and who meet as a group four times during the academic year for follow-up workshops. The Teaching Associate appointment is based on "documented accomplishments as a teaching assistant that demonstrate qualification for the assumption of increased teaching responsibilities within the academic department" (p. 109). An important part of the Teaching Associate program is the opportunity to work closely with individual Faculty Teaching Mentors. The Certificate is awarded to Teaching Associates who "pursue a program of professional development that results in the documentation of their preparation to assume a teaching position at a college or university" (p. 110). The teaching portfolio, which should include the Teaching Associate's teaching philosophy, syllabi, videotapes, student evaluations, list of teaching awards, and an assessment by the Faculty Teaching Mentor, is an essential part of the certificate process. Thirteen departments participated in the original program, with an additional 24 added by 1994.

Build a core. Use the university's resources to create a mandatory, centrally-organized core program for teaching assistants. Begin with a preterm orientation to the university's expectations and policies, followed by ongoing orientation and training programs, to provide consistency in the information given to teaching assistants. The decision to have a campuswide program is usually made because of the unevenness of departmental training. The University of Wisconsin-Madison, for instance, chose to provide what they call an "umbrella" of orientation and generic training activities to supplement existing departmental programs (Craig & Ostergren, 1993). Illinois State University developed a conceptual framework for communicating the "knowledge base" needed by all of their TAs (Jerich, 1993). The three-level program moves TAs from factual information, to conceptual and then value-laden information through a series of tasks and teaching practice. Undergraduate students reported that the TAs "were able to significantly increase their overall level of teaching performance," notably in the areas of demonstrating content mastery and effective teaching skills (p. 130).

Support departmental efforts. In addition to the university-wide program, support the development and presentation of discipline- and course-specific programs in the departments. Help departments develop criteria for selecting, orienting, training, supervising, and evaluating their TAs. Ask for departmental TA development policies to be placed on file in the graduate school and to be reviewed by a committee of faculty and graduate students.

At the University of Washington, the Center for Instructional Development and Research uses a "train-the-trainer" model in which it provides ideas, materials, and instructional facilities for a network of faculty TA training coordinators and student TA training representatives appointed by the chairs of each department employing TAs (Nyquist & Wulff, 1989). The Center has developed a calendar of activities to support the network's efforts, including orientation, videotaping and consultation services, and special programs for international TAs. By working through the network to provide services, the Center is able to support its belief that "the way academics stimulate inquiry, generate knowledge, and present understanding is specific to the respective disciplines" (p. 145).

An innovative concept supports departmental efforts at a smaller university (approximately 7,500 undergraduates) through a cluster approach to TA training. The University of California, Riverside, provides training focused on key disciplinary clusters: laboratory sciences, mathematical/

problem solving, social sciences and humanities, and foreign languages. This model has proven effective and economical because it allows training to focus on particular needs of TAs teaching in different situations, while enjoying economies of size not available in small departments (Frongia, 1994).

At the University of Pittsburgh, a team composed of the Dean and Associate Dean of Graduate Studies of the Faculty of Arts and Sciences (FAS), along with faculty and student representatives, and the Director of the Office of Faculty Development (OFD) meet with two to three departments each year to review their teaching assistant development programs. These in-depth reviews include gathering documents, meeting with the department chair and teaching assistant coordinator(s), and an extended, private meeting with currently employed teaching assistants. Discussions include TA selection and hiring practices, orientation and training programs, assignments, supervision, and documentation of the TAs' teaching abilities. The review team issues a report of its findings, including recommendations, which is made public (and to which a department may respond, if it wishes). Based on these reviews, the FAS Task Force requires all new TAs to attend a campus-wide orientation. Those TAs who will be teaching a course independently for the first time must participate in a semester-long seminar. In addition, FAS requires that departments assist TAs in constructing teaching portfolios (discussed below). Participation is optional for students from departments which provide orientation and training comparable to the OFD programs. Students in departments that can show they are providing orientation and training comparable to the OFD programs may be exempted, although they may still participate. Under this system, each program is reviewed approximately every ten years by top level administrators, conveying the message that quality TA department programs are vital to the university's mission.

Document the work. Just as graduate students document their research with the dissertation and publications, TAs should be encouraged to document their teaching scholarship and skills with the use of portfolios and videotapes. As discussed above, this process should start when TAs first begin teaching and should continue with updates as they are able to refine their documents and improve their abilities. Outstanding programs, such as the Future Professors project at Syracuse, use the portfolio as its culminating document because it provides the opportunity for development through reflection. The portfolio encourages TAs to evaluate their own work as they decide what constitutes good examples of teaching and learning. It will be this reflective process that will enable the TAs of today to continue to improve their teaching when they complete their graduate degrees and assume their places in the faculty of the future.

Assess the results. Finally, it is extremely important to evaluate the impact of faculty development programs on the improvement of teaching by TAs. Bort and Buerkel-Rothfuss (1993) analyzed the criteria by which 90 US universities assessed the performance of TAs and found that of 102 teaching elements included on evaluation forms, only 54 were included in TA training programs. Abbott, Wulff, and Szego (1989) categorized research on TA program effectiveness into those that reported on program components, effects of TA characteristics, and relationships among self, supervisor and/or student ratings of instruction. They found positive effects for training combined with videotaping, as well as for training in specific disciplines and using specific approaches. However, they found little systematic investigation of the impact of TA programs on TA performance.

A good example of how TA training can be designed based on pedagogical theories and modified in the light of assessment information is the TA preparation program in the accounting department at Illinois State University. The curriculum in their TA seminar was first grounded in "instructional theory that stressed techniques for conducting lectures/discussions representative of the didactic mode of learning." Different instructors changed the curriculum, first to include "communication principles of teaching" grounded in the theories of "instructional media," and then to include new clinical-based components focusing on "teaching as information processing" (Jerich & Leinicke, 1993, p. 62). To find the effect of the different training programs, the department used results from a teaching evaluation instrument completed by students in the classes of TAs who were trained in the three different programs. They found significantly higher scores on each of the dimensions of teaching abilities in the Teacher Performance Appraisal Scale (Johnson, 1968) for the TAs who were in the most recent group, those who used the "information processing" curriculum. The accounting faculty, therefore, concluded that "the current model is a very effective plan and should remain" as their training design (p. 66).

It is important for the future of higher education to prepare today's graduate students—the faculty of the future—to meet the instructional demands of the changing academy. This chapter has discussed how teaching assistant programs have evolved and some basic tenets of effective programs. Because the culture of each university and each department is unique, there is no one clear-cut method for preparing professors-to-be. In addition, the stresses and demands of graduate education should be considered when planning teaching enhancement programs. But this does not mean that there are not guidelines for developing an effective program.

The models discussed in this chapter were designed to answer the needs and fit the cultures of specific institutions. Those planning to begin a new TA training program, or interested in improving existing training, should familiarize themselves with models and results of TA training at other universities and decide which program elements best suit their needs. It is only through scholarly, well-designed, and practical TA policies and activities that graduate programs can meet the challenge of preparing the new generation of teacher-scholars.

REFERENCES

Abbott, R.D., Wulff, D.H., & Szego, C.K. (1989). Review of research on TA training. In J.D. Nyquist, R.D. Abbott, & D.H. Wulff (Eds.), *New Directions for Teaching and Learning: No. 39. Teaching assistant training in the 1990s* (pp. 111-124). San Francisco, CA: Jossey-Bass.

Allen, R.R., & Rueter, T. (1990). *Teaching assistant strategies: An introduction to college teaching.* Dubuque, IA: Kendall/Hunt.

Andrews, J.D.W. (1987). Part 1: A developer's perspective. Teaching in higher education: From hobby to profession. In N.V.N. Chism (Ed.), *Institutional responsibilities and responses in the employment and education of teaching assistants* (pp. 19-21). Columbus, OH: The Ohio State University.

Andrews, J.D.W. (1985a). Why TA training needs instructional innovation. In J.D.W. Andrews (Ed.), *New Directions for Teaching and Learning: No. 22. Strengthening the teaching assistant faculty* (pp. 47-62). San Francisco, CA: Jossey-Bass.

Andrews, J.D.W. (1985b). Editor's notes. In J.D.W. Andrews (Ed.), *New Directions for Teaching and Learning: No. 22. Strengthening the teaching assistant faculty* (pp. 1-5). San Francisco, CA: Jossey-Bass.

Andrews, J.D.W. (1985c). Additional resources. In J.D.W. Andrews (Ed.), *New Directions for Teaching and Learning: No. 22. Strengthening the teaching assistant faculty* (pp. 83-87). San Francisco, CA: Jossey-Bass.

Andrews, J.D.W. and Contributors. (1985). The process of launching a TA development program. In J.D.W. Andrews (Ed.), *New Directions for Teaching and Learning: No. 22. Strengthening the teaching assistant faculty* (pp. 75-81). San Francisco, CA: Jossey-Bass.

Arrowsmith, W. (1967). The future of teaching. In C.B.T. Lee (Ed.), *Improving college teaching* (pp. 57-71). Washington, DC: American Council on Education.

Belenky, M.F., Clinchy, B.M., Goldberger, N.R., & Tarule, J.M. (1986). *Women's ways of knowing: The development of self, voice, and mind.* New York, NY: Basic Books.

Berelson, B. (1960). *Graduate education in the United States.* New York, NY: McGraw-Hill.

Bess, J.L. (1978). Anticipatory socialization of graduate students. *Research in Higher Education, 8*(4), 289-317.

Bess, J.L. (1990, May/June). College teachers: Miscast professionals. *Change*, pp. 19-22.

Boehrer, J., & Sarkisian, E. (1985). The teaching assistant's point of view. In J.D.W. Andrews (Ed.), *New Directions for Teaching and Learning: No. 22. Strengthening the teaching assistant faculty* (pp. 7-20). San Francisco, CA: Jossey-Bass.

Border, L., & Chism, N. (Eds.). (1992). *New Directions for Teaching and Learning: No. 47. Teaching for diversity: The opening of the American classroom.* San Francisco, CA: Jossey-Bass.

Bort, M.B., & Buerkel-Rothfuss, N.L. (1993). Evaluating the evaluation measures: What do we expect from TA teaching and how are we measuring what we get? In K.G. Lewis (Ed.), *The TA experience: Preparing for multiple roles* (pp. 41-50). Stillwater, OK: New Forums Press.

Bowen, H.R., & Schuster, J.H. (1986). *American professors: A national resource imperiled.* New York, NY: Oxford University Press.

Bowen, W.G., & Sosa, J.A. (1989). *Prospects for faculty in the arts and sciences.* Princeton, NJ: Princeton University Press.

Boyer, E.L. (1990). *Scholarship reconsidered: Priorities of the professoriate.* Princeton, NJ: Princeton University Press.

Carroll, J.G. (1980). Effects of training programs for university teaching assistants. *The Journal of Higher Education, 51*(2), 167-183.

Chism, N.V.N. (Ed.). (1987). *Institutional responsibilities and responses in the employment and education of teaching assistants.* Columbus, OH: The Ohio State University.

Chism, N.V.N. (1993). Designing programs on social diversity for TAs. In K.G. Lewis (Ed.),*The TA experience: Preparing for multiple roles* (pp. 269-277). Stillwater, OK: New Forums Press.

Chism, N.V.N., Cano, J., & Pruitt, A.S. (1989). Teaching in a diverse environment: Knowledge and skills needed by TAs. In J.D. Nyquist, R.D. Abbott, & D.H. Wulff (Eds.), *New Directions for Teaching and Learning: No. 39. Teaching assistant training in the 1990s* (pp. 23-36). San Francisco, CA: Jossey-Bass.

Clifford, G.J. (1990). "Let Hayward State do it...?" *The Review of Higher Education, 13*(3), 387-396.

Constantinides, J.C. (1987, March). Designing a training program for international teaching assistants. In N.V.N. Chism (Ed.), *Institutional responsibilities and responses in the employment and education of teaching assistants* (pp. 275-283). Columbus, OH: Ohio State University.

Cox, M.D., & Richlin, L. (1993). Emerging trends in college teaching for the 21st century. A message from the editors. *Journal on Excellence in College Teaching, 4,* 1-7.

Craig, J.S., & Ostergren, R.C. (1993). Establishing an effective, voluntary teaching assistant program in a large, decentralized university setting. In K.G. Lewis (Ed.), *The TA experience: Preparing for multiple roles* (pp. 122-133). Stillwater, OK: New Forums Press.

Cross, K.P. (1990a). Grand Panel. Paper presented at "The Scholarship of Teaching" Conference, Iona College, New Rochelle, NY.

Cross, K.P. (1990b). Teachers as scholars. *AAHE Bulletin, 43*(4), pp. 3-5.

Davis, W.E. (1987a). TA training: Professional development for future faculty. In N.V.N. Chism (Ed.), *Institutional responsibilities and responses in the employment and education of teaching assistants* (pp. 129-131). Columbus, OH: The Ohio State University.

Davis, W.E. (1987b). *Teaching assistant training and preparation for future faculty roles.* Unpublished manuscript, University of California, Teaching Resources Center, Davis, CA.

Diamond, R.M., & Adam, B.E. (Eds.). (1993). *New Directions for Higher Education: No. 81. Recognizing faculty work: Reward systems for the year 2000* (pp. 97-100). San Francisco, CA: Jossey-Bass.

Diamond, R.M., & Gray, P. (1987). *National study of teaching assistants.* Syracuse, NY: Syracuse University, Center for Instructional Development.

Dressel, P.L. (1982). *College teaching as a profession: The doctor of arts degree.* New York, NY: Carnegie Corporation.

Eble, K.E. (1971). *Career development of the effective college teacher.* Washington, DC: American Association of University Professors.

Edgerton, R. (1990, April). *The making of a professor.* Paper presented at the National Conference on Higher Education, San Francisco, CA.

Ervin, G., & Muyskens, J.A. (1982, October). On training TAs: Do we know what they want and need. *Foreign Language Annals, 15*(5), 335-344.

Freyburg, M., & Ponarin, E. (1993). Resocializing teachers: Effects of graduate programs on teaching assistants. *Teaching Sociology, 21,* 140-147.

Froh, R.C., Gray, P.J., & Lambert, L.M. (1993). Representing faculty work: The professional portfolio. In R.M. Diamond & B.E. Adam (Eds.), *New Directions for Higher Education: No. 81. Recognizing faculty work: Reward systems for the year 2000* (pp. 97-118). San Francisco, CA: Jossey-Bass.

Frongia, T. (1994). *Report for the campuswide strategic planning committee.* University of California, Riverside, CA.

Fuller, F.F., & Brown, O.H. (1975). Becoming a Teacher. In K. Ryan (Ed.), *Teacher education: The seventy-fourth yearbook of the National Society for the Study of Education* (Part II, pp. 25-52). Chicago, IL: University of Chicago Press.

Gaff, J.G., & Wilson, R.C. (1971). The teaching environment. *AAUP Bulletin*, pp. 475-493.

Glazer, J.S. (1989, November). *The fate of the Doctorate of Arts degree*. Paper presented at the meeting of the Association for the Study of Higher Education, Atlanta, GA.

Glazer, J.S. (1993). The Doctor of Arts: Retrospect and prospect. In L. Richlin (Ed.), *New Directions for Teaching and Learning: No. 54. Preparing faculty for the new definitions of scholarship* (pp. 15-26). San Francisco, CA: Jossey-Bass.

Green, M.F. (1988). *Minorities on campus: A handbook for enhancing diversity*. Washington, DC: American Council on Education.

Hatton, E. (1989). Levi-Strauss's bricolage and theorizing teacher's work. *Anthropology and Education Quarterly, 20*, 74-06.

Hiiemae, K., Lambert, L.M., & Hayes, D. (1991). How to establish and run a comprehensive teaching assistant program. In J.D. Nyquist, R.D. Abbott, D.H. Wulff, & J. Sprague (Eds.), *Preparing the professoriate of tomorrow to teach* (pp. 123-134). Dubuque, IA: Kendall/Hunt.

Hollis, E.V. (1945). *Toward improving PhD programs*. Washington, DC: American Council on Education.

Jackson, A. (1990, March). Graduate education in mathematics: Is it working? *Notices of the American Mathematical Society, 37*, pp. 266-268.

Jaros, D. (1987, March). The teaching assistant and the university. In N.V.N. Chism (Ed.), *Institutional responsibilities and responses in the employment and education of teaching assistants* (pp. 369-371). Columbus, OH: Ohio State University.

Jerich, K.F. (1993). A knowledge base for educating graduate assistants to be effective instructors at Illinois State University. In K.G. Lewis (Ed.), *The TA experience: Preparing for multiple roles* (pp. 122-133). Stillwater, OK: New Forums Press.

Jerich, K.F., & Leinicke, L.M. (1993). A comparative study of the teaching effectiveness for three groups of graduate teaching assistants in accounting. In K.G. Lewis (Ed.), *The TA experience: Preparing for multiple roles* (pp. 59-67). Stillwater, OK: New Forums Press.

Johnson, W.D. (1968). *An evaluative report of the laboratory portion of the professional semester Fall, 1967*. Unpublished manuscript, University of Illinois, Teaching Techniques Laboratory, Urbana-Champagne, IL.

Katz, J. (1976). Development of the mind. In J. Katz & R.T. Hartnett (Eds.), *Scholars in the making* (pp. 107-126). Cambridge, MA: Ballinger Publishing.

Katz, J., & Hartnett, R.T. (1976). Recommendations for training better scholars. In J. Katz & R.T. Hartnett (Eds.), *Scholars in the making* (pp. 261-280). Cambridge, MA: Ballinger Publishing.

Katz, J., & Hartnett, R.T. (Eds.). (1976). *Scholars in the making.* Cambridge, MA: Ballinger.

King, J.E. (1967). The need for in-service programs. In C.B.T. Lee (Ed.), *Improving college teaching* (pp. 96-98). Washington, DC: American Council on Education.

Lambert, L.M. (1993). Beyond TA orientations: Reconceptualizing the PhD in terms of preparation for teaching. In K.G. Lewis (Ed.), *The TA experience: Preparing for multiple roles* (pp. 107-112). Stillwater, OK: New Forums Press.

Lee, C.B.T. (Ed.). (1967). *Improving college teaching.* Washington, DC: American Council on Education.

Lewis, K.G. (Ed.). (1993). *The TA experience: Preparing for multiple roles.* Stillwater, OK: New Forums Press.

Loeher, L.L. (1987). Factors in locating a program within the university organization. In N.V.N. Chism (Ed.), *Institutional responsibilities and responses in the employment and education of teaching assistants* (pp. 104-108). Columbus, OH: The Ohio State University.

Malaney, G.D. (1987, November). *A decade of research on graduate students: A review of the literature in academic journals.* Paper presented at the annual meeting of the Association for the Study of Higher Education, Baltimore, MD.

McMillen, L. (1986, October 29). Teaching assistants get increased training: Problems arise in foreign-student programs. *The Chronicle of Higher Education, 32*(21), 18.

Merriam, R.W. (1986). Academic research vs. the liberal arts. *Journal of College Science Teaching, 16,* 105-109.

Nyquist, J.D., Abbott, R.D., & Wulff, D.H. (Eds.). (1989). *New Directions for Teaching and Learning: No. 39. Teaching assistant training in the 1990s.* San Francisco, CA: Jossey-Bass.

Nyquist, J.D., Abbott, R.D., Wulff, D.H., & Sprague, J. (Eds.). (1991). *Preparing the professoriate of tomorrow to teach: Selected readings in TA training.* Dubuque, IA: Kendall/Hunt Publishing.

Nyquist, J.D., & Wulff, D.H. (1989). The training of graduate students at the University of Washington. In N.V.N. Chism (Ed.), *Institutional responsibilities and responses in the employment and education of teaching assistants* (pp. 144-154). Columbus, OH: Ohio State University.

Parrett, J.L. (1987). A ten-year review of TA training programs: Trends, patterns, and common practices. In N.V.N. Chism (Ed.), *Institutional responsibilities and responses in the employment and education of teaching assistants* (pp. 118-125). Columbus, OH: Ohio State University.

Perry, W.G. (1970). *Forms of intellectual and ethical development in the college years.* New York, NY: Holt, Rinehart & Winston.

Piccinin, S., Farquharson, A., & Mihu, E. (1993). Teaching assistants in Canadian universities: An unknown resource. *The Canadian Journal of Higher Education, 23*(2), 104-117.

Pister, K.S. (1991). "Report of the Universitywide Task Force on Faculty Rewards." Oakland, CA: University of California, Office of the President.

Rice, R.E. (1990). Rethinking what it means to be a scholar. *Teaching excellence: Toward the best in the academy.* Stillwater, OK: New Forums/POD Network.

Richlin, L. (1987). *Survey of largest TA programs.* Unpublished manuscript, The Claremont Graduate School.

Richlin, L. (1991). *Preparing future faculty: Meeting the need for teacher-scholars by enlarging the view of scholarship in PhD programs.* Unpublished doctoral dissertation, Claremont Graduate School.

Richlin, L. (Ed.). (1993). *New Directions for Teaching and Learning: No. 54. Preparing faculty for the new definitions of scholarship.* San Francisco, CA: Jossey-Bass.

Ronkowski, S.A. (1993). Scholarly teaching: Developmental stages of pedagogical scholarship. In L. Richlin (Ed.), *New Directions for Teaching and Learning: No. 54. Preparing faculty for the new definitions of scholarship* (pp. 15-26). San Francisco, CA: Jossey-Bass.

Rudge, D. (1991). "Report on the 3rd national conference on the training and employment of graduate teaching assistants." Pittsburgh, PA: University of Pittsburgh, Office of Faculty Development.

Ryan, K. (Ed.). (1975). *Teacher education: The seventy-fourth yearbook of the National Society for the Study of Education.* (Part II). Chicago, IL: University of Chicago Press.

Schön, D.A. (1983). *The reflective practitioner: How professionals think in action.* New York, NY: Basic Books.

Schön, D.A. (1987). *Educating the reflective practitioner: Toward a new design for teaching and learning in the professions.* San Francisco, CA: Jossey-Bass.

Sell, G.R. (1987, November). *Preparing teaching assistants as future faculty: Is this really the university's objective?* Paper presented at the meeting of the Association for the Study of Higher Education, Baltimore, MD.

Shulman, L.S. (1987). Knowledge and teaching: Foundations of the new reform. *Harvard Educational Review, 57*(1), 1-22.

Smith, R.M., Byrd, P., Nelson, G.L., Barrett, R.P., & Constantinides, J.C. (1992). *Crossing pedagogical oceans: International teaching assistants in US undergraduate education* (ASHE-ERIC Higher Education Report No. 8). Washington, DC: The George Washington University, School of Education and Human Development.

Smock, R., & Menges, R. (1985). Programs for TAs in the context of campus policies and priorities. In J.D.W. Andrews (Ed.), *New Directions for Teaching and Learning: No. 22. Strengthening the teaching assistant faculty* (pp. 21-34). San Francisco, CA: Jossey-Bass.

Sorcinelli, M.D. (1986). Tracing academic career paths: Implications for faculty development. *To Improve the Academy, 5*, 169-181.

Sprague, J., & Nyquist, J.D. (1989). TA supervision. In J.D. Nyquist, R.D. Abbott, & D.H. Wulff (Eds.), *New Directions for Teaching and Learning: No. 39. Teaching assistant training in the 1990s* (pp. 37-56). San Francisco, CA: Jossey-Bass.

State of California. (1987). *Resolution Chapter 102 of Assembly Concurrent Resolution No. 39*. Sacramento, CA: Author.

Stokely, L. (1985, March). *Development of teaching assistants as apprentice faculty*. Paper presented at the Western Association of Graduate Schools Dean's Meeting, Reno, NV.

Svinicki, M., Sullivan, T.A., Greer, M., & Diaz, M. (1989). *Combining departmental training with central support: A research project*. Paper presented at the Third National TA Conference, Austin, TX.

Weimer, M., Svinicki, M.D., & Bauer, G. (1989). Designing programs to prepare TAs to teach. In R.M. Diamond & B.E. Adam (Eds.), *New Directions for Higher Education: No. 81. Recognizing faculty work: Reward systems for the year 2000* (pp. 57-70). San Francisco, CA: Jossey-Bass.

Wise, W.M. (1967). Who teaches the teachers? In C.B.T. Lee (Ed.), *Improving college teaching* (pp. 77-89). Washington, DC: American Council on Education.

AUTHOR

Laurie Richlin is the Director of the Office of Faculty Development, University of Pittsburgh (US). She is the Executive Editor of the Journal on Excellence in College Teaching, *a peer-reviewed journal that provides a scholarly, written forum for discussion by faculty about all areas affecting teaching and learning. In addition, she is the Director of regional Lilly Conferences on College Teaching. Dr. Richlin's research and recent publications focus on graduate school preparation of the faculty of the future.*

11.

The Development of
New and Junior Faculty

Milton D. Cox

This chapter presents strategies to improve the teaching abilities of faculty in their first critical years as college and university professors. The effectiveness of these strategies is discussed, an award-winning program is described, and recommendations are made for successful new and junior faculty teaching development.

INTRODUCTION

New and junior faculty are one of the most important resources for colleges and universities. Yet, many of these faculty experience great stress in their initial years (Sorcinelli & Austin, 1992). They are a neglected resource (Boice, 1992b)—untapped in efforts to change campus cultures, isolated even from departmental colleagues, and, after a brief flurry of activity during orientation, forgotten by faculty developers and central administrators. What can we do to encourage colleagues and administrators to pay attention to the welfare of these faculty and to help them move from first year to tenure? The experiences of today's new and junior faculty will influence the quality of teaching and learning—in fact, all aspects of the academy—throughout the first half of the twenty-first century.

This chapter discusses strategies to enhance the teaching interests and abilities of new and junior faculty. However, in addition to enhancing teaching, junior faculty programs that are continued over time may have other benefits. Studies of the longest, award-winning, continuing junior faculty development program in the United States will provide examples for analysis of many of the strategies for helping new and junior faculty. Evidence of the impact and long-term effectiveness of this program, particularly in relation to the tenuring of its participants, is encouraging. It is hoped that the successes of this program will inspire others to undertake similar initiatives at their colleges and universities.

DESCRIBING NEW AND JUNIOR FACULTY

Several definitions of new and junior faculty are found in the literature. In this chapter, a new faculty member is one in the first year at a two- or four-year college or university. Typically, this person will have recently completed the PhD or terminal professional degree and be full time, non-tenured, and in a tenure-track position (probationary appointment). However, the term *new faculty* also includes a few faculty in their first year at a particular institution who have just made a career change or who have had experience at a different institution. The term does not include part-time faculty, although there are exemplary faculty development programs that address the needs of new and junior part-time and/or adjunct faculty (Gappa & Leslie, 1993). Junior faculty are defined as former new faculty who are in year two through the year before their tenure decision (typically year five) at an institution.

What are today's new and junior faculty like? Finkelstein and Lacelle-Peterson (1992) characterized them as a focused and well-motivated group, choosing to enter academe at a time when a decreasing proportion of new PhDs are making this choice and competition for tenure-track positions is stiff (a job squeeze that has been increasing over the last 20 years). The cohort of the 1990s also has a significantly higher proportion of women, is older than previous groups, and includes more dual-career and commuter couples.

> *An interesting paradox can be found in the literature on new and junior faculty. Nearly all newcomers report high levels of satisfaction with their careers. When asked to identify aspects of academic life that consistently afford satisfaction, most new faculty describe their work as providing personal autonomy, a sense of accomplishment, the capacity to have an impact on others, and the opportunity for personal and intellectual growth. At the same time, however, virtually all of the same faculty rate their work as stressful. Words such as* tension, pressure, anxiety, *and* worry *stand*

> *out in an even cursory reading of the literature. (Sorcinelli, 1992,*
> *p. 27)*

New and junior faculty find these pretenure years both difficult and critical to later success in academe (Boice, 1991a; Fink, 1984; Sorcinelli, 1988; Turner & Boice, 1987; Whitt, 1991).

With respect to the teaching difficulties of new and junior faculty, Fink (1992) reported, "Stress was not due to time taken to engage in creative teaching; most new faculty were lecturing almost all the time, thereby teaching little more than 'facts and principles'" (p. 40). Even the new faculty with experience as teaching assistants had only been taught "how to survive" in the classroom.

In a decade of interviewing and observing a wide range of new faculty over several successive semesters at both research and teaching campuses, Boice (1992b) noted some generalities worthy of mention. When new and junior faculty begin as teachers, most tend to:

- teach as they were taught, equating good teaching with good content
- teach defensively, worried about public failures at teaching, and trying to get their facts straight, not wanting to be accused of not knowing their material
- blame external factors such as poor students, heavy teaching loads, and poor evaluation instruments, for teaching failures such as bad student ratings
- be passive about change and improvement, in part because of a lack of teaching awareness
- shun outside help from resources such as faculty development programs
- specify no avenues to improvement beyond modifying lecture content and making assignments and tests easier
- claim, where they have some experience, that their defensive and factual styles of teaching are temporary regressions from how they had taught most recently at other campuses
- worry about public complaints and about heavy investments in new lecture notes
- establish comfort, efficiency, and student acceptance slowly (even by the fourth year, the majority of inexperienced new faculty reported feeling tense, worrying about not being in control of classes, and doubting that students liked them)
- state that their most important teaching goals are to cut down on teaching preparation time; yet they expend large amounts of time

on lecture preparation (18 to 27 hours per week for those with three-course loads)
- go to class with too much material and rush to say it all (Boice, 1991b, 1992b)

According to a limited survey by Gibbs, Gold, and Jenkins (1987), who interviewed five new geography faculty in Britain, the characteristics of new faculty there are similar to those in the United States.

However, five to nine percent of Boice's observed faculty behaved quite differently, exhibiting high energy, a sense of humor, and relaxed pacing in the classroom, with verbal and non-verbal cues encouraging students to participate. They had uncritical, optimistic attitudes toward undergraduates, few complaints about colleagues, and interest in seeking advice about teaching. They did not over prepare for teaching and integrated scholarly interests into undergraduate classes. Boice called these new faculty *quick starters*.

In conclusion, it is clear that new and junior faculty often begin their years in the professoriate under serious pressures and in dysfunctional academic communities. The resulting stress and lack of preparation for teaching lead to "survival teaching" unless there are thoughtful interventions.

HISTORY AND THE LITERATURE

Have new faculty always entered the professoriate under such trying conditions? Throughout history, most new faculty have started with little preparation for teaching. Fink (1990), in his bibliographic essay about beginning college teachers, wrote that "there have been periodic efforts for several decades to correct this deficiency by adding certain activities to graduate programs so that new professors will be prepared for teaching *before* their first appointment, rather than *after* the fact" (p. 235). He found it sobering to realize that this problem was being addressed as long ago as the 1920s through programs at several US universities—Chicago, Clark, Idaho, Iowa, Ohio State, and Oregon—but that today these efforts are all but forgotten, even though nearly identical initiatives have been established decades later.

Prior to World War II, most new faculty entered academe without today's pressure to publish, and they probably had small, supportive communities of experienced departmental or college colleagues. However, after World War II, the pace and focus of higher education changed. In the 1950s and 1960s, the number of undergraduates swelled, yet academic prestige came to be measured in terms of research grants and discovery scholarship. Faculty developed loyalties to their disciplines rather than to their institutions. By the 1970s, the expansionary stage of the previous decade was over and new academic positions became scarce, putting increasing pressure on new faculty to focus their efforts on research and publication. Undergraduate education was neglected.

In the 1980s, legislators, parents, and national higher education associations, such as the Association of American Colleges and the Carnegie Foundation for the Advancement of Teaching, voiced criticism of the quality of higher education and called for teaching reform. Academe has been slow to respond. Although many central administrators and deans have come to consider ways to balance the rewards and emphases on teaching and research, this is not usually true at the department level, where entrenched faculty and chairs have control.

The quality of records of the particular experiences and characteristics of new and junior faculty is steadily increasing. Information about new and junior faculty comes from national surveys, general empirical studies of the professoriate, and special empirical studies of new and junior faculty. Two kinds of national surveys provide data in the United States. The National Research Council annually surveys new doctoral recipients, providing data on academic discipline, career plans, current job prospects, ethnicity, and gender. In addition, US national faculty surveys are conducted by organizations such as the Carnegie Foundation for the Advancement of Teaching, the Higher Education Research Institute at the University of California at Los Angeles, and the National Center for Education Statistics, providing data on a representative sample of faculty, including a comparison of current and past cohorts of junior faculty. Comprehensive general studies of the professoriate now usually contain information about new and junior faculty (e.g., Bowen & Schuster, 1986).

Most scholars agree that specific studies of new and junior faculty began with Fink's study of 97 new geography faculty (Fink, 1984), although published reports about programs to help new and junior faculty occurred before 1984; for example, Beeman's (1981) report about the Post-Doctoral Teaching Awards Program of the Lilly Endowment, Inc. Most of the research deals with the experiences of new faculty in one discipline at more than one institution or with new faculty in several departments at one institution.

Two books about new and junior faculty—*Developing New and Junior Faculty* (Sorcinelli & Austin, 1992) and *The New Faculty Member* (Boice, 1992b)—provide comprehensive, detailed summaries of research findings and strategies for improving the lives and careers of new and junior faculty. Both should be required reading for administrators and practitioners.

How have programs to help new and junior faculty evolved? Astin and Lee (1967) noted in a discussion of the results of a survey of deans in US higher education institutions that "most institutions [68%] have pre-registration orientation sessions, but other methods for supervising or training of new faculty are little used" (pp. 307-308). The other formal methods mentioned were seminars for new teachers given by the institution, supervision by an assigned or designated faculty member, seminars given by the department, and summer institutes or other such intensive programs.

There was an increase in the number of university-wide faculty development programs in the early 1970s because of the lack of departmental interest. In 1975, Centra conducted the first national survey to find out what was actually happening in these programs but included only one faculty development practice which directly addressed new faculty: master teachers or senior faculty working closely with new or apprentice teachers, a practice more likely to be used in small colleges. Yet, new teachers received the lowest ratings in the Student Instructional Reports sent to the Educational Testing Service (Centra, 1977, 1978).

Erickson's (1986) survey of faculty development practices in four-year colleges and universities in the US included only one item related to new faculty. Assigning lighter-than-normal teaching load for first year faculty was reported by 20% of institutions with faculty development activities.

In 1989, Kurfiss and Boice (1990) surveyed members of the Professional and Organizational Development (POD) Network in Higher Education (one member per campus) to determine existing and desired faculty development practices. With respect to new faculty, 53% reported having orientations on teaching skills, and 36% planned or desired to institute such programs; 25% involved senior faculty as mentors, and 50% indicated that they desired or planned to implement a mentoring program.

Wright and O'Neil's 1993 international survey of faculty development specialists, discussed in Chapter 1, asked respondents to rate 36 teaching-improvement practices according to the confidence the faculty developer had in the practice's potential to improve the quality of teaching in his or her university. Only one item directly involved new faculty: mentoring programs/support for new professors. In the survey results, this item ranked fifth among all countries, and sixth in the US portion of the survey.

These four faculty development surveys, spanning the entire period of the faculty development movement to date, did not focus on faculty development activities specifically designed to assist new faculty. This confirms that new faculty have become a neglected resource. The following sections describe methods of enhancing the quality of teaching through developmental programs for new and junior faculty.

AN AWARD-WINNING PROGRAM

This section examines an award-winning program for junior faculty. Later sections cover aspects of the program in more detail, its impact on the faculty participants, and other evidence of the program's success.

Established in 1978 by Miami University, in Ohio (US), the Teaching Scholars Program was developed to raise the level of the importance and quality of teaching at the university and to assist junior faculty during their early years in academe. This longest-running junior faculty development program in the United States enhances its participants' teaching interests and abilities through involvement in a two-semester series of special activities and individual projects related to teaching. The Miami Teaching Scholars Program won the 1994 Hesburgh Award, given to the faculty development program in the United States judged best in meeting the three award criteria: significance of the program to higher education; appropriate program rationale; and successful results and impact on undergraduate teaching and learning.

Founded in 1809, Miami University is a state-assisted, Doctorate-Granting I^1, residential university in Oxford, Ohio. The enrollment is approximately 16,000 (including 14,000 undergraduates), with an additional 4,000 students who spend their first two years on two nearby, non-residential, urban, regional campuses. Miami University has a history and tradition of emphasis upon undergraduate teaching, and its mission statement includes "to provide an environment conducive to effective and inspired teaching and learning, and to promote professional development of faculty..." During the 1950s and 1960s, as enrollment tripled and doctoral programs were developed, Miami University experienced a change in its academic culture. This was a period of growing expectations for the university to play an important role in producing new knowledge to contribute to the betterment of society. Concern that this change of culture could negatively affect learning by undergraduates led to a concerted search for solutions. A committee of senior faculty, students, and administrators appointed by the Provost in 1978 developed the Teaching Scholars Program. The initial three years, 1979-80 through 1981-82, were funded by the Lilly Endowment as part of the Lilly Teaching Fellows Program.

The *objectives* of the Miami Teaching Scholars Program are to provide junior faculty with opportunities to obtain information on teaching and learning; to observe successful teaching and practice using new skills and technology; to investigate—as individuals—teaching problems and projects; to share ideas and advice with senior faculty mentors; to experience the scholarship of teaching and to establish colleagueship across disciplines;

and to share, via outreach, their enthusiasm and experience with other new faculty.

For the university, the long-term *goals* of the program are to increase faculty interest in undergraduate teaching and learning; inform faculty about teaching and active learning in the multicultural classroom; build university-wide community through teaching; increase faculty collaboration and the coherence of learning across disciplines; nourish the scholarship of teaching; and broaden the evaluation of, and increase the rewards for, teaching.

Program activities include group events, such as seminars on teaching and learning, retreats, and attendance at national conferences; individually, each participant selects and collaborates with a senior faculty mentor, and develops, carries out, evaluates, and gives presentations about a teaching project.

Participants receive release time from one course for one semester and are released from committee and service assignments for the other semester. The release time can be either first or second semester, and is negotiated by the participant and the department chair. The program covers participants' expenses, for example, travel and meals, as well as modest funding ($100-$400 US) for individual teaching project costs and books.

Since 1980, I have directed the program as University Director (formerly Associate Provost) for Teaching Effectiveness Programs (a half-time position). The program is advised by the University Senate's Committee on the Improvement of Instruction.

The program is supported by a one-third time secretary and a budget of $36,000 (US), which funds programming, participants' release time, and the participants' costs as mentioned above. The director's and secretary's salaries, office expenses, and supplies are funded by the Provost. One objective is to keep administrative costs low relative to the amount of direct support available to faculty.

Selection of Participants

Full-time faculty in tenurable positions are eligible to participate in the program during their second through fifth years of teaching at Miami. Nine to 13 applicants are chosen by a faculty committee in April for participation the next year. Applicants are asked to describe their current teaching responsibilities, their reasons for wanting to participate in the program, their most pressing teaching needs, and their involvement in any innovative teaching activities. They are also asked how the program, and the mentoring aspect specifically, will help them achieve their professional goals; which area of teaching they wish to explore in their teaching project; and what they think they can contribute to the program.

Criteria for selection include commitment to quality teaching, level of interest in and potential for contributions to the program, need, and plans for the award year. During the first few years of the program, an attempt was made to avoid identification of the program as remedial in nature— selection was viewed as an award. Once the program was well established on campus, this was no longer a concern. Each group is selected to ensure gender balance and diversity across disciplines, campuses, needs, and experiences.

The number of applicants has varied from 11 to 27 over the years. Those not accepted one year are encouraged to apply the next, and most who continue to apply are eventually accommodated. From 1979-1989, 22% of new hires participated in the program (Table 1); about one third apply. Some faculty who are not quick starters apply at the urging of their department chairs or colleagues who have already participated in the program. On the other hand, some chairs discourage participation because a faculty member is already an excellent teacher and/or, for tenure reasons, needs to focus primarily on a research program.

Program Assessment

The Miami Teaching Scholars Program engages in a continuous evaluation of its program elements and the program's impact on the junior faculty participants. Each seminar and retreat is evaluated; an extensive mid-year progress report and final report are prepared by the participants. To honor a commitment to the mentors to keep paperwork at a minimum, they are not asked to evaluate their role; no doubt this is a tradeoff at the expense of better mentoring.

It is surprising to note that the 1989 faculty development survey (Kurfiss & Boice, 1990) found that only 13.5% of the respondents reported that their own programs were evaluated systematically. Assessment of programs provides continuous quality improvement, important statistical evidence for scholarly reports, and hard evidence for faculty and administrators that programs are working.

Table 2 provides a long-term picture of the impact of the programming elements as reported by the junior faculty participants, whereas Table 3 describes the impact of the Teaching Scholars Program on the junior faculty participants as teachers and members of the university community. Note that the strongest program impact is colleagueship, which alleviates the isolation that new faculty experience. In terms of program outcomes, the strongest impact is on the participants' interest in the teaching process, followed by their interest in the scholarship of teaching, their comfort in the university community, and their effectiveness as teachers. These evaluations provide evidence that the program is meeting many of its objectives.

STRATEGIES FOR DEVELOPING
NEW AND JUNIOR FACULTY

Often-Discussed Initiatives

The landmark essay, *Who Teaches the Teachers*, states that "colleges must assume a fair portion of the responsibility for inducting new teachers" (Wise, 1967, p. 88). To meet this responsibility, Wise proposed three initiatives: reducing teaching loads for the first term or year, giving selected senior faculty responsibility for working with new faculty, and arranging cooperatively with other colleges for seminars and workshops to be conducted by outstanding leaders. In one form or another, these practices have been employed by some institutions.

Release time. In Erickson's (1986) survey of colleges and universities, a little over 20% of the institutions reported offering new faculty a lighter than normal teaching load. In Austin's (1990) survey of 25 former Lilly Teaching Fellows Programs in the 1974-1985 period, nine of the 16 respondents indicated that they provided release time, and three others provided summer stipends.

At Miami University, the one-course release time for one semester is important to the participation of the Teaching Scholars. Table 2 indicates that over 13 years, release time ranks second (a tie) out of the seven program elements in its positive impact on the participants. Over the years, "release time for the other semester" is the one response that appears repeatedly on the open-ended part of the program evaluation questionnaire in reply to "What could be improved about this program?" Participation in the program takes much time, and most comment that they could not do it without release time. However, Boice (1987, 1992b) found the opposite results about release time for scholarship development.

While some faculty and administrators question release time from teaching to participate in a teaching program, one must argue that to engage in scholarly teaching and in the scholarship of teaching, one has the same needs as for release time for research. Such scholarship requires the same opportunities for learning the literature, careful planning, experimentation, assessment, analysis, and disseminating the results.

Mentoring has been used for years in the business world and to foster the scholarly development of apprentices in the graduate programs of the academy. Although mentoring is of increasing interest on campuses and is often requested by new faculty who feel isolated, mentoring programs are not well developed or widely used. "Few campuses conduct mentoring in any systematic... way... Practitioners often imply that it demands too much time, that some newcomers neither want nor need it, that pairings afford too many chances for exploitation or dependency, and that most... pairs will quit meeting... [M]ost advice about establishing programs is conjecture" (Boice, 1992b, pp. 107-108).

In the 1989 Kurfiss and Boice survey, 25% of the respondents reported that their campuses already had senior faculty mentors for new faculty, and 50% planned or desired to have them. Several new programs were described at the 1993 Conference of Academic Chairpersons (Kansas State University, 1993). Some special programs have been established to mentor new faculty who are women and minorities; others have involved *emereti* faculty as mentors. The mentoring concept sounds good, but the goal of implementing effective programs has proved elusive.

Of the 16 former Lilly Teaching Fellows Programs reporting in the Austin (1990) survey, four of 12 mentoring programs failed. She found that where mentors were used with some degree of success, the patterns varied considerably, with no single model being 'the best.' "Any effective use of the Mentors depends completely on institutional culture, the personality and needs of the particular Fellow, and the personality and willingness of the Mentor to get involved in the Program" (p. 83).

Finding no empirical advice on the mentoring process, Robert Boice initiated a mentoring study at a large, comprehensive university. He described five general outcomes of value to other campuses:

- Arbitrary pairings and pairings across disciplines worked as well as departmental ones
- Requiring pairs to meet regularly early on helped ensure pair bonding
- Pairs working alone displayed narrow mentoring styles; for example, concentrating only on promotion and tenure issues
- Monthly group meetings helped broaden their interaction
- Mentors were reluctant to intervene, waited for requests for teaching help, then responded with vague admonitions which rarely translated into improved teaching

He concluded that "Mentoring pairs may need considerable mentoring" (Boice, 1992a, p. 55).

Mentoring has been an important part of the Miami Teaching Scholars Program since its inception in 1978. During the 15 years of the program, there have been 196 mentoring pairs involving 149 different junior faculty and 118 different mentors.

New participants select a mentor in consultation with the program director, their department chair, and colleagues. New participants find that former Teaching Scholars and Mentors are familiar with the program and usually are pleased to serve. They bring an informed perspective to the mentoring relationship.

The trend has been to select a mentor from a different department. Pairing outside one's discipline is selected more often because of interest in exploring teaching in a new area, the safety of discussing weaknesses with colleagues not involved in one's tenure decision, and the new insights non-experts can bring to one's teaching. To encourage a broader experience, selecting two mentors is now encouraged, especially for those on a regional campus (who select a mentor there and on the main campus) or for those whose initial selection is within their department. Some participants work with one mentor the first semester and the other during the second.

Mentoring pairs engage in a variety of activities, such as attending each other's classes, meeting for lunch to discuss teaching or to explore university issues, and attending sessions at the Lilly Conference on College Teaching. The extent to which these activities occur depends on schedules, interests, and compatibility.

If one word could sum up the philosophy of mentoring in the Teaching Scholars Program, it is *flexibility*. Frequent meeting attendance and rigorous reporting demands are not made. However, if the program had more staff, more structure could be provided, as Boice recommended. As reported in Table 2, the mentoring element of the program has had a great impact on the participants over the years. Each year, at least one participant writes in the final report that mentoring is the most important element of the program.

Seminars, workshops, and retreats. As program director, I learned after my first year that seminar topics that were well received one year may not be of much interest the next. After that, the group was given a strong hand in selecting seminar topics. The new participants discuss successful seminars with the outgoing group at the May opening/closing retreat; then they begin planning their seminars and reach consensus on four or five topics for first-semester seminars. Flexibility is important, so some topics may change to accommodate varying interests. In a developmental way, as the year progresses, the Teaching Scholars move from "how to" topics (for example, how to lead discussions, how to use writing assignments) led by campus experts, to more controversial or philosophical topics, such as ethical dilemmas in teaching, often led by a member of the group.

At least two off-campus retreats occur each year, and both contribute to the social and intellectual bonding of the group. One retreat answers Wise's (1967) call for arranging seminars cooperatively with other colleges. The September retreat takes place on another campus whose students and curriculum differ from Miami's. This not only provides interesting teaching contrasts to discuss, but also enhances the Teaching Scholars' understanding of the Miami environment. Another retreat is held in May at a nearby country inn; here the newly selected participants spend a day with the graduating group, learning the pros and cons about teaching projects, mentoring, and seminar topics, as well as the traditions of the Teaching Scholars Program. This passing of the torch is an important rite, stimulating the new initiates to plan for the coming year and rewarding the missionary and playful zeal of the graduating class.

Austin (1990), in her survey of former Lilly Teaching Fellows Programs, reported that only 5 of the 16 responding programs held retreats. It is difficult to imagine another activity that could establish such important networks, friendships, and lore, as well as generate enthusiasm for the program.

New Faculty: The First Year

Orienting new faculty. Researchers have described the characteristics of successful orientation programs for new faculty. These include: participants are not overloaded; sessions which illustrate the topic; sessions less than one day long; small group interaction with other new faculty and with second-year faculty as guides; an unhurried pace; previews of workshops coming later in the year; and an emphasis on collegiality (Fink 1992, Boice 1992b).

The Miami orientation for first-year faculty—to which second-year faculty are also invited—incorporates many of these elements. Topics cover ways to enhance the effectiveness of teaching and scholarship. Two one-hour seminars in the late afternoon and evening are separated by a dinner and a reception introducing support personnel.

The goals of the orientation are: to emphasize the importance of and expectations for scholarship and teaching; to provide an overview of resources available for the support of teaching and scholarship at Miami; to provide an opportunity to reflect on ways to enhance scholarship and teaching; to introduce new faculty to leaders of programs that support teaching and scholarship; and to begin to build community by having new faculty meet one another and discuss teaching and scholarship across disciplines, divisions, and campuses. Formal feedback from participants indicates that these goals are well achieved and that the session should be repeated in subsequent years.

Role of the department chair. The department chair (or head) is crucial to the success of new faculty. Wheeler (1992) recognized the major roles that chairs can play in developing their new faculty, as resource link, mentor, facilitator of mentor relationships, institutional authority, evaluator, and model of balance. Boice (1992b) also suggested helpful strategies for chairs working with new faculty, for example, how to handle the results of teaching evaluations. Boud (1988) described a pilot program at an Australian university designed to involve new faculty in ongoing planning sessions with the department head, including ways to establish accountability for teaching effectiveness. The paper examined ways in which fears and resistance can be addressed sensitively. The value of the approach appears to lie in the potential long-term benefits: Fewer problems should develop in later stages of faculty careers, and an infrastructure for working with all faculty can be established best when faculty are new and most receptive to improvement. In the Kurfiss and Boice survey (1990), only 16% of the respondents were training department chairs to facilitate teaching, but this was the most highly rated desired activity (60%). Working with chairs remains one of the top priorities—and challenges—for faculty developers.

Junior Faculty

Year two through the year of tenure consideration are crucial for junior faculty. After trying to get one's bearings in the department the first year, the next four years should offer opportunities for learning about teaching and establishing networks with colleagues in other departments in the university. A year-long teaching development program can provide these opportunities, but not during the first year. As one Miami faculty member wrote in his application this year, "After a year of adjustment here, I feel I have settled in but am not yet set in my teaching ways—this is a very appropriate time to develop an effective teaching program and good teaching skills for my career at Miami. Close communication with a mentor, peer reviews, specialized seminars, and interdisciplinary discussions with fellow participants would provide a wonderful environment in which to develop and grow as an educator."

Year-long teaching programs. An ambitious initiative to improve the teaching of junior faculty was started in 1974 by the Lilly Endowment's Post-Doctoral Teaching Awards Program (now called the Lilly Teaching Fellows Program). It invites selected research universities to design year-long programs for six to ten junior faculty in their second through fifth years of teaching. Selected programs are funded up to three years, with the university expected to continue funding afterwards. The Miami Teaching Scholars Program began in 1978 as part of this initiative.

Various program components incorporated by participating universities include release time, senior faculty mentoring, individual teaching projects, seminars, and retreats (Austin, 1992a). In a study of 30 programs from 1974 to 1988, Austin (1990) noted that, "Each of the programs we evaluated had some degree of positive impact on the Fellows and, with few exceptions, some significant institutional impact" (p. 61). "This study shows that a program modest in cost, staff, and time can significantly assist faculty in dealing with their most challenging professional concerns" (Austin 1992b, p. 101).

Over 52 institutions have participated since 1974, including 65% of Research I institutions (Lundgren, 1994). Austin (1990) reported that by 1990, only seven of 30 programs were continuing after endowment funding had ceased. However, half of the institutions had established some other faculty development or teaching-related activities (such as teaching centers) with roots in the original program. The study also identified key factors associated with program continuation: attention to institutional culture, a committed and respected director, administrative support, cultivation of a broad institutional base, prestige of the program, excellent publicity, community built among the participants, and cultivation of university fiscal commitment. Plaudits must go to the Lilly Endowment for its unique efforts to assist junior faculty.

The scholarship of teaching. Because a long-term goal of the Teaching Scholars Program is to increase campus rewards for teaching, and because scholarship is highly rewarded in disciplines and departments, the program always has taken a scholarly approach to teaching. The program has nourished the scholarship of teaching (Boyer, 1990) in a variety of ways. This scholarship is developed gradually over the year for the junior faculty participants through a sequence of steps: design and implementation of a teaching project; selection and use of classroom assessment techniques; reading of teaching literature; attendance at a national teaching conference, with opportunities to meet nationally known teacher-scholars; presentation of teaching seminars on campus, and a national teaching conference; and encouragement to prepare a manuscript for publication. Although the scholarship of teaching was not a buzzword when the program was first developed, the outward focus of the program participants was part of the movement that created high-quality teaching scholarship. Program seminars have featured teacher-scholars working at the cutting edge of teaching and learning theory. The participants rank the scholarship of teaching second of all elements of the program in its impact on their teaching (Table 3).

Two initiatives were taken by the program to promote the scholarship of teaching in a broader context. First, the program developed a national teaching conference, *The Lilly Conference on College Teaching*. Since its inception in 1981, the Lilly Conference on College Teaching at Miami has grown from 50 participants to 400. In addition, Miami University has developed and co-sponsored with various California institutions the Lilly Conference on College Teaching-West (1989) and The Lilly Conference-South (1995).

Teaching Scholars Program participants present at these conferences, where both novice and expert teacher-scholars from a wide variety of campus cultures share their classroom experiences and teaching and learning theories.

Second, the program developed the *Journal on Excellence in College Teaching* in order to provide a written forum for discussion about all areas affecting teaching and learning. This nationally-refereed journal gives faculty the opportunity to share proven, innovative pedagogies and thoughtful, inspirational insights into teaching. Among the contributors are a large number of well-known experts.

The program's commitment to the scholarship of teaching bears out a corollary to the hard-easy rule (Boice, 1990): faculty developers must work to make teaching harder. "Teaching, so long as it remains ostensibly easy (i.e., seen as requiring little training, as unspecifiable in terms of excellence, as uncompetitively evaluated, as only occasionally labeled a failure), will not merit the same rewards and status as hard tasks like writing for publication" (p. 6). "Perhaps the greatest challenge facing faculty developers in expanding their roles is how to integrate scholarship into programs formerly focused exclusively on teaching" (Mann, 1990, p. 13).

IMPACT AND EVIDENCE OF SUCCESS

Long-Term Results

Katz and Henry (1988) stated, "We felt that the faculty development movement that had begun in the early 1970s had not had the transforming influence upon teaching that many have expected. We thought that the problem lay in the fact that efforts at faculty development usually were too short-term and episodic" (p. x). One reason for the recognition of the Miami Teaching Scholars Program is its distinction as the longest-running year-long junior faculty teaching development program in the United States. Because cultures change slowly, successful programs must be continued for several years to have an effect on campus cultures. On the Miami campus, the change in culture—restoring the balance between teaching and research—is notable, although exact balance has not yet been achieved. A university-wide community has been created and strengthened through teaching. In Table 3, the fourth-highest program impact is reported to be on the scholar's comfort as a member of the Miami University community. Evidence of this community and program impact includes:

- One-fourth of former participants still on campus have now served as program mentors; some have been seminar leaders; two are now department chairs.
- Program graduates have contributed to implementing a new general education program broadening cross-disciplinary curriculum and collaboration.
- Of the eight departments volunteering to participate in the first year of the teaching portfolio project, four had former Teaching Scholars as initiators and project coordinators.
- Teaching development grant and program funding from alumni has increased tenfold, from $15,000 to $150,000 US.
- The success of the Teaching Scholars Program led to the establishment of the similar Senior Faculty Program for Teaching Excellence at the request of senior faculty themselves.
- The number of annual awards for excellent teaching at Miami have increased fivefold.
- Undergraduate student learning has been enhanced in many ways. The Teaching Scholars become enthusiastic, interested teachers, some of whom report that their student evaluation ratings have increased an entire point on a four-point scale.
- The strength of the program has enabled it to be combined with Miami's Office of Research and Sponsored Programs to create a new Office for the Advancement of Scholarship and Teaching. This sends a clear message to the campus that teaching and scholarship are equally valued and supported. Several joint initiatives have been sponsored.

The Teaching Scholars Program has changed the Miami culture in a positive way, enhancing the role of teaching in the departmental and university-wide communities.

The Tenure Study

The tenure experiences of all faculty hired at Miami University in the academic years 1977-78 through 1988-89 were examined to determine the relationship between participation in the Teaching Scholars Program (TSP) and tenure decisions at Miami (Bailer & Cox, 1990; Richlin & Cox, 1989). One hundred and six (22%) of the 477 new hires during this period participated in the TSP. The majority of new hires and TSP participants were from the College of Arts and Science (the largest division at Miami). Table 1 provides a breakdown of new hires and program participation by academic division. On a percentage basis, the School of Education and Allied Professions has been most involved in the TSP.

A comparison of tenure decisions ("tenured" versus "left without tenure") is provided in Table 4. Of the 371 faculty for whom a tenure decision was made, there was a significant association ($p<.005$) between TSP participation and a positive tenure decision. Seventy-two percent of TSP participants were tenured versus 55% of the non-participants. To explore this association in greater detail, Table 5 shows tenure decisions by academic division. The School of Interdisciplinary Studies is not included, because they hired only 4 faculty during the study period. From this table, one notes that the strongest association ($p<.05$) between TSP participation and a positive tenure decision occurred in the College of Arts & Science and the School of Education & Allied Professions. As an aside, a few departments have never participated in the TSP program; however, the results remain unchanged even if these departments are removed from the analysis.

From the results presented above, one certainly sees no adverse effects of TSP participation. No causal claims that TSP participation leads to a positive tenure decision can be made. It could be that the TSP is populated by a majority of quick starters, and/or by faculty who are comfortable with their research programs. The TSP encourages development of the qualities of quick starters such as collegiality, interest, and comfort in teaching. The most important conclusion from this study is that the time invested by faculty in a year-long junior faculty development program does not affect tenure outcomes adversely, and in fact, may have a positive influence on such decisions.

RECOMMENDATIONS

Many recommendations are in print about planning, initiating, and conducting specific programs to assist new and junior faculty. Just about every article on a specific aspect of these programs contains suggestions about implementation and use. Helpful, in-depth recommendations can be found in Austin (1990, 1992a), Boice (1992b), and Jarvis (1991). I now offer recommendations, based on 15 years of experience directing such programs on my campus, and on the studies and stories of colleagues involved in similar ventures on other campuses.

Campus cultures are complex, differing by history, curriculum, mission, funding, governance, leadership, size, location, faculty, and student body (Kuh & Whitt, 1988). Tierney & Rhoads (1993) state that, "While we have noted that the institution is only one of the key forces that shape faculty culture and behavior, it nonetheless plays a critical role in the socialization of faculty" (p. 18). Good strategies for implementing and running programs for new and junior faculty will vary greatly from institution to institution, and the institutional culture must be well understood and taken into account as one proceeds.

Initial planning for a program is crucial. Broad administrative and faculty support must be obtained. The president, academic vice-president, and deans must strongly endorse, fund, and otherwise promote the program. A "critical mass" of department chairs must be aware of and support the program, because their valuable resources—new faculty—are the essential ingredients. However, unanimity of chair support is rarely achieved; for example, some chairs do not value teaching as highly as research. Senior and junior faculty should be consulted and involved in planning. In fact, control should remain with the faculty, in the form of a respected advisory committee that is part of university governance, such as an existing teaching support committee. Long-term goals for the university should be included in the planning discussion. Program planners should survey new faculty to determine specific needs (Boice, 1992b) and should draw upon the literature (Shea & Knoedler, 1993). Resource decisions must be made with priority given to programs for junior faculty and / or new faculty: if resources are limited, they should be directed to first-year programs.

As planning and resources are addressed, a committed, conscientious director must be identified.

> *Much of the overall success of a teaching fellows program and the individual successes of the participants rest [sic] on the dedication, interest and hard work of the program director. An effective director is highly committed to the program and its purposes, [and] understands the challenges that confront junior faculty... Typically, directors are senior administrators, leaders of faculty development or teaching centers, or interested faculty members. (Austin, 1992a, p. 84)*

Each of these roles has a different capacity to influence budget allocations; provide expertise about teaching and knowledge of useful resource people; and attract positive recognition across campus (Austin, 1992a).

The initial two or three years should be viewed as pilot testing, with the expectation of changing and fine-tuning various elements of the program. For the junior faculty program, one should select participants with the most potential for successful careers in higher education, seminar leaders of proven quality, and the most generous, well-respected faculty as mentors. I must caution, though, that some department chairs may want a remedial program instead. If the initial years are successful, the program can include some struggling faculty in subsequent years, once the program is well established.

With respect to hiring and first-year programs, one must work with department chairs to encourage mentoring of first-year faculty and the use of portfolios and pedagogical interviews. A campus-wide orientation program for new arrivals should be designed to fit the campus culture, to incorporate the approaches illustrated in seminars (for example, use of small groups), and to make faculty feel welcome (for example, inviting them to a dinner in their honor). Second-year faculty should be invited, too. The initial orientation should be followed by other sessions throughout the year.

Some general principles for ongoing, year-long programs for junior faculty include the following:

- The program application form should be designed to identify candidates' commitment to quality teaching, level of interest in the program, need, potential for contributions to the program, and plans for use of the award year.
- The approval of chairs and deans for application to the program should be required.
- Selection should create a diverse group across disciplines, campuses, experience, gender, race, and needs.
- At the start of the program year (for example, in May for the fall semester), a full-day opening/closing retreat or session should be held at which the graduating participants share their experiences and wisdom with the new group, so that they can plan ahead.
- Each year, the new participants should have a strong hand in determining the programming, including seminar topics, speakers, projects, and mentor selection.
- Mentoring is a complex process and should be designed according to campus culture.
- Release time from at least one course for at least one semester should be provided to the junior faculty participants.
- The scholarship of teaching should be developed gradually through a sequence of teaching projects, classroom assessment techniques, reading of the literature, campus presentations by the participants, and presentations at national teaching conferences.
- The participants should assess program seminars, components, and personal impact, and this feedback should be used for planning and making a case for continuing the program.
- Activities, accommodations, and recognition should be designed to make participants feel valued and respected by the college or university.
- Some activities should be designed to build community; for example, retreats or conferences off campus.

- Reunion activities should be provided for past participants, both for all alumni and for each group.

Since cultures change slowly, commitment to a junior faculty teaching program must be long term. Key words for development, selection, programming, leadership, and assessment of the program include *support, quality, flexibility, openness, comfort, balance,* and *diversity.*

Once faculty are admitted to the academy, every attempt must be made to help them develop as teachers and scholars. Working with new and junior faculty is one of the most rewarding forms of teaching and one which will shape the character of higher education in the new century.

REFERENCES

Agresti, A., & Finlay, B. (1986). *Statistical methods for the social sciences* (2nd ed.). San Francisco, CA: Dellen.

Astin, A.W., & Lee, C.B.T. (1967). Current practices in the evaluation and training of college teachers. In C.B.T. Lee (Ed.), *Improving college teaching* (pp. 296-311). Washington, DC: American Council on Education.

Austin, A.E. (1990). *To leave an indelible mark: Encouraging good teaching in research universities through faculty development. A study of the Lilly Endowment's teaching fellows program 1974-1988.* Nashville, TN: Vanderbilt University, Peabody College.

Austin, A.E. (1992a). Supporting junior faculty through a teaching fellows program. In M.D. Sorcinelli & A.E. Austin (Eds.), *New Directions for Teaching and Learning: No. 50. Developing new and junior faculty* (pp. 73-86). San Francisco, CA: Jossey-Bass.

Austin, A.E. (1992b). Supporting the professor as teacher: The Lilly teaching fellows program. *The Review of Higher Education, 16*(1), 85-106.

Bailer, A.J., & Cox, M.D. (1990, April). *Tenure decisions and faculty development programs.* Paper presented at the AAHE National Conference on Higher Education, San Francisco, CA.

Beeman, A.L. (1981). *Toward better teaching: A report on the post-doctoral teaching awards program of the Lilly Endowment, Inc., September 1974-August 1980.* Indianapolis, IN: Lilly Endowment.

Boice, R. (1987). Is released time an effective device for faculty development? *Research in Higher Education, 26,* 311-326.

Boice, R. (1990). The hard-easy rule and faculty development. *To Improve the Academy, 9,* 3-12.

Boice, R. (1991a). New faculty as teachers. *The Journal of Higher Education, 62*(2), 150-173.

Boice, R. (1991b). Quick starters: New faculty who succeed. In M. Theall & J. Franklin (Eds.), *New Directions for Teaching and Learning: No. 48. Effective practices for improving teaching* (pp. 111-121). San Francisco, CA: Jossey-Bass.

Boice, R. (1992a). Lessons learned about mentoring. In M.D. Sorcinelli & A.E. Austin (Eds.), *New directions for teaching and learning: No. 50. Developing new and junior faculty* (pp. 51-61). San Francisco, CA: Jossey-Bass.

Boice, R. (1992b). *The new faculty member: Supporting and fostering professional development*. San Francisco, CA: Jossey-Bass.

Boud, D. (1988). Professional development and accountability: Working with newly appointed staff to foster quality. *Studies in Higher Education, 13*(2), 165-176.

Bowen, H.R., & Schuster, J. H. (1986). *American professors: A national resource imperiled*. New York, NY: Oxford University Press.

Boyer, E.L. (1990). *Scholarship reconsidered: Priorities of the professoriate*. Princeton, NJ: The Carnegie Foundation for the Advancement of Teaching.

Centra, J.A. (1977, December). Plusses and minuses for faculty development. *Change*, pp. 47, 48, 64.

Centra, J.A. (1978). Types of faculty development programs. *The Journal of Higher Education, 49*(2), 150-161.

Erickson, G. (1986). A survey of faculty development practices. *To Improve the Academy, 5*, 182-196.

Fink, L.D. (1984). *New Directions for Teaching and Learning: No. 17. The first year of college teaching*. San Francisco, CA: Jossey-Bass.

Fink, L.D. (1990). New faculty members: The professoriate of tomorrow. *The Journal of Staff, Program, & Organization Development, 8*, 235-245.

Fink, L.D. (1992). Orientation programs for new faculty. In M.D. Sorcinelli & A.E. Austin (Eds.), *New Directions for Teaching and Learning: No. 50. Developing new and junior faculty* (pp. 39-49). San Francisco, CA: Jossey-Bass.

Finkelstein, M.J., & LaCelle-Peterson, M.W. (1992). New and junior faculty: A review of the literature. In M.D. Sorcinelli & A.E. Austin (Eds.), *New Directions for Teaching and Learning: No. 50. Developing new and junior faculty* (pp. 5-14). San Francisco, CA: Jossey-Bass.

Gappa, J. M., & Leslie, D. W. (1993). *The invisible faculty: Improving the status of part-timers in higher education*. San Francisco, CA: Jossey-Bass.

Gibbs, G., Gold, J.R., & Jenkins, A. (1987). Fending for yourself: Becoming a teacher of geography in higher education. *Journal of Geography in Higher Education, 11*(1), 11-26.

Jarvis, D.K. (1991). *Junior faculty development: A handbook.* New York, NY: The Modern Language Association of America.

Kansas State University, Center for Faculty Evaluation & Development. (1993). *Proceedings of Tenth Annual Conference: Academic Chairpersons: Selecting, Motivating, Evaluating and Rewarding Faculty.* Manhattan, KS: Kansas State University, National Issues in Higher Education, Division of Continuing Education.

Katz, J., & Henry, M. (1988). *Turning professors into teachers: A new approach to faculty development and student learning.* New York, NY: ACE/Macmillan.

Kuh, G.D., & Whitt, E.J. (1988). *The invisible tapestry: Culture in American colleges and universities* (ASHE-ERIC Higher Education Report No. 1). Washington, DC: Association for the Study of Higher Education.

Kurfiss, J., & Boice, R. (1990). Current and desired faculty development practices among POD members. *To Improve the Academy, 9,* 73-82.

Lee, C.B.T. (Ed.). (1967). *Improving college teaching.* Washington, DC: American Council on Education.

Lundgren, R. (1994, February 24). Personal communication. Indianapolis, IN: Lilly Endowment, Inc.

Mann, M.P. (1990). Integrating teaching and research: A multidimensional career model. *To Improve the Academy, 9,* 13-28.

Richlin, L., & Cox, M.D. (1989, June). *What works and when should we do it: Innovative programs to prepare new instructors to teach more effectively.* Paper presented at the STLHE National Conference, Edmonton, AB.

Shea, M.A., & Knoedler, A.S. (1993). *Becoming a teacher: From pedagogy to praxis.* Manuscript submitted for publication.

Sorcinelli, M.D. (1992). New and junior faculty stress: Research and responses. In M. D. Sorcinelli & A. E. Austin (Eds.), *New Directions for Teaching and Learning: No. 50. Developing new and junior faculty* (pp. 27-37). San Francisco, CA: Jossey-Bass.

Sorcinelli, M.D., & Austin, A.E. (Eds.). (1992). *New Directions for Teaching and Learning: No. 50. Developing new and junior faculty.* San Francisco, CA: Jossey-Bass.

Theall, M., & Franklin, J. (Eds.). (1991). *New Directions for Teaching and Learning: No. 48. Effective practices for improving teaching.* San Francisco, CA: Jossey-Bass.

Tierney, W.G., & Rhoads, R.A. (1993). *Faculty socialization as cultural process: A mirror of institutional commitment* (ASHE-ERIC Higher Education Report No. 6).

Washington, DC: The George Washington University, School of Education and Human Development.

Turner, J.L., & Boice, R. (1987). Starting at the beginning: The concerns and needs of new faculty. *To Improve the Academy, 6*, 41-55.

Wheeler, D.W. (1992). The role of the chairperson in support of junior faculty. In M.D. Sorcinelli & A.E. Austin (Eds.), *New Directions for Teaching and Learning: No. 50. Developing new and junior faculty* (pp. 87-96). San Francisco, CA: Jossey-Bass.

Whitt, E.J. (1991). Hit the ground running: Experiences of new faculty in a school of education. *The Review of Higher Education, 14*(2), 177-197.

Wise, W.M. (1967). Who teaches the teachers? In C.B.T. Lee (Ed.), *Improving college teaching* (pp. 77-89). Washington, DC: American Council on Education.

AUTHOR

Milton D. Cox is University Director for Teaching Effectiveness Programs, Miami University, Ohio (US), where he directs the 1994 Hesburgh Award-winning Teaching Scholars Program and the university's Teaching Portfolio Pilot Project. He founded and directs the national Lilly Conference on College Teaching, and is editor-in-chief of the Journal on Excellence in College Teaching. For the past 28 years, he has taught mathematics at Miami University, designing courses that celebrate and share with students the beauty of mathematics. Nationally, Dr. Cox has helped develop programs to enable the presentation of undergraduate student papers at national professional meetings. In 1988, he received the C.C. McDuffee Award for distinguished service to Pi Mu Epsilon, the National Mathematics Honorary Society.

NOTES

[1] The Carnegie Foundation for the Advancement of Teaching (1987 ed.). *A classification of institutions in higher education*. Princeton, NJ: Author.

TABLE 1

New Hires (n=477) and TSP Participation by Academic Division

TSP Participation	Did Not Participate (n=371)	Did Participate (n=106)
Division		
Business	19%	21%
Arts and Science	44%	31%
Education	12%	25%
Applied Science	12%	9%
Fine Arts	11%	11%
Interdisciplinary Studies	1%	3%

TABLE 2

Miami University Teaching Scholars Program
Evaluation of Program Elements

How would you rate the impact of each of the following elements of the Teaching Scholars Program on you? "1" indicates a very weak impact and "10" indicates a very strong impact.

Elements	*	81-82	82-83	83-84	84-85	85-86	86-87	87-88	88-89	89-90	90-91	91-92	92-93	93-94
The colleagueship and learning from the other Teaching Scholars	(1) 8.8	(3) 8.8	(2) 8.9	(2) 8.1	(3) 8.9	(2) 9.0	(6) 6.5	(1) 9.0	(1) 9.1	(1) 9.9	(1) 9.8	(1) 9.3	(1) 9.0	(1) 8.5
The retreats and conferences	(2) 8.3	(5) 7.7	(6) 7.6	(6) 7.2	(3) 8.9	(1) 9.4	(2) 8.1	(3) 8.7	(3) 8.1	(4) 8.6	(2) 8.8	(2) 8.7	(3) 8.1	(2) 8.3
Release time	(2) 8.3	(1) 9.0	(4) 7.9	(3) 8.0	(1) 9.7	(4) 8.3	(1) 9.5	(7) 7.1	(3) 8.1	(2) 9.5	(7) 5.7	(4) 7.8	(2) 8.5	(3) 8.2
The teaching project	(4) 8.2	(1) 9.0	(1) 9.1	(1) 8.3	(5) 8.6	(7) 7.4	(4) 7.5	(6) 7.8	(2) 8.4	(3) 9.0	(4) 8.1	(5) 7.6	(4) 8.0	(4) 8.0
The Mentor relationship	(5) 8.0	(4) 8.7	(2) 8.9	(4) 7.8	(2) 9.5	(5) 8.0	(3) 8.0	(2) 8.9	(5) 7.1	(6) 7.1	(5) 8.0	(6) 7.1	(6) 7.3	(6) 7.7
Seminars	(6) 7.6	(6) 7.3	(7) 7.1	(5) 7.4	(7) 7.9	(5) 8.0	(7) 5.8	(5) 7.9	(4) 7.4	(5) 7.9	(3) 8.4	(3) 8.1	(5) 7.7	(5) 7.9
Observation of Mentor's or others' classes	(7) 6.9	(7) 6.3	(5) 6.8	(7) 6.8	(6) 8.3	(3) 8.8	(5) 7.0	(4) 8.3	(6) 5.6	(7) 5.9	(6) 7.0	(7) 6.3	(7) 6.6	(7) 6.6
OVERALL MEAN FOR COHORT	8.0	8.1	8.0	7.7	8.8	8.4	7.5	8.2	7.7	8.3	8.0	7.8	7.9	7.9

*Overall mean and rank across years; number in parentheses is ranking by each year's group; number on second line is mean for that element.

TABLE 3
Miami University Teaching Scholars Program
Ratings of Program Outcomes

Estimate the impact of the Teaching Scholars Program as a totality on each of the following areas.
"1" indicates a very weak impact and "10" indicates a very strong impact.

Areas	*	81-82	82-83	83-84	84-85	85-86	86-87	87-88	88-89	89-90	90-91	91-92	92-93	93-94
(1) Your interest in the teaching process	(1) 8.5	(1) 8.4	(2) 8.4	(1) 9.5	(3) 8.6	(2) 8.0	(2) 7.4	(3) 7.9	(1) 8.5	(3) 8.1	(1) 9.0	(1) 9.1	(1) 8.4	(1) 9.4
(2) Your understanding of & interest with respect to the scholarship of teaching	(2) 8.1												(3) 8.0	(2) 8.2
(2) Your view of teaching as an intellectual pursuit	(2) 8.1	(2) 7.8	(1) 8.9	(4) 7.0	(1) 9.0	(1) 8.2	(1) 8.0	(1) 8.5	(2) 8.2	(1) 8.4	(2) 8.3	(2) 8.3	(6) 7.3	(6) 7.4
(4) Your comfort as a member of the Miami University community	(4) 8.0													
(5) Your total effectiveness as a teacher	(5) 7.8	(3) 7.1	(4) 7.2	(3) 7.3	(2) 8.9	(3) 7.9	(3) 7.3	(2) 8.3	(3) 7.9	(2) 8.3	(4) 7.5	(3) 7.8	(4) 7.9	(3) 7.9
(6) Your awareness of ways to integrate the teaching/research experience	(6) 7.2												(5) 7.4	(7) 6.9
(7) Your technical skill as a teacher	(7) 7.2	(4) 6.6	(6) 6.3	(5) 6.8	(6) 7.6	(3) 7.9	(6) 6.1	(4) 7.7	(4) 7.1	(5) 7.0	(3) 7.8	(5) 7.1	(6) 7.3	(5) 7.7
(8) Your understanding of the role of a faculty member at Miami University	(8) 7.1	(6) 6.3	(5) 7.6	(2) 7.4	(4) 8.3	(4) 7.7	(5) 6.4	(5) 7.4	(6) 6.1	(6) 6.7	(4) 7.5	(4) 7.3	(9) 6.8	(8) 6.6
(9) Your research and scholarly interest	(9) 6.9	(5) 6.5	(3) 7.9	(6) 6.3	(5) 8.2	(6) 6.3	(4) 6.9	(6) 6.8	(5) 6.2	(4) 7.2	(6) 7.1	(6) 6.3	(8) 7.0	(9) 6.4
OVERALL MEAN FOR COHORT	7.7	7.1	7.7	7.4	8.4	7.6	7.0	7.7	7.3	7.6	7.9	7.7	7.6	7.6

*Overall mean and rank across years; number in parentheses is ranking by each year's group; number on second line is mean for that area.

TABLE 4

Tenure Decision and TSP Participation

Did Not Participate		Did Participate		
Tenured	Left W/O	Tenured	Left W/O	*p*-value*
55%	45%	72%	28%	.005
(*n*=295)	(*n*=295)	(*n*=76)	(*n*=76)	

TABLE 5

Tenure Decision and TSP Participation by Academic Division

	Did Not Participate		Did Participate		
Division	Tenured	Left W/O	Tenured	Left W/O	*p*-value*
Business	55% (*n*=60)	45% (*n*=60)	56% (*n*=16)	44% (*n*=16)	.929
Arts & Science	60% (*n*=124)	40% (*n*=124)	88% (*n*=25)	12% (*n*=25)	.008
Education	37% (*n*=38)	63% (*n*=38)	67% (*n*=15)	33% (*n*=15)	.049
Applied Science	46% (*n*=39)	54% (*n*=39)	67% (*n*=9)	33% (*n*=9)	.231
Fine Arts	61% (*n*=33)	39% (*n*=33)	67% (*n*=9)	33% (*n*=9)	.529

*p-value for test of the independence of tenure decision and TSP participation (small p-values => dependence). P-value based on Chi-square test of independence (Agresti & Finlay, 1986).

12.

Improving Teaching: Academic Leaders and Faculty Developers as Partners

Mary Deane Sorcinelli
Norman D. Aitken

Faculty developers have long recognized the key role to be played by chairs, deans, and senior academic administrators in the success of instructional development programs. This chapter describes the role administrators can play in faculty development and outlines strategies to involve the academic leadership in efforts to enhance teaching in the university.

INTRODUCTION

In recent years, there has been increasing pressure on institutions of higher education to improve teaching. External constituencies such as parents, employers, and legislators have focused a critical eye on colleges and universities, calling for graduates who are better prepared for the demands of an increasingly complex society. Associations that represent higher education—Association of American Colleges, American Association for Higher Education, Carnegie Foundation for the Advancement of Teaching—have challenged the academy to improve support for teaching, especially at the undergraduate level (Association of American Colleges, 1985; Boyer, 1987; Edgerton, 1988). Even within the academy, faculty, chairs, deans, and academic administrators feel that the balance between teaching and research is inappropriate and needs to be modified (Gray, Froh, & Diamond, 1992).

The authors (a director of a center for teaching and a deputy provost) have worked collaboratively over the past six years to develop a culture that values teaching in the research university—a setting that has a tradition of supporting the primacy of research and publication. Our experience has strengthened our conviction that administrators play a critical role in encouraging institutions to take teaching seriously. It has also reinforced our belief that faculty developers must be fully supported at key administrative levels in order to create programming and cultivate an environment that promotes good teaching.

In this chapter, we will focus on the role that academic leaders and faculty developers can play in creating a campus climate that supports and rewards good teaching. We want to draw both on research-based information and on concrete examples of teaching development initiatives from our own campus. In doing so, we can identify and examine several tasks for academic leaders and faculty developers to engage in if they are to effect changes needed to enhance teaching. We can also illustrate the multi-level linkages that can be fashioned from an administrator/developer partnership—linkages among junior and senior faculty, departments and disciplines, faculty and teaching assistants, and chairs, deans, and central administrators.

ADMINISTRATORS AND FACULTY DEVELOPERS: FORGING ALLIANCES

Although some academic leaders might believe that they have a very limited role in improving teaching, there is much evidence to the contrary. In the mid-1970s, researchers and writers in the field of faculty development hypothesized that support and recognition for good teaching would be greater if administrators played a crucial role in the teaching agenda, and further, that teaching development programs would be more effective if they enjoyed strong administrative support (Bergquist & Phillips, 1975; Centra, 1976; Gaff, 1975; Lindquist, 1978). Some 20 years later, those who have looked at the evidence have found considerable positive support for these hypotheses (Diamond & Adam, 1993; Eble & McKeachie, 1985; Schuster, Wheeler, & Associates, 1990; Seldin & Associates, 1990).

From our own research and experiences, we know that chairs, deans, provosts, and the like can create a climate that fosters support and reward for teaching (Sorcinelli & Austin, 1992; Sorcinelli, 1989). We also know that such an environment does not occur by happenstance. Regardless of vision and charisma, administrators by themselves cannot simply make good teaching happen; regardless of their professional skills and leadership, neither can faculty developers. What, then, are the important strategies for academic leaders to focus on if they wish to recognize and reward good teaching? We have come up with four basic strategies aimed at supporting teaching. We will provide examples of how these strategies are embodied, in one form or another, in our programs. We have now incorporated these strategies into all our planning because they have proven so successful in helping a teaching community to flourish. As this account reveals, the four principles upon which we have come to depend overlap. And in a way, that is the point: linkages are the linchpin of effective and long-lasting efforts to integrate a teaching culture into the life of a campus.

Identify Faculty Leadership

On any campus there are a number of administrators who have a strong commitment to teaching and notions of how good teaching can be fostered. But as Green (1990) notes, the nature of academia is such that faculty will generally resist administrative leadership: "Leadership from peers on issues that affect the daily lives of faculty is likely to be more palatable" (p. 57). Given this caution, it is not surprising that a number of other researchers and writers also recommend that administrators and faculty developers encourage faculty to "lead the charge" (Aitken & Sorcinelli, 1994; Eble & McKeachie, 1985; Green, 1988; Rice & Austin, 1990; Schuster et al., 1990; Seldin & Associates, 1990; Sorcinelli, 1989). Engaging faculty is a solid first step in building community, and in identifying excellence in teaching.

At the University of Massachusetts Amherst (US), a Teaching Fellows Program served as the first catalyst in this process. Since 1986, our campus has offered a faculty development program to assist untenured faculty in developing their teaching expertise while they also develop the scholarly agendas expected of faculty in research universities. The program was funded by the Lilly Endowment, Inc., for three years; since that time, the campus has fully funded the fellowship. Fellows attend a bi-weekly "Seminar on College Teaching," develop or redesign a course for their home department, engage in individual consultation (e.g., class visits, videotaping, student feedback), and work with a senior faculty mentor (Aitken & Sorcinelli, 1994; Austin, 1992; see also the chapter by Cox in this volume).

When our first teaching fellowships were awarded, we asked the junior faculty to select mentors. At that point, we realized that there were senior faculty who had been seeking a forum for sharing their commitment to teaching with others. We designed a retreat which brought together six distinguished senior faculty mentors with six energetic and enthusiastic junior faculty. During the retreat, there was a revealing moment: after an extensive discussion of teaching, a mentor who is a highly distinguished scholar said, "In all the years I have been at this university, I have been asked to speak about my research numerous times, but this is the first time I have ever been asked to talk about teaching."

Over the next two years, dedicated and outstanding senior faculty mentors helped to establish the credibility of the program campus wide. The notion of seeking support from key faculty members was reinforced as we worked to create a campus-wide Center for Teaching in 1988. We planted the idea with and solicited support from teaching fellows and mentors as well as members of several faculty senate committees. The model that emerged was one which resembled that of a research institute where the very best research faculty are brought together as a way of encouraging scholarship in particular areas. Thus, while we welcome and support faculty who need help in their teaching, our Center has become known both for its ability to bring together the very best teachers on campus for the purpose of improving teaching for all faculty, and for using outstanding faculty to provide programming and advice. In short, academic leaders and faculty developers must seriously listen to respected campus citizens, provide them with a forum in which they can advocate for teaching, connect them with like-minded colleagues, and empower them as leaders.

Enlist Administrative Support at Multiple Levels

A national survey of perceptions as to the relative importance of undergraduate teaching and research asked faculty, deans, chairs, and central administrators at some 100 research-oriented institutions to describe their perceptions of the balance between research and teaching at their campuses. The survey revealed a perceived overemphasis on research at the expense of teaching at all administrative levels (Gray et al., 1992). In other words, at most institutions there was a considerable amount of latent support for teaching among academic leaders. This latent support can yield numerous opportunities to create a more supportive environment for teaching. To be effective, however, interventions must take place at all levels.

Central administration is frequently told by external constituencies—parents, alumni, trustees, legislators—that there is a need to improve teaching on the campus. But just as frequently, administrators may be reluctant to take a strong stand on the issue within the campus for fear that they will be perceived by faculty as not supporting the research mission of the institution. In this situation, faculty developers have two tasks in obtaining central administration support. The first step, as mentioned, is to identify a critical mass of faculty who support teaching development, especially faculty of high stature within the institution—those who are apt to be perceived as leaders by their colleagues. The second step is to develop means by which central administrators can provide what Green (1990) and Rice and Austin (1990) refer to as "symbolic leadership," leadership in which the administrator's actions and words have symbolic as well as overt meaning.

Our first "Celebration of Teaching Dinner" in Spring semester, 1987, was a breakthrough not only in terms of providing evidence to the central administration that there was widespread support for good teaching, but also in encouraging our Provost and Chancellor to articulate a powerful and positive message about teaching to the rest of the campus. This annual dinner provides an occasion at which members of the University community across disciplines, departments, and ranks come together publicly to acknowledge and celebrate the importance of teaching. The dinner's over 250 attendees include campus-wide administrators, deans, chairs, former fellows and mentors, Distinguished Teaching Award winners, winners of the Chancellor's Medal for outstanding research contributions, and students. The most popular part of the program is presentations by the faculty teaching fellows in which they share memorable experiences from their fellowship year or their teaching career.

The provost (who was later appointed chancellor) attended. When he saw the size and composition of the audience, listened to the stories of all eight fellows, and observed the response to the event, he became convinced that there was a large community of faculty who supported teaching. Over the last eight years he has returned to and participated in every celebration dinner. More importantly, when the three-year Lilly Endowment grant ended, he decided to fully fund the teaching fellows program out of his office. The internal funds have been protected for six years now, despite the fact that the provost's area and all of academic affairs have been particularly hard hit by budget cuts in recent years.

Teaching centers and their directors can create a range of programs and activities by which the central administration can honor teaching and bring it into prominent view. Our teaching center constantly looks for new ways to invite the central administration to articulate and reinforce their symbolic and real commitment to teaching. For example, through a structured luncheon/discussion each semester, it provides contact between fellows, mentors, and central administrators, enabling chief administrators to call on the fellows and mentors for advice, consultation, and advocacy of teaching issues. In addition, the Center works with the central administration to provide campus-wide teaching programs. The Center and the Provost's office co-sponsor an annual campus-wide Teaching Assistant Orientation and a Deans and Chairs Conference. With the Chancellor's office, the Center sponsors a newly created College Outstanding Teaching Award. Through these and other symbolic gestures and concrete actions—speaking at dinners, appearing at luncheons or workshops, meeting with teaching fellows and mentors, co-sponsoring teaching assistant training, deans and chairs development, fellowships and teaching awards—central administration can signal its commitment to teaching.

Deans and department chairs. Many deans and department heads would like a more supportive environment for teaching but feel that their efforts would not be supported by either the central administration or by individual faculty members in their departments or colleges (Gray et al., 1992). In order to improve support at this level within the institution, department heads must be convinced that both the central administration and the faculty at large support teaching. Since this requires support from both above and below, the so-called "middle management" of the university is one of the most difficult to change in the direction of supporting teaching at a research institution. Yet their commitment is crucial. An evaluation study of Lilly Teaching Fellows programs at 34 research universities found that department chairs and deans, through informal encouragement and positive recognition, provide invaluable support to faculty in their teaching efforts (Rice & Austin, 1990).

The role of deans in improving the quality of college teaching has yet to be explored in depth, but there is growing and useful literature on the role of the academic chair in dealing with teaching effectiveness in the department (Creswell, Wheeler, Seagren, Egly, & Beyer, 1990; Lucas, 1989, 1990; Tucker, 1992). It presents chairs with concrete ideas for programs they can initiate, such as in-service seminars or workshops, teaching awards, and graduate student training. It also outlines specific interventions which chairs can use to improve teaching, offers ways to overcome faculty resistance, discusses topics to explore in departmental meetings, and suggests particular avenues to pursue in improving the teaching performance of both new and tenured faculty.

While these strategies are creative and helpful, they presuppose that faculty developers, chairs, deans, and central administrators are all in agreement and working toward the same goal of teaching improvement. On many campuses, however, faculty developers may be still struggling to make connections at the departmental or college level. How to galvanize department chairs and deans around a teaching agenda is a critical question.

On our own campus, we began to court department chairs by enlisting their support in the Teaching Fellows Program. This move immediately allowed chairs to personally identify with a major teaching initiative. We emphasized that candidates must be nominated by their department chairs because we were convinced that without a supportive climate within the department it would be difficult for the fellow to sustain newly learned views and skills in teaching. We also stressed the ability of the program to provide recognition to the home academic department and to reward the department with curriculum development opportunities. As fellows developed teaching skills in an interdisciplinary and collaborative environment, chairs began to see that at the end of the year the department received back a faculty member who was now a trained teacher and who could share ideas with other faculty within and beyond the department.

Further connections with academic departments have been created by the Center over time. For example, we design departmental workshops and consultations on specific topics requested by various departments. We also ask for departmental commitment as a requisite to involvement in our campus-wide Teaching Assistant Orientation. Department chairs appoint a faculty liaison to our Center, invite TAs to the program, and host a departmental luncheon as part of the day. In this way, not only TAs, but also the department chair and faculty representatives are invested in the orientation. We also publish a teaching handbook that is available free of charge to TAs and faculty in all departments.

An annual Deans and Chairs Conference provides another opportunity to address the need for support for teaching from this stratum of academic leadership. We knew that the close involvement of department chairs was essential to change the teaching culture on campus, but there were few early intervention strategies that allowed us to work directly with this group of individuals. Being invited to participate in a FIPSE[1] Focus on Teaching Project (Roberts, Wergin, & Adam, 1993) provided the provost's office and the teaching center with a timely opportunity to work with the department chairs on campus.

In 1991, the campus initiated a day-long conference to enable all chairs, deans, and academic administrators to discuss the role of academic leaders in supporting undergraduate teaching and learning. A committee of chairs, deans, and administrators and the director of the teaching center plans the conference, which is now an annual event, and over 80% of academic leaders, including the Provost and Chancellor, have attended each year. The first conference tackled the issue of the balance between teaching and research. That day-long conference began with presentations by the Chancellor and Provost followed by opportunities for the chairs to meet in small groups across disciplines to discuss the issues raised in the larger group sessions. At the end of the day, the chairs were assembled by college with their deans and asked to develop strategies for improving the balance between teaching and research. The conference encouraged participants to describe the initiatives that they had successfully introduced to improve the balance, and to discuss opportunities for future policies and programs. Subsequent conference themes were *Creating a Multicultural Campus* and *The Changing University*.

In addition, the Center now works with the chairs, deans, and the chancellor's office to coordinate a new college-level teaching award. This award grew directly from a recommendation from the first Deans and Chairs Conference. A group of chairs from the social sciences proposed that the campus create more awards to acknowledge excellence in teaching, particularly within colleges and departments. The new program provides a monetary award, a plaque, and recognition at commencement for one or two faculty members from each of the colleges. The nomination and selection process is governed by the departments and colleges, the award is funded by both the deans' and chancellor's offices, and the formal accolades come from the highest academic officer—the chancellor. This illustrates one more way in which symbolic and real recognition of teaching can find a wider and higher berth in the organizational structure.

In sum, since the support for teaching that exists at each level of the university depends in part on the support from other levels of the university, the faculty developer will be successful in improving faculty teaching to the extent that she has been able to garner support for teaching within the central, college, and departmental administrations. The converse is also true, that obtaining support by administrative units is more easily accomplished if the campus already has broad based faculty support for teaching. Initiatives need to be directed at more than one of these levels, but might sometimes emphasize one or the other—central administration, colleges, departments, or faculty—depending on the circumstances at hand. Whatever the evolving constellation of strategies may be, administrators at all levels must eventually be enlisted.

Create Community, Collegiality, and Coalitions

Rice and Austin (1990) argue that when universities encourage interactions among faculty and administrators who are committed to teaching, they provide incentives for good teaching and for the development of teaching "communities and networks" (p. 39). Over the years, we have put increased effort into devising ways to bring individuals together, not only faculty, but also chairs, deans, and campus administrators. Whether through peer visits, informal study groups, conferences, or social events, the input of others offers new and original ideas, provides intellectual stimulation around teaching issues, and creates a sense of community that helps to break down the isolation felt by many college teachers and the barriers that often build up between faculty and their administrators.

Teaching and faculty development programs are one effective way to bring the campus community together (Aitken & Sorcinelli, in press; Eble & McKeachie, 1985; Green, 1990; Rice & Austin, 1990; Seldin & Associates, 1990). In the Teaching Fellows Program which is housed in our teaching center, for example, collegiality is encouraged by selecting an interdisciplinary group of fellows, having the fellows meet regularly to talk about their teaching, and involving them in the design of the teaching development workshop series for the fellowship year, some of which will be available to the broader campus community.

The teaching center fosters community by enlisting outstanding senior faculty to act as presenters in campus-wide workshops, to sit on University committees related to teaching, and to serve as "faculty associates" at the Center each year, offering workshops and consultations to their colleagues. One of the teaching center's foremost aims is to provide a variety of programming over time to serve all disciplinary interests on campus, from the sciences to the arts to the professional disciplines. This programming, as well as topics of general interest to the community as a whole, such as teaching in the diverse classroom, writing across the curriculum, and teaching large classes well, is often planned in concert with other departments or campus agencies. This provides another way of keeping communication open across disciplinary boundaries.

Green (1990) notes that "coalition and consensus building is one of the most important tasks of academic administrators" (p. 52). While we have discussed the very public actions we have taken to create support for good teaching among a variety of constituencies, a good deal of quiet, behind-the-scenes work is also needed to build coalitions and consensus around teaching. For example, one or the other of us, that is, the Deputy Provost or the Director of the Center for Teaching, sits on the Faculty Senate Council on Teaching, Learning and Technology; the Chancellor's Task Force on Teaching and Learning; and the President's Task Force on Faculty Roles and Rewards. These groups meet on a regular basis to listen to and share ideas, and to seek support from their varied constituencies. Ultimately, the groups help shape the direction of the institution in terms of issues, such as evaluation of teaching, both for improvement and personnel decisions; teaching portfolios; teaching assistant training; teaching and learning in the diverse classroom; and faculty roles and rewards. In a more public forum, we have attempted to respond to needs and create linkages both among individuals, departments, and colleges, and within disciplinary units, through such events as the annual Teaching Assistant Orientation, the Deans and Chairs Conference, and the Celebration of Teaching Dinner.

Provide Recognition and Rewards

The motivation for good teaching is primarily intrinsic. Still, when faculty are asked for ideas on improving the climate for teaching, they often mention something vaguely described as a need for rewards. The need is in part for salary or resources, but is also clearly for more than that. Not only formal but also informal rewards for good teaching can serve as strong incentives (Rice & Austin, 1990; Sorcinelli, 1985).

It is difficult for administrators in research universities to balance rewards between "stars" and the wider group of "good citizens" who teach undergraduates and sit on committees. We make a conscious effort to take notice of all efforts to improve teaching, whether by individual faculty or departments and colleges within the institution, and to give them as much publicity as possible. Such efforts include not only distinguished teaching awards, but also opportunities for faculty and academic leaders to present their ideas and programs on teaching.

The Teaching Fellows Program provides extensive recognition of the junior faculty selected as fellows and the senior faculty who serve as mentors. The program also distinguishes the departments and colleges from which the faculty fellows are selected. Recognition is provided through the Celebration of Teaching Dinner, newspaper publicity, and opportunities for the fellows to meet with both the Chancellor and the Provost during their fellowship year.

In addition, like many campuses, ours is in the process of launching an initiative to field test the teaching portfolio concept as one way to make the reward system more responsive to teaching (Seldin & Associates, 1993). Our teaching center and faculty senate have jointly authored a handbook on the teaching portfolio and will offer a series of campus-wide workshops on teaching portfolios during the upcoming academic year (Faculty Senate Committee on Teaching Evaluation and Improvement and the Center for Teaching, 1993).

Finally, as a part of a strategic planning process, our new Chancellor has established a task force on faculty roles and rewards. It is too early to tell what the outcomes of this effort will be, but the goal is to provide a fair and just system of rewards compatible with the roles for which the faculty are responsible. We hope that a campus-wide consensus can be achieved concerning the rewards for teaching and research, and that a reward structure can eventually be developed which will ensure that both activities are encouraged and rewarded fairly.

CONCLUSION

Administrators and faculty developers should work as partners to improve teaching. Such partnerships help to create community and build alliances among campus constituencies that might otherwise operate in isolation. Much of what we have discovered about creating an institutional culture that values teaching can be found in these lessons learned: the prime importance of identifying support, crossing boundaries and creating linkages, providing opportunities for collegiality, and providing ways for faculty to develop and receive recognition as teachers.

For explanatory purposes, we have dissected our plans and programs into four key strategies. In reality, however, they are always interconnected in both design and execution. One example of this interwoven quality is the Celebration of Teaching Dinner. The dinner not only honors the fellows and mentors who have participated in the teaching fellows program, but also brings together the larger campus community which is committed to teaching for a festive evening that is solely and unashamedly about teaching and learning. The notion of creating multidimensional linkages is fostered by the simple strategy of inviting representatives from all constituencies of the campus, including academic leaders, faculty who have been recognized by the campus as either outstanding teachers and/or outstanding scholars, and some academic staff and students as well.

It may seem ironic that the subtlest blend of the four strategies is to be found in a social, rather than a strictly academic, event. However, university life can be fragmented by disciplinary allegiances and scholarly activities, by campus politics, and by financial hardship. This single event crosses all those boundaries, affirming that teaching, and the relationships which cause it to thrive, transcend the concerns that can divide us into competing camps within the same institution. As administrators and faculty developers seek ways to create both a campus culture and institutional structure that values teaching, here might be a place to begin.

REFERENCES

Aitken, N.D., & Sorcinelli, M.D. (1994). Academic leaders and faculty developers: Creating an institutional culture that values teaching. *To Improve the Academy, 13*, 63-77.

Association of American Colleges. (1985). *Integrity in the college curriculum: A report to the academic community.* Washington, DC: Author.

Austin, A.E. (1992). Supporting junior faculty through a teaching fellows program. In M.D. Sorcinelli and A.E. Austin (Eds.), *New Directions for Teaching and Learning: No. 50. Developing new and junior faculty* (pp. 73-86). San Francisco, CA: Jossey-Bass.

Bergquist, W., & Phillips, S. (Eds.). (1975). *A handbook for faculty development.* Washington, DC: Council for the Advancement of Small Colleges.

Boyer, E.L. (1987). *College: The undergraduate experience in America.* New York, NY: Harper & Row.

Centra, J.A. (1976). *Faculty development practices in U.S. colleges and universities.* Princeton, NJ: Educational Testing Services.

Cresswell, J.W., Wheeler, D.W., Seagren, A.T., Egly, N.J., & Beyer, K.D. (1990). *The academic chairperson's handbook.* Lincoln, NE: The University of Nebraska Press.

Diamond, R.M., & Adam, B.E. (Eds.). (1993). *New Directions for Higher Education: No. 81. Recognizing faculty work: Reward systems for the year 2000.* San Francisco, CA: Jossey-Bass.

Eble, K.E., & McKeachie, W.J. (1985). *Improving undergraduate education through faculty development.* San Francisco, CA: Jossey-Bass.

Edgerton, R. (1988, April). All roads lead to teaching. *AAHE Bulletin*, 3-9.

Faculty Senate Committee on Teaching Evaluation and Improvement and the Center for Teaching. (1993). *Teaching portfolio.* Amherst, MA: University of Massachusetts Amherst, Center for Teaching.

Gaff, J.G. (1975). *Toward faculty renewal.* San Francisco, CA: Jossey-Bass.

Green, M.F. (Ed.). (1988). *Leaders for a new era: Strategies for higher education.* New York, NY: ACE/Macmillan.

Green, M.F. (1990). Why good teaching needs active leadership. In P. Seldin & Associates, *How administrators can improve teaching* (pp. 45-62). San Francisco, CA: Jossey-Bass.

Gray, P.J., Froh, R.C., & Diamond, R.M. (1992). *A national study of research universities on the balance between research and undergraduate teaching.* Syracuse, NY: Syracuse University, Center for Instructional Development.

Lindquist, J. (Ed.). (1978). *Designing teaching improvement programs*. Berkeley, CA: Pacific Soundings Press.

Lucas, A.F. (Ed.). (1989). *New Directions for Teaching and Learning: No. 37. The department chairperson's role in enhancing college teaching*. San Francisco, CA: Jossey-Bass.

Lucas, A.F. (1990). The department chair as change agent. In P. Seldin & Associates, *How administrators can improve teaching* (pp. 63-88). San Francisco, CA: Jossey-Bass.

Rice, R.E., & Austin, A.E. (1990). Organizational impacts on faculty morale and motivation to teach. In P. Seldin & Associates, *How administrators can improve teaching* (pp. 23-42). San Francisco, CA: Jossey-Bass.

Roberts, A.O., Wergin, J.F., & Adam, B.E. (1993). Institutional approaches to the issues of reward and scholarship. In R.M. Diamond & B.E. Adam (Eds.), *New Directions for Higher Education: No. 81. Recognizing faculty work: Reward systems for the year 2000* (pp. 63-86). San Francisco, CA: Jossey-Bass.

Schuster, J.H., Wheeler, D.W., & Associates. (1990). *Enhancing faculty careers*. San Francisco, CA: Jossey-Bass.

Seldin, P., & Associates. (1990). *How administrators can improve teaching*. San Francisco, CA: Jossey-Bass.

Seldin, P., & Associates. (1993). *Successful use of teaching portfolios*. Bolton, MA: Anker.

Sorcinelli, M.D. (1985, April). *Faculty careers: Personal, institutional, and societal dimension*. Paper presented at the meeting of the American Educational Research Association, Chicago, IL.

Sorcinelli, M.D. (1989). Chairs and the development of new faculty. *The Department Advisor, 5*(2), 1-4.

Sorcinelli, M.D., & Austin, A.E. (1992). *New Directions for Teaching and Learning: No. 50. Developing new and junior faculty*. San Francisco, CA: Jossey-Bass.

Tucker, A. (1992). *Chairing the academic department* (3rd ed.). New York, NY: ACE/Macmillan.

AUTHORS

Mary Deane Sorcinelli is Director of the Center for Teaching and associate adjunct professor in the Department of Educational Policy and Administration, University of Massachusetts, Amherst (US). Dr. Sorcinelli has consulted with hundreds of individual faculty members on teaching and has worked at departmental, school, and campus-wide levels to encourage support and recognition for good teaching. She has published an Evaluation of Teaching Handbook *(1986), a book on* Academic Memories: Retired Faculty Members Recall the Past *(1988), and edited a volume on* Developing New and Junior Faculty *(1992). She has directed a number of grants, including a Fund for the Improvement of Postsecondary Education (FIPSE) grant to enlist the support of key campus academic leaders in encouraging reward structures that support undergraduate teaching.*

Norman D. Aitken is Deputy Provost and Professor of Economics, University of Massachusetts, Amherst (US). He has primary administrative responsibility for undergraduate education on the Amherst campus. Dr. Aitken instituted a faculty teaching fellowship program on the Amherst campus with a grant from the Lilly endowment and was responsible for creating the Center for Teaching, established in 1988. He has published articles on the undergraduate student experience, and has also been responsible for developing a variety of residentially-based academic programs for undergraduate students, enabling small groups of freshmen to live together and share a common and enriched academic experience.

NOTES

[1] US Department of Education's Fund for the Improvement of Postsecondary Education.

13.

Promoting Inclusiveness in College Teaching

Nancy Van Note Chism
Anne S. Pruitt

This chapter describes the instructional and curricular issues and related administrative strategies involved in dealing with diversity. It first discusses problems associated with teaching inclusively and how these problems are manifested in college settings. The chapter then addresses the process of institutionalizing programs designed to help college teachers recognize the dimensions of the issue and teach in ways that are sensitive to different cultures and perspectives.

INTRODUCTION

Throughout history, discriminatory arrangements have routinely been viewed as normal and proper by people of given societies. Slavery, the imprisonment of individuals with Downs Syndrome, rigid caste systems, and hierarchies based on race, ethnicity, or gender all have been taken-for-granted features of the social structures of different countries and historical eras. While today most people view these arrangements with repugnance, they consciously or unconsciously engage in actions that exclude or devalue certain groups of people. The struggle continues into the present to create and maintain a society that serves all individuals and groups and welcomes their contributions.

The quest for equality in higher education reflects the particular societies in which the institutions are rooted. For example, in South Africa, the issues revolve around color; in the Czech Republic, around ethnicity; in the Netherlands, around language; in Ireland, around religion; in eastern Canada, around language and ethnicity; in the United States, around race, gender, sexual identity, and a host of other issues. Examination of just three of these contexts, however, shows that there are many commonalities.

In South Africa, the President of the National Union of South African Students, Erika Elk (1990) observed: "Thousands of black students from the universities... have been excluded or expelled. The reasons given for this range from political expulsions to exclusions on so-called academic grounds" (pp. 20-21). The Union calls for universities to examine teaching methods, admissions criteria, and the process for reviewing students. One of the many hopes for majority rule in South Africa (established in 1994) is to redress this situation.

In the Czech Republic, where Romanies (Gypsies) constitute an ethnic minority, deep-rooted prejudices and xenophobia result in unequal schooling. At Palacky University (Jarabová, 1993), the faculty in Pedagogy have proposed a set of experiences that will help future teachers to understand the Romany culture and adopt teaching behaviors that will help all students to succeed.

Minority students in the Netherlands (consisting of students from Surinam or the Antilles, or second-generation students of Turkish, Moroccan, Surinam, Antillean, or Chinese parents) experience severe problems in the universities due to language differences and poor early academic preparation. There is a need to increase teachers' understanding of the students, as well as to improve their lecturing and communication skills (van der Land & Kok, 1993).

The problems in South Africa, the Czech Republic, and the Netherlands are similar in theme to those in the United States, where groups that have historically constituted a minority are increasing in population at a much higher rate than European Americans. African-Americans and Hispanic-Americans currently comprise one-fourth of the nation, but by century's end, they will comprise one-third. Asian-Americans are the fastest-growing ethnic group.

In the experience of colleges where the dominant group is in the majority, these population shifts have led to concerns about the disenfranchised groups' access, achievement, retention, and graduation. In most cases, they have not met with the same success as the dominant group. Wide gaps exist between measures such as college attendance, academic grades, and dropout and graduation rates. So, while diversity is increasing, so is the search for ways to eradicate the gaps.

The United States example, and echoes in other countries of similar crises centered on population shifts and attendant educational problems, calls for societies throughout the world to take action to enhance the success of under-served groups.

In response to these issues, multicultural education has increasingly been the topic of international attention, encouraging programs that strive to ensure equal student access to education, teaching practices that are respectful and supportive of all students, and attention to the issues and accomplishments of a variety of cultures and social groups in courses of study. A variety of sessions devoted to these issues have been presented at such international meetings on higher education as the International Conference on Improving University Teaching held in Schwäbisch Gmünd, Germany, in July, 1993, and the European Association for Institutional Research Forum held in Turku, Finland, in August, 1993.

THE HIGHER EDUCATION CHALLENGE

For many reasons, higher education is in a unique position to exercise leadership with respect to human equality. The much-touted origin of the word *university*—associated with the bringing together of many peoples, academic disciplines, and viewpoints—is at the philosophical heart of the matter. Value is clearly placed on the creativity and intellectual progress that can result from multiple talents and the free exchange of ideas and perspectives.

In addition to internal beliefs about equality, higher education is faced with external pressures to deal with access issues. The increased need for highly developed talent in many societies has created an emphasis on human potential development. In many countries, educating only the elite or members of the dominant class will not be sufficient; the pressure to educate non-traditional students is increasingly strong.

Political unrest around the world is also having repercussions for higher education. As dissent and even warfare escalate, pressures to reach a peaceful solution through education and acceptance have critical implications for the universities. They are being called upon to model equality of opportunity and to foster productive dialogue about social justice.

There are substantial challenges inherent in creating a supportive climate for previously under-represented students at institutions of higher education. Faculty and students bring with them the biases that permeate their societies. Even well-meaning individuals offend inadvertently. In recent years, however, conscious attention has been paid to articulating the ways in which discrimination affects the learning environment in higher education. Frank consideration of these problems is a crucial first step in undertaking change.

FACTORS THAT CONSTRAIN INCLUSIVE PRACTICE IN HIGHER EDUCATION

Inclusive educational practice, that is, approaches to education that are welcoming to students from all social groups, has been constrained by two main factors in higher education: narrow curriculum choices and pedagogy that favors traditional students. The first factor focuses on the *what* of teaching—the content; the second on the *how*—the teaching methods.

Curriculum Issues

Curriculum issues center around choices that are made about topics for study in both individual courses and degree programs, around print and audiovisual materials, and around topics for assignments, research projects, or theses and dissertations.

Curriculum choices. Decisions about what shall be taught reflect the decision makers' values about what knowledge is most worthy. These values are rooted in the societal traditions, mainstream scholarship, and personal preferences of those who make curriculum choices. In the United States, for example, the dominant group comes from a male, European tradition. The result is an emphasis on European art, philosophy, science, literature, and social science. Students of medicine, for example, are unlikely to study methods of healing that come from tribal African or North American Indian cultures. Literature survey courses are much more likely to include European and United States authors than South American or Laotian authors; African-, Asian-, and Hispanic-American writers are studied far less frequently than European-American writers. Until recently, the work of most female artists has been neglected in many cultures worldwide.

Valued perspectives. In perspective as well, curricula have traditionally reflected the dominant class. Ways of knowing associated with women (Belenky, Clinchy, Goldberger, & Tarule, 1986) and non-technological societies are often devalued in universities. Feminist (Maher, 1985), American Indian (Tierney, 1991), and Afrocentric (Asante, 1987) approaches to philosophy, history, and culture are often ignored in the official curriculum or are rejected as legitimate approaches to scholarship in courses where they could be considered.

Bias in texts. Text materials often mirror (or perpetrate) these omissions. Until recently, content analysis of texts could document the ways in which the issues and scholarship of non-dominant groups were entirely absent from leading textbooks. Examples and language favored the dominant group, such as the use of the male pronoun to refer to all people (Schau & Scott, 1984). Visual aids, such as photographs and illustrations, also ignored women and minority subjects. Even though this pattern is changing, such biases are still present.

One example of an initiative to address this problem can be found in PEARL, an independent, national advisory council in Amsterdam, the Netherlands. PEARL's members analyze and evaluate learning materials by carefully scrutinizing text as well as illustrations in order to determine whether racial stereotypes and prejudices, ethnocentrism, and racism are confirmed or combatted. Through service to educators as well as local and national governments, they are attempting to adapt educational materials to a multi-ethnic society (van Praag, 1989).

Research topics. Choice of research topic, as well, is often constrained by the social bias of advisors and teachers. Assignments focus on traditional ways of exploring traditional subjects. An analytic paper on power in social groups, for example, is more likely to be assigned than an autobiographical essay or oral history focused on a non-dominant group experience. Students who propose researching topics that reflect the interests of such non-dominant groups as gay and lesbian people, disabled people, or racially-different people are often discouraged from working in "marginal," "unimportant," or "emotionally-charged" areas. Often the messages are subtle: a student on the videotape *Making a Difference* (Center for Teaching Excellence, 1990) said: "A large problem I've had with faculty has been subjects that I have identified which deal with black people or minority-related issues. You'll get a glance, a look from them when you say, 'This is what I want to do.' And that look gives you the feeling that this [kind of research] isn't exactly what they really want you to pursue."

Failing to be inclusive with respect to curriculum issues results first in a narrowness of scholarship, and second in the loss of potential new scholars. Narrowness of scholarship is reflected in a canon that effectively ignores much of human accomplishment, a canon that preoccupies a community of mainstream scholars and presents itself as complete when really it is quite parochial in nature, given the range of achievements that various cultures have produced. The loss of potential scholars results when those with the desire and ability to do the research necessary to bring neglected voices and issues to the academy are coerced into doing traditional scholarship or rejected or discouraged from continuing to follow their interests within a higher education context.

Teaching Methods

A second set of issues revolving around diversity in higher education concerns the interpersonal and pedagogical approaches used by faculty in classrooms and office interactions. These range from overt hostility and discriminatory behaviors to more subtle, institutionalized practices that result in exclusion.

Stereotypes. At the root of many teaching behaviors that are not supportive of diversity are the stereotypes teachers hold and the expectations for student performance associated with these stereotypes (Green, 1988). Whether, at one extreme, faculty think that students of certain racial backgrounds are genetically inferior or whether they just hold unarticulated stereotypes based on their socialization as members of a given culture, stereotypes are extremely powerful. In attributing negative or even positive characteristics to an entire group of people, teachers who stereotype convey messages to students that can impair their academic performance. Students easily pick up these messages, even if faculty are unaware that they are sending them. For example, a teacher who lavishes excessive praise on a female student in a physics class might convey the message to the student that he or she does not expect females to do well in science. Similarly, a teacher who expresses astonishment when an Asian student does poorly in physics reveals the expectation that all Asian students perform well in science (Chan & Wang, 1991). Since teacher expectations are critical in student achievement, stereotyping can have very harmful results.

Unequal participation. Differential access to learning can be overcome by fostering free and open class discussion, inviting students from diverse groups to participate in special opportunities, and nominating them for awards and scholarships. Too often, teachers in higher education inadvertently pay the greatest attention to those students who are like themselves— who come from similar backgrounds, think in the same way, value the same things, and communicate similarly. The consequence is that students who are different are neglected. Research in United States classrooms has shown, for example, that in class discussion, women and ethnic minority students participate at far lower rates than European-American males (Sadkar & Sadkar, 1992). Women and ethnic minority students are interrupted more, called upon less frequently, and given less teacher praise and attention. Similarly, studies of mentoring have found that women and ethnic minority students are less likely to have mentors to advise them, nominate them for honors, or help them academically (McCormick, 1991).

Tokenism. In an effort to correct unequal participation, some faculty engage in tokenism (Center for Teaching Excellence, 1990; Lopez & Chism,

1993). This behavior, which idealizes a particular member of a non-dominant group or pays the person superficial attention to make a point, can be just as offensive and harmful to student performance as deliberate exclusion. Calling on a student to speak for his or her gender, racial, or ethnic group (for example, asking a blind student to talk about how the blind feel about health care) assumes that the student can speak for all members of the group—a responsibility that most students do not want—and that all members of the group think alike. It also may make the student feel uncomfortable at having been singled out as a member of the non-dominant group.

Communication. At the heart of participation and performance issues in the classroom are styles of communicating, thinking, and learning. Again, teachers may have been socialized to value a certain way of thinking or communicating, and they consequently may see other styles as inadequate or deficient. Language differences are one area of concern. In the United States, African-American students who use "Black English" are often thought by many students and teachers to be ignorant. In Great Britain, a great deal of importance is placed on an accent. Throughout the world, students studying in a language other than their own native language experience condescending attitudes based on language differences.

Although more subtle than language differences, differences in communication styles exert a greater impact on classroom teaching. Recent research on male and female patterns of communication (Tannen, 1990) and European and African styles of communication reveal that cultural differences can influence classroom performance if the dominant style is favored to the exclusion of others (Cummins, 1990). For example, students who are expressive rather than analytical in their portrayal of a situation might be devalued as "soft" or frivolous in a Eurocentric classroom. Students, such as American Indians or Asians, who have been taught to value silence and reticence, might be judged ignorant, passive, or even hostile by teachers who associate extensive verbalization with knowledge. Students whose culture teaches that eye contact is rude, or conversely, believe that eye contact is a sign of politeness, might feel uncomfortable or insulted if teachers use the opposite behavior.

Learning styles. Similarly, the ways in which people learn are thought by many scholars to be associated with specific cultures (Anderson & Adams, 1992). Although too strict an association results in stereotyping, general patterns can be informative. In the United States, for example, females and students from African, Hispanic, and American Indian backgrounds are more apt to rely on intuition and emotional cues than structured logic; on concrete rather than abstract information; and on unique characteristics rather than commonalities. They tend to value collaboration and interpersonal relationships more highly than do male European- or Asian-American students. These non-dominant students, therefore, are likely to be more comfortable in group learning situations than in formal debates; to perform better on a creative project than a traditional term paper; and to value the evidence from a case study rather than a statistical analysis. When the dominant classroom teaching style is at odds with the style of non-dominant groups, learning is constrained.

Other cultural norms, such as religious beliefs, values about promptness or neatness, styles of clothing and music, can also affect classroom performance if exceptions to the dominant style are not treated with tolerance.

For more information on learning styles, see Knapper's comments on the subject elsewhere in this volume.

WHAT COLLEGE TEACHERS CAN DO

Sensitivity to individual differences, coupled with an attitude that values diversity, forms the basis for helpful teacher behaviors. While there are no hard and fast rules because the variety of situations is so great, there is some helpful general advice for college teachers who want to encourage the success of all students. Key guidelines include:

- College teachers should examine their own thoughts and actions. The more reflective they are about biases, the more able they are to deal with them. The more they convince themselves of the importance of valuing other perspectives and socially different people, the more willing they will be to take extra measures to foster inclusion.
- Teachers should continually try to know their students. Talking with learners from previously under-represented groups and learning about their backgrounds, their values, and their motivation helps teachers to know which actions will help, and which will constrain, the academic success of all students.
- Faculty members should examine their curricula, syllabi, and text materials for overt bias or omission of representation of people from non-dominant groups.
- College teachers should strive to create a welcoming attitude and classroom climate conducive to equality of participation.
- Teachers should welcome and try to accommodate differences in interests, communication, and learning styles rather than thinking of them as deficiencies. Varying instructional methods is helpful

to both dominant and nondominant students (see Anderson & Adams, 1992).

FACULTY DEVELOPMENT PROGRAMS ADDRESSING DIVERSITY

To help college teachers understand diversity issues and adopt behaviors supportive of all students, a variety of faculty development programs have arisen. (Many of these are detailed in Mintz, 1993, and Border & Chism, 1992). While the programs differ in format, most focus on the following goals:

- Raising awareness of the issues through problem definition
- Obtaining institutional commitment to change
- Creating a sense of individual involvement and responsibility
- Identifying helpful and undesirable teaching behaviors
- Developing personal action plans

Specific activities designed to achieve each of these goals are detailed below.

Raising Awareness

Faculty development programs engage participants in problem definition chiefly through information and personal testimony. Many use information, either in the form of institutional or departmental data, such as retention rates, attitude surveys, participation rates, and performance statistics, or in the form of research results in the scholarly literature. Before workshops at the University of Missouri (US), for example, data that will help to frame the discussion is gathered from departments (vom Saal, Jefferson, & Morrison, 1992). This information is presented to faculty to offer evidence of discrimination. Many programs also offer personal testimony: videotapes of students or others speaking about their experiences of alienation and discrimination or live student panels that address the issues. Some programs precede meetings with a survey of students in the unit under discussion; actual student comments are brought to the session to create an understanding of how particular issues are manifested in that unit.

Establishing Commitment

Many programs rely on institutional or unit-level leadership to stimulate commitment to addressing diversity issues. Reading a statement or hearing a presentation by a key administrator or committed faculty colleague can help others to become involved. Discussion of the issues and of the forces, such as public pressure or student interest groups, that are arguing for solutions can also help to establish commitment.

Creating Individual Ownership

To help faculty engage the issues in a personal way, many programs rely on active learning strategies that involve some reflective activity. Several programs have developed simulation exercises, using print or video prompts, and others have developed case studies, such as *Dialogues for Diversity* (Kramer & Weiner, 1994), or short vignettes, such as Harvard University's (US) *Race in the Classroom*, that illustrate the dynamics of these issues in specific contexts. Faculty are asked to take on the perspectives of both the student and the faculty member in the incident described, focusing on how these roles make them feel. They then work together to suggest positive responses to the situation. Many programs have developed self-inventories or attitude or behavior checklists that faculty can use to identify ways in which they may be a part of the problem and move to alternative behaviors.

Identifying Helpful Teaching Behaviors

Lists of helpful teaching behaviors can be generated in conjunction with the exercises used to establish individual involvement. Pre-constructed lists distributed at the end of sessions on diversity can also help those who want more structure and guidance than the open-ended discussion offers. Such lists have been constructed by many programs and of necessity must be general in nature. An example from The Ohio State University (US) is contained in the appendix to this chapter.

Action Plans

Many programs conclude sessions for faculty by distributing a personal action plan document on which faculty members write down one or more things that they can do personally to address diversity issues. Sometimes, program leaders ask participants to circle on a pre-printed list a few behaviors that they can adopt. Some programs set up partners among the participants and ask the partners to meet or talk on the telephone at an agreed-upon date to report on their progress.

DEVELOPING DIVERSITY PROGRAMS
FOR SUCCESSFUL INSTITUTIONALIZATION

Creating more supportive classroom environments and more positive interactions with previously disenfranchised students requires change in attitudes and behavior (Pruitt, 1993). Applying ordinary understandings of organizational change does not provide sufficient guidance. On the contrary, this task is emotionally charged: negative attitudes are so embedded in the history of every society that efforts to address them usually elicit hostile reactions. The leaders of an institution will take a stand only when the political climate of the institution, as well as the community in which it is located, regards exclusion as a significant problem.

Occasionally, individual teachers will become convinced that they can serve diverse students better by initiating changes on their own in the classes they teach. Sometimes they succeed in convincing colleagues to do the same, and together they become islands of responsiveness committed to making a difference in student learning. Often their efforts spread to other institutions. As necessary as individual initiative is, the nature of the current situation requires something more: not one or two teachers who strive to foster the educational success of all students, but efforts on the part of *all* teachers.

The entire institution must reject the notion that low attendance, retention, and graduation rates are caused by students alone and replace it with the belief that institutional policies and practices, as well as teaching procedures, may be at fault—a change from the idea of "fixing the student" to that of "fixing the institution."

Given this backdrop, we turn to institutional planning. *Understand, support*, and *accept* are watchwords that characterize the planning effort that we recommend. All constituencies must understand the plan, they must accept it, and they must support it. The process of implementation begins with a phase in which the institution prepares for the changes.

Preparation

Six main considerations should be addressed during the preparation phase:

Analyzing the policy. An institution that hopes to bring about changes in curriculum and pedagogy must conduct careful policy research. The goal is to identify and define the problem clearly. Then, existing efforts should be evaluated. Are the ways in which the institution is currently addressing the problem satisfactory or should they be changed? Following this assessment comes the formulation and evaluation of alternative courses of action. The final step is to draft a plan of action.

Proposing the plan. Students, staff, and faculty should be urged to attend hearings and forums on drafts of the plan of action. Their responses should be carefully considered in subsequent revisions.

Issuing the call for action. As Curry (1992) indicates, "Leaders are sponsors of change. They prepare the organization for change and for its institutionalization by creating a climate in which change can take place or by influencing the perceptions and attitudes of the organization's members" (p. 23). Clearly, then, the leadership of the institution must articulate the vision with respect to creating a teaching environment inclusive of all students.

Assigning responsibility. It is important to charge one person with key coordinating responsibility for the program, even though the entire program might involve collaboration with many individuals and units. To track progress, a monitoring system should be built in, including provision for formative and summative evaluations.

Specifying the timetable. At this point, it is important to ask whether the program will be short-term or long-term. Envisioning how it will grow and change will be important in forecasting the amount of time needed to achieve the given objectives.

Obtaining adequate funding. Resources to support staff and operating expenses should be provided from the institution's own funds rather than from an external grant. A willingness to designate its own funds is indicative of a university's serious commitment to inclusiveness.

Designing a Plan According to Institutional Characteristics

Once the institution has been prepared for change, steps can be taken to implement the plan. The likelihood of obtaining attitudinal and behavioral change is proportional to the involvement of those from whom these changes are expected. When considering involvement, one should be guided by an understanding of how colleges and universities operate. Because systems of higher education around the world vary, it is impossible to be prescriptive; yet we can illustrate by using an example to spell out certain assumptions about higher education that would govern the approach to change in the United States.

Academic governance and authority. Planning must take its direction from an understanding of academic governance. Although governance is participatory, involving faculty, deans, department heads, central administrators, and students, it is also hierarchical. "The faculty are the university" is a basic belief. A good deal of the authority of the institution is exercised through academic administrators with titles such as department chairperson, dean, and provost. Organizational arrangements designed for participation include university-wide senates, councils, and student governments. Communications, therefore, and decisions as to whether or not the program is to be required or optional must respect the governance characteristics of the institution.

Academic disciplines. Members of academic disciplines vary in their attitudes toward racial matters. Departmental culture with respect to decision-making varies as well. Allegiance to those beyond the institution is often stronger than allegiance to the home institution, resulting in initiatives within disciplines that may be at variance with those being proposed by the institution. Knowledge of disciplinary initiatives with respect to teaching for inclusiveness and curriculum change could influence the institutional effort. Programs can build on disciplinary initiatives and can use specific examples tailored to specific departments, such as case studies from the discipline, as components of the programming.

Informal system. Coalitions of individuals that speak for various interests—such as African-American faculty, administrators, and students—play a part in the governance of institutions. Involving the institution's stakeholder groups in the planning, design, and implementation is critical.

Faculty authority. According to a long tradition, final authority for the conduct of teaching belongs to individual faculty members. This is such a guarded and prized prerogative that one treads lightly when it comes to inquiry and recommendations regarding the manner in which teaching takes place. Curry (1992) observes that faculty "do not expect change to come as dicta from inaccessible individuals... decisions related to implementing and institutionalizing innovations cannot be made unilaterally and be expected to go uncontested" (p. 22). Sensitivity and involvement are critical in environments where faculty autonomy prevails.

Interinstitutional system. Colleges and universities are conscious of their relationship with other institutions of higher education. While it is important to remember that no two institutional settings are exactly the same, it is often helpful to learn about and assess solutions tried at peer institutions. Doing so can be both instructive and time-saving.

Driving and restraining forces. Change is not always greeted with open arms. In designing a program, it is necessary to assess the forces that drive and restrain change at the institution. For example, competing interest groups might oppose the move. Segments of the student body besides those being addressed in the action plan might consider themselves similarly victimized and protest the focus on other groups. In economically depressed times, funds sought by the program compete with requests for funding other projects, such as more graduate fellowships or more faculty. Others might try to deny or minimize the problem, pointing out, for example, that access and graduation rates of African-Americans from United States colleges and universities over the years reveals some progress, or that others have struggled against legally-sanctioned barriers, such as segregation and discrimination, and have managed to overcome them without help. Efforts to obliterate language that is offensive in matters such as gender, race, and ethnicity, to eliminate sexual harassment, and to broaden curricula to include feminist perspectives have spawned the opposition of groups who have named the efforts the "political correctness" movement. The opposition groups continually confront those who are attempting to make higher education more responsive to diversity. Moreover, faculty tend to be detached from what they regard as administrative responsibilities, such as retention of a diverse student body, and believe that participation in efforts like this is a waste of their time. Some will agree that change is needed but might differ about the form of innovation, or they might hold a variety of visions of organizational structure and function. Restraining forces like these must be understood and addressed.

Composition of the staff. Designing a plan requires attention to the composition of the staff at the institution. Leadership for change is best found in those who are most like the population to be changed. In the case of United States higher education faculty, this population is most frequently white, middle-aged, and male. To be sure, staffing also requires the understanding and credibility that members of the disenfranchised groups can bring to the undertaking. Working in teams or dyads consisting of both majority and disenfranchised group representatives is often a good approach.

Incentive systems. Motivating people to depart from the *status quo* requires incentives. Although intrinsic rewards are important to teachers, external rewards are also important. Within academe, promotion, tenure, and merit increases are the usual external rewards. It is important, then, to lobby for the inclusion of items about teaching for diversity on standard student evaluation forms, or to request that evidence of curricular inclusiveness be presented in teaching dossiers or portfolios.

Experts external to the institution. Receptivity to change can be aided by external authorities. Respected analysts and scholars brought to the campus for seminars and lectures help to give credibility to the proposed changes.

Implementation Steps

When understandings have been reached about institutional change, governance and authority, and attitudinal change, particularly as it pertains to multicultural matters, one can begin to take the steps outlined below (Anderson, Oliver, Pruitt, Vallery, & Godard, 1974).

Build a case. Appoint a committee to assist in establishing a *raison d'être* for the program. A good way for members to begin is to conduct a needs analysis or institutional audit by quantifying appropriate data, such as retention statistics; collecting anecdotal information, such as stories told by students; and listening to opinions and perceptions. The committee should consult the people most affected (students); those who experienced the system (alumni); those who must institute the change (faculty and teaching associates); and other institutions that are addressing the same problem. The committee should then determine how to proceed at its own institution. Following this process, the committee may be dismissed, its task complete.

Organize for advice and decision making. Appoint a second committee to see the project through. Unlike the needs assessment committee, this committee's role is to advise the entire project throughout the implementation process. This committee would be composed, ideally, of faculty who serve in areas where the largest dropout rates or diversity problems occur and who represent a range of academic areas and responsibilities. The committee should be chaired by a respected member of the faculty.

Specify the objectives, time frame, program, and evaluation procedures. Staffed by specialists in faculty development, the second committee formulates the program's objectives. It also clearly delineates a span of time during which it expects objectives to be achieved. For instance, one objective might be to sensitize the entire faculty to factors in classroom interactions that are offensive to women, and one could specify that this be achieved in one year's time. The program must then be designed with these specifications in mind. By what method does one achieve this objective in 12 months? What measures should be employed to determine whether the objectives have been achieved? Answering questions like these shows that program planning is a dynamic process. Once the plan has been completed, each part derives from and influences the other. Clarity on these tasks helps the program to be realistic, accountable, and self-correcting.

Consult with constituencies. Once the program plan is in draft form, respecting protocol, consult with governing and quasi-governing bodies and interest groups and incorporate their suggestions in a revised plan. Secure acceptance, support, and understanding.

Pilot test the program. Select for the testing a variety of departmental or college settings that will allow you to judge the responses across different faculty groups. Departments as varied as mathematics, English, and philosophy might be chosen for the pilot. These might be the ones that enroll large numbers of the disenfranchised group.

Evaluate and report. Carry out a multidimensional evaluation plan that includes many perspectives and uses several kinds of data: ratings, interviews, written responses. Disseminate information about the program to colleagues in higher education by circulating materials and exchanging ideas at conferences and other forums. Reach decision makers with the results of the evaluations and news of contacts with other institutions.

In this chapter, we have presented different approaches to change to show that circumstances of a particular institution will dictate how one proceeds. Change does not always proceed smoothly. The degree of acceptance and success depends on careful and thoughtful planning.

As we look to the future, we realize that we will encounter greater diversity among students seeking higher education around the world. We must encourage the success of students from all populations, treating them fairly, and benefitting from the ways in which they enrich us all. Otherwise, many of the existing problems in teaching, such as instructor-student bias in the classroom, low teacher expectations, and instructor bias toward a traditional learning style, will continue to characterize interactions with students.

But faculty are not the only resource, nor should they be expected to assume the whole burden for correcting inequities. Collaboration among faculty developers and student affairs staff, department heads, and deans is essential. Such collaboration acknowledges the seamless nature of learning; that is to say, learning is not limited to classrooms. The total campus environment, including residence halls, student unions, counseling and career planning offices, all play a role (Pruitt, 1994). Initiatives that call for joint planning and program execution make use of a broad range of institutional resources.

Administrators can help by tracking and being responsive to population shifts and needs of non-traditional students, by keeping track of their progress, by encouraging experimentation and flexibility, and by being willing to expend time, energy, and money on an effort that will have important short- and long-term benefits.

REFERENCES

Anderson, J., & Adams, M. (1992). Acknowledging the learning styles of diverse student populations. In L. Border & N. Chism (Eds.), *New Directions for Teaching and Learning: Vol. 49. Teaching for diversity* (pp. 19-34). San Francisco, CA: Jossey-Bass.

Anderson, W., Oliver, J.R., Pruitt, A.S., Vallery, H.F., & Godard, J.R. (1974). *University-wide planning for the minority student.* Atlanta, GA: Southern Regional Education Board.

Asante, M. (1987). *The Afrocentric idea.* Philadelphia, PA: Temple University Press.

Belenky, M., Clinchy, B., Goldberger, N., & Tarule, J. (1986). *Women's ways of knowing: The development of self, voice, and mind.* New York, NY: Basic Books.

Border, L.B., & Chism, N. (Eds.). (1992). *New Directions for Teaching and Learning: Vol. 49. Teaching for diversity.* San Francisco, CA: Jossey-Bass.

Center for Teaching Excellence, The Ohio State University. (1990). *Making a difference: Teaching for Black student retention* (videotape). Columbus, OH: Author.

Chan, S., & Wang, L. (1991). Racism and the model minority: Asian-Americans in higher education. In P.G. Altbach & K. Lomotey (Eds.), *The racial crisis in American higher education* (pp. 43-67). Albany, NY: State University of New York Press.

Cummins, J. (1990). Multilingual/multicultural education: Evaluation of underlying theoretical constructs and consequences for curriculum development. In P. Vedder (Ed.), *Fundamental studies in educational research.* Lisse, Amsterdam: Swets & Zeitlinger.

Curry, B.K. (1992). *Instituting enduring innovations: Achieving continuity of change in higher education* (ASHE-ERIC Higher Education Report No. 7). Washington, DC: The George Washington University, School of Education and Human Development.

Elk, E. (1990). South Africa: Education crisis at tertiary institutions. *World Student News: Magazine of the International Union of Students, 44,* 20-21.

Green, M.F. (Ed). (1988). *Minorities on campus: A handbook for enhancing diversity.* Washington, DC: American Council on Education.

Jarabová, Z. (1993, August). *Romanies in the Czech Republic.* Paper presented at EAIR Forum, Turku, Finland.

Kramer, M., & Weiner, S. (1994). *Dialogues for diversity: Community and ethnicity on campus.* Phoenix, AZ: Oryx Press.

lopez, g., & Chism, N. (1993). Classroom concerns of gay and lesbian students. *College Teaching, 41,* 97-103.

McCormick, T. (1991). *An analysis of some pitfalls of traditional mentoring for minorities and women in higher education.* Paper presented at the Annual Meeting of the American Educational Research Association, Chicago, IL.

Maher, F. (1985). Classroom pedagogy and the new scholarship on women. In M. Culley & C. Portuges (Eds.), *Gendered subjects: The dynamics of feminist teaching.* London, UK: Routledge and Kegan Paul.

Mintz, S.D. (Ed.). 1993. *Sources: Diversity initiatives in higher education.* Washington, DC: American Council on Education.

Pruitt, A.S. (1993, August). *Stimulating faculty involvement in the retention of minority students.* Paper presented at EAIR Forum, Turku, Finland.

Pruitt, A.S. (1994, March). *Enhancing the educational experience of underrepresented groups.* Paper presented at ACPA Convention, Indianapolis, IN.

Sadkar, M., & Sadkar, D. (1992). Ensuring equitable participation in college classes. In L. Border & N. Chism (Eds.), *New Directions for Teaching and Learning: Vol. 49. Teaching for diversity* (pp. 49-56). San Francisco, CA: Jossey-Bass.

Schau, C., & Scott, K. (1984). Impact of gender characteristics of instructional materials: An integration of the research literature. *Journal of Educational Psychology, 76,* 183-193.

Tannen, D. (1990). *You just don't understand: Women and men in conversation.* New York, NY: Ballantine Books.

Tierney, W.G. (1991). Native voices in academe. *Change, 23,* 36-44.

van der Land, P. & Kok, H. (1993, August). *The integration of ethnic minorities into higher technical and commercial education.* Paper presented at EAIR Forum, Turku, Finland.

van Praag, T. (1989). *PEARL: A paragon in education.* Amsterdam/Utrecht: PEARL.

vom Saal, D., Jefferson, D., & Morrison, M. (1992). Improving the climate: Eight universities meet the challenges of diversity. In L. Border & N. Chism (Eds.), *New Directions for Teaching and Learning: Vol. 49. Teaching for diversity* (pp. 89-102). San Francisco, CA: Jossey-Bass.

Appendix

MULTICULTURAL TEACHING PROGRAM SUGGESTIONS FOR FACULTY

Faculty-Student Relationships in Class

- Be careful about language you use, avoiding terms or expressions that may be offensive.
- Deal with, rather than ignore, racist remarks made by others during the class.
- Troubleshoot problems between students from different sociocultural groups in class.
- Be clear in stating policies on attendance, late papers, class conduct, and grades, and be fair in enforcing them.
- Cultivate a communication style that allows you to maintain eye contact with all students, to use and understand nonverbal language effectively, and to personalize as much as possible.
- Try to take a multicultural perspective in discussions or lectures, incorporating multicultural examples or materials as much as possible.
- Provide different perspectives based on research findings rather than personal opinion or experience in presenting material on the issues of diverse social groups.
- Keep an open mind about all students by avoiding stereotypic thinking, such as assuming that all African-American students are athletes, underprepared, or on financial aid.
- Encourage the involvement of all students in discussion, but avoid putting them on the spot, especially by asking them to provide, for example, the "Asian-American perspective."
- Try to structure project groups, panels, laboratory teams, and the like so that membership and leadership roles are balanced across ethnic and gender groups.
- Understand that there are different kinds of cultural backgrounds and learning styles in your class and vary your instructional strategies, appreciate different perspectives, and provide options for assignments when possible to allow students to have successful experiences.

Faculty-Student Relationships Outside of Class

- Be open and friendly with students outside of class.
- Encourage out-of-class conferences and help to make students comfortable in these situations.
- Be available and willing to provide honest feedback and help when needed.
- Take the initiative to recruit students from different sociocultural groups to major in your program.
- Bring opportunities, such as internships or special programs, to the attention of students from different sociocultural groups.
- Nominate students from different sociocultural groups to honorary societies or for awards.
- Provide good academic and career counseling by being informed about academic programs and support services available for all students so that you can make good recommendations.

Course Design Issues

- When forming course goals, provide for diverse preparation levels and learning styles.
- Incorporate material on minority issues or contributions from minority scholars, scientists, professionals, and artists in course content.
- Review texts to make sure that they are unbiased, and supplement or correct them if no other text is available.
- Communicate to book publishers your findings on biased materials or omissions in coverage.
- Pursue multicultural scholarship in your discipline and incorporate it in your teaching.

AUTHORS

Nancy Van Note Chism is Director of the Office of Faculty and TA Development and teaches research methods in the College of Education, The Ohio State University (US). As a faculty developer, she consults with teachers; coordinates workshops, seminars, and conferences on teaching; and works with administrators on teaching and learning issues. Her special interests have included reflective practice, teaching assistant issues, and diversity issues. Dr. Chism is President for 1995-96 term of the Professional and Organizational Development Network in Higher Education and is co-coordinator of the National Consortium on Preparing Graduate Students to Teach, sponsored by The Pew Charitable Trusts.

Anne S. Pruitt is Professor of Educational Policy and Leadership, The Ohio State University (US). During her tenure at Ohio State, she also served as Director of the Center for Teaching Excellence, Associate Provost, and Associate Dean of the Graduate School. An advocate of increased access to education for minorities, Dr. Pruitt has testified before the US Congress and consulted with numerous groups working to effect desegregation in American higher education and to enhance opportunities for minorities. She has lectured and conducted workshops involving faculty in the retention of minority students in both the United States and Europe.

14.

National-Scale Faculty Development for Teaching Large Classes

Graham Gibbs

This chapter describes a large-scale national faculty development project in the United Kingdom (UK) concerned with teaching large classes. Evidence is presented of the extensive impact of this project, which led to the training of 8,500 faculty. The cost-effectiveness of large-scale faculty development of this kind is examined.

INTRODUCTION

Large classes have been a fact of life for faculty in many North American universities for a long time, whereas in the UK they are a fairly new phenomenon in many universities. Much of the research on large classes in the United States (US) (Feldman, 1984), and much of the advice on how to teach large classes effectively (Weimer, 1987) has focused narrowly on large lectures. In the UK, large-class issues are more broadly focused and concerned with assessment, discussion, access to library resources, student motivation, overall course design, and the effective use of faculty time. It is helpful to examine the background to these differences.

At the time of the first large-scale expansion of UK universities in the 1960s, class sizes were extremely small, and students received a great deal of personal attention from faculty. Lectures were given, on average, to 28 students and final-year lectures to only 18 students. No less than 73% of all tutorials were one-to-one. In science, more than 10 students was considered to be a large laboratory class (HMSO, 1963). Until the mid-1980s, higher education in the UK still differed in many respects from that in the US and Canada. Classes were, in general, relatively small—and even where they were not, students still had plenty of opportunity to meet faculty, including senior faculty, face-to-face in small discussion groups. Students received reasonably extensive individual written comments on essays or reports on a regular basis. Libraries supported scholarly activity, and the use of textbooks was limited. It was still unusual to find many of the features common to higher education in the US, such as mass lectures, mechanized objective testing, a lack of opportunity for discussion with senior faculty, the use of teaching assistants, and reliance on key textbooks.

Throughout the 1980s, however, student numbers increased steadily. By the start of the 1990s, some institutions had doubled in size, while funding per student had declined dramatically. Student-faculty ratios doubled or tripled over a decade in many courses. Some institutions expanded at extraordinary rates in a bid to achieve university status, and this had a devastating impact on class sizes. For example, a management course at what is now the University of Derby expanded from 60 to 360 students in four years and tripled the ratio of students to faculty over the same period. Increasing access to higher education meant that, nationally, the proportion of 18-year-olds in higher education rose from below 10% to above 25%. A considerable increase in the proportion of mature students also meant that the range of ability and background knowledge of students was very much wider than the system had accommodated in the past. A system designed to meet the needs of a homogeneous student body was coping poorly with heterogeneity. At the same time, many institutions adopted US-style credit accumulation and modular systems with more flexibility and choice. The rationalization of courses which went along with this structural change produced huge (by UK standards) first-year introductory modules. At my own institution, Oxford Brookes University (then Oxford Polytechnic), while the number of students doubled to 8,000 over a decade, the number of modules with more than 100 students enrolled tripled in five years, and the largest modules quadrupled in size. Lectures became much larger, seminar groups doubled and tripled in size, marking loads became crippling, and personal tutoring was squeezed out. A model of teaching, learning, and assessment designed for a small, elite, well-resourced system was falling apart at the seams. Whether it had ever worked well, it certainly wasn't working well any more. A study of all student grades at Oxford Polytechnic over five years showed that students performed significantly less well

in large classes (Lindsay & Paton-Saltzberg, 1987). Contrary to the equivo-
cal studies of student feedback data on class size in the US (Feldman, 1984),
students in the UK clearly dislike large classes.

Throughout the 1980s, the Educational Methods Unit at Oxford Polytechnic, which I led, had supported the development of a range of innovations to help cope with the problems outlined above. The unit was
responsible for a variety of initiatives including:

- A 200-hour compulsory training course for new faculty leading to
  a qualification
- A teaching development fund, open to competitive bidding,
  which supported about 20 educational development projects a
  year
- Weekly lunchtime seminars on topical themes concerning
  teaching methods, for which as many as 25% of all faculty
  enrolled
- Consultancy to individual faculty, course teams, and departments
  on teaching and learning initiatives
- Single-event workshops on specialist topics
- A once-a-term publication entitled "Teaching News" containing
  articles by faculty about their teaching innovation
- Promotion on the basis of teaching excellence through the use of a
  teaching profile (a decade before the current teaching portfolio
  initiatives in the US)[1]
- A client-centered evaluation service and the establishment of
  user-friendly optional computer-based evaluation systems
- Institutional evaluation initiatives such as large-scale student
  diary studies and the use of the Approaches to Studying
  Inventory (Entwistle & Ramsden, 1983) across the entire
  institution

This was all centrally funded by the institution, without external support, and senior management showed their commitment to the development of teaching in a variety of ways, attending sessions and pushing
through policy changes.

Many of the developments in teaching and learning which resulted
from all this effort concerned coping with reduced resources and increased
student numbers. For example, Oxford Brookes had severe accommodation problems, and we had find ways to make student learning more independent so that fewer classrooms would be required. Probably one third
of the 1,300 modules now have tutor-prepared, print-based learning packages to compensate for a much reduced frequency of lectures. Extensive
use of independent student groups for projects, seminar preparation, and

shared learning resources compensates for reduced small-group teaching. A distinctive teaching culture was developed, possibly unique in the UK, which valued and supported attention being paid to enhancing the quality of student learning. The extent and range of innovations at Oxford Brookes were such that there was a considerable demand for consultancy and training from other polytechnics and universities. In 1989, the Oxford Centre for Staff Development was established as a self-funded training and consultancy agency for higher education, undertaking all its work outside Oxford. By 1992, it was running 300 events a year for 100 institutions. These events were delivered by a team of 20 consultants drawn from the leading educational development centers in the UK.

THE TEACHING MORE STUDENTS PROJECT

Genesis of the Project

By 1990, the national press had started to carry articles about student dissatisfaction with excessively large classes. Even traditional, well-established universities did not escape public criticism. Bill Stubbs, Chair of the Polytechnics and Colleges Funding Council (PCFC), which provided the funding for all public-sector institutions, made an unexpected visit to the Educational Methods Unit in 1990. He wanted to see the problems for himself, and he wanted to hear what we were trying to do about them. When he left, he invited us to prepare a proposal for a large-scale national training project to help lecturers change their methods to teach large classes more successfully. Our outline proposal, supported by the influential Committee of Directors of Polytechnics, was approved by the PCFC and we were in business.

Project Outline

The Teaching More Students Project was designed to deliver 100 workshops, within twelve months, to 3,000 faculty from all 82 polytechnics and colleges. This framework ensured that a reasonable number of faculty from every institution gained an understanding of the problems and were exposed to many ideas about how to tackle them as quickly as possible. Daylong sessions consisted of two half-day workshop units, selected by the institution from a choice of eight. The institutions would provide the accommodation and undertake all the local marketing and administration. In return, they would receive the workshop free of charge. A budget of £100,000 ($160,000 US)[2] was made available by the PCFC.

A team of twelve consultants was rapidly assembled with a reasonable geographical spread, to make covering all the institutions easier. The team members had a good deal of educational development consultancy and training experience, but none had previously run workshops on all the topics listed below. The problem was how to make workshops run reliably well in a context with little opportunity to train the consultants, no available resource materials, an enormous variety of institutional contexts, and a very short time scale. We decided to develop extensive resource materials for the workshops in the form of publications which participants could keep. The workshop exercises would be tightly designed around these publications, and the publications would contain sufficient material to allow considerable flexibility in choice and timing for workshops delivered to different groups.

There were to be eight publications to support these workshops:

1. *Problems and strategies:* concerned with identifying and diagnosing the problems associated with more students and analyzing and illustrating the strategic options available for tackling these problems at the level of overall course design
2. *Lecturing:* concerned with problems in large lectures, alternatives to lecturing, and a range of practical methods for minimizing and overcoming problems
3. *Discussion:* concerned with problems in large discussion groups and ways to break up large groups into smaller ones, handle difficulties, and support independent discussion groups
4. *Assessment:* containing six strategies for more economical and effective assessment, including self- and peer assessment and assessing groups
5. *Independent learning:* concerned with group work, resource-based learning, and the development of students' independent learning skills
6. *Laboratory work:* concerned with achieving the aims of conventional labs through more cost-effective alternatives
7. *Supporting students:* concerned with more structured and targeted alternatives to personal tutoring systems
8. *Evaluation:* concerned with monitoring and improving large courses

In the cost cutting which went on before a contract was signed, the last three publications and workshop topics were cancelled, though 6 and 7 have subsequently been written without funding (Bochner, Gibbs, & Wisker, 1995; Gibbs, 1992a, 1992b, 1992c, 1992d, 1992e, 1995). A video was also produced illustrating the use of a range of classroom techniques for large classes.

Developing Materials and Training the Consultants

Clarifying values. To avoid being seen as representing the causes of faculty's problems rather than being part of the solution, we had to develop a series of quick value-clarification exercises that demonstrated that we shared with faculty a belief in the efficacy of smaller classes but also believed that if classes had to be large then there were ways of holding onto quality.

Tackling real problems, not selling methods. Many of the potential solutions to large-class problems had been peddled by educational development for the past 20 years, without much success, under the guise of active or independent learning. What made this project different was that, for perhaps the first time, faculty were experiencing problems so severe that they simply could not carry on as before. Identifying the problems in a way which faculty recognized and acknowledged as real was a vital prerequisite to seeking viable solutions. Teaching methods would have to be presented as tackling otherwise intractable problems, not as being good for your soul. The most useful part of the video which was produced turned out to be two minutes at the start in which students simply talked to the camera about what it was like in large classes. There were no arguments about the scale of the problem after these two minutes; whenever faculty started defending current practice, someone would quote something a student had said on the video as evidence that current practice did not work very well. I subsequently had the pleasure of showing this video to the PCFC whose expansion and funding policies had produced these problems.

Providing practical advice, not educational theory. In our experience, faculty who attend workshops on large classes are different from those who attend workshops on particular methods, such as problem-based learning or using learning contracts, because the topics sound interesting. They come because they have real problems and they want practical answers, *now*, and the more answers the better. Over the years, I have written a number of books in the "Interesting Ways To Teach" series (Gibbs & Habeshaw, 1989; Habeshaw, Habeshaw, & Gibbs, 1993) which make the assumption that if you want faculty to find something that interests them, which fits their context, and which they are not already doing, then you have to offer a great many ideas, because they will reject most of them. Faculty want to see straightforward, practical ideas and examples of their use. We had been visiting 50-100 institutions a year running workshops and collecting examples of good practice wherever we found them. We had also collected publications and accounts from Australia, where a British-style higher education system had expanded a few years ahead of the UK system and had been tackling similar problems in imaginative ways (Andreson, Nightingale, Boud, & Magin, 1989; Magin, Nightingale, Andreson, & Boud, 1989). A review of the US literature on the subject, in contrast, provided very little in the way of usable ideas.

Providing arguments and evidence. Faculty coming to such workshops are often isolated: they are different from their colleagues who choose not to come. But many of the solutions to large-class problems involve a course team working together cooperatively. If the workshops were going to be effective, they had to arm faculty with arguments and evidence which they could use to persuade their colleagues to change.

Modelling good practice. The workshops were designed to demonstrate the methods under consideration. For example, the workshop on lecturing involved structured lectures which included interaction; the workshop on discussion used a wide variety of structured discussion methods; and the workshop on independent learning involved participants in teams working on a design project using resource materials and peer assessment.

Educational Rationale

The rationale which provided a framework for the workshops and publications involved two main features: contrasting strategies for tackling large-class problems and examining overall course design and course costs rather than only details of teaching methods. We identified eight problem areas with increased class sizes and then contrasted two sets of strategies for dealing with these difficulties. One is to control the situation—a strategy popular in undergraduate classes in North America—and the other is to foster students' freedom and independence, as illustrated in Table 1.

Faculty in the UK are very reluctant to go down the "control" route (which in the UK is perceived as the American approach), and the stark contrast provided here encouraged faculty to examine some of the "independence" strategies more carefully.

Case studies cost-evaluated the alternative course designs in terms of faculty's teaching and assessment time. Of ten case studies, eight roughly halved the time investment while maintaining quality. In workshops, faculty were invited to undertake similar costings of their current courses, to invent alternatives which cost half as much to deliver, and then to analyze the gains and losses involved in these alternatives.

Workshop Programs

Workshop programs were negotiated with institutions. Leaflets were sent explaining the five basic workshop components. Usually, each institution selected two to fit into a day, often with a certain amount of customizing to suit the context.

TABLE 1

Problem area resulting from large classes	Characteristic methods adopted	
	Control strategies	Independence strategies
1. Lack of clarity of purpose	Use of objectives Highly structured courses	Use of learning contracts Problem-based learning
2. Lack of knowledge of progress	Objective testing Programmed instruction and computer-aided instruction	Development of student judgment Self-assessment
3. Lack of advice on improvement	Standard feedback forms Automated tutorial feedback	Peer feedback and peer assessment
4. Inability to support reading	Use of required texts Use of learning packages	Development of students' research skills More varied assignments
5. Inability to support independent study	Structured projects Lab guides	Group work Learning teams
6. Lack of opportunity for discussion	Structured lectures Structured seminars and workshops	Student-led seminars Team assignments
7. Inability to cope with variety of students	Pre-tests plus remedial material Self-paced study (PSI)[2]	Variety of support mechanisms Negotiated goals
8. Inability to motivate students	Frequent testing High failure rates	Contracts, problem solving, group work

([2] Personalized System of Instruction)

Publications

The first publication, on lecturing, was produced in pilot form, and components were used in workshops to test out exercises and gauge the kind of material most appropriate for supporting workshops. The remaining publications were written in ten weeks and published in a further four weeks at the start of 1992, just in time for the delivery of workshops to institutions. They were in the form of attractively designed manuals, 42 to 74 pages long, printed in two colors to high production standards. They were the most highly rated aspect of the whole project (see Evaluation, below) and sold over 20,000 copies. The high volume of sales may be attributed to the very low price, a result of the agreement to make no profit on sales.

Video

The video was designed as a workshop resource rather than as a program to be watched in its entirety. It contained two minutes of *vox populi*, in which students were interviewed about their experience of large classes, followed by five examples of classroom practice: four large lectures and one large discussion group. These were real teaching sessions, not studio or prepared jobs, and were selected to illustrate very different styles rather than perfect teaching. Each example consisted of about five minutes of extracts interspersed with voice-over from or interview with the teachers explaining their approach. The examples tended to be used as short 'triggers' to discussion during the workshops on lecturing and discussion. About 300 copies of the video have been sold, equivalent to two for every higher education institution in the UK.

Logistics

Workshops were allocated to institutions according to size. For example, large polytechnics were allocated three workshops (90 places), and small colleges were pooled together or allocated places at workshops in nearby larger institutions. Specialist institutions, such as music conservatories, were pooled nationally and allocated one workshop at whichever institution negotiated to be the host.

The PCFC contacted the director or principal of each institution, enclosing a brochure explaining the purpose and operation of the project and asking him/her to nominate a contact person. We then contacted this person and started negotiations for topics and dates. Early on, we took a great deal of trouble with these negotiations and visited institutions to discuss the best ways to explain the workshops, negotiate programs, and consider how to integrate them with other institutional staff development initiatives. Later on, we offered options based on models developed earlier. As consultants became more experienced, they were able to be more flexible and cope with extremely varied arrangements and customized programs.

Logistical Problems

Inevitably, not everything went smoothly. The main problems resulted from poor administration within institutions. Sometimes the nominated contact person was not the most appropriate person to arrange workshops, and supervising workshop administration at a distance could be difficult, time consuming, and diplomatically sensitive. Poor marketing of the workshops was a particular problem which, in some institutions, led to poor attendance and the wrong faculty attending, sometimes under sufferance. Institutions sometimes made unreasonable demands, wanting all five workshops run within one day or requesting unsuitable combinations of topics which were not related to faculty interests. We had to be quite assertive on occasion to prevent institutions from wrecking their own workshops.

Patterns of Delivery

While some institutions offered the workshop as a single event, in isolation from all other faculty development initiatives, many sought ways to make the most of the opportunity, and a wide variety of strategies were eventually adopted, few of which could have been anticipated, and many of which involved purchasing extra workshops, publications, and the video. The workshop exercises, instructions, and overhead transparencies were all provided free of charge on request so that it was relatively easy for institutions to run workshops for themselves once they had experienced them. Variations included:

Middlesex Polytechnic used its two free workshops as open-access events with faculty from all four faculties. It then purchased four half-day workshops which each ran in all the four faculties.

City of London Polytechnic focused on assessing more students. It used both its free workshops for events on assessment and then purchased a third workshop on the same topic. The institution followed up by purchasing additional consultancy support to review current assessment practice and to become involved in a senior management review of assessment policy across the institution.

Coventry Polytechnic purchased three additional workshops so that the faculty experienced all five. The Polytechnic's own faculty development person then ran the five workshops repeatedly throughout all parts of the institution, purchasing publications as necessary, and eventually running a total of 24 workshops attended by 250 faculty, nearly half the entire body of teachers.

Use of the workshops was not limited to the polytechnics. Many other institutions saw what was going on and bought into the project in a variety of ways. By 1993, the majority of all follow-up workshops were being delivered in institutions which were not part of the original project. For example:

Newcastle College started with a trial event in which 40 faculty attended an introductory hour, and then 24 selected faculty participated in the rest of the day. After this had gone well, the College purchased an additional day in which 140 attended the first hour and 30 participated in the remainder of the day. A copy of the publications was purchased for each of the 460 faculty in the institution.

The University of East Anglia purchased a large number of the publications for use in the five workshops which it organized and conducted. It then funded a series of development projects to implement ideas generated in the workshops and provided consultancy support. While these projects were under way, the University purchased additional consultancy support from the Oxford Centre for Staff Development to facilitate the exchange of ideas and help solve problems common to all those involved in development work.

It was also common for faculty who had attended open, institutionwide workshops to return to their departments fired with enthusiasm and obtain support to purchase a workshop directly from the Oxford Centre for Staff Development to run within their department. In the first nine months of the project, 78 workshops were delivered to faculty from 73 institutions within the project, and 34 additional workshops were purchased to supplement those delivered within the project. At peak times, we were running 10 workshops a week, all led by different consultants in different locations.

Delivery

Although faculty often worry about large lectures because they are perhaps the most stressful part of their working lives, this was not the main focus of requests for assistance. Requests for workshop topics revealed a very different pattern of concern from that evident in US publications about large classes (e.g., Weimer, 1987).

One of the most significant outcomes of the project was the great extent to which faculty were willing to examine the overall design and rationale of their courses, rather than only details of classroom practice. Because faculty recognized that in-class activity and features of the student assessment system were no longer generating effective out-of-class learning activity, they determined that new overall strategies rather than minor adjustments were required.

EVALUATION

Evaluation took four forms: questionnaire feedback from participants at the end of workshops; open-ended questionnaire feedback from the institutional organizer; feedback from the consultants who ran the workshops;

TABLE 2

Workshop topic	Number of workshops addressing each topic
Problems and strategic options	68
Assessing more students	50
Independent learning with more students	27
Discussion with more students	25
Lecturing to more students	22

and a three-month follow-up, requiring the institution to collate information about the impact of the workshops.

Feedback from Participants

At the end of every workshop, participants were asked to complete a feedback form. The analysis reported here is from 1,547 participants at 88 workshops. Reactions to the way the workshops were run were overwhelmingly positive in all but a few institutions. The effect of the workshops on participants was also impressive: all of the participants said that the workshops addressed their interests, and 98% said they had gained a fuller understanding of the problems and strategic options for tackling large-class problems. Ninety-seven percent said they would introduce changes into some aspect of their courses as a result of the workshop, with 26% saying they would make changes to a considerable extent. Similar proportions said they would tell others about ways of dealing with more students. Only 3% found the workshops not to be worthwhile, and 91% thought the workshops offered plenty of good ideas. Some of the highest ratings were reserved for the materials: 95% of participants found them helpful, and 91% requested copies of other booklets in the series.

In the context of the culture of British higher education which is, in my experience, much more critical and grudging with praise than American culture, participants' response to the workshop, its processes and materials, can be seen to be very positive, and the participants' expectation of impact is also encouraging. While there was some variation between consultants, the overall variability was much lower, and the average ratings higher, than for other workshops run by the Oxford Centre for Staff Development by the same consultants. The design of the workshops and the support of the materials clearly worked well to maintain a uniformly high

TABLE 3

Statement	Percentage of respondents who strongly agreed
The working methods in this workshop encouraged me to take an active part.	86%
The workshop has encouraged me to put the ideas and knowledge I have gained into practice after the workshop.	85%
I would like to participate in other workshops in the series.	77%
The workshop will help me to encourage my colleagues at work to learn and make use of new methods.	48%

standard. In a small number of unfortunate workshops, faculty were too angry with what was happening in their institution and with the way they were being treated by their management to calm down enough to get much further than complaining about their plight. In a few instances, the workshops and materials did not adequately address the specific institutional and departmental contexts. However, these kinds of difficulties were less frequent than anticipated and less problematic than in workshops undertaken on the same topics prior to the project.

As highlighted above, a very large number of workshops were run by institutions themselves using our publications and sometimes our workshop exercises, overheads, and consultants' notes. We were sent evaluation data by a number of institutions which had run their own workshops, and these showed similarly positive responses from faculty. This evidence is not possible to pool as it involved a variety of evaluation instruments, but the following sample (from the first 10 of an extensive series of workshops run by faculty development staff at Coventry Polytechnic) illustrates a typical response.

Feedback from the Institutional Organizer

One page of feedback was requested from the contact person within the institution, mainly to help us with future administrative arrangements and to guide future workshops within the same institution. This helped us to change various procedures and introduce more checks on facilities and so on to improve reliability. The contact person was also asked to indicate what kinds of follow-up action were planned to reinforce the impact of the workshops. Almost every institution had follow-up plans, sometimes quite extensive and imaginative. Plans included:

- Evaluating the impact of changes introduced
- Establishing an "innovative teaching week" followed by a series of feedback seminars and poster sessions reporting on the innovations
- Holding a series of follow-up workshops within participants' departments in response to requests
- Setting up course leaders' groups to arrange further initiatives and run further workshops
- Purchasing more workshops to run within each faculty
- Using the Teaching More Students materials in centrally-arranged workshops run by educational development staff
- Participants spending two days disseminating information within their own department
- Publishing and distributing a booklet summarizing the plans for change generated at the workshop
- Conducting an institutional audit of large-class teaching strategies
- Holding evaluation meetings for course leaders to monitor the impact of changes
- Developing a teaching and learning policy for the institution focusing on new methods of delivery
- Establishing a network of contacts within departments to help the educational development unit to monitor and support innovations
- Setting up a progress review meeting for six months after the workshops
- Discussing the workshop outcomes at Academic Standards Committee, Teaching and Learning Committee, etc.
- Providing consultancy support for individual participants who had significant development plans and who requested help
- Establishing a lunchtime seminar series for faculty to share their innovations
- Establishing a wide-ranging program of initiatives focusing on assessment and student support
- Setting up a heads of department meeting to discuss the management implications
- Large-scale purchasing of materials to distribute within the departments of those who attended

Feedback from the Consultant

Consultants wrote a brief reflective report after each workshop, mainly for the purpose of helping other consultants. They commented on exercises which worked well or which caused problems, shared new exercises and materials, warned about difficulties, and wrote up ideas or course designs they had come across to use as examples in future workshops. A good deal of practical information, informal reporting, and good-natured banter comparing hotels was circulated around the consultants' team throughout the project.

Three- to Six-Month Follow-up

Three to six months after the workshops, a questionnaire was sent to the institutional organizer. The questions required the collation of a range of information from within the institution about the impact of the project. Because this information was difficult to obtain, there was often a delay in responding, but 45% of institutions returned the questionnaire between four and ten months after the workshops had taken place. Where other parallel initiatives were operating within institutions, it was sometimes hard for those responding to gauge the extent to which the Teaching More Students project had been directly responsible for some of the changes reported, but this did not stop them from attributing changes to the project.

The impact reported was extraordinary and quite unexpected. It is often difficult to identify any impact from one-time events of this kind, but here the workshops had galvanized action on an unprecedented scale.

From information provided by the institutions, we can extrapolate that the project led to a further 360 workshops being run by institutions themselves (an average of over 4 per institution) for a total of 5,500 participants (65 per institution). Forty-four percent of these workshops were organized centrally, and 56% ran in departments or faculties. As well as being more frequent, departmental workshops attracted more participants (17 compared with 12 for centrally-run workshops). The distribution of these workshops was very uneven, with the four most active institutions being responsible for 65 workshops and 840 participants, and one institution involving almost half of all faculty in workshops.

Thirty-two percent of institutions reported collating or publishing examples of best practice in teaching large classes, 57% reported holding discussions at the faculty and department levels about teaching more students, and 64% reported holding such discussions centrally at Academic Board, Academic Standards, or Teaching and Learning Committees.

The list of specific change initiatives resulting from the project (beyond simply running more workshops) reads like an encyclopaedia of faculty development:

- Formation of a teaching and learning methods group
- Establishment of seconded posts to facilitate developments within faculties
- Consultancy at the course, team, and department levels
- Formation of a sub-group specifically concerned with the issue of academic quality;
- A review of learning resources provision
- A requirement for annual course reviews to include a section on new methods introduced to cope with increased student numbers, or to specify plans for reducing lecture hours and assessment in appropriate ways
- Funding for the production of materials to support flexible learning
- Appointment of a member of senior management of the college responsible for overall course quality to respond to issues raised in the workshop
- A "University Challenge" week, following an intense round of workshops, in which faculty were encouraged to be innovative and report back in seminars the following week; 40% of faculty made innovations during this special week
- Large-scale purchase of the Teaching More Students materials for circulation to, in one case, every member of faculty

Even where institutions had well-established, well-staffed, educational development centers the project had a galvanizing effect. The following extracts from a letter from one leading center describes having used the Teaching More Students workshops as the start of a "cascade process" across the whole institution.

> *We have just completed the first stage of our cascade process. The whole thing has been much more successful than we dared hope. It has released a totally unexpected tide of enthusiasm for dealing with our problems here in teaching and assessment. There is no doubt whatsoever that your contributions were instrumental in getting us off to a flying start ... The process that followed your input include[d] a half-day on how change agents were going to organize their dissemination ... most opted for either a one- or two-day 'away day' rather like the system you used when you were with us. Indeed many used the sorts of exercises and workshop approaches that you demonstrated so well, and they affirmed the*

> *value of seeing these approaches modeled ... Overall they (14 groups) were successful—some of them were terrific, and one was 'magic'! ... The next stage was a half-day report back by the change agents. During that they raised a number of questions to be addressed by the Chancellery. The most recent stage, last week, was a meeting of the change agents with the Chancellery ... the Chancellery accepted that there had been significant change for the better in morale and that this sort of process should be repeated each year ... Well, all this has been totally unforeseeable, and I couldn't have done it without you.*

The impact was considered to have extended far beyond the faculty who attended. In 50% of institutions, respondents claimed that more than 25% of faculty increased their awareness of issues of teaching more students (while less than 10% actually attended the workshops). In 43% of institutions, teaching methods were changing in more than one quarter of courses. In 39% of institutions, more than one quarter of course designs were changing, and, in 32% of institutions, assessment methods in more than one quarter of courses were changing. This pattern of change in response to large classes echoes that reported elsewhere (e.g., Jenkins & Smith, 1993): faculty become aware of issues first, then change classroom methods, then adapt overall course features and leave assessment until last. In 30% of institutions, the overall impact was considered to have been "significant and worthwhile." These were mainly smaller institutions where the proportion of faculty directly involved was high and where representatives of most courses were involved. Large institutions tended to report more modest overall impacts even where large numbers of faculty attended.

CONSTRAINTS ON THE EFFECTIVENESS OF THE PROJECT

While the above evaluation evidence was very heartening and the impact was much greater than originally envisaged, there were still major obstacles constraining the project's overall effectiveness. These obstacles are not specific to this project and affect faculty development everywhere, but they were particularly influential here.

Infrastructure Problems

Many of the kinds of changes which faculty needed to introduce to make their courses effective with more students were blocked by features of the infrastructure of the institution. The rigidity of the timetable, the ways teaching accommodations were allocated, the types of teaching accommodations available, examination regulations, the ways teaching duties were calculated and allocated, library book acquisition policy, the way the print room operated—all tripped faculty up and prevented them from operating effectively. We sometimes kept a running list on a flip chart of all these infrastructure blocks as they cropped up during workshops and then sent it to the vice chancellor or director afterwards, as a way of relieving frustration and dumping problems we couldn't tackle.

Management Style

Many faculty worked in departments or institutions where there was very little scope for individuals to bring their imagination and commitment to bear on a problem and tackle it in idiosyncratic ways. There was far too much inappropriate central control over what should have been decided locally by those having to face and resolve problems. Centrally imposed 'solutions' were inappropriate. Too often, the management style was part of the problem. By far the most effective solutions and the best quality teaching seem to occur where there is local responsibility and devolved budgets within a sensible institutional system for monitoring quality. The most severe large-class problems we encountered occurred where faculty had no freedom to address the problems.

There was a considerable demand, after the first year of workshops, for consultancy and training for senior management on managing more students, often as a result of pressure from faculty. Materials were developed which addressed infrastructure issues and management styles and practices. Though these materials have not been published, they have been used in a number of universities.

Narrow Range of Topics

The budget constraints on the project meant that there was no focus on laboratory or field work, practical work, or work-based learning. Neither was there a focus on alternatives to personal tutoring. Higher education in the UK has lower drop-out and failure rates than any other European country, and this has been due, in part, to an expensive but informal system of pastoral care which has largely collapsed. Organized replacements for components of this system are vital if drop-out and failure are not to rise dramatically. This was a major concern of many faculty who take their personal tutoring responsibilities seriously but who do not have the time to fulfill them adequately.

Lack of Disciplinary Focus

While the publications and workshops included practical examples from as many disciplines as possible and addressed some problems experienced across discipline boundaries, many discipline-specific problems were not tackled. Some of these, such as the collapse of the apprentice model of art and design education due to declining resources, pose a fundamental challenge which general-purpose teaching methods cannot adequately meet. Proposals for a follow-up project with a series of disciplinary foci were stalled as the PCFC merged with the Universities Funding Council to form the Higher Education Funding Council. Currently, the Oxford Centre for Staff Development is managing a £195,000 ($312,000 US) initiative on course design for resource-based learning through nine parallel discipline-specific projects. This is probably the way to go in the future: focused, discipline-based projects on a national scale.

Lack of Follow-up Support

In some institutions, the in-house educational development units cooperated with the project and were able to provide follow-up support for faculty who wanted to implement ideas encountered in the workshops or who needed help in persuading colleagues to adopt new methods in a team approach to change. But in most institutions the follow-up support was very limited. We received countless telephone calls from individuals asking for advice when they should have been able to obtain support within their own institution. Any future project on this scale should pay more attention to supporting in-house faculty development staff so that they are in a better position to support faculty. The number of workshops delivered in-house was three times greater than that delivered directly by the project, and this potential could have been exploited to an even greater extent.

DEVELOPING THE MODEL

Having established the practicability, cost-effectiveness, and potential of such large-scale national faculty development projects, it is crucial to learn from experience and map out how further projects of this kind could operate with even more impact. At the December, 1992 joint annual conference of the national organizations for faculty and educational development in the UK (SEDA: Staff and Educational Development Association and the SRHE: Society for Research into Higher Education), the outcomes of the project were summarized in a keynote presentation. Participants (nearly all of whom had been involved in the project as users of the workshops or materials) worked cooperatively to produce proposals for future national-scale projects which would overcome some of the problems experienced in the Teaching More Students Project and have greater impacts on institutions and the faculty within them. The main conclusions highlighted strengths and weaknesses of the project:

- Workshops, materials, and follow-up support should, wherever possible, be discipline-specific in order to help faculty recognize the significance of issues for their own context and to convince them that methods can work in their discipline, as well as in the cases cited from other disciplines.
- A range of teaching and learning methods, often associated with specific disciplines, such as studio-based design work and scientific fieldwork, was not covered by the project and should be picked up in future projects.
- Close liaison and coordination with an institution's existing faculty development are crucial. More local ownership is essential to this process, and this project did not provide sufficient funding to support the necessary negotiation and flexibility. It was clear that only those institutions with fairly well established faculty development units were able to mount large-scale follow-up initiatives.
- A national center should be established, coordinating regional networks, to provide a data base on methods, provide a helpline, and act as a repository of case studies and materials on teaching methods.
- There should be a greater focus on overall course design and less on details of teaching methods.

CONCLUSIONS

In the international instructional developers' survey described in Chapter 1, workshops were ranked quite highly and their effective use is described in detail in Chapter 8 by Eison and Stevens. However, they are frequently criticized in faculty development circles as an ineffective mechanism for change because they embody inappropriate implicit assumptions about the relative expertise of faculty and the consultant, establish inappropriate relationships between faculty and consultant, and tend to lead to little transfer into subsequent teaching behavior. Over the past decade, workshops have formed a very small component of faculty development initiatives at Oxford Brookes University for these very reasons. And yet in this project, workshops proved an enormously influential stimulus for change, on a very large scale, in a very short time period, and at a very low cost per participant. It seems that even open-access workshops run by outsiders can be very effective when they are offered in response to a clearly-identified problem which faculty want to overcome and where the workshops are part of a local strategy for change involving a variety of interlocking components. For the most part, the workshops acted as a stimulant to local change which went beyond what local faculty development had managed. This was in large part simply because the materials, workshops, and consultants were so reliably excellent. This was achieved only because the project funding allowed more time and effort to go into material, workshop, and consultant development than is normally the case. While the project cost £100,000 ($160,000 US), it reached 8,500 faculty at a cost of less than £12 ($19.20 US) per person to the funding agency. It is hard to imagine a cheaper approach to faculty development. At a time of constrained resources for faculty development, as well as for teaching students, this project has lessons for low-cost training for large numbers of faculty in higher education.

ACKNOWLEDGEMENT

I would like to acknowledge the commitment, skill, expertise, and friendship of the consultants' team in the Teaching More Students project: David Baume, Liz Beaty, Sally Brown, Diana Eastcott, Bob Farmer, Trevor Habeshaw, David Jaques, Alan Jenkins, David MacAndrew, Chris Rust, and Gina Wisker.

REFERENCES

Andreson, L., Nightingale, P., Boud, D., & Magin, D. (1989). *Teaching with reduced resources: No. 1. Strategies for assessing students*. Kensington, UK: University of New South Wales, Kensington Professional Development Centre.

Bochner, D., Gibbs, G., & Wisker, G. (1995). *Teaching More Students: No. 7. Supporting more students*. Oxford, UK: Oxford Centre for Staff Development.

Entwistle, N.J., & Ramsden, P. (1983). *Understanding student learning*. London, UK: Croom Helm.

Feldman, K.A. (1984). Class size and college students' evaluations of teachers and courses. *Research in Higher Education, 21*(1), 45-97.

Gibbs, G. (1983). *Submitting teaching profiles for promotion*. Headington, UK: Oxford Polytechnic, Educational Methods Unit.

Gibbs, G. (1992a). *Teaching More Students: No. 1. Problems and course design strategies*. Oxford, UK: Oxford Centre for Staff Development.

Gibbs, G. (1992b). *Teaching More Students: No. 2. Lecturing to more students*. Oxford, UK: Oxford Centre for Staff Development.

Gibbs, G. (1992c). *Teaching More Students: No. 3. Discussion with more students*. Oxford, UK: Oxford Centre for Staff Development.

Gibbs, G. (1992d). *Teaching More Students: No. 4. Assessing more students.* Oxford, UK: Oxford Centre for Staff Development.

Gibbs, G. (1992e). *Teaching More Students: No. 5. Independent learning with more students.* Oxford, UK: Oxford Centre for Staff Development.

Gibbs, G. (1995). *Teaching More Students: No. 6. Laboratory teaching with more students.* Oxford, UK: Oxford Centre for Staff Development.

Gibbs, G., & Habeshaw, T. (1989). *Preparing to teach.* Bristol, UK: Technical and Educational Services.

Gibbs, G., & Openshaw, D. (1983). *Rewarding Excellent Teachers* (SCEDSIP Paper No. 14). Birmingham, UK.

Habeshaw, S., Habeshaw, T., & Gibbs, G. (1993). *53 interesting ways to assess your students* (2nd ed.). Bristol, UK: Technical and Educational Services.

HMSO. (1963). *Students and their education.* The Robbins report. London, UK: Author.

Jenkins, A., & Smith, P. (1993). Expansion, efficiency, and teaching quality: The experience of British geography departments 1986-91. *Transaction of the institute of British geographers.* New Series, pp. 500-515.

Lindsay, R., & Paton-Saltzberg, R. (1987). Resource changes and academic performance at an English polytechnic. *Studies in Higher Education, 12*(2), 213-227.

Magin, D., Nightingale, P., Andreson, L., & Boud, D. (1989). *Strategies for increasing students' independence.* Teaching with reduced resources (No. 2). Kensington, UK: University of New South Wales, Kensington Professional Development Centre.

Weimer, M. (1987). *Teaching large classes well.* London, UK: Jossey-Bass.

AUTHOR

Graham Gibbs is the Head of the Oxford Centre for Staff Development, Oxford Brookes University (UK), which is the largest provider of faculty development services in Europe. He is the author of many books on teaching, learning, and assessment in higher education and has specialized in teaching large classes and in the kinds of changes in course design and delivery needed to cope with reduced resources and increased diversity of students. In 1992, he directed the UK's Teaching More Students project which led to the training of 8,500 faculty in over 100 universities and colleges.

NOTES

[1] Oxford Polytechnic introduced the use of teaching profiles for promotion to Principal Lecturer in 1983 following an international conference held in Oxford concerned with rewarding excellent teachers. See Gibbs & Openshaw (1983), and Gibbs (1983).

[2] All Pounds Sterling (£) amounts in this volume were converted to US dollars on the basis of a 1.60 exchange rate.

15.

The Impact of National Developments on the Quality of University Teaching

George Gordon
Patricia A. Partington

Recent interest in teaching improvement on the part of higher education faculty and managers in the United Kingdom (UK) has been striking. This chapter examines how several national developments have contributed to the recent evolution of faculty and educational improvement in universities. These initiatives constitute a series of changes which may finally embed faculty development into the operational ethos of individuals, departments, programs, policies, and institutions.

CATALYSTS FOR CHANGE

Long-term faculty development and educational change often fail as a result of strategies which focus upon changing sympathetic individuals who, it is assumed, will effect change in the organizations in which they work. Jones and Lewis (1991) have argued that such strategies are flawed and ineffective: some of the reasons have been expressed by Fullan (1990):

> *Effective approaches to managing change call for combining and balancing factors that do not appear to go together—simultaneous simplicity/complexity, looseness/tightness, strong leadership/participation (or simultaneous bottom up/top downness)... More than*

> *anything else, effective strategies for improvement require an un-*
> *derstanding of the process, a way of thinking that cannot be cap-*
> *tured in any list of steps or phases… (p.22)*

Resolution of such opposites requires a dialectical process, in which thesis and antithesis lead to synthesis, and desired systematic change is gradually and progressively achieved. 'Carrots' (factors which facilitate and motivate) and 'sticks' (controlling factors) are examples of opposites which between them 'unfreeze' an organization and make it more open to change (Lewin, 1952). Additionally, change rarely comes from within the body which requires changing; it is commonly necessary for an external agency or development to initiate it (Alschuler in Jones & Lewis, 1991).

National developments in higher education in the UK appear to illustrate the validity of the writings quoted above. In the 1960s, 1970s, and 1980s, educational and faculty developers endeavored to spread their enthusiasm for innovations in curricula and pedagogy in higher education. They encountered frequent suspicion and apathy from academics who believed that their career development depended mainly on research excellence. The arousal of short-term interest in teaching on the part of higher education lecturers and managers in the UK has been striking and, in some senses, unanticipated. These changes are largely attributable to external catalysts.

The national initiatives which have influenced behavior and led to change in universities and colleges have comprised both sticks and carrots. It is, perhaps, this combination of controlling measures and facilitating ones which has led to their initial effectiveness as change factors. The major influencing developments have been:

- The wider, integrated UK university system incorporating the universities and the former polytechnics
- The increasing accountability of higher education institutions to their funding councils
- The obligations to new quality systems for learning and teaching (quality audit, subject area assessment)
- The financial and academic impact of cyclical assessments of the quality of research in universities
- Consequent quality assurance procedures and processes for all personnel, including schemes of appraisal and development of individual employees
- Investment by the Higher Education Funding Councils in programs for the improvement of learning and teaching, funded on the basis of competitive bidding

- Pressures as well as incentives from employers' bodies for undergraduate and postgraduate programs which relate better to job and career requirements
- The UK Government's Department of Employment and its Enterprise in Higher Education (EHE) initiative

It is proposed in this chapter to examine how these national developments have contributed to the recent evolution of faculty and educational development in universities. These new initiatives constitute a series of changes which may finally embed faculty development into the operational ethos of individuals, departments, programs, policies, and institutions.

In the section which follows, we will describe a number of assessment and accountability systems which fall into the category of controlling measures, or 'sticks.' We will then review a number of quality enhancement programs and conclude with an enumeration of the implications for faculty development.

SYSTEMS OF ASSESSMENT AND ACCOUNTABILITY

Historically, British universities, or more accurately those founded prior to 1992, possess substantial independent powers. In particular, their academic autonomy is invariably enshrined in their Royal Charters. In effect, the institution, through its supreme academic body, determines which programs are offered and approves proposals relating to these offerings (content, methods of delivery, methods of assessment, entry standards, examination arrangements, etc.). In the case of vocational subjects, programs are normally scrutinized by the relevant professional body for the purposes of accreditation. But, in essence, the system amply illustrates Clark's (1993) depiction of self-monitoring, largely discipline-based academic communities. Conversely, until at least the late 1980s, the non-university sector of higher education in the UK (polytechnics, colleges of higher education, and specialized colleges, and the central institutions in Scotland), had limited independent powers. In addition to any accountability to professional bodies, their degree programs had to be validated either by the Council for National Academic Awards or by a university. Similarly, the sub-degree level programs had to be approved by appropriate designated bodies. These institutions were limited also by the fact that their academic profiles were subject to comment by, and the influence of, various local and national education departments.

Many of these initiatives have been influenced, directly or indirectly, by the views of government. In particular in the 1980s, policy for higher education, as for many other spheres of activity, was affected by what have broadly been summarized as the five E's of Thatcherism (economy, efficiency, effectiveness, enterprise, and excellence). To show "value for money" in public spending, institutions had to demonstrate that they were searching for economy, greater efficiency, and more effective use of resources. Employers argued that they needed more enterprising students who could display mastery of crucial skills such as problem-solving, communication, and computer literacy. In sum, while she was Prime Minister, Mrs. Thatcher frequently voiced the view that British enterprises and institutions would succeed on the world stage only if they pursued a policy of excellence. The foregoing briefly summarizes a complex set of political influences, even imperatives, which did not receive universal acclaim, certainly within the academy. Nonetheless, they set an overarching climate for institutions against which policies and initiatives were articulated and developed.[1]

Quality Audit

Quality Audit deals with systems of quality assurance (policies, procedures, and practice) operated by institutions. It is conducted by the Division of Quality Audit of the Higher Education Quality Council (HEQC), a body which is wholly owned by UK institutions of higher education and which was formed in mid-1992. Quality Audit built upon the methodology of Academic Audit as practiced from early 1991 in what we now term the older universities. That initiative operated under the aegis of the Committee of Vice-Chancellors and Principals (CVCP).

Quality Audit examines quality assurance in institutions in relation to several broad topics, namely: the institutional context, systems, and arrangements for quality assurance; the design, approval, and review of programs of study; teaching, learning, and the student experience; student assessment and the classification of awards; feedback and enhancement processes; staff appointment, development, promotion, and reward; content of promotional material relating to academic provision; and validation, franchising, and other forms of collaborative program provision (HEQC, 1993).

Each institution submits documentation to the Division of Quality Audit about its mission, objectives, and system of quality assurance, including illustrations of the system in practice. A team of auditors reads this documentation, agrees on a program for the audit visit, and, if necessary, seeks further supporting documentation from the institution. The actual visit normally lasts three days, and the auditors meet with faculty, staff, and students in order to examine and evaluate the effectiveness of the institution's procedures and policies of quality assurance. The subsequent report describes the nature of the institution, details the visit and the topics covered in the discussions, commends examples of good practice, and draws to the attention of the institution matters which may merit review or *lacunae* to be addressed. Most institutions receive a separate audit of their procedures dealing with franchising and with the validation of programs in associate institutions.

When Academic Audit was initiated, it was assumed that institutions would be visited after a period of five years. The enlarged system of institutions now covered by the Quality Audit may lengthen that cycle, but it is unlikely to exceed seven years unless significant changes are made to the procedures. Quality Audit has recently been reviewed, and that report is being considered by HEQC. The Review of Quality Audit outlines a number of options for the future. It also concludes that,

> Audit has... produced many benefits for HEIs [higher education institutions] — and has much to offer in the future. It has the potential to provide [the institutions] and the wider public with an important and valuable tool for accountability and to give increased assurance about the seriousness with which institutions take their quality control. It has an important role to play in the present national quality assurance framework. (Coopers and Lybrand, 1993, p. 12)

The Review suggests five immediate operational changes:

1. Clearer language and more explicit judgments in the conclusions and recommendations of reports
2. Increased attention to the selection and training of auditors with a higher proportion from outside higher education
3. Reduced paperwork
4. More attention to Division of Quality Audit (DQA) quality assurance
5. Production of an annual report (p. 9)

To date, audit is perceived to have few sanctions to use against institutions which do not respond to its suggestions or do not operate adequate systems of quality assurance. The Coopers and Lybrand Review argues that this issue must be resolved.

The same Review also outlines a number of options for medium- to long-term change in the content of audits, their frequency and duration, and the responsibility for the process. Higher education institutions which were consulted on the contents of the Review are unlikely to favor the adoption of some of its harder-edged managerial options and proposals.

Further consultations will take place with institutions about the future plans for Quality Audit. A consensus appears to have emerged that any changes to practice within the first round should be limited. These may involve some thinning of the supporting paperwork and sharpened attention to quality assurance within the Quality Audit Group. Greater emphasis may also be placed upon the definition and monitoring of academic standards and the quality assurance of inter-institutional collaborative arrangements (including franchising and overseas operations). Wider changes are likely to affect the second round of audits with the introduction of core and extension/elective items in the process attracting interest among institutions.

Quality Assessment

The March, 1992, legislation which led, among other things, to the establishment of higher education funding councils in Scotland, in England, and in Wales, charged these bodies with considering the assessment of educational provision in the institutions for which they have funding responsibility. In anticipation of that outcome, the preceding funding bodies were asked in July, 1992, to devise a possible methodology for quality assessment. That methodology was piloted in a sample of volunteer institutions in Scotland and England early in 1992. Subsequently, the new funding councils pursued somewhat different detailed strategies in relation to quality assessment, although substantial common elements have also been retained. With respect to the latter, the assessments are essentially subject-based, albeit often broadly defined. The process starts with self-assessment in the institution of each of the programs being assessed in that year, according to the criteria, schedule, and format specified by that funding council. The principal differences in the operation of assessment relate to the subject areas being assessed in a particular year, the categories of assessment, the role of documentary scrutiny in the process, and the provision of feedback during visits. On every occasion to date in Scotland, the scrutiny of institutional self-assessments by external assessors has been a preliminary to an actual visit by a team of assessors.

By contrast, in England many decisions about the standard of provision have been made solely on the basis of the critical reading of the self-assessment documents. Not surprisingly, that practice invoked protests from several institutions which claimed excellence of provision but were adjudged to be only of satisfactory standard. The institutions have argued that assessors would have formed a different, and more favorable, view had a visitation taken place. The logistical problem facing the Higher Education Funding Council England (HEFCE) is the sheer scale and cost of undertaking visits to all providers of each subject area under assessment in any year. Admittedly, costs would be reduced if the number of subjects assessed annually were radically pruned, but that would inevitably, and unacceptably, lengthen the time between assessments. Whilst it might appear that the main pressure for shorter cycles comes from politicians and other external sources, it is likely that the academy would be unhappy about the potentially adverse effects of quality labels such as 'satisfactory,' that were reviewed infrequently. The other major area of divergence on quality assessment stems from the fact that, in the 1993/94 assessments, the Scottish Higher Education Funding Council (SHEFC) has adopted four categories (Excellent, Highly Satisfactory, Satisfactory, Unsatisfactory), whereas those for England and Wales have retained the original threefold classification (Excellent, Satisfactory, Unsatisfactory).[2]

Impact of the Two Quality Systems

The academic community has questioned, even opposed, the introduction of quality audit and quality assessment. Nonetheless, both processes are operating and affect all institutions. Moreover, there is good reason to suggest that they have resulted in a variety of inter- and intra-institutional developments. Preparation for audit or assessment inevitably causes reflection and a form of academic stock-taking. Policies are reviewed, procedures overhauled, practices critically analyzed. At institutions where actual visits take place, further developmental possibilities can arise, although the visits are constrained by practical limitations of time and the numbers involved in meeting auditors, and by the fact that such developmental benefits are *not* the prime purpose of either procedure. Subsequently, consideration of the reports and reflection upon the overall experience offers additional development possibilities. Others benefit, perhaps less broadly, from the process: the auditors' learning experiences increase; the subject peer groups gain from the networking with other institutions; and those responsible for quality assurance profit from the contacts with others within and beyond their institutions. Additionally, there are the various conferences, seminars, and workshops that feature papers and discussions on these topics. Faculty developers have a part to play in every instance, as informers, facilitators, consultants, supporters, developers, scholars, and researchers (Gordon, 1993).

It is probably too early to measure whether the developments and changes that have occurred stem more from skillful compliance than a shared commitment to enhancement, or even to gauge whether the aggregate outcomes are cost-effective. However, quality audit has existed for a sufficiently long period, and has happened in enough institutions, to justify the conclusion that genuine attempts have been made to improve, and presumably enhance, many policies, procedures, and practices relating to the assurance of the quality of educational provision. It would be surprising if improvements did not occur as a result of assessment. The doubts, shared by academics and managers, relate to the scale of benefits compared with the cost of the exercise; to the centrality and significance of these benefits to any widely shared definition of the quality of education experience; and to the ability of these processes to sustain continuing commitment and enhancement.

Assessment has more apparent 'sticks' and 'carrots' than audit. In Scotland, achieving excellence results in additional funded places. In England and Wales, the reward is currently confined to the publicity that can accrue from the publication of the assessments. Attaining an unsatisfactory grade is something of a public embarrassment for institutions, and fear of that outcome may cause them to attach considerable importance to the exercise.

Research Selectivity

In the mid-1980s, the universities (and *not* the then polytechnics) in the UK took part in the first round of an assessment of the quality of research, conducted by the University Grants Committee (UGC) (the funding body at that time). The actual assessment was undertaken by small teams of distinguished peers in each academic area (discipline or cost center). Departments were graded, and these grades affected the level of subsequent funding for research allocated by the funding council. That exercise has been repeated on two subsequent occasions, and it is anticipated that the next exercise will be conducted in 1996. Over time, the actual gradings have altered, as have the descriptors, the rules governing submissions, and the detailed funding consequences. With these important *caveats*, cumulatively this process has had profound consequences for institutions, departments, and individual academics. Whilst the consequences have been greatest in disciplines which demand very large sums of money in order to support excellent research of international standing, all disciplines and, at least to some degree, all researchers have been affected. Institutional pride and prestige is affected by the research assessments, as is institutional funding. Perhaps the most fundamental challenge is to the notion that all university academics in the UK should be funded for approximately one third of their time in order to pursue fundamental scholarship and research. Whilst most of the older universities did include the overwhelming majority of academic staff in their submissions in the 1992 research assessment exercise, a substantial number were, in effect, not adjudged by groups of peers to have either national or international reputations as researchers.

Over a period of time, the research assessment exercise is starting to create 'leagues' of universities in the UK. It has been suggested that there are now approximately 12 to 16 institutions in which research in most disciplines is of international stature. An approximately equal-sized second group of institutions has some areas of this standing, but most of the research is, at best, of national standing. If these arguments are valid, in excess of 50 universities in the UK do not meet these criteria. Because of historic features of funding, most of the new universities would fall into that third category. However, many of them believe that some of their distinctive subjects or research fields can develop national and international standing now that they receive some core funding for research from the funding councils.

In aggregate, these forces have caused institutions to examine carefully their strategies for research and to require departments, subject areas, and research centers to do likewise. In that process of re-examination and refocusing, some would argue that the freedom of the lone researcher has been curtailed, even stifled.

The pressures upon research funding have also impinged upon research studentships and the supervision of research students. For some time, the various research councils in the UK have demanded a significant improvement in the completion rates of research degrees, especially PhDs. Indeed, most have set minimal standards which must be met to qualify for continuing eligibility for funded studentships. Subsequently, the research councils have demanded that greater attention be paid to the induction and training of research students and to the induction, preparation, and monitoring of supervisors. Here, an overlap occurs with quality audit which is also concerned with such matters and with the codes of practice which guide the supervision and monitoring of postgraduates' performance.

Once again, the changes and imperatives have influenced the work of faculty developers. Workshops on topics such as research supervision, writing research proposals, or writing for publication are well attended and in demand. Institutions, faculties, schools, and departments now commonly have research committees, active seminar programs, and regular debates about strategy, policy, and practice. Finally, it should be noted that the amounts of funding that are influenced by the quality of research considerably exceed those allocated to the quality of teaching and learning.

Management Accountability

Quality audit and assessment and research selectivity are important matters that illustrate increased external demands for individual and collective (managerial) accountability in higher education in the UK. Other components of that phenomenon should be noted. First, government in the 1980s dictated the broad context of that accountability through what have been termed the five Es of Thatcherism—economy, efficiency, effectiveness, enterprise, and excellence. Second, a study (CVCP, 1985, committee chaired by Jarratt) commissioned by the British universities concluded that they needed to pay greater attention to managerial efficiency and effectiveness, to choose managers carefully and train them, to devolve responsibility and accountability to these managers, and to clarify and simplify their organizational structures. Universities responded to Jarratt in varying ways and to varying degrees. Over a period of time, devolution of responsibility and accountability has strengthened.

Similarly, formal systems of appraisal were introduced in the late 1980s, albeit with a developmental rather than judgmental emphasis. Such appraisal schemes have proved, in some cases, to be potent supports for educational and faculty development, providing a systematic basis on which programs can be planned. From the mid 1980s, universities have also reported annually on a wide range of performance indicators. Currently, these exceed sixty in number, including a set designed to illuminate their financial state.

Finally, the recent Further Education and Higher Education Charters require institutions to set standards of student service on an array of matters relating to pre-admissions queries and post-admissions advice and complaints. Government departments and other relevant bodies are also expected to follow this model of practice with a series of Citizens' Charter initiatives. These Charters state the standards which particular public services will provide to customers and the recourse procedures available if these are not met. Thus, a public sector hospital might promise that outpatients will be taken within 30 minutes of their appointment time.

The relationship between some of these managerial developments and the enhancement of the quality of university teaching can be complex and, at times, debatable. That said, there is now a general acceptance of the need for, and importance of, good leadership (Middlehurst, 1993) and management at all levels, involving what Bergquist (1992) has described as the four cultures of the academy (collegial, managerial, negotiating, developmental).

QUALITY ENHANCEMENT INITIATIVES

As has been illustrated in the preceding sections, accountability systems have been costly in financial terms as well as in staff time. It has been argued (Lewin, 1952) that such systems alone do not effect change in the long term, but must be complemented by investment in enhancement initiatives. Such enhancement programs seek to engage faculty in the development of projects which will motivate their colleagues to explore and apply innovative approaches in the various aspects of their work. Central bodies in the UK have invested in such initiatives which have run in parallel with the measures already described. The quality enhancement initiatives reviewed here fall into the category of facilitating or motivating measures—what we refer to as 'carrots.'

Government-Funded Development Programs

Interestingly, the largest development investment in higher education has come not from the Department for Education or the higher education funding councils, rather from the Department of Employment. During the 1980s in the UK, the voice of industry became increasingly influential on university practices. A number of reports from organizations[3] contained commentary on the preparation of undergraduates for subsequent employment and emphasized the importance of the development of core skills as well as knowledge. In 1984, the funding bodies of the polytechnics and universities acknowledged the significance of such skills and the role higher education has to play in their development.

> *The abilities most valued in industrial, commercial and professional life as well as in public and social administration, are the generic intellectual and personal skills. These include the ability to analyze complex issues, to identify the core of a problem and the means for solving it, to synthesize and integrate disparate elements, to clarify values, to make effective use of numerical and other information, and above all to communicate clearly both orally and in writing. A higher education system which provides its students with these things is serving society well. (National Advisory Board and University Grants Committee [NAB/UGC], 1984, p. 4)*

The Department of Employment's Further and Higher Education Branch responded to the comments of employers and the responses of higher education by financing a series of higher education development projects. Between 1989 and 1994, these totaled an investment of more than £100 million ($160 million US) in higher education-based development programs.

The Enterprise in Higher Education Initiative (EHE) is the Department of Employment's most substantial investment, funding more than 50 higher education institutions with £1 million ($1.6 million US) over five-year periods. Its aims are based on the above quotation and expressly on three implicit aspects:

1. The aim of developing generic intellectual and personal skills should be explicit in the curriculum, and should be achieved within the teaching of the discipline being studied, rather than separate from it
2. The curriculum should relate to the world of work and should involve employers and employment
3. Universities and colleges participating in EHE should ensure that most students in most programs are affected by the initiative

Although general, these three aims of EHE have profound significance for faculty and institutional development. In order to achieve them, participating individual members of faculty are expected to:

- Formulate the curriculum in terms not only of subject knowledge but also generic skills and to make this extended curriculum explicit
- Incorporate skills learning—whether subject-specific or generic, core skills—into the curriculum and programs of a particular school or faculty
- Work with employers in the design of the curriculum and the learning, teaching, and assessment methods
- Assimilate the preceding into planning for the curriculum and teaching across all subject areas: EHE is an institution-wide initiative

The obligations of the institution and its departments and schools are:

- Encouragement of a culture which supports staff and students in developing approaches to curriculum design and teaching and learning methods (see Elton & Partington, 1993)
- Review and improvement of existing incentives for the development of teaching
- Creation of mechanisms for the cross-fertilization of these innovations from one faculty or school to another
- Development of closer links with employers

EHE was introduced in phases, and significant shifts in emphasis occurred between each phase. Nonetheless, in aggregate, successful initiatives have led to, and been founded upon, effective faculty development activities, although the form and delivery of these have varied greatly from institution to institution.

When EHE was introduced, it encountered a mixed reception from the academy, but as the program developed the balance of opinion has shifted in favor of the educational benefits which could be pursued.

Funding Council Programs

Two areas of change have led to development investment by the funding councils, namely technological change and quality systems.

The University Grants Committee (subsequently the Universities Funding Council) had already acknowledged in the early 1980s its obligation to support the establishment of policies, strategies, and infrastructures in universities for the effective and efficient use of technology in both academic and administrative activities. Two initiatives were funded to develop both academic uses of computing—the Computers in Teaching Initiative (CTI)—and administrative uses of information technology—the Management and Administrative Computing (MAC) initiative.

The CTI funded the establishment and maintenance of academic discipline-based computing centers concerned with the development of computer technology within a specific subject area. A network of 20 CTI centers exists across the UK providing software and hard- and software information for academics within each major university discipline. The main strategy in this initiative for enhancing computer-assisted learning and teaching is that the centers are staffed predominantly with academics, who combine their computing expertise with their existing subject specialization and so focus their innovations on particular subject areas rather than on generic computing-skills development.

This approach, although eminently understandable, is partially flawed in that it underestimates the influence of institutional leaders and managers, and of the diverse cultures which exist in different universities. The approach suffers also from the image of a network of clubs of and for initiated enthusiasts. More positively, the work and products of many CTI centers have influenced the adoption of computer-assisted approaches to learning and teaching. As is frequently the case with technological developments, however, it was a long time before the University Grants Committee's Computer Board and the Directors of the CTI centers realized fully the importance of encouraging and training staff to use the materials created through the initiative. Existing academic staff development networks were used only sparingly and late, groupings of senior leaders and of heads of departments were also rarely used, and the potential impact of the CTI was consequently minimized in its early stages. Much might still be achieved if faculty members' capabilities to use computer-assisted learning techniques and materials are developed, and if collaboration is encouraged with other national and regional bodies and networks, particularly those concerned with faculty and educational development. With these emphases, the products of the initiative might still be more effectively embedded within universities.

The MAC initiative of the late 1980s concerned itself with the cost-effective creation of management information systems and software designed for the specific administrative and management tasks of higher education. Once again, the significance of academic staff development and training was recognized late, and many of the difficulties still being experienced with the introduction of some of the systems are attributable to insufficient emphasis on user needs and skills. Some universities and 'families' of universities using the same systems are now remedying this deficit by organizing staff training programs for the induction of users. These are both necessary and well received and contribute substantially to more effective and efficient applications.

In the 1990s, the funding councils have built on these beginnings by investing considerably more funds in four new initiatives:

- the Information Technology Training Initiative (ITTI)
- the Teaching and Learning Technology Programme (TLTP)
- the Flexibility Learning Initiative (FLI)
- the Effective Teaching and Assessment Programme (ETAP)

Because all four programs are in progress, it is difficult to gauge their long-term results. However, much interest is focused on the projects funded through these programs.

The Information Technology Training Initiative. The furthest advanced of the four programs, the ITTI, funded 29 projects over three years (1990-93), with a total expenditure of approximately £3 million ($4.8 million US). The projects were all concerned, as the title implies, with training for improved uses of technology (see Shields, 1993).

One significant feature of this initiative was its emphasis from the start on uniting faculty developers—the intended users of the products—with the computing specialists who were creating them. Indeed, two of the 29 funded projects were concerned with facilitating networking across various groups of training providers within higher education and disseminating the products of ITTI via existing central bodies and networks. Information Technology specialists and trainers met regularly with faculty developers to discuss how to apply ITTI materials to identified training needs. The initial seminars highlighted the difficulty of arranging content perceived as relevant by all the three categories of staff. The language of each specialist area (computing and faculty development) also proved to be a significant barrier to the other. These initial difficulties are slowly being overcome and the barriers eroded, but the problems with communications should not be underestimated, despite the positive intentions of cross-fertilization. That both the dissemination and networking projects are continuing with growing success, and that their proponents have sought further funding for these two projects, may serve as a crude measure of their perceived value.

The Teaching and Learning Technology Program. In launching its new program to develop uses of technology in teaching and learning, the funding council announced:

> *The aim of the program is to make teaching and learning more productive and efficient by harnessing modern technology. This will help institutions to respond effectively to the current substan-*

> *tial growth in student numbers, and to promote and maintain the quality of their provision. Particular importance is attached to ensuring that the benefits of the program spread throughout learning in higher education, and priority will therefore be given to supporting projects which promise a high degree of transportability, and which may involve consortia of institutions. (Universities Funding Council, 1992, p. 1)*

The above extract gives an indication of the program's major intentions: efficiency gains for teaching staff; maintenance of teaching quality; and establishment of technology as an integral and widespread feature in delivering higher education.

The selection committee originally had £5 million ($8 million US) at its disposal to grant to projects through a UK-wide bidding process, similar to the one previously developed for the selection of ITTI bids. Both programs were introduced to support universities only, since the Universities Funding Council (UFC) could provide funding only to the current university sector. (The former polytechnics had at that time their own Polytechnics and Colleges Funding Council, which had no similar program in the area of teaching and learning technology development.) The number of proposals received by the committee exceeded all expectations, but, more importantly, the quality of most of the approximately 180 bids was so high that the committee's Chair was successful in persuading the UFC to increase the amount of funding available to £7.5 million ($12 million US). Finally, 40 projects were selected of varying duration, up to 3 years, at a range of funding from £100,000 ($160,000 US) to £1 million ($1.6 million US). The projects commenced in August, 1992.

The Flexibility Learning Initiative and the Effective Teaching and Assessment Program. These two programs sponsored by the funding councils in England, Scotland, and Wales (successors to the UFC) have no particular technological focus and have each allocated approximately £1 million ($1.6 million US) to a small number of projects to improve learning and teaching. The Flexibility Learning Initiative in 1992 preceded the Effective Teaching and Assessment Program (ETAP) of late 1993. Under the former program, relatively small amounts of funding were distributed to several small projects; whereas the ETAP concentrated its funding on five proposals only, each with substantial financial support. Under both, monies have been allocated to subject-specific projects, such as the Effective Engineering Education project under ETAP, and generic pedagogical or curriculum development work, such as the improvement of independent learning resources.

Impact of these Development Programs

It is rather early to assess the full impact of all these programs. Certain features influential for faculty development are important to note at this stage:

- The commitment of approximately £15 million ($24 million US) to teaching and learning projects represents a significant step by the Funding Council(s) towards recognizing the value of professional development for faculty.
- The great interest aroused across the university system and the quality of the proposals in each case have indicated the level of expertise across higher education which might be harnessed.
- The programs' emphasis on attracting consortium bids, in some cases comprising components of work from over fifteen universities, has led to the creation of influential networks across institutions and faculties. (One of the most encouraging features of the selection process—according to the committees involved— has been the way and the speed with which bidders have responded to this aspect of the program brief. They received many more large consortium proposals than anticipated, given the limited bidding time.)
- Both the TLTP and ITTI have full-time national coordinators with mandates to assure completion and quality of all the projects; support networking across all project-holders; ensure the most widespread and effective dissemination of the projects' findings and products; and link their programs to the work of other relevant national initiatives and bodies, thereby ensuring that the work of their programs is embedded within higher education. Because coordinators are appointed for the duration of the programs, the faculty development potential of the initiatives has increased, in that they devote much of their time to dissemination strategies including organizing national, regional, and local seminars and workshops, in addition to publications and promotional literature.
- A measure of the perceived effectiveness of the programs is that some have already been extended. In 1993, a second phase of TLTP was organized and funded, and the new universities were included. Many submitted successful bids. Some ITTI projects have also received extensions.

European Initiatives

The extensive raft of European initiatives sponsored by the European Community also deserves mention. Perhaps the most significant has been *Erasmus*, a scheme whereby students undertake part of their academic studies in an institution in another European Community country. Notably, the initiative has necessitated both extensive contact between teaching staff in collaborating institutions and detailed consideration of a range of matters relating to curriculum design, credit transfer, methods of assessment, forms of teaching, and student support systems. For those actively involved, it has constituted an important opportunity for personal and academic development. Likewise, research collaboration has been sponsored under other European initiatives.

Similarly, an array of initiatives is directed towards higher education in Eastern Europe. Projects, such as *Tempus*, require academic collaboration between at least two European Community institutions and a partner(s) in Eastern Europe. The underlying purpose is to assist higher education institutions in Eastern Europe to address the changing needs of the economy of their nation. Business management and technology have featured prominently in Tempus initiatives. Whatever the academic focus, collaboration has often resulted in extended periods of faculty exchange between institutions in European Community countries and institutions in Eastern European Countries. Interestingly, whilst the scale of available funding barely covers the basic costs to institutions in European Community countries, there has been no shortage of interested participants in these initiatives.

University-Owned Central Bodies

Returning to our focus on the British scene, since 1964 the Committee of Vice-Chancellors and Principals (CVCP) has played a role in supporting educational and faculty development. Early in the 1970s, this led to the establishment of a National Coordinating Committee which had representation from the CVCP, faculty unions, and student associations. Matheson (1981) has documented the subsequent growth of academic staff training in the 1970s. At the same time, in the former non-university sector of higher education, educational development units flourished.

A small number of institutions were more innovative, introducing induction courses for new lecturers and management programs for heads of departments. In 1985, the Jarratt Report encouraged such courses by recommending "the introduction of arrangements for staff appraisal, development and accountability" (p. 36). It also recommended that more attention be paid to the development of academic managers.

The period 1987-1989 was an important one for academic staff development in British universities. Institutions agreed to introduce staff appraisal. They were urged by the CVCP to develop an array of staff development activities directed appropriately to satisfy the needs of both inexperienced and experienced staff and to base these initiatives upon a formal policy for academic staff development. Over time, every institution did so and, in the process, reviewed their means of providing the necessary support. Thus, by the start of the 1990s, every institution had a coordinator or director of academic staff development, and some had established substantial central, integrated units. The latter were variously accountable to pro-vice-chancellors, vice-principals, registrars, secretaries, or directors of personnel, depending upon the focus of the particular service and the prevailing managerial structure of the specific institutions.

Leadership and management development programs became more prevalent, as did induction courses for new teaching staff. Appraisal systems were designed and developed, varying in detail from institution to institution, but all with a strong developmental ethos. In turn, these led to the need for support for academic staff development and the allocation of additional resources to this activity. Not only were human and financial resources dedicated to the task, but tailored resources and programs were produced. In larger units, faculty developers could also act as consultants, undertaking sustained projects with individuals and departments and conducting research into the links between theory and practice. While the balance varied, every institution made use of a range of appropriate expertise, be that in-house, in-system, or from external sources. Strong collaborative networks have emerged between individual faculty developers. In some cases, formal regional networks have developed such as those in Scotland, Northern England, and the Midlands of England. These networks now not only share information but also organize extensive programs of high-quality events directed towards particular developmental needs. Thus, the Scottish network collaborates on events relating to teaching, learning, research, management development, appraisal, and administrative training.

For many years, the CVCP funded two part-time national coordinators, one for administrative training and one for academic training. After considerable discussion and consultation, in 1990 this provision was greatly enhanced with the formation of a central unit, the Universities' Staff Development and Training Unit (funded initially by the University Grants Committee) with a mandate:

- *to stimulate provision for the training and development of all categories of university staff in order to improve their performance and that of the institution*

- *to promote such provision principally by encouraging universities' own activities both locally and regionally... (CVCP, 1990, p. 2)*

In its first five years, the Universities' Staff Development Unit (USDU) (it has dropped the word 'Training' from its title) has significantly developed its mandate and its influence, helped in this by the quality systems described earlier. Now its aims are:

- *to promote staff development and training within and across universities*

- *to provide specialist advice, support and resources to universities in their planning and delivery of staff development for all personnel*

- *to influence key central bodies in higher education in their understanding and support of this function (CVCP, 1993, p. 2)*

The USDU's relationship with the funding councils has been maintained throughout its existence. The unit has also increased its capacity to attract funding for research and development projects.

As a result of a review of the CVCP in 1993, the USDU became an optionally funded part of that organization, along with other central services. An indicator of the current value placed on academic staff development in UK universities is that a high number of universities (over 90%) chose to maintain their USDU memberships.

Prior to 1993, the polytechnics had their own body, the Committee of Directors of Polytechnics (CDP). In 1990, the CDP introduced its own central Training Unit which was directly concerned with supporting the managements of polytechnics in their changed status, independent of local authorities, and for their consequent managerial and administrative responsibilities. As this task progressed, the Unit was disbanded.

In addition to its central promotion of staff development through its own optional agency, the CVCP also supports faculty development by commissioning reports regularly. These reports include the Flowers Committee Report (1993) on changes in the pattern of the academic year, which explores models of modularization, and the Crawford Committee Report on the current quality systems in higher education.

One particularly significant recent study was commissioned by the Committee of Scottish University Principals and was chaired by Alistair MacFarlane, Principal of the Heriot-Watt University, Edinburgh (UK). The questions which the MacFarlane group addressed are identified in the preface to the report as follows:

- *How can high quality environments for the support of learning be created and maintained… to handle the expected growth in numbers?*

- *What role has technology to play in creating such environments?*

- *How can an increasing effectiveness and the containment of costs be reconciled with a high quality of learning experience?*

- *How can the status of teaching, both as a professional activity and as a sphere for research, be raised in the higher education sector?*

(Committee of Scottish University Principals, 1992, p. vii)

The report was widely disseminated in the UK and has resulted in the establishment of a number of projects to support the improvement of students' educational experience. It has proved also to be of considerable value to the work of educational and faculty developers.

IMPLICATIONS FOR FACULTY DEVELOPMENT

Many catalysts have been mentioned in this chapter, but not all the resulting changes have necessarily been welcomed by the academy. Nor should we presume that all changes will inevitably be beneficial. Even well-designed and well-implemented ones can have some unintended consequences. To date, while the collective impact has been substantial—notably in terms of workload and stress—faculty have not always been affected in the same way nor to the same degree. Nonetheless, faculty development has been firmly put on agendas in institutions, resulting in the production of an extensive array of materials, programs, and networks, albeit of varied quality and with differing foci and degrees of coordination.

Partington (forthcoming) argues that more attention should be paid to policies and strategies for staff development: "Herein lies the basis for the ways forward, if staff development is to… play its full and valuable part in enriching individuals' and institutions' activities and in contributing to the achievement of goals in each case." What actions might offer a way forward? We suggest nine key points which need careful consideration. These are:

1. Effectively relating institutional and departmental goals to faculty developmental policies, planning, and provision
2. Listening to individuals' expectations, needs, and motivations, and seeking to address these in an appropriate manner

3. Providing adequate resources for faculty development
4. Assuring the quality of provision and the credibility of the providers
5. Addressing the links between appraisal or review and faculty development
6. Addressing the links between the quality enhancement of specific activities and effective faculty development
7. Conducting research on effective ways of providing for the development of faculty
8. Ensuring that any specific organizational change under consideration is consistent with the culture of the institution and that supporting faculty development is perceived as relevant and helpful
9. Creating a climate of personal commitment to continuing one's professional development amongst all staff

If progress toward these goals is made, the issues raised at the outset of this chapter may be resolved. The dialogue will not be conducted in the abstract, but within the day-to-day flesh and blood of institutional politics and against the background of myriad external factors. These factors may continue to appear at times like unwanted intrusions or uncomfortable burrs and threats, but they will also offer opportunities to individuals and institutions as can be seen from the combination of judgmental and developmental initiatives presented in this chapter. In any process of innovation, adoption happens in a complex manner, at different times, in different places, and by different individuals.

The centrality of the education process to the purpose of institutions of higher education leads us to conclude that quality audit and quality assessment may be particularly important external catalysts. If these are truly embedded within institutions, they are likely to result in substantial and continuing faculty and institutional development. Skeptics may ask for evidence that supports that conclusion. We offer two main pieces of evidence. Firstly, there is the evidence in the audit and assessment reports which recognize and applaud good practice and which appear to be more than capable of getting below the surface and investigating whether policies are substantiated in practice (e.g., training of teaching assistants or the supervision of doctoral students) and whether policy and practice constitutes a coherent entity that leads to a high quality experience for learners. Secondly, there is the testimony from a greater number of academics than one might have anticipated who have seized upon the opportunity (even challenge) offered by audit and assessment to review, revise, even rebuild, policies and practices, putting into effect at operational unit level the ideas behind the philosophy of the learning organization. The foregoing argument should not be interpreted as diminishing the potential contribution that other external stimuli have made / can make; rather it takes one important area as a means of highlighting both the possibilities offered and the means whereby these are likely to be attained.

Even when an innovation stumbles or dies, some will have adopted it. These lessons are pertinent when we evaluate the likely impact of external forces for change in higher education. The challenge for faculty developers is not so much to spot the innovations that will succeed, as to pursue focused strategies which have widely based support; which address developmental needs of individuals, functional units, and institutions; and do so within a dynamic framework which is appropriately responsive to environmental changes.

REFERENCES

Bergquist, W. (1992). *The four cultures of the academy.* San Francisco, CA: Jossey-Bass.

Clark, B.R. (1993). The research foundations of post-graduate education. *Higher Education Quarterly, 47*(4), 301-315.

Committee of Scottish University Principals. (1992). *Teaching and learning in an expanding higher education system.* Edinburgh, UK: Scottish Conference of University Principals.

Committee of Vice-Chancellors and Principals. (1985). *Report of the steering committee on efficiency studies in universities.* London, UK: Author.

Committee of Vice-Chancellors and Principals. (1990). *Update 1: Annual Report of USDTU.* Sheffield, UK: USDTU.

Committee of Vice-Chancellors and Principals. (1993). *The UK Universities' Staff Development Unit: Strategies and Services 1993-94.* Sheffield, UK: USDU.

Coopers and Lybrand. (1993). *Review of quality audit.* London, UK: Higher Education Quality Council.

Crawford Committee. (forthcoming). Paper for the CVCP's September Retreat on *Future quality systems in UK higher education.* London, UK: CVCP.

CTI Annual Report. (1993). Oxford, UK: CTISS Publications.

Elton, L., & Partington, P.A. (1993). *Teaching standards and excellence in higher education: Developing a culture for quality* (2nd ed.). Sheffield, UK: USDU.

Flowers Committee. (1993). *The review of the academic year.* Bristol, UK: HEFCE.

Fullan, M. (1990). The management of change: An implementation perspective. In J. Megarry (Ed.), *Facing the challenge.* Oxford, UK.

Gordon, G. (1993). New trends in assuring and assessing the quality of educational provision in British universities. *To Improve the Academy, 12,* 207-216.

Gordon, G., & Partington, P.A. (1993). *Quality in higher education: Overview and update.* Sheffield, UK: USDU Briefing Paper.

Higher Education Quality Council. (1993). *Auditors' manual.* Birmingham, UK: Author.

Jones, P., & Lewis, J. (1991). Implementing a strategy of change in higher education. *Studies in Higher Education, 16,* 41-61.

Lewin, K. (1952). *Field theory in social science.* London, UK: Tavistock.

Matheson, C.C. (1981). *Staff development matters.* Norwich, UK: University of East Anglia.

Megarry, J. (Ed.). (1990). *Facing the challenge.* Oxford, UK.

Middlehurst, R. (1993). *Leading academics.* Buckingham, UK: Open University Press / SRHE.

National Advisory Board and University Grants Committee (NAB/UGC). (1984). *Higher education and the needs of society.* London, UK: Author.

Partington, P.A. (forthcoming). Staff development and enterprise in higher education. In H. Gray (Ed.), *Going with the grain.* Sheffield, UK: Employment Department.

Shields, B. (1993). *ITTI project abstracts.* Sheffield, UK: ITTI/USDU.

Universities Funding Council. (1992). *Circular 8/92: The teaching and learning technology programme.* Bristol, UK: HEFCE.

AUTHORS

George Gordon is Director of the Centre for Academic Practice at the University of Strathclyde, (Scotland) the largest integrated faculty and student development center in British universities. He served as an academic auditor with the Committee of Vice-Chancellors and Principals and has written widely on matters relating to quality assurance in higher education. He is a former Dean of Arts and Social Studies.

Patricia Partington is Director of the UK Universities' Staff Development Unit established by The Committee of Vice-Chancellors and Principals of the Universities of the United Kingdom. The Unit has a remit to support and advise UK universities on training and development for all categories of staff. Dr. Partington previously worked as a researcher and lecturer in Education at the Universities of Nottingham and Sheffield. Between 1986 and 1989, she established a human re-

sources development unit at the University of Sheffield. She has wide experience in planning and delivering continuing professional development for all faculty in higher education. Her particular interests are learning and teaching developments and management training and consultancy, in which areas she has worked with higher education colleagues both nationally and internationally.

NOTES

[1] Legislation passed in March, 1992, set in train substantial structural and organizational changes in higher education in the UK. These were foreshadowed in the White Paper published in Spring, 1991. Amongst the consequential changes were the dissolution of the Council for National Academic Awards; the enabling of polytechnics to seek the title of university (which they did with alacrity); the creation of unified funding councils in Scotland, England, and in Wales; the development of a unified admissions handling body (Universities and Colleges Admissions Service); and the introduction of the quality audit and quality assessment of educational provision in institutions of higher education. (For further details, see Gordon & Partington, 1993.)

[2] The Quality Framework adopted by SHEFC contains eleven aspects relating to educational provision: aims and curricula; curriculum design and review; the teaching and learning environment; staff resources; learning resources; course organization; teaching and learning practice; student support; assessment and monitoring; students' work; and output, outcomes, and quality control. Although expressed differently, the quality assessment operated by each funding council explores comparable topics.

[3] These organizations include the Council for Industry and Higher Education, the Department for Trade and Industry, the Confederation of British Industries, the Engineering Council, and the British and the European Round Table.

Index